BROADCAST ADVERTISING & PROMOTION!

A Handbook for Students and Professionals

BROADCAST ADVERTISING & PROMOTION!

A Handbook for

Students and Professionals

by FRED L. BERGENDORFF, Ph.D
CHARLES H. SMITH
LANCE WEBSTER
Edited by Lance Webster

With Contributions from the membership of
the Broadcasters Promotion Association

Communication Arts Books
Hastings House, Publishers
New York 10016

Library of Congress Cataloging in Publication Data

Bergendorff, Fred.
  Broadcast advertising and promotion.

  Includes index.
  1. Broadcast advertising. I. Smith, Charles
Harrison. II. Webster, Lance. III. Title.
HF6146.B74B47   1983   659.2′93845453   82-9303
ISBN 0-8038-0801-1   AACR2

Published simultaneously in Canada by
Saunders of Toronto Ltd., Markham, Ontario

Designed by Al Lichtenberg
Printed in the United States of America

Contents

Acknowledgements

This textbook originated with the determination of the Board of Directors of the Broadcasters Promotion Association (BPA) to assist colleges and universities in training talented students in the basics of radio and television advertising, promotion and publicity.

The book is also intended as a useful tool for station promotion staffs.

Former BPA President W. Thomas Dawson, Vice President, CBS Radio Network, and 1983-4 BPA President Fred Bergendorff set the process in motion in 1979. Succeeding BPA Board members and officers, including Presidents Gail Morrell (CFCF-TV, Montreal), Clarence Martin (KYTV, Springfield, MO.), and Anne Coleman (WAVE-TV, Louisville, KY) added their support.

The information in this text has come largely from BPA member stations and organizations and their promotion staffs. Illustrative material from many stations was drawn from the BPA Library at San Diego State University in California.

Special thanks are due to:

—Mort Slakoff, VP of Creative Services, MCA-TV, New York, for an outstanding and comprehensive breakdown of the many responsibilities of the station promotion director and department (Chapter 6).

—Lynne Grasz, Director, Communications, CBS Broadcast Group, New York, for her insightful analysis of key station staff members and their interactions with advertising and promotion personnel. (Chapter 8).

—Carol Bauer, New-York-based broadcast promotion consultant who drew on her station and network experiences to outline group promotion activities (Chapter 9).

—Dr. Ray London, President, Human Factor Programs, Ltd., Santa Ana, CA, who prepared an original draft which forms the basis of Chapter 10, exploring the Promotion Director as manager/creator.

—Professor James Webster, Ohio State University, and the National Association of Broadcasters, for their permission to reprint a major portion of the NAB's classic background booklet, "Audience Research", and Hugh Beville, Executive Director of the Broadcast Ratings Council for permission to use material from that organization's superb booklet, "Understanding Ratings Research" (Chapter 11).

—Dennis Fitch, Director of Advertising for the ABC-TV Network, for permission to reprint, in edited form, his BPA-sponsored booklet, "Creatively Servicing the Budget" (Chapter 12).

—Jon Beacher, Senior Vice President of Reymer & Gersin, a marketing research firm in Southfield, MI, for allowing us to draw on material from his speeches and presentations to BPA seminars as a basis for Chapter 13 on motivational techniques.

—Terri Brady, Los Angeles-based media consultant and buyer, and Linda Nix, Public Information Director of WYES-TV, New Orleans, LA, for their invaluable contributions to understanding the various media, as detailed in Chapters 14 and 15.

—David Milberg, Director of Operations at WBBM/CBS Newsradio in Chicago for his valuable observations on radio on-air promotion in Chapter 16.

—Dave Course, Promotion Director, KARK-TV, Little Rock, Arkansas, for permission to use material from his booklet on on-air promotion scheduling, "Stroking Themselves," in Chapter 16.

—Beryl Spector, Public Information Director, WMHT-TV/AM/FM, Schenectady, New York, for her expertise in publicity which set directions and provided details for Chapter 17.

—Clarence Martin, Promotion Director, KYTV, Springfield, Missouri, and former BPA President, for important examples and rules for mounting the station Fall Preview Party effort (Chapter 17).

—Linda Nix of WYES-TV again for explaining how to set up a station speaker's bureau (Chapter 17).

—Gary Claussen, Senior Vice President, Stone Associates Public Relations, Los Angeles, for explaining in Chapter 17 how a PR firm can best serve a broadcast station.

—Lee Pocock, Promotion Director, KSL Radio, Salt Lake City (and BPA 1983–4 President-Elect), and Larry Heywood, Vice President of Creative Services for the Radio Bureau of Canada, for their major contributions to Chapter 18 detailing all aspects of broadcast station contesting.

—Dan Agan, PBS TV Network Director of Marketing and Information Services, for permission to excerpt from various papers he prepared for PTV stations on direct mail efforts (Chapter 18).

—Jane Graber, KEBC-FM, Oklahoma City, and Dr. Donald Patton, Professor of Mathematics, University of Oklahoma, for their original work in preparing a formula for determining penetration levels for bumper-sticker promotion campaigns.

—Joseph Logsdon, Promotion Director, WTTV, Indianapolis, Indiana, for permission to condense his BPA Newsletter article on balloon promotions.

—Stan Harrison, Director of the Office of Corporate Communications, Corporation for Public Broadcasting, Washington, D.C., and CPB's Nel Jackson, for permission to excerpt from and adapt their booklet, "Radio Program Guide Critique," in Chapter 20.

—Dawn Delong, Assistant Director for Public Affairs for the Communications Center of the University of Texas, for her contributions on "Low Budget, or No Budget Promotions" in Chapter 20.

—Rod Warner, Sarasota, Florida cable marketing consultant, for the basic material comprising Chapter 21 on "Marketing Cable Television."

—Janet Lane-Tornell, Promotion Director, KMTV, Omaha, Nebraska, for her extensive analysis of promoting the new broadcast station facility, in Chapter 22.

—And W. Thomas Dawson, Vice President, CBS Radio Network and former BPA President, for his special message to students, Part Six of this Text.

The materials used as case studies at the end of the text were drawn from the files of the BPA Library at San Diego State University. In addition, special thanks are due to Andy Ockershausen, General Manager, WMAL-AM 63 Stereo Radio in Washington, D.C., for his explanation of how WMAL uses its on-air personalities in the community to help keep the station one of the nation's most successful.

Also, special thanks are due to the many people who aided in compiling visual material used in the text. These include Catherine Heinz, Director of the Broadcast Pioneers Library in Washington, D.C., and Fay Greenlee and Lynda Irvin of her staff; Cindy Potthast, Librarian, BPA Resource Center and Library at San Diego State University; Susan Nicholson, WSB-TV, Atlanta, Georgia; Betty Hudson, NBC-TV, New York, and Penny Springer and Tom Gauger, WMAL-AM Radio, Washington, D.C.

Another group of people helped expedite the flow of materials and information used in this text, or helped identify those whose contributions would be valuable. Thanks to Jane Cohen, NAB; Eleanor Miller, CPB; Betty Hudson, NBC; and Lynda Stewart, President of the International Association of Business Communicators.

Though they did not participate directly in writing this text, the following deserve special mention for invaluable background information: Baltimore, Maryland ad agency president Robert Kingwell (former Promotion Director of WBAL-TV); the late Ned Ryan, former Promotion Director of WRC-TV, Washington, D.C.; Dick McBride, Executive Producer of Promotion Production, WNET, New York; and Tom Aylward, Chairman, Department of Communication Arts and Theatre, University of Maryland.

This text would not have been possible without the substantial input of the aforementioned contributors, and the continuing advice and support of many of the more than 1,300 members of the Broadcasters Promotion Association.

The authors wish to express their appreciation to Los Angeles attorney Walter Hurst for reviewing the text and making valuable suggestions; and the Foster & Kleiser outdoor advertising company for assistance in promoting the text, and for valuable advice.

The authors also wish to thank Dick Bell, Bell-Jessness Advertising, Los Angeles for the cover design of this text.

Finally, the authors dedicate this text to BPA's sincere concern for continually improving the quality and calibre of those in the broadcast promotion and advertising business. In the 1980's, these men and women are clearly moving to the forefront of station management teams with their marketing, advertising, promotion, research, and publicity skills and knowledge.

FRED BERGENDORF, Ph.D.
Director of Promotion, KNX Newsradio, L.A.
CHARLES HARRISON SMITH
Retired Professor of Communication Arts,
San Francisco State University
LANCE WEBSTER
Executive Coordinator, BPA

January 1, 1983

Part One

Introduction
and Background

CHAPTER 1

Introduction

A career in broadcast advertising and promotion is exciting, stimulating, challenging, fast-paced, constantly varied and rewarding.

Radio and television stations are on the cutting edge of a modern society characterized by change, new trends, fascinating discoveries and daily news developments of local, national and international significance. Most people get their news from the broadcast media. Working at the source of this constant flow of information is stimulating. It is also a big responsibility for everyone involved. The engineer helping to put on the broadcast, the salesman selling commercial time, the producer responsible for program content and the Promotion Director telling the public where to find the station and its programming, all share in the responsibilities to listeners and viewers, working in an environment of rewarding excitement.

Creative, energetic, productive people are attracted to broadcasting. These qualities are essential for success in many areas of this unique industry. Working with actors, directors, producers, artists, reporters and other promotion executives stimulates one's best efforts.

This era is one of rapid technological change. To broadcasters in the Eighties, change means constant new opportunities to improve the techniques of bringing images and sounds to the home viewer and listener. With these new opportunities come many challenges for broadcast Promotion Directors to prove their abilities. Old strategies must be adapted to new situations. New ways to do the job must be found.

The challenges are especially significant to the Promotion Director because this professional helps shape the viewing and listening patterns of thousands, tens of thousands, even millions of people. Promotion efforts create public awareness of programs which can entertain, improve and enrich lives. The position is one of power, influence and responsibility.

Further, as the person chiefly charged with creating public perception of the station's image and attracting new viewers and listeners, the Promotion Director shares with programmers and sales people the responsibility for generating station income, making more and better programs possible, and enabling the station to meet its payroll and, as in regards to commercial stations, make a profit.

The broadcast Promotion Director's job is a multi-faceted one, as the pages ahead clearly show. Functions range from supervisory and planning, to creative, to public relations—all usually intermingled throughout each working day.

The Promotion Director might start the morning working on plans for next year's budget; then supervise the creative design of an ad layout with the station's art director. Later in the morning a meeting with a music production expert who is working on a new station jingle might take place. Next on the agenda could be lunch with a network star and the town's top newspaper critic. In the mid-afternoon there may be studio time allotted for on-air promotion production work, and the late afternoon might include a staff brainstorm session on ideas for a Fall season preview party, or an upcoming contest. At six p.m. a late meeting with the News Director to review themes for the next news campaign ends the day . . . almost. At seven, the Promotion Director is on the way home, with the unfinished budget that started off the day in a briefcase for work at home.

Broadcast promotion is not a field that lets one relax. And it certainly is not routine. The pace is demanding, the hours can be long, and the scope of activities broad. But the constant challenges bring rewards—both emotional and financial—to those who can successfully meet them.

In addition, the job is personally broadening by requiring up-to-date knowledge of trends, fashions, lifestyles, news developments, and the activities and habits of people throughout the community. Creative ideas that are current, fresh and appropriate are essential.

Finally, personal leadership qualities must be developed and exercised. The best creative efforts of others must be elicited and shaped to effective promotional purposes. Patience, tolerance, sound judgment, an outgoing personality, wit or sense of humor, a genuine liking of people, and plenty of self-confidence are all important qualities of a successful Promotion Director.

This handbook is designed to thoroughly explain the varied activities of a broadcast promotion professional. Included are general principles, specific examples, illustrations, and unique situations drawn from the experiences of professionals in the field. Numerous members of the Broadcasters Promotion Association (BPA), the international professional association of broadcast Promotion Directors, have contributed to its writing by supplying expertise, specific examples, case histories and visual materials.

In addition, other resources are provided to which the reader can turn for help in solving specific kinds of advertising, promotion and publicity problems.

This first Part includes definitions of basic terms and a brief survey of the history of broadcast promotion.

The second Part examines the Promotion Director's job—from titles and responsibilities to relationships with others at the station and at networks and ownership groups.

Part Three includes a study of the complexities of motivating human behavior—invaluable background for the creation of written and visual material necessary to advertise, publicize and promote. It also examines in detail the basic skills needed to do the jobs: knowledge of ratings and research, advertising, publicizing, promoting, and planning.

Part Four provides insight into how to cope with unusual challenges which may arise. And for those interested in careers in public television or radio, or with cable or syndication companies, this section also looks at the unique demands on Promotion Directors of these kinds of organizations.

Part Five looks at various major tasks a Promotion Director must perform by presenting case studies of specific station's activities.

The concluding section, Part Six, looks at the future of broadcasting, and what the Promotion Director's role might be.

No text can cover all the creative possibilities that a job in broadcast promotion offers, nor all the unique situations that arise to tax one's abilities. But this book does provide a solid understanding of the basics of the Promotion Director's job, and the jobs of promotion support personnel, along with a wealth of creative suggestions and places to turn for more information.

Finally, for the professional already in the field, this handbook can serve as an invaluable reminder of the basics of the profession, and an indispensable training guide for new staff members.

Welcome to the fascinating and challenging world of the broadcast Promotion Director!

CHAPTER 2

The Scope of the Job

Throughout this book, in industry trade magazines and on the job, there are constant references to a number of basic terms which define the scope of a Promotion Director's work.

First are terms which describe large-scale, overall responsibilities: Public Relations; Audience Promotion; Image Promotion; Sales Promotion; Marketing; Merchandising.

Then there are three terms which refer to the means a Promotion Director has to actually get messages to potential audiences: Advertising; Publicity; Promotion.

The following definitions have sample illustrations to provide an initial understanding of each concept. In Part Three, details are provided on how a Promotion Director becomes involved in each of the above areas and performs functions related to each concept.

PUBLIC RELATIONS

"Public relations" is a general term which encompasses virtually all contact between a radio or television organization and its various publics. These include listeners, viewers, and potential audiences, as well as more specialized groups: community leaders, advertising agencies, potential clients, media buyers, minority groups, the press, and others.

In addition to the obvious advertising, publicity and promotion techniques defined in this section of the text, effective public relations efforts encompass speaking appearances by station personalities and executives, station participation in, or in support of, community activities, membership by station management on the boards of community organizations, participation in local college broadcasting courses, and even the design of the station's lobby and the way station personnel answer the telephone.

Overall, an effective public relations effort is designed to create a positive, significant relationship between the station and the public. It enhances the station's image as a valuable asset and resource for the community. This supports the station's goals of increased audience, growing revenue, and public appreciation.

Further, a well-designed public relations plan is one that gives the station feedback from the public about its image, format, personalities and program-

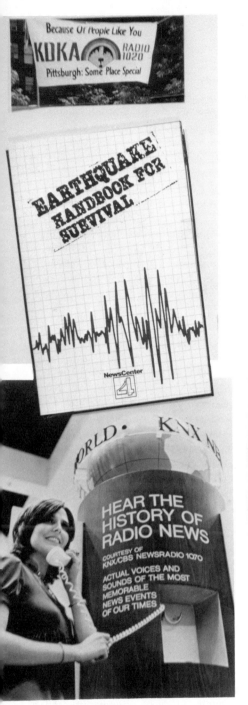

There's More to New England News Than Just the Burning Issues...

All local TV stations carry basically the same hot news items and, of course, we think our coverage is the best. But Newscenter 5's reporters strive for that interesting angle, the color, the human touch — the life of a story. It's just part of the new tradition.

channel 5 &you

A broadcast station's *public relations* activities include many interfaces with the local community. Station image ads (Channel Five), station community service efforts (Newscenter 4's Earthquake Handbook, CJBK's "blood Donor Day") KNX's History of Radio News booth and KDKA's banner at a community function are all parts of various public relations efforts.

ming. The cycle of communication between a broadcast station and the public includes not only sending out messages about the station, but receiving messages—through phone calls, letters, community contacts, and, most importantly, careful research. This input in turn helps the station to continually reshape or refine its overall public relations goals and its specific advertising, promotion and publicity messages.

PROMOTION

The word "promote" has, in part, this definition: "To contribute to the progress or growth of; To further; To attempt to sell or popularize by advertising or by securing financial support." (From the American Heritage Dictionary of the English Language, 1973.) It is from this definition that radio (and later television) stations originally derived the title, "Promotion Director." So in its broadest sense, to broadcasters, the word "promotion" encompasses all efforts to "advance the growth of," "further," or "popularize" a station and its programs. There are, however, various kinds of promotion, as you'll see in the paragraphs ahead.

AUDIENCE PROMOTION

The term "audience promotion" is a general one. It refers to advertising, promotion and publicity efforts specifically designed to increase station or program audiences. Ads, press releases and kits, contests, on-air radio and TV spots, public appearances, and much more are designed to call attention to programs and the personalities on them, and to persuade people to watch or listen. Audience promotion stresses program times, days, stars, content or story lines, personalities, and specific contests or features.

IMAGE PROMOTION

The term "image promotion" is also general. It refers to advertising, promotion and publicity designed to establish, reaffirm, or strengthen a station's image. The intent is to create in the public's mind an impression of the station as an important community resource. The emphasis might be on news, specific kinds of programs, entertainment, sports, musical format, or any other image that reflects how the station is trying to serve the public with its air time. In radio, is it the "all news station?" Or the "rock music station?" Or "the 'good' music station?" Or the "country music station?" In television, is it "the movie station?" Or the station which carries local sporting events? Or the station with the best, most comprehensive local news coverage? Or the station which does the most for its community?

There are many more radio stations than television stations. That is why most radio stations tend to specialize in particular kinds of programming appealing to specific and somewhat narrow audience interests. Radio station image promotion is largely the advertising of its format, or type of programming.

In contrast, most commercial network-affiliated television stations are

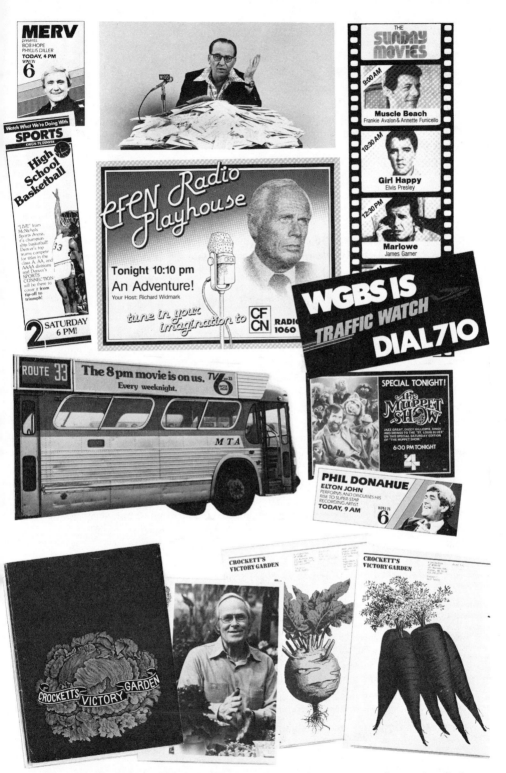

Any activity a station engages in directly to increase its program audiences is called *audience promotion.* Newspaper and TV Guide magazine ads, bus posters, contests, press kits, and billboards are all audience promotion.

competing for the same mass audience. Each is striving to project a relatively similar overall image, which usually centers around the best local news, being concerned about the community, and providing the best entertainment programming.

Independent television stations let their programming direct their image. The movie station, the sports station, the alternative programming station—all are examples.

Public radio and television stations usually strive to project an image of quality programming, and of providing specialized program services for in-school or minority interest audiences.

Elements of image promotion might focus on specific kinds of programming, the quality and experience of the news team, awards the station has won, or focus on ties between the station and the community. Slogans are frequently employed which briefly and memorably encapsulate the station's image.

SALES PROMOTION

"Sales promotion" is the term used to classify advertising promotion and publicity directed at advertising agencies, media buyers and potential clients—those in a position to buy advertising time on the station.

Competition among broadcast stations, and between broadcasting and other advertising media, is becomming more intense, a trend that will continue through the Eighties. At each station, Sales, Research and Promotion staffs must spend ever-increasing amounts of time identifying specific client groups, researching appropriate ratings and demographic statistical information, and fashioning attractive or impressive means of conveying the right information to the right potential clients.

Maps of the station's coverage area; flyers about program and day-part ratings, demographics, programs, pricing advantages over the competition, personality bios; and parties to provide advance looks at programming are among the many sales promotion activities Promotion Directors must frequently supervise.

Advertisements in the trade press such as *Broadcasting, Television/Radio Age,* and *Marketing and Media Decisions* magazines are key sales promotion elements for many stations.

For the station not in first place in overall ratings, research is essential to find ways that ratings and demographic information might show other advantages for specific advertisers.

Sales promotion is designed to assist station salespeople in selling commercial time to potential advertisers.

In the world of public broadcasting, the term "Development Department" is used in place of the commercial station's "Sales Department." Here, the Public Information (or Promotion) Director often aids the Development Department in designing and producing similar program descriptions and demographic information to interest corporate underwriters and other public stations

Above top, Boston's WSBK-TV has prepared a folder of informative material about how its coverage of the Red Sox games out-performs other local stations in drawing certain desirable audiences. This information in the hands of media buyers can help influence them to place commercials on WSBK. In the lower photo, KDKA Radio's sales staff, dressed as shown, delivered pizzas to media buyers to help get across the message that "KDKA Delivers" the right kind of audiences. These are both sales promotion activities.

in funding program production. In addition, specific development projects to attract foundation money, auction support, and viewer memberships often require promotion expertise.

And, as in commercial broadcasting, the importance of effective research on audience specifics is growing rapidly for public broadcasters.

Sales promotion and development materials stress the quantity and/or quality of viewers reached by specific programs or groups (packages) of programs.

MARKETING

Like sales promotion, "marketing" is a term of growing importance in broadcasting. It is a broad term which describes a specific plan to position the station with its potential audiences and advertisers.

Marketing is the end result of a process which starts with research to determine what programming and/or personalities the station should provide. This is followed by the development of that programming.

A television station may use such research to determine the presentation of its news coverage and the selection of its newspersons. A radio station uses research to select its format: news, talk, or type of music, etc. Once the programming is fine-tuned, advertising and promotion are scheduled to attract audience and advertiser interest. The Sales Department simultaneously moves to agressively communicate the values of the programming to customers and prospects.

Marketing also encompasses the station's sale of goods and services directly to the public. The range can include the station "store" (selling station and program-related T-shirts, coffee mugs, posters, and similar items), to a

Above left, WJXT-TV in Jacksonville's van-shaped booklet markets the station's services as a commercial production resource. Right, a Channel 11/Atlanta ad based on market research which showed that people were watching the competition's news out of habit. This ad tries to break that habit.

WHWH's "Which Hunt" contest helped get customers to the store (a station client) where this sign was posted along with entry blanks. And WBRE-TV's trumpet was sent to food store managers to let them know that P & R's advertising schedule for macaroni would soon create demand in the stores for the product. Both are merchandising efforts designed to help advertisers on the station sell their products.

coming revolution that will see many larger stations (with production facilities) producing videotape cassettes and discs of programs for direct sale to the public, or for sale to cable systems. Selling of production time to commercial clients is another potential profit area that might be part of a station's marketing effort. And cable television companies must "market" their various levels of services to the public.

MERCHANDISING

"Merchandising" refers to a station's efforts to work with its advertisers to help them sell merchandise or services. Many commercial radio stations and some television stations are heavily involved in merchandising activities.

Broadcasting from supermarkets, department stores or shopping mall locations; offering sales incentive prizes; writing letters to the advertiser's sales staff; providing distributors or dealers with point-of-purchase signs; helping products get shelf space or prominent display in stores; and product tie-ins with many other kinds of station programming are all merchandising efforts a Promotion Director may have to originate and supervise.

At many larger stations the task is so involved that a merchandising expert is brought in on either a full-time or free-lance basis.

ADVERTISING

"Advertising" is the first of three terms which define the ways stations get audience, image and sales promotion messages to the various publics.

"Advertising" vehicles are the time or space purchased or traded for by the station to put forth a message exactly as the Promotion Director intends it.

"Time" is air time on a radio or television station. The station, as an advertiser, compensates another station with money or traded time for use of specific amounts of time—usually in 10-, 20-, 30- or 60- second "spots"—to give listeners or viewers a specifically prepared message.

"Space" refers to places where printed or outdoor material appears. Most often, broadcasters buy space for print advertising in newspapers, magazines, on billboards, and on mass transit vehicles and taxis. Space can also be purchased in lobbies of hotels, airports, bus or train stations, the sides of street trash cans, and elsewhere.

In addition, there are more imaginative advertising mediums. Examples include the skywriter hired to spell out a message in the air or tow a banner behind a plane for a given length of time; and illuminated changing message boards on the sides of buildings, in ballparks, or other public places.

In addition to bartering with each other, radio and television stations often "trade" with other media. For example, air time might be traded for outdoor billboard space, magazine space, or ad space in newspapers. The ratio of traded or bartered time and space varies greatly, depending on careful negotiations usually supervised by the Promotion Director after careful coordination with the station's Sales Manager.

The principal advantages of advertising are that the Promotion Director has complete control of an ad by writing the words, designing the look, picking the artwork and photos or video and sound material, and any other elements which comprise the finished ad. The advertiser has the option of designating exactly where the message will appear, in what size or length it will appear, and for how long it will be used. In short, the advertiser has complete control of content and placement of the message.

Another advantage of advertising is its ability to reach large numbers of people at relatively small cost per person.

In relation to publicity and many forms of promotion, however, advertising can be very expensive. Production of TV and radio spots is usually costly.

Advertising includes billboards, newspaper and magazine space, and any other time or space purchased by a station to get its messages across to potential audiences.

And large stations in major markets have to budget hundreds of thousands of dollars to buy newspaper space or radio or television air time.

But such expenditures are usually justified by placement, content control and effective reach.

PUBLICITY

To a broadcaster, "publicity" means free newspaper or magazine space, or air time on another radio or TV station devoted to comment on the station, its programs, personalities, staff or activities.

Publicity may occur as a result of spontaneous comment by others. More often it is generated by the Promotion Director. The usual way a Promotion Director encourages publicity is by calling to the attention of publications and other broadcast stations information which might interest their readers or audiences.

News and feature releases (both sometimes called "press" releases), photos, press kits, and personal contact with members of the press are the most common publicity-generating tools. Through them, Promotion Departments have almost daily contact with members of the press.

Promotion events and advertising campaigns might also be designed to generate publicity.

Like advertising, publicity has certain advantages and disadvantages.

A significant disadvantage is that the station usually loses direct control over what is said, when and where the information will appear, and even whether anything will appear at all. And, of course, the station runs the risk of incurring negative comments about programs, format changes, personalities, or station activities by reporters, critics, columnists or editors.

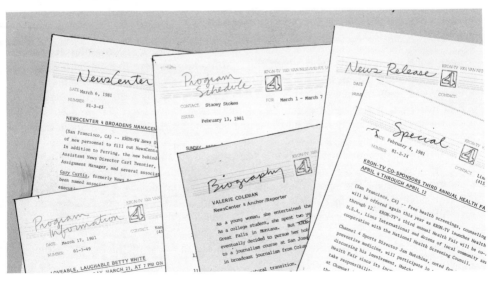

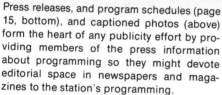

Press releases, and program schedules (page 15, bottom), and captioned photos (above) form the heart of any publicity effort by providing members of the press information about programming so they might devote editorial space in newspapers and magazines to the station's programming.

However, the major advantages of publicity are important. Compared to advertising, costs of maintaining press and media contacts are very low. And most important of all, there is a distinct advantage to having information about the station, and especially its programs, come to the viewer not from the station directly as in an ad or promotional announcement, but from a third party such as a newspaper columnist or critic—presumably impartial and trusted sources.

PROMOTIONS

"Promotions" refer to a station's efforts to impart a specific message to the public directly. As with advertising, promotions involve the station putting across exactly the message it wants to impart. Like publicity, promotions involve no costs for space or time, although there are usually costs for production of materials or staging of events and activities.

Promotions are divided into two distinct categories: on-air promotion, and off-air promotion.

On-air promotion is a station's use of its own air time to advise viewers or listeners about its programs, format or personalities, and persuade them to listen or watch. The approaches and motivational techniques are the same as with advertising. In fact, some stations refer to on-air promotion spots (called "promos") as "*broadcast* advertising," even though they don't have to pay for their own air time.

The costs involved in on-air promotion are those of producing the audio and/or video materials to be aired.

Parades and street signs serve as promotion vehicles.

Major television stations consider on-air promotion their most cost-effective means of reaching large numbers of people.

For radio and television stations with smaller or more fragmented audiences, extensive off-air promotion, advertising and publicity are essential to reach non-viewers or potential listeners.

Off-air promotion is sometimes called non-air promotion, or often just "promotion." It includes a laundry-list of activities and items designed to call public attention to a station and its programs or personalities. Examples include: brochures, flyers and posters; pens, pencils, coffee mugs, T-shirts and other items imprinted with the station's logo, call letters, channel number, dial position, and/or slogan; contests; appearances by station personalities at fairs and other public gatherings; and many additional similar devices, gimmicks and opportunities.

Off-air promotion activities are frequently supported by advertising and designed to attract publicity to increase their impact.

SUMMARY

These definitions begin to show the overall scope of the job of the broadcast Promotion Director. Each area is examined more closely in the chapters ahead, especially in Part Three.

Even though specific responsibilities of Promotion Directors at different stations may vary, all of the above elements come into play for the professional in the field at one time or another. Various kinds of advertising, publicity and promotions become part of larger public relations, promotional, merchandising and marketing strategies designed to increase station audiences, improve the flow of persuasive information to the various publics, and better the station's ability to attract income.

Station promotions include everything from snowman contests to sock hops, and from golf course sign donations to look-alike contests.

CHAPTER 3

A Brief History

RADIO'S BEGINNINGS

Radio as an advertising medium was not anticipated, it sprang upon America at a time of great need and was of considerable usefulness.

Print advertising became well-established during the second decade of this century. It was living up to the modest expectations of advertising—bringing buyer and seller together to acquaint the buyer with the "what, where and how much" of an expanding economy.

The United States was a nation of diminishing rural and burgeoning urban living. A quarter of a million miles of railroads distributed an expanding list of manufactured goods to a widely dispersed population in rapidly growing cities. These cities provided a fast-increasing supply of skilled and semi-skilled labor to run the increasingly efficient machinery of production. Soon whole industries were concentrated in a few cities—textiles clustered in the urban areas of New England; steel furnaces lit the skies of Pittsburgh and Birmingham; Ivory Soap crowned Cincinnati as the capital of cleanliness; Battle Creek and Minneapolis ground the kernels of the Midwest to flour and cereals.

Americans were making things of grains and fibers and metals at a rate that soon threatened to outstrip demand. A new force was needed to help bring consumption into line with production.

Advertising was that force. Through the Twenties, as the economic level of the country was creating the means to provide the individual with more than he needed, advertising began to *create demand* to take up the slack in the supply/demand balance. A steadily rising level of literacy helped print advertising gain initial dominance as the touchstone to ensure demand for just about anything offered for sale. In the words of a leading advertising man of the times: "Advertising is *salesmanship*—in print!"

This early editorial cartoon in the Denver Post, supplied by station KOA in Denver, captures the spirit of gleeful enthusiasm that greeted radio in its early days.

The emergence of radio, with its ability to send the human voice over the horizon, out of sight of the sender, meant *people*—by the thousands, beyond the reach of the print media, offering access to themselves via their ears—access by advertisers from near at hand and across the continent.

Radio's listeners increased in numbers by leaps and bounds. Teenagers and hobbyists alike, with minor financial investment and minimal technical skills, stayed up late at night to listen to anything on the air, as long as it originated from beyond the horizon, from a place unfamiliar and far away. The audience was ready and waiting to be entertained, informed. Since a large number of the early stations were owned by newspapers, hotels and manufacturers of radios, early radio *promoted* its owners, bidding for the attention of potential buyers of radio equipment, hotel guests, and diners.

And, as they achieved success in helping themselves, radio station owners quickly realized the potential profit in sharing this bonanza with other businesses which might wish to talk to—and sell to—the cascading number of radio listeners. Enter the sponsor. And enter the need to attract more listeners for the sponsor's message, as station's began to vie with each other for advertisers. So promotion has been a part of broadcasting since its earliest days.

EARLY PROMOTION EFFORTS

The first problem for stations was how to determine the number of people listening, or at least to develop comparative estimates that could be used with competing stations and to draw advertisers from the print media to radio. Lacking any better gauge, much emphasis was placed on the mail received from listeners addressed to the station and its on-air personalities. This seemed to be evidence akin to the newspaper and magazine counts of numbers of copies sold. At least it was tangible evidence in an area of intangibles. So broadcasting brains focused on ways to increase the flow of mail to the station—"keep those cards and letters coming, folks!" Claims and counterclaims were made by stations about the "tons" of mail received in "just one week from 18 states and three Canadian provinces!" Promotion campaigns were mounted to induce listeners to write in for premiums and give-aways. (Both are still an important part of radio station promotion.)

As early as 1922, Westinghouse published "Radio News," a weekly magazine of station programming free to listeners and replete with ads for Westinghouse products—but none for its competitors.

Numerous publications sprang up addressed to the interest of the listener, most including skeleton logs of stations on the air.

Ads for stations were plentiful, especially for the big clear channel stations which served large areas.

For all practical purposes, industry trade publications began with *Broadcast Advertising* in 1928. This magazine later became *Broadcasting* in 1931. Ads for stations to encourage advertisers were an early feature and remain so today. Early ads set a lasting style, with flamboyant type faces, extravagant claims, and very common use of the numeral "1" and words such as "first," "largest," "best," "oldest," "friendliest," etc., etc.

From the earliest days of radio, station identification was a promotional challenge. Stations selected call letters that listeners could remember with ease. Each letter stood for a word and the words formed an identifying phrase or slogan:

WEBH/Chicago—The Edgewater Beach Hotel.
WEEI/Boston—The Edison Electric Institute.
WCFL/Chicago—The Chicago Federation of Labor.
WBIG/Greensboro, N.C.—We Believe in Greensboro.
WTOP/Washington, DC—Washington, at the TOP of the dial.
WEAF/New York—Wind, Earth, Air, Fire.
WIOD/Miami Beach—Wonderful Isle O'Dreams.
KECA/Los Angeles—Earle C. Anthony (a local automobile dealer).
WGN/Chicago—The World's Greatest Newspaper (Chicago *Tribune*).
WOW/Omaha—The Woodman of the World
WGBS/New York—The Gimbel Brothers Store
WCCO/Minneapolis—The Washburn Crosby Company (millers)
KFSG/Los Angeles ("Four Square Gospel"—Aimee Semple McPherson's
    station.)

Along with promoting the station's call letters, early ads called attention to such things as increased power ("WOR to 50kw—More Power to You"); new studios and/or transmitters and locations; announcements of talent additions to programs and station staffs; and, of course, promotion of programs and of advertiser success stories.

And intense internecine strife was rampant. In Chicago, all three network affiliates individually conducted surveys which "proved" beyond a shadow of doubt, that each was FIRST among the city's stations. The leading independent station let the dust settle a bit after the media advertising blasts, then ran its own ad which said, "We don't know who is first, but we're pleased that *all three competitors agree that we are second!"*

EARLY RATINGS

The increasing sophistication of the buyers of time, plus a desire to provide more and better information about its audiences soon brought radio past the "mail-counting" stage to the beginnings of audience research as it is known today. Engineering advances made possible accurate measurements of signal strength and station coverage areas, allowing stations to know for sure how many potential listeners were available in the market. The stage was set for "where is our audience?", and the more crucial "how many are listening?"

It would be many more years before research was able to determine with precision just what kinds of people composed broadcast audiences.

As early as 1929, Archibald M. Crossley was experimenting with telephone recall studies in some midwestern markets. By 1934 his work was expanded to a continuing survey of 30 major U.S. cities, endorsed and partially funded by the Association of National Advertisers. While the Crossley Reports were limited to essentially a popularity poll of network programs, they occupied a position of prominence similar to that enjoyed today by A.C. Nielsen's National Television Index (NTI).

Originally the radio networks were excluded from subscription to Crossley's Cooperative Analysis of Broadcasting—or CAB—reports. But the data was leaked in torrents and provided grist for the mills of columnists across the land. These columns were quoted by the network and affiliate promotion staffs to establish the superiority of their programs (NBC), leadership in radio drama (CBS), local savour (Mutual Broadcasting) and their competitive positions when all carried major events simultaneously.

PROMOTION DEVELOPS

Through the 1930s, many of the main tools of radio promotion were developed by stations and networks. After initial controversy, newspapers agreed to carry listings of radio programs without pay. Broadcasting from store windows proved a popular way for many stations to call attention to their on-air personalities. Remote broadcasts—though cumbersome by today's standards— were regular features. Newspaper advertising helped call attention to network programs.

Since a majority of stations were affiliated with a major national network, it was those network programs that drew the largest audiences, just as is the case with television in more recent times. Most newspaper ads trumpeted NBC or CBS or Mutual programs, stars and special guests.

As television replaced radio as the dominant broadcasting medium in the 1950s, and radio programming changed from dramatic and entertainment programs to music formats, contests began to play a larger role in radio promotion. Money give-aways helped draw listeners, and continue to do so to this day.

In the world of radio, promotion, programming and sales drew even closer together as the need to program audience-attracting and client-attracting material became critical.

Television station promotion directors began their efforts in many of the same ways as their radio station counterparts: print advertising was the staple, with listings information supplied to local newspapers. The prime-time entertainment programs drew the most attention until the mid-1960s, when station revenue derived from news programming began to grow. Then, especially at commercial network-affiliated TV stations, advertising and promotion dollars began to shift into the news area, promoting news concepts and equipment, special news features, and on-air news personalities.

Hand-in-hand with this shift of emphasis came the beginnings of marketing concepts that saw increasing use of outside consultants who came in to advise stations on their whole news product. They not only suggested anchorpeople and reporters, but titles, themes, and advertising and content approaches—all based on careful research of a station's market.

As successes in this marketing approach brought greater audiences to news, the concept began to spread into other forms of programming in the 1970s. Prime-time access programs, and counter-programming by a number of independent stations became dependent on the more sophisticated, research-oriented marketing processes. Promotion and advertising, too, drew its inspiration from much more careful analysis of audience needs, wants, and preferences.

In today's broadcast promotion world, the station Promotion Director not only needs to know the basics of public relations and advertising, but must command a working knowledge of the entire marketing process, from researching the community, to programming to meet community preferences, to basing campaigns on those preferences.

It is still useful to know how many responses a radio station disc jockey or contest can draw. And the cultivated newspaper article or *TV Guide* ad are still important. But in the highly competitive and unpredictable world of the 1980s, a Promotion Director must be prepared in a much broader way to analyze the market and approach it with well thought-out campaigns that effectively stimulate potential audiences and motivate viewing or listening. They must work hand-in-hand with programming, sales and news directors to ensure a total station effort in each area. Broadcast promotion has matured into a vital and highly rewarding profession.

CHAPTER 4

The Broadcasters Promotion Association

Founded in 1956, the Broadcasters Promotion Association (BPA) is a non-profit international professional association. Its membership includes Promotion Directors of radio and television stations and networks in the U.S. and Canada, as well as in England, Australia, New Zealand, Mexico, and a growing list of other countries.

BPA is the only professional association specifically geared to providing services and professional educational opportunities for the people about whom this handbook is written. However, there are other organizations, associations, and services of great value to Promotion Directors. As a result, it is not unusual for a Promotion Director to wear many association hats and to avail him or herself of added ideas and information gained from additional memberships.

The BPA's stated goals are to:

- Increase the effectiveness of broadcast promotion personnel.
- Improve broadcast promotion methods, research principles and techniques.
- Enhance the image and professional status of its members, and members of the broadcast promotion profession.
- Facilitate liaison with allied organizations in broadcasting, promotion, and government.
- Assist management in finding competent broadcast promotion personnel.
- Increase awareness and understanding of broadcast promotion at stations, in the community, and at colleges and universities.

It is in the context of several of these goals that BPA has sponsored the preparation of this handbook. Many BPA members have contributed their expertise, and samples of their efforts, to the authors.

BPA membership includes advertising, promotion, publicity, public information, and design personnel from:

- Commercial TV and radio stations and networks.
- Public TV and radio stations and national and regional networks.
- Vendors of promotion-related materials and services.
- College and university broadcasting instructors and students.
- Advertising agency personnel
- Cable company personnel.

BPA members exchange ideas and experiences annually at a major national seminar—one of the largest in the broadcasting industry—as well as in a monthly newsletter, special magazines, and through a growing library of audiovisual and print samples from its membership.

BPA and its members and committees study, report on, and exchange information about relevant matters related to the broadcast industry. The overall goal is to help BPA members better serve the companies for whom they work, as well as the interests of the public.

The organization also has as a major goal the broadening of horizons and professional skills and abilities of its individual members. It does this by providing opportunities for contact with other experts in the field and exposure to new concepts and ideas.

Annual Seminars

BPA members gather annually for a three-day Seminar of promotion-related activities. Workshops, major industry speakers, displays of promotion-related materials and services provide the formal structure for discovering fresh approaches to common challenges. Informal opportunities abound to meet and exchange ideas with hundreds of fellow promotion, advertising, publicity, research and public relations experts from the broadcast industry throughout the world.

Each BPA Seminar is carefully planned to explore important new trends; seek solutions to industry-wide problems; and exchange ideas or learn new techniques on topics of special interest, including various forms of advertising, on-air promotion, contests, research, sales promotion, graphics, and much more.

At its 24th consecutive annual Seminar, held in 1979 in Nashville, BPA formed an alliance with the newly created Broadcast Designers Association (BDA) to hold joint Seminars, bringing promotion and design expertise together for the benefit of both.

Seminars are held in cities in various parts of the United States and Canada. At this writing, upcoming Seminar sites include: 1983—New Orleans, Louisiana; 1984—Las Vegas, Nevada; 1985—Chicago, Illinois; 1986—Dallas, Texas. Students from local college communications departments are frequently invited to work at each Seminar, offering excellent exposure to people in the industry and to promotion ideas.

Publications

BPA's monthly *Newsletter* is a principal means of exchanging ideas among BPA members. Each issue places special emphasis on photos and articles about promotion, advertising and publicity successes. Advertising in the *Newsletter* keeps the membership aware of many companies whose services can be especially valuable, from vendors of promotional give-aways, to market research firms, to animation production companies.

In addition, BPA publishes four or five "Big Ideas" magazines each year on specific topics. Traditionally, one issue covers many of the formal activities at the annual Seminar. Other magazine topics include sales promotion, on-air promotion, contests, station anniversaries, and advertising, each issue filled with samples of what stations are doing around the nation.

Employment Service

A Committee of the BPA Board of Directors maintains contact with broadcast promotion professionals and graduates who are seeking employment in the industry, and provides them with names of stations or companies that are hiring. Conversely, the service also supplies names of appropriately qualified job applicants to member stations.

Library

BPA has the nation's most extensive library of broadcast promotion and advertising material, housed at the Communications Department of San Diego State University. Hundreds of video and audio tapes of promotion spots are available for reference by members at modest dubbing fees. Also, audio tapes of BPA Seminar workshops, and extensive files of print, outdoor, and other statio advertising ave available for the cost of reproduction.

Awards

In conjunction with the San Diego State University, BPA runs a major annual awards competition to honor the best advertising, promotion and publicity efforts of all broadcast stations. (BPA membership is not a requirement for entering the competition.)

Award categories include overall campaigns, on-air efforts, sales promotion, and community involvement. Awards are given for each category in large, medium and small market sizes to avoid pitting small stations with limited resources against major market stations with huge budgets.

Additional information about the Broadcasters Promotion Association, its services, and membership can be obtained by writing:

> Administrative Secretary
> BPA Headquarters
> 248 W. Orange Street
> Lancaster, PA 17603

Part Two

The Broadcast
Promotion Director

Before beginning a detailed analysis of the varied work of a Promotion Director, it is instructive to place the job in context. By exploring responsibilities and the positioning of the job at a broadcast station, as well as the relationships of the person who holds the job to other station management positions, the reader will better understand why certain tasks are necessary, how they help the station's overall efforts, and how some tasks are accomplished as part of a team, rather than by a Promotion Director alone.

The focus of this section is on leadership qualities needed by a Promotion Director to help the station achieve its goals, special qualities required for a dual management and creative position, and the unique tensions that are inherent in such a dual position.

CHAPTER 5

Different Titles

The person in charge of advertising, promotion and publicity at a radio or television station might have any one of a number of titles other than Promotion Director. Some of them are:

- Director of Advertising, Promotion and Publicity
- Director of Creative Services
- Public Information Director
- Director of Information Services
- Director of Corporate Communications
- Marketing Director

Some stations substitute "Manager" for "Director" in the title. In some cases, the position is held by a "Vice President." Occasionally, "Supervisor" or "Coordinator" are used. And, at many smaller stations—especially radio— the promotion duties are performed by a Program Director, Sales Manager, or even the General Manager.

Other stations might have a staff member who serves as Promotion Director, but some traditional Promotion Department functions may reside elsewhere at the station. On-air promotion, for example, might be the responsibility of the Program Department; or sales promotion might be totally the responsibility of the Sales Department.

It is important to never assume what a Promotion Director's job includes, but to look carefully at the job description at any particular station. There are, however, some clues—by no means universal—which can help predict what functions are actually included in the job.

The most traditional term, "Director of Advertising, Promotion and Publicity,'' is a straight-forward attempt to let the title describe all the major kinds of work the job includes. When the shorter titles "Advertising Director" and "Publicity Director" are used, they generally imply that the person's scope is limited to one or the other of those two more specific areas, usually under someone with a broader title. However, when the shorter term, "Promotion Director" is used, it is generally shorthand for the longer title, "Director of Advertising, Promotion and Publicity."

Since "Promotion Director" has come to be an umbrella title, or shorthand, in the industry, it is the way this text consistently refers to the position.

At some broadcasting stations, the title "Director of Information Services" is gaining popularity. It usually encompasses all the above functions, but is phrased in a more self-serving way to give a public relations gloss to the fact that the person "providing information" is really in the business of attracting audiences and advertisers.

The title "Director of Creative Services" is relatively new, and also growing in popularity with the growing importance and scope of the Promotion Director's job. It usually implies that a station has included the graphics, art or design department under promotion and given the Director greater control over all non-program creative production by the station. It may also mean that additional responsibilities in sales promotion and research have been added.

At many public television and radio stations, the title "Director of Public Information" is common. This stems from the early days of "educational" broadcasting when small viewing audiences rendered on-air promotion relatively unimportant, so it was not part of the job. The most important task was supplying information to the press and public so that, if they chose to watch, they might know what was on the air. Attracting audiences was not a priority. However, public broadcasting's continuing and growing need for funds has made attracting larger audiences imperative, so the "Public Information Director's" job has become almost identical to that of a commercial station Promotion Director. (Some major differences are discussed in Part Five.) In recent years, the trend for many public stations has been to change the job title to one of those listed above.

The title "Director of Corporate Communications" (or "Corporate Information") implies that there is more than one distinct entity for which the person has promotion responsibility. Such combinations might include a radio and TV station, a TV station and a production facility, or all three. It might also mean that the bearer of the title works for a group that owns several stations, or even newspapers and broadcast stations in different markets. This person, often a Vice President, helps unify the efforts of those stations in the group, and where possible, enacts cost-saving measures by avoiding duplication and overlapping work at various stations.

When the title "Director of Marketing" is used, it implies that the parent company has branched out to provide services in addition to just programming sent over the air. Perhaps new services or products are being developed for public consumption, such as premium items, videotapes or discs. The station might sell studio production time to commercial enterprises, involving special marketing efforts. Or the job might involve working with the Program Director, News Director, and research staff to develop new programs and fine-tune existing ones to conform to public needs and expectations.

Usually the marketing job is so complex that it requires a seperate person to supervise it. In such cases the Promotion Director may support the Marketing Director's office by producing print materials, supervising logo usage, or coordinating the look of programs and program-related materials.

The term "Promotion Director" is considered by some in the industry to be old-fashioned and not indicative of the scope of a job that has grown to be much more than simply "promotion" as defined in the opening section of this text. Through the years, as the job has grown, the title has evolved from "Sales Promotion Director" or "Promotion Director" to "Director of Creative Services" or "Director of Information Services."

Others in the industry argue, however, that these new titles are too vague. They feel that the heart of the job is, and will remain promotion (along with advertising and publicity). The title, they believe, should clearly say so.

One experienced promotion pro recently referred to the new titles as "dressing up the old carnival barker in a tuxedo and having him do his spiel in an Oxford accent. It leads," he cautioned, "to a case of mistaken identity."

"Basically," he continued, "broadcasting is showbiz. All else derives from that, whether it be shows or news or weather or information specials. It's something that attracts people to see and hear whatever is being offered for public consumption. Who will get the lion's share of viewers or listeners? Well, that depends on who waves the flag in front of the customer—and he who waves the reddest flag, the largest flag, the flakiest flag, is going to wind up on top. That, simply put, is the essence of Showmanship—and the key to promotion."[1]

The other side of the "promotion" issue is equally clear and compelling. Many stations feel a need for a dignified image reflecting responsible corporate concern for the community and its citizens. They also recognize that the art of research has become extremely sophisticated, and now enables highly targeted promotion efforts. It is not necessarily the largest, reddest, or flakiest flag that gets attention, but precisely the right flag held in front of just the right person or group at just the right moment. Effective promotion has become an exacting science rather than noise-making exploitation.

Certainly the growth of station promotion and advertising budgets, the emergence of station research staffs, the inclusion of broader areas of responsibility under Promotion Director umbrellas, and the sophistication of job titles supports the latter contention.

But it is also true that the effective Promotion Director, whatever his or her title may have become, does not forget the roots of the profession. They are firmly planted in the elements of creativity and imagination that in the past,

[1] Sid Mesibov, former ABC-TV exploitation expert, in a speech to BPA's 1979 Nashville Seminar.

present and future are capable of devising fresh, original approaches to the continuing challenges of attracting the attention of audiences, advertisers and the press.

Each individual radio and television station, network and group must examine its own needs, goals, directions, and staff, and must choose the title it considers most appropriate. In this text the term "Promotion Director" is used consistently, but with full recognition that there is now much more to the job than just flag-waving and flakey promotion of days gone by.

CHAPTER 6

Job Responsibilities *

What does the Promotion Director do at the average television or radio station? Here, in outline form, is a broad list of the responsibilities that can be, and often are, included in the job. At small stations, one versatile person has to do just about everything on this list with very little assistance. At larger stations, this "King Solomon" has to have done nearly everything in the list at one time or another, and must be able to supervise a staff—sometimes as many as 10 or 15 people—in most or all of these activities. (Radio and TV station activities have been combined into one all-inclusive list):

AUDIENCE PROMOTION

Promotion Directors must have a thorough command of audience motivation processes, and extensive background in research techniques necessary to guide motivational efforts. The following skills are also necessary:

On-Air Promotion and Broadcast Advertising:

- Copy writing.
- Previewing and selecting tape and film excerpts, music tracks and sound effects.
- Selecting talent (actors, announcers).
- Scheduling promotion announcements (or placing TV and radio advertisements).

*This chapter is adapted from material originally prepared for the BPA Newsletter by Mort Slakoff, Vice President of Creative Services for MCA.

- Evaluating media for ad placement.
- Recommending and coordinating trade arrangements with other broadcast stations.
- Maintaining promo library or inventory.
- Assuring the consistency and overall creativity of each promotion spot as well as each entire campaign.
- Directing the creative processes of promo production.
- Evaluating the effectiveness of promotion spots.
- Editing music, sound and video materials.

Newspaper and Magazine Advertising:

- Preparing ad schedules based on priorities and available program schedules.
- Securing artwork/graphic materials for ad production.
- Copy writing.
- Artwork and design supervision, including type selection and overall appearance.
- Determining appropriate ad size and frequency.
- Coordinating trade arrangements.
- Securing approvals and ensuring delivery of finished artwork to publication by deadline.
- Directing ad agency efforts.

Outdoor and Transit Advertising:

- Coordinating trade arrangements.
- Researching cost effectiveness.
- Selecting locations.
- Supervising creative concepts, including copy and design.
- Supervising production of materials.

Special Campaigns:

- Developing press and publicity campaigns for station originated group or network programming.
- Maintaining knowledge of network and/or group needs, to best supply them with effective materials.
- Arranging ad co-ops when outside money is available to support programs.
- Maintaining national and trade press contacts to assist in promotion of group or network programs, if station regularly produces them.

Other Forms of Audience Promotion:

Coordinating and supervising contests, including:

- Originating or adapting the idea.
- Ensuring conformance to legal restrictions.

- Making contests appealing to local audiences.
- Arranging trades for prizes.
- Arranging for judging.
- Ensuring fairness and honesty.
- Maintaining accurate records.
- Publicizing participating clients.

Originating many ingenious and unusual promotion ideas to bring attention to individual programs and the station. This category is limited only by budget and imagination. The Promotion Director must organize, arrange, compensate—through cash or trade—and follow through on these forms of promotion and more like them:

- Ticket Envelopes.
- Supermarket bags.
- Shopping-mall tie-ins.
- Retail outlet tie-ins.
- Book and record company tie-ins.
- Painting the sides of buildings.
- Skywriting or sky banners.
- Parades.
- Fireworks displays.
- Personalized mailings.
- Posters, flyers, brochures.
- Personal appearances.
- Station guide magazine production.
- Bill stuffers.
- Station program guide magazine.

SALES PROMOTION

Promotion Directors must have a thorough understanding of research, sales, merchandising and marketing techniques in order to write and supervise the layout and production of:

- Customized written and audio/visual sales presentations.
- Sales brochures, flyers, posters.
- Coverage maps.
- Major client presentations.
- Generalized sales presentations (written and audio/visual).
- Direct mail campaigns.
- Coordination of graphics for commercial operations, e.g., camera cards, commercials, etc.
- Supervision of agency and client reception, including:

  - Theme development.
  - Location selection and arrangements.

- Budget for the event.
- Catering arrangements.
- Entertainment selection.
- Decor.
- Guest lists and invitations.

- Maintenance of familiarity with suppliers and sources of new, imaginative gifts for station giveaways and premiums for agency personnel and clients.
- Preparation of post-program promotion reports for clients or underwriters.

RESEARCH

Promotion Directors should have the ability to plan, develop and analyze research on audiences, media reach, and rating demographics, or to supervise such work with station or outside research staff. Included are:

- Reading and accurately interpreting ratings.
- Maintaining knowledge of additional in-depth studies available from rating services.
- Maintaining familiarity with services of outside research firms.
- Developing, or supervising development of accurate, impressive, creative, easy to understand presentations of research results.

COMMUNITY RELATIONS

Promotion Directors work closely with Community Relations Directors (if there is one), or directly supervise:

- Public service campaigns.
- Community tie-in promotions.
- Station tours.
- Logging of public service activities for FCC filing.
- Ascertainment.
- Community Relations.
- Answering viewer letters or phone calls.
- Coordination of community speaking engagements by station personalities and management staff.

STATION IMAGE

Promotion Directors coordinate the overall graphic look or sound of a station, including:

- All uses of station logo.
- Station on-air identifications.

· Corporate identification, including stationary, letterheads and business cards,

In addition, they prepare and submit presentations for awards. This includes:

· Maintaining complete roster of awards competitions, entry dates, rules, etc.
· Preparing impressive entry presentations, either in print or audio/visual.
· Promotion of station awards when won.
· Preparing awards display area at station.

Design and look of station building exterior and lobby might also fall in this category.

PRESS RELATIONS

Promotion Directors develop and maintain close personal contact with members of the press and broadcast media. This includes:

· Lunches and personal meetings and phone calls.
· Developing an interest in the likes, dislikes, habits, hobbies and other activities of key members of the press.
· Providing magazines, newspapers and cable systems with accurate advance program information and late changes.
· Developing feature stories and press outlets for them for stories on:

· Station personnel.
· News programming and personalities.
· Specials, or program highlights.
· Visiting celebrities.
· Unusual station events and promotions.
· Unusual production activities.

· Keeping complete press clipping files to measure effectiveness of press activities, and for use in sales and other presentations, ads, etc.
· Organizing press screenings and receptions for special program events. This includes:

· Providing catering.
· Preparing invitations and guest lists.
· Preparing special press kits.
· Ensuring presence of appropriate station or program personnel or talent.

· Providing the press with news releases on station programs.
· Preparing major press kits for new seasons or special groups of programs.

INTERNAL PR AND STAFF SUPERVISION

Promotion Directors not only must assemble, organize and lead their own staffs, but often have responsibility for station staff morale. This includes:

- Building and maintaining a closely knit, effective promotion staff:

    - Knowing where to find talented new staff members.
    - Supervising staff work loads.
    - Advising, teaching, helping staff members grow in capabilities.
    - Training new personnel, interns.
    - Administering salaries, raises, vacations, sick time, etc.
    - Helping promotion staff understand and adhere to company policies and procedures.

- Writing, or supervising production of station in-house newsletter.
- Assisting General Manager with intra-company communications.
- Keeping entire station staff informed of current promotions, themes, and community tie-in events.
- Organizing the station sports teams (softball, basketball, etc.)
- Making premiums available to the staff (T-shirts, coffee mugs, etc. imprinted with station logo, theme, etc.)

GENERAL ADMINISTRATION

- Preparing and administering department budget.
- Supervising art or graphics department.
- Preparing post-campaign evaluation of department activities.
- Maintaining close liaison with network (if affiliated,) or group (if owned by one), and coordinating appropriate efforts.
- Coordinating promotion projects with other station departments.
- Preparing monthly reports for General Manager and other executives.
- Attending station staff meetings, providing input, and keeping up-to-date on all activities of all other station departments.
- Maintaining liaison with program suppliers for promotion information.
- Cultivating reliable, reasonably-priced suppliers for printing, catering, photographic, artwork, and other potential outside needs.
- Maintaining file of updated bios and photos of station on-air staff and management personnel.
- Maintaining up-to-date knowledge of competition's promotional activities, including their staffs, budgets, and campaigns.
- Keeping abreast of all new technologies, equipment, trends in graphics, and current fads and popular themes.
- Maintaining awareness of legal restrictions on advertising and promotion.

• Maintaining awareness of company policies regarding use of trademarks, copyright information, and other legalities.
• Informing trade publications of station management personnel changes.

Some stations do not require all of the above from one person. Many, however, do. And while the above list does mix some responsibilities that are unique to radio, television, and public broadcasters, nevertheless it is a list that covers all the activities in which a Promotion Director *may* become involved.

CHAPTER 7

The Promotion Director's Staff

Most Promotion Directors have one or more staff members to assist them with the mountain of tasks they must perform. At smaller stations, it might only be a secretary. At large stations in big markets, at public stations which regularly produce national network programs, and at station groups or networks there may be as many as 15 or more people.

Rather than examine the extremes, or all the possibilities, this section looks at a basic division of responsibilities that might exist at a typical medium-sized broadcast station.

Different kinds of skills are important in four basic areas: advertising, on-air promotion, publicity and PR, and sales promotion.

Advertising requires print design, copy and layout skills, and a specialized knowledge of media-buying.

On-air promotion calls for skills in slide, videotape, and film copywriting, production, and in on-air scheduling or placement of promotion spots.

Press, publicity and public relations work needs a different kind of writing ability—more factual and less openly persuasive than advertising and promotion writing. The person in this position also has frequent contact with members of the press—critics, columnists, reviewers—and must work closely with visiting stars or personalities. Charm, an outgoing personality and a degree of sophistication are helpful characteristics.

Sales promotion requires most of the above traits and abilities, plus skill in developing useful research and translating it into easy-to-grasp visual or print formats. A flair for coming up with attractive, unusual, attention-getting gimmicks, devices, concepts and themes is of great value.

If the budget permits, the Promotion Director may have the luxury of being able to hire different people for each of these four major job areas. Selecting the precise person for each enables a close match of skills to job requirements. In medium and smaller stations and markets, however, there may only be enough money in the budget for one or two assistants to handle all four areas.

In addition to administrative and supervisory work, the Promotion Director at such a smaller station normally takes on whichever of the four areas he or she is most comfortable with, or the area the station considers most important. Nonetheless, the Promotion Director must have a familiarity with all areas in the Department.

For example, the Promotion Director might handle all advertising and media buying as well as overall planning and Department supervision. Press relations, on-air promotion and sales promotion would then be handled by assistants. Other Department tasks are assigned as time and individual capabilities permit. Promotional literature and sales promotion pieces might best be written, for instance, by the person handling on-air promotion; while station brochures, annual reports, and sophisticated award entries might best be prepared by the press person who has a more factual writing style. Station contests and promotions could be the province of the advertising or promotion person; while public appearances, station tours, and station participation in community events would fall to the press and public relations member of the staff.

Of course, at most stations, many Promotion Department activities require active participation by all staff members. Fall preview parties, for instance, require the production skills of the on-air person, the party-giving talents usually found in the press representative, the design flair of the advertising staff, and development of meaningful and persuasive sales information by the sales promotion person. The Promotion Director plans, budgets and supervises.

Brief, typical job descriptions of the four basic positions follow in outline form.

Advertising Manager

- Prepares schedule of programs which are to be advertised (usually in conjunction with Program Director and Sales Director.)
- Acquires photographs or art material for use in ad.
- Supervises design of ad, and writes ad copy.
- Places ads in local (and national trade) publications and *TV Guide.*
- Arranges ad barter or trade agreements.
- Handles ad billings.
- Places bold-face listings in newspapers.
- Buys radio and/or television time on local stations.
- Handles relations with advertising agency, if the station uses one.
- In public broadcasting, solicits advertising grants from companies underwriting programs, and administers advertising co-ops with other stations carrying those programs.

On-air Promotion Manager

- Writes and produces videotape promos (for TV) and audiotape promos or copy (for radio).
- Writes on-air and voice-over credit promotion copy.
- Supervises design and production of station identification slides and animation.
- Schedules promotion spots and identification spots (IDs) on air, or supervises such scheduling by traffic personnel.
- Handles on-air contests.
- Writes and produces video presentations for sales and press use.

Publicity Manager

- Writes all news and feature releases.
- Supervises photography and prepares photo cut lines (captions).
- Develops contacts and maintains liaison with members of the local press.
- Plans and coordinates station press parties, screenings, tours, and other activities designed to get publicity.
- Plans and supervises schedules of visiting celebrities.
- Writes in-house staff newsletter.
- Supervises preparation of weekly or monthly "listings" or "logs," chronologic summaries of the station's broadcast schedule.
- Administers station speaker's bureau, and provides material for speeches by station personnel and others.
- At public stations, prepares monthly program guide magazine, if there is not a separate editor.
- Maintains file of press clippings and prepares publicity reports as campaign follow-ups.

Sales Promotion Manager

- Works with sales and research staffs to develop meaningful information for agencies and clients.
- Writes and oversees design of flyers, brochures, direct mail pieces, and other literature to attract business.
- Supervises previews, receptions, and station events designed for agency and client personnel.
- Prepares post-buy reports of promotion activities for clients, including ratings and demographic information.

Secretary

A key person on any promotion staff is the department secretary, sometimes called administrative assistant. This person:

- Maintains files of program information.
- Maintains correspondence and other pertinent files.
- Maintains photo morgue, or library.
- Prepares weekly or monthly listings or logs, and follows through with changes and updates.
- Prepares finished typing of releases and other material for duplication.
- Provides budget administration assistance.

With this kind of staff support, the Promotion Director assigns, directs, and supervises all the above tasks, and bears responsibility for their success. He or she also administers the budget, handles personnel matters (salaries, vacations, hiring, promoting, evaluating, training, etc.), and works with staff members and others at the station to develop overall campaigns, themes, marketing and merchandising approaches, and departmental policies and procedures.

The Promotion Director also approves all ads and promos developed by the staff, deals directly with the press on sensitive matters, and maintains a close rapport with the General Manager and other department heads.

LOCATION IN THE STATION HIERARCHY

As titles and responsibilities differ, so does the location of the Promotion Department at various stations. If there is a "normal" position for the Promotion Director and the promotion staff, it is at the "department head" level, directly under the station's General Manager, in a position equal to the Program Director, Business Affairs Director, Community Services Director, Sales Director and Chief Engineer.

The official position taken by the Broadcasters Promotion Association, the international professional association of broadcast promotion executives, is that the input a Promotion Director can give the General Manager is critical. Promotion efforts have a direct effect on station image, programs, audience and sales. The Promotion Director must be knowledgeable about all station activities in order to effectively represent the station to the press and public. Promotion Directors warrant a position of close and continuing contact with General Managers with the same status as other department heads.

If the Promotion Director reports to another department head and not directly to the General Manager, promotion activities could become subservient to the other activities of that department.

For example, if the Promotion Department is under Sales, the Sales Manager might be tempted to have the promotion staff spend more time on sales promotion than on audience promotion or station image. Similarly, if the Promotion Department is under the Programming Director, sales promotion and station image may be forced to take a back seat to audience or program promotion.

In many ways, a Promotion Department can be considered a service department of the station, not unlike the Engineering Department—which provides its expertise and equipment for various other departments and station needs. The Promotion Department provides expertise to programming, sales, community relations, news, and to the entire station. Allocation of the Promotion Department's budget and personnel resources should not, therefore, be under the control of any other department, but rather, under the strict control of the Promotion Director, and ultimately the General Manager.

At stations too small to have a separate Promotion Director or Promotion Department, and where a Program Director, Sales Director or other person handles those functions, great care must be taken by that person to see that all station advertising, promotion and publicity needs are met. The Program/Promotion Director must recognize an obligation to work closely with the Sales Director; the Sales/Promotion Director must not overlook audience promotion; and neither one must let promotion responsibilities slide in favor of programming or sales work. All are equally important to a station's success.

A station might have superb programming and personalities, but if the public does not know of them, audiences will be small and sales weak. Conversely, the station might have superb salespeople and sales promotion tools, but if audiences are low, or programs unattractive, clients will be scarce. And if audiences are low and clients scarce, the dollars to buy or produce good programs and pay the best personalities will not be there.

The situation is similar in public broadcasting, where the Sales Department is called the "Development Department." The need to get dollars from audiences and corporations to fund station operations is so great that if the Development Department controls the Public Information (promotion, publicity and advertising) efforts, key station decisions can be made in favor of what will help raise the most money, rather than in favor of what the public should know about the station and its programs.

Unless care is exercised, all this can happen at commercial or public stations without coming to the notice of the General Manager who does not have direct and frequent contact with a specific Promotion Director.

Conversely, the well-trained and efficient Promotion Director who reports directly to the General Manager becomes a strong asset to both programming and sales staffs, as well as others at the station who need public and press exposure.

CHAPTER 8

Promotion and the Management Team*

The Promotion Director at each broadcast station is in a unique situation. He or she is in a position to have daily contact with every other department at the station. Whether it's the News Department, Sales, Traffic, Engineering, Programming, Graphics, Community Relations, or the General Manager, the Promotion Director must have strong internal visibility and contact to do the job effectively. All angles must be checked, all departments consulted to carry through the wide variety of responsibilities of promotion. The Promotion Director may frequently know more about daily happenings within the station than anyone else who works there.

For example, at a TV station, in the course of promoting a specific program, the Promotion Director and staff will have contact with the following departments: Programming and Sales to learn which programs need or deserve promotional emphasis; Graphics to design the artwork, slide or ad; Production to schedule time for promo production; Engineering to run the equipment; Traffic to schedule spots; and News for details, if it's a news program that's being promoted.

In addition, the Promotion Director is the person at the station with closest ties to the press and news media. When anything newsworthy happens at the station, the Promotion Director is the logical one to get the word out. Programming might acquire a new series; Engineering might acquire a sophisticated new piece of equipment; Community Services might want to announce a new emphasis on promoting local charities; and new employees are hired by all departments.

*Material in this chapter is based on an original draft prepared for this text by Lynne Grasz, Director, Communications, CBS/Broadcast Group.

Each broadcast station acquires a group of people who must work together daily as a *team*. Not unlike a professional sports team, the broadcasting *team* must develop a winning spirit, plan strategy to overcome the competition, use its best players effectively, execute tactics with the precision and surprise of a military general, and work together efficiently on the road to winning. Winning a time period, winning a ratings sweep, winning audience share, winning public support, winning prestige, winning advertiser/underwriter confidence, winning awards—all are important to a station's success.

To better understand how various members of the team work with each other toward the station's common goals, it is useful to examine the respective roles of each of the key players. And to better understand the Promotion Director's role on the team, one must look at how Promotion Department activities relate to each other department.

THE GENERAL MANAGER

The General Manager, frequently referred to as the GM, is responsible for holding the FCC license. At the typical commercial station, this person is also responsible for operating the station at an appropriate profit level, increasing sales, and increasing viewers or listeners.

The GM must unite staff members toward common goals, motivate them, and make them stretch themselves mentally and sometimes physically to achieve them. A GM must inspire the staff or surely its members will leave to find someone with whom they can work more comfortably.

The GM has many pressures, from within and without. These include being held accountable for the station and its profit margin to the owner, stockholders or board of directors. As a community leader, the GM is responsible for the station's image in the market and participation in vital activities of the community. As a leader, the GM is responsible for the staff, knowing when to lead, when to delegate, when to spur, when to pull in the reins, and how to inspire. Whether alone or in consultation with department heads, an effective GM develops a vision for the station, faces daily decisions, searches for alternate solutions to problems, and bears the responsibility for every action the station takes.

A GM must listen to many voices: pressure groups, special interest groups, peers, staff, family, and concerned citizens. There is tremendous pressure on this person. The decisions the GM and his managers make are reflected in what is broadcast daily into thousands, sometimes millions, of homes. This inevitably exposes the GM to criticism, praise, ridicule, and reward—often for the same program.

Yet it is a position to which many aspire because of both the psychological and financial rewards of a position of power.

To accomplish the station's goals, the GM employs trusted management associates. And because a Promotion Director's efforts touch so directly on many of the GM's concerns, from image to audience size, and from internal morale to actualization of the station's self-concept, the Promotion Director is usually a very important part of the management team.

To maintain this relationship, one important key is not to spring surprises on the General Manager. Keep the GM informed of budget planning, campaign planning, and shifts in promotional emphasis. Clearly understand the GM's goals for the station, and for specific station undertakings before beginning promotion planning for a project or a season. Seek the GM's input. It may be specific and incisive, or it may be vague and searching for your expertise to shape it. In either case, the GM will feel a part of whatever final promotional decisions are made, and will therefore support them and invest even more faith in the Promotion Director's wisdom and judgment.

Be sure the GM regularly sees the promotion staff's output—ads, promos or promo copy, slides, press releases and resultant press coverage (clippings). Continual reminders of the scope and complexities of promotion activities give the GM a clear understanding of the promotion budget and staff needs. Through a process of constant review, the GM will be assured that promotion activities are meeting his goals for the station.

Finally, working closely with the GM to solve station image problems before they arise—such as in connection with the replacement of a program series, a popular DJ, or a news anchorperson—can maximize the trust the GM has in the Promotion Director.

THE NEWS TEAM

One area at many radio or television stations which plays a key role in establishing a local image is broadcast news. Local news is becoming increasingly important to viewers and listeners. Most stations are budgeting more dollars for better equipment, larger crews, and growing staffs of writers, editors and talent. Now it is big business.

A few years ago local news was a loss leader for television. Now it determines and commands the top advertising dollars in the market. In radio, all-news and news-talk formats are becoming increasingly powerful and profitable.

The News Director works very closely with the General Manager. In many stations, this means hourly contact. Like the General Manager, the News Director works with constant pressure. The position carries ultimate responsibility for news programs. Creativity, news judgment, administrative skills and the ability to relate to people are mandatory for the News Director. Also like the GM, the News Director must motivate people, encouraging reporters and producers to stretch themselves in areas best suited to their expertise.

The News Director must be familiar with everything that is happening in the world—locally, regionally, nationally and internationally.

In the area of news judgment, the News Director is the final decision-maker on taste, relevance, poignancy, controversy, and suitability. He or she must be able to see broad implications of local concerns, and local implications of national events.

A good News Director is able to help reporters and writers improve their styles; suggest improvements in the ways stories are edited on film or tape; advise producers on story positioning and emphasis in newscasts; and all the while keep track of what the competition is doing. The position also involves making adjustments and improvements in crew scheduling, program format, visuals, set design, reporter assignments and anchor positions.

Administrative duties include personnel work, budgeting, FCC reports, and letter or phone contact with many community and state leaders and politicians. News Directors, like most others in the News Department, are on call 24 hours a day, seven days a week. Eight-hour days are rare, 40-hour weeks unheard-of, and even holidays are not sacred.

The Promotion Director must get close to the News Director, especially if—as is usually the case—the GM places a high priority on news. The Promotion Director must include the News Director in every step of assembling a news advertising campaign. The Promotion Director must win the support of the News Director or a campaign may be doomed before it begins. Such rapport usually has its roots in cultivated friendship, and an easy working relationship. Learn the News Director's work patterns and habits and adjust to them.

To ensure cooperation from reporters, editors and producers, the Promotion Director must continually cultivate genial, easygoing, trustful working relationships with these professionals as well.

There are two key ingredients in establishing good relationships with members of the news team.

First, include them in campaign planning. Solicit their ideas. Get their feedback on promotion. Treat their contributions with respect. Carefully explain goals and procedures to them so they understand what is intended and how it will be achieved.

Second, treat them as professional journalists. Do not plan promotions which ridicule, embarrass or belittle them. Respect their erratic and hectic work schedules and do not make excessive demands on their time. Always be well-prepared for meetings or promotion production sessions which involve them.

Finally, it can be a big boost to interdepartment cooperation if members of the news team are familiar with Promotion Department efforts and successes on their behalf. Be sure they see news ads before the ads appear in print, as well as after. Be sure they see or hear new promos for news before they go on TV or radio. And be sure they see press clips that result from joint efforts to promote news specials and features.

PROGRAMMING AND PRODUCTION

The Program Director has overall responsibility at most stations for all non-news air product (except, of course, promotion spots and some community service activities). This person must creatively program the station for a strong demographic audience flow through all parts of the day, whether it is syndicated, network, or locally produced programming.

Local programs are usually the most desirable from a license standpoint. The FCC says that local stations exist to provide service to local communities. However, a Program Director faces many problems with local programming. Chief among them are how to create a program, build its audience, keep it interesting on a regular basis with local talent, deal with union restrictions and still remain within a limited budget.

A Program Director may have many different departments reporting to him or her. The Production Manager, Film Manager, Art or Graphics Department, talent, Traffic and Operations, Engineering, and Community Services are some examples at most television stations. At radio stations, the Program Director's scope is usually more limited, but includes record libraries and announcing talent.

Program Directors must frequently handle talent union negotiations, commercial acceptance and clearance, FCC licensing materials including ascertainment, and the station's public file. Being up-to-date on all legal requirements is essential.

Since a Program Director may have one of the station's largest staffs, working effectively with a wide range of people is an important prerequisite. The clerical workers in traffic/operations areas, and the highly skilled technicians ranging from writers and editors to producers and directors represent extremes in a range of personalities that includes performers, announcers and technicians.

In many instances, a Program Director must understand all the capabilities of the station's equipment—microphones, cameras, audio and video tape recording and editing machines, and much more. Keeping up on the state-of-the-art of technical equipment enables the Program Director to know the station's production capabilities.

The Promotion Director must have a good rapport with the Program Director. Program Directors must understand promotion needs when they negotiate syndicated program purchases, and when they plan local productions. They must recognize promotion demands on station announcers and talent. They must be sure that promotion needs for studio time are met. And they must see that traffic and operations areas respond to necessary Promotion Department demands.

Conversely, they can draw on the Promotion Department's knowledge of local talent outside the station, including announcers, artists, animators, and others important to various stages of program (and promotion) production.

The Promotion Director needs an intimate understanding of why a specific program or series was acquired, why it is scheduled where it is, and what its intended audiences are. The Program Director's answers to these questions help shape promotion campaigns.

In radio, promotional contests are often an integral part of station programming. Close cooperation is necessary to plan, schedule and monitor each contest.

Finally, at television stations, the Production Department is frequently under the Program Director. When production timetables are tight and facilities for the promotion staff are unavailable, Promotion Directors must rely on production talent to produce promos. Interdepartment cooperation is essential.

SALES DEPARTMENT

The easiest product to sell is a radio or television station with high ratings, likeable personalities, great programs, and a strong, positive image. At stations like this, the sales staff may only have to quote commercial availabilities over the phone and take orders. However, this is the ideal. It is not the situation at most stations.

The Sales Manager is responsible for making sure a station hits its targeted goal in sales and profitability. He or she must gauge the market, usually a year or more in advance, and make projections on how much the market will bear in terms of increases for commercial sales. Some stations operate on a rate card; others operate on a grid system where rates fluctuate on a supply-and-demand basis.

A good Sales Manager will accurately project the station's income on a weekly, monthly, quarterly and yearly basis, then divide the client list among the sales staff so individual attention can be given to accounts and agencies. The department must also be on the constant lookout for new business and new clients.

In addition to sales and research staffs, Sales Managers are sometimes in charge of traffic—the station personnel responsible for actually preparing the log and seeing that commercials are correctly inserted into the schedule among program elements.

Like the News and Promotion Director, the Sales Manager keeps a close eye on what the competition is doing, sometimes adjusting station advertising rates and tactics accordingly.

Also like the News and Promotion Director, the Sales Manager must be a motivator, supplying account executives with necessary tools and incentives to do their jobs. The Promotion Director usually provides invaluable help by producing special sales promotion materials and merchandising to attract or close a sales.

The Promotion Department may be asked to put together a special audio/visual presentation to sell a program, a sound, or a new "season" of programs. The Promotion Department may coordinate and plan a Fall Preview Party highlighting the new season or new sound for agencies, clients and the press.

And, as with others on the management team, the Sales Manager is expected to be up-to-date on the station's general technical capabilities, FCC rulings, advertising and commercial acceptance guidelines and network restrictions.

Sales Managers and Promotion Directors are natural allies. Sales Departments need listeners and viewers in order to attract commercial sponsors or corporate underwriters. Many of the tools Promotion people develop to attract audiences are easily adapted to attract advertisers as well. On the other hand, ratings research done by sales staff researchers is invaluable to the Promotion Director who must schedule on-air promotion announcements efficiently and target advertising and promotion campaigns.

At non-commercial, or public radio and television stations, there is no ''Sales Manager'' with a staff selling air time for commercial messages. But public stations rely heavily on corporate money for funding program production, program advertising, and general station operations. Most public stations have a Development Director who oversees these efforts, as well as on-air fund raising targeted to the public, and in most cases, auctions or other similar fund-raising activities.

The Promotion (or Public Information) Director with skills in motivation is an invaluable colleague for the Development Director who, like his commercial counterpart, must rely on printed sales pieces, audio/visual presentations, parties and receptions, and direct appeals on-air or by mail to raise funds. And, just as in commercial broadcasting, the Development Director can be a source of invaluable ratings and demographic research to aid the promotion staff.

OPERATIONS AND TRAFFIC

One of the most demanding, critical areas, and one often under-rated in terms of salary and personal recognition at a broadcast station is operations/traffic. Sometimes combined and sometimes separate, operations and traffic personnel schedule studio use (operations) and everything that airs (traffic). The latter includes programs, commercials, promotion announcements, public service announcements, emergency broadcast alerts, station identifications, license renewal announcements, sign-ons and sign-offs.

The product of the Traffic Manager is the station log, used more and more in conjunction with computers to actually dictate when each slide, recording, tape, piece of copy or film, and network or syndicated program airs. Traffic personnel must be familiar with FCC rules and logging requirements, and must have—at most stations—a working knowledge of the computers which translate logs to machine action. They must be precise and good at detail work because any mistakes can be costly in the case of missed commercials, and harmful to the station's image because they are seen or heard by thousands of viewers or listeners.

At many stations, the Traffic Department reports to the Sales Manager. At other stations Traffic reports to the Program Director. In either case, Traffic personnel work under tremendous daily pressure. When changes occur—more often the rule rather than the exception—the staff must stay until all logs have been changed. That can mean working into the evening hours. Many times changes occur so close to airtime that they cannot be made in the computer and must be made by hand, further compounding chances for error. And weekend logs must be prepared in advance, along with holiday logs.

To many Promotion Departments, traffic personnel become invaluable allies. Traffic is often responsible for the actual insertion of promotion spots (promos) into the schedule, or log, and for placing announcer copy in daily books. Traffic personnel must know which programming or station promotions need special emphasis; which programs have current promos available; when new promotion slides are available; which time periods are best for promoting certain key programs; and which promos can be deleted, should it be necessary to make room in the schedule for last-minute commercials or public service announcements.

Regular meetings with traffic personnel can keep them advised. It is also useful to monitor their scheduling efforts, provide suggested schedules for them to follow, and provide regular constructive criticism of their work.

It is also important to recognize their most difficult and pressured times (usually just before weekends and holidays) and stay away from them when they are struggling to get ahead.

Operations personnel generally schedule production facilities, including studio time. When traffic departments are under Sales, Operations might be under Programming or Production Directors. Promotion Department needs for on-air promo production time make this group of people important allies as well. Good relations with operations staffers might mean extra cooperation in finding that extra hour or two of production time that is frequently needed.

GRAPHICS AND DESIGN (ART)

Every television station has a Graphics or Design Department. It is often called the "Art Department." Some large radio stations have them, too. The larger the station, the more artists and designers, especially when the station produces many local programs, or is independant of networks and groups and must generate all its own advertising, promotion and publicity materials.

Usually the artists are specialists in various areas: print, on-air, or scenic design. This department may report to the Promotion Department, the Program Department, or may be on an equal level with those departments reporting directly to the General Manager.

It is the function of this department to coordinate the total "look" of the station. All graphics used on-air, in print, all sets and station IDs, sometimes even news blazers, vans, and company softball team uniforms bear the stamp of the Graphics staff.

Graphic styles constantly change. Art Directors must keep aware of trends by sampling magazines, record-album jackets, fashions, and even modern art museums for style trends. In addition, station designers must know current techniques in an age when electronics is beginning to make a strong mark on television graphics. Animation and computer graphics capabilities, and the latest video image-creating equipment can all be useful tools of the imaginative, up-to-date designer.

Usually the most important design created by this department is the station logo. A lot of attention to detail must be given to logo design, and there is more on that later in this text. But it is one area where Promotion and Graphics Departments must work closely together. Effective use of the logo in its many forms is usually worked out by the promotion staff, which has image expertise and makes the most use of the logo.

Most good advertising uses the strength of continuity. Ads usually are designed in a hurry, and this is made easy by a strong, simple format. The Graphics Department works with Promotion to devise effective ad formats and ensure their continuity of use in on-air and print materials.

And the Promotion Director may want to seek the Art Director's advice or active participation when turning to outside artists, animators, or even ad agencies for special projects.

A strong Graphics Department is one of a station's biggest assets, especially in television. The station that encourages creativity from these people will certainly be ahead of the competition, and the Promotion Director who works well with the station's creative artists will find the promotion job easier and more fun.

ENGINEERING AND TECHNICAL OPERATIONS

The Engineering Department is usually one of the largest groups of employees at a station. At TV stations the department is frequently headed by someone who has risen through the ranks of broadcasting, remembers the early days of television, and probably worked in radio before that.

This Chief Engineer has probably been at the station longer than most other personnel, and has seen General Managers and Promotion Directors come and go. With a strong senior staff, the Chief Engineer can bring a great deal of perspective and much invaluable experience to bear on the problems on-air promotion people face.

Chief Engineers (or Engineering Directors) are responsible for the broadcast signal, the station's reception, the development of new and/or additional coverage through the use of transmitters and/or translators, cable, satellites or microwave. As with others in station management, and perhaps even more so, it is imperative that the Chief Engineer keep up-to-date on technical advances which occur almost daily.

At many stations technical staffers are union members. They belong to the International Brotherhood of Electrical Workers (IBEW), or the National Association of Broadcast Engineers and Technicians (NABET). The Director of Engineering must be fully qualified in union regulations and negotiations, as well as all legal requirements for FCC and NAB rules and codes and their continuing interpretations.

This department is responsible for scheduling technicians, maintaining the station log for the FCC (keeping an audio and/or video log of everything broadcast by the station) and maintenance and repair of all technical equipment. It also handles technical aspects of all station production, from programs to promos—manning cameras, setting lights, running tape, film and slide machines, editing videotape, and staffing control rooms and remote locations.

To the Promotion Director, the Chief Engineer's staff can provide invaluable technical advice, suggestions and support in producing promotion spots and putting on effective audio/visual presentations. Good cooperation from technicians can mean considerably more promotional output during a taping or edit session.

To help maintain good relationships, it is important to know exactly what activities the non-union promotion person *cannot* perform, and adhere strictly to such restrictions. It is also important to know how to work with technicians without doing things only union people are allowed to do—aiming cameras, pushing buttons, turning knobs, aiming lights, adjusting microphones, etc.

Explain carefully what is to be accomplished during a taping or editing session before it begins and cooperation by technicians will be much greater. Come to production sessions fully prepared and technicians will be inspired with confidence that the Promotion Department knows what it is doing. Vague goals and ideas half-developed can result in lasting damage to cooperative promotion/technicians relationships.

Finally, if technical advice is required, don't wait until a session begins to request it. Get advice well in advance so that the proper equipment and crew complement can be scheduled and valuable time isn't lost.

COMMUNITY RELATIONS (COMMUNITY AFFAIRS)

At some smaller radio and television stations the Promotion Director is also the person who supervises community relations activities. But at most larger stations, the Community Relations, Community Affairs or Community Services Director is the person in a separate department who keeps a finger on the pulse of the community. This person represents the station at community functions, providing a station presence and station point-of-view. From these contacts, the Community Relations Director develops a station VIP list for use as program sources and possible ascertainment subjects. Since this is a very visable extension of the station in the community, it is important that the Community Relations Director be personable and work well with people. Being a mediator, a good listener, a moderator, a good public speaker, and having a thorough knowledge of the broadcasting business are important assets.

This department also performs an important public relations function for the station. The staff must be personable with viewers or listeners who write or call—frequently the only direct contact a member of the community might have with the station.

And this department often deals with many special interest groups who want the station to promote their special position, or their particular causes. A good understanding of the Fairness Doctrine, equal time restrictions, and all FCC restrictions and codes regarding public affairs programming and public service announcements is necessary.

At many stations, it is to this department that citizens and groups in the community turn when they want public service messages broadcast. And frequently the Community Relations staff works with such groups to help them produce their messages, or even to produce entire programs. Often the most difficult part of the job is the ability to say "no" to such requests for time, avoiding negative repercussions for the station.

Community Relations Directors are often responsible for filing the station's license renewal with the FCC, maintaining the station's public access file, scheduling and following through on ascertainment interviews, keeping all station correspondence with community leaders, and scheduling license renewal announcements on air when required.

The Community Relations Director acts as liaison with community organizations and institutions including local universities, schools, civic and community groups and city, county or state governments. The Director may be asked to make numerous speaking engagements on behalf of the station. In addition to speech-making ability, skill at handling audience questions is useful.

Because of its close contact with the community, this department frequently develops, researches and prepares station editorial opinions on issues of community concern.

Promotion Directors must be especially careful to coordinate outside efforts with the Community Relations Director to ensure a unified station appearance to the public.

Further, the Community Relations Department can help develop VIP invitation lists for important station functions; and can help spread the station's latest promotion theme or slogan by using it in community appearances. It can also help the Promotion Director pinpoint areas of the community where additional advertising, promotion or publicity efforts for certain programs might have significant impact in increasing awareness of the station or improving the station's ratings and image.

SUMMARY

All these departments work intimately with each other. Each must learn to compromise with the others—to fight battles worth winning, but give in on non-essential ones. Each must report to the General Manager and account for the Department's time and energies.

There are several simple devices and tactics a Promotion Director can and should use to ensure continuing cooperation from other departments and department heads:

· Avoid springing surprises on others. Work with them to develop promotion plans that can benefit everyone.
· Keep other department heads and their staffs informed about all important station promotion activities—their start dates, major emphasis, progress and results.
· Be appreciative of valuable assistance the Promotion Department receives. A brief note of thanks to deserving individuals with a copy to the appropriate department head and/or or the General Manager will go a long way toward ensuring future cooperation.

ORGANIZATIONAL CHART
(Typical Television Station)

GENERAL MANAGER

STATION MANAGER (optional)

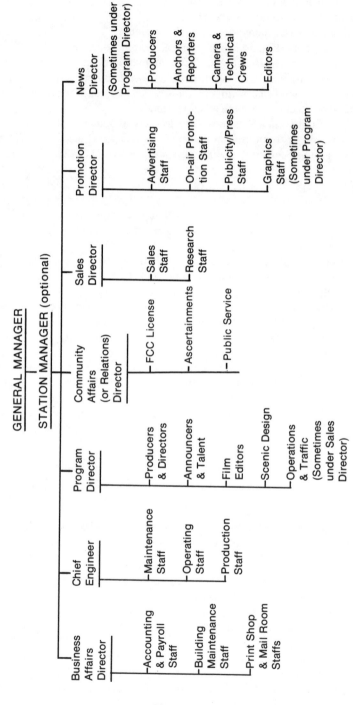

ORGANIZATIONAL CHART
(Typical Radio Station)

GENERAL MANAGER

Business Affairs Director
- Accounting & Payroll Staff
- Building Maintenance Staff
- Print Shop
- Mail Room

Chief Engineer
- Maintenance Staff
- Operational Staff

Program Director
- News
- Announcers
- Record Library

Sales Director
- National Sales Staff
- Local Sales Staff
- Traffic
- Research

Promotion Director
- Publicity
- On-air, Contests & Promotions
- Advertising
- Artist(s)

Community Relations Director
- FCC License
- Ascertainments
- Public Service

57

CHAPTER 9

Promotion and the "Outside Team"

The Promotion Director not only works with the station's management team but may also be in a position to make use of various outside groups. Among these are networks, their owned and operated station groups, and other ownership groups.

NETWORKS

Major commercial television networks include the American Broadcasting Company (ABC), CBS, and the National Broadcasting Company (NBC). Each of these networks owns five TV stations and oversees their operations through an Owned and Operated Stations Division headquartered in New York City. There is also the Public Broadcasting Service television network, called PBS—in effect, a network owned and operated by its stations with a PBS Board of Directors comprised almost entirely of station executives over the network President.

Major radio networks include ABC, CBS, Mutual, NBC, RKO and National Public Radio (NPR). In addition, many companies today operate several networks. ABC, for example, has at least four.

Each network provides specific services to aid the Promotion Departments of its stations. Because services vary from network to network and from year to year at each network, what follows is a general look at the kinds of services the Promotion Director can anticipate.

Publicity

All radio and television networks have staffs of publicists who prepare informational releases on programs and personalities for distribution to national and local publications. Releases and photos are usually sent as press packets to general press mailing lists one or more times a week. Copies are sent to stations for information and local use. Networks also provide national magazines and major market newspapers with exclusive feature stories and photos for key network programs.

Networks can usually arrange to have stations' anniversaries or other very special occasions mentioned on some network programs, such as NBC's "Today" and "Tonight," and ABC's "Good Morning, America."

All four major television networks routinely provide stations with a closed-circuit Fall Preview. These overviews of upcoming Fall programming usually highlight new programs and new elements of returning programming, and are valuable for stations to use with local press, clients, ad agency personnel, and community leaders. They can also be used to enthuse station staff members about the new season. Many local stations add their own key local programs to these previews.

Also for the press, the TV networks provide regular closed circuit previews of programs. Local stations are encouraged to invite appropriate members of the press to see the programs and review them.

Posters, flyers, leaflets, and educational materials may also be available from networks in limited or bulk quantities to help stations promote certain programs; or to help stations reach out to special interest groups in the community and encourage their cooperation in promoting the programming.

Most networks have audience services personnel who perform public relations services for the stations by answering viewer inquiries, questions, complaints, requests for information and photos. They also handle requests for information from students, writers, researchers, and other specialized publics.

Each year the four television networks jointly host one or more major "press junkets." TV editors and columnists from across the nation are invited to central locations in Los Angeles and New York for several days. There they are given access to many major network stars, personalities, producers, and others affiliated with upcoming or ongoing program series and specials. This results in publicity space on TV pages in many markets.

All networks can, at stations' requests, help arrange for local press people to have telephone interviews with program personalities or producers.

At the start of each new Fall season, each TV network provides members of the nation's TV press and local stations with press kits for all major programs. The kits traditionally contain some or all of the following:

- Overall program schedules.
- Program, personality and feature releases.
- Program, personality and feature photographs.
- On-air copy for use by local station announcers.
- Ads in reproducible form.
- Sample ad layouts (suggestions for combining network and local ads).
- Type sets in the network's type style to enable easy construction of local ads that have a network look.

• Theme or slogan elements.
• Suggestions for carrying the theme over into locally prepared outdoor advertising.
• Film strips which can be cut into frames and mounted as slides for TV on-air use or for presentations.

Networks also can help arrange for a visit to the local station's city by network program personalities.

Commercial television networks generally provide a special service called the "Promotion Festival." It involves flying a local station personality to a central location where he or she can interview major network stars on tape, then take the tapes back to the local station for insertion into local news or feature programming.

Each network also has a merchandising department which specializes in custom items promoting network shows which local stations can buy in quantity at low prices. T-shirts, coffee mugs, decals, posters, stickers, jackets, and many other custom imprinted items are frequently available with program promotion messages for local stations to use as gifts, prizes, giveaways, or resale.

Advertising

In addition to ad materials supplied in the kits referred to above, networks buy ads in major market newspapers and national magazines. Networks may make local newspaper buys outright, or as part of a cooperative buy (co-op) with the local station. Co-op arrangements might combine network and local station money for ads in various forms of local media, including newspapers, radio, and outdoor advertising. Such co-ops are designed in part to encourage local stations to spend more money for advertising by stretching their ad dollars. In actual practice, stations place the advertising, are billed locally, and then are reimbursed by the network for a predetermined portion of the ad costs. Other kinds of co-op ad arrangements involve the network picking up the cost for all, or most, local advertising of network programming during various parts of the year.

On-Air Promotion. All radio and television networks provide stations with prerecorded announcements for use on-air. Generally these video and/or audio tape promotion spots (promos) are fed to stations over the network when it is not being used for programs. In addition to promos for specific programs, some networks supply block promos for an entire night of programming; special theme campaign promos; separate feeds of promotion theme audio and video material so local stations can make their own promos with a network "look" or "sound"; and program and theme slides. Personalized promos for individual stations by network stars can often be arranged. And TV networks routinely provide specialized animation of words such as "today," "tomorrow," and "tonight" for local station use in building promos with a network "look."

Station Responsibilities. Stations have implied or explicit responsibilities to networks in the promotion area, as well. Networks need station co-operation in giving a fair share of station advertising, promotion and publicity attention to network as well as local programs.

Networks also look for prompt response to surveys and requests for information about station advertising, promotion and publicity activities.

GROUPS AND OWNED-AND-OPERATED (O&O) DIVISIONS

When several radio or television stations are owned by one corporation, the industry calls them a ''group.'' Within the parent corporation, the group is often referred to as the television or radio ''stations division.'' In charge of each Division of the multifaceted corporation there is, of course, a President. And, on the President's staff are Vice Presidents who—just as at individual stations—supervise and counsel in their respective areas of expertise.

Thus, each group has a Vice President in overall charge of the advertising, promotion and publicity efforts of all the stations in the group. In addition, of course, each station has a local Promotion Director. Relationships between the station Promotion Director and the group Vice President of Advertising, Promotion and Publicity (or, more frequently, Vice President of Creative Services) vary from group to group. Some groups take a strong, active hand in directing the look and sound of promotion at local stations. Some have very small staffs and tend to keep hands off most operational decisions. Most fall between the two extremes.

Those groups actively involved in their stations' promotion efforts recognize that in spite of each station's individual circumstances there are common challenges which can best be attacked by pooling resources and working together.

The Vice President of Creative Services for a broadcast group must, therefore, get to know each particular station's needs, audiences, competition, and must be an expert in ad production, and media buying. He or she must be able to act as a consultant to all stations in the group to combine talent and promotional efforts for the benefit of all.

Carol Bauer, former Vice President of Creative Services for the ABC-TV Network's Stations Divisions Group, expresses the group's role through this illustration:

> For several years, each of our stations had run a late afternoon movie and a checkerboard of syndicated game shows at 7:30 each evening. Each station's Creative Services (Promotion) Department was taking most of its limited production time to create on-air promotion for these programs. There was a 45% duplication in movie titles alone. The time and talent of each production staff was being gobbled up by the effort. Little was left for locally produced programs.
>
> From the vantage-point of the Division, I researched two different avenues. First, the feasibility of hiring an outside agency to produce syndicated program on-air promotion for all five stations. Then, I looked into setting up our own special production unit within the Group. Comparing the two, we opted for the consistent expertise of an outside firm. Now we have that firm making promos for all five stations' duplicated syndication programming. The product is of the highest qual-

ity. The individual stations' Creative Services staffs are freed to concentrate their promo production facilities and staff time on local, live and news programming. It proved to be a perfect project for a group; eliminating duplication, improving quality, while supporting the individual stations' efforts.

This is not a one-project effort. I organize a similar effort every time two or more of our stations are running the same program.

Ms. Bauer provides a second example of the kind of service a Group Creative Services Department can provide in this illustration:

Recently a ratings study revealed that all five of our stations rated number one in their respective markets in a very important demographic group: 18–49 year old male/female and combined adults. Very impressive, especially to media buyers who read trade press magazines such as *Broadcasting Magazine, TV/Radio Age, Advertising Age, Variety* and so on. They are the ones who will place advertising on our local stations. It is information which must be shared—even trumpeted— and quickly. Within one week the Group had prepared and placed in four trade publications a major several-page advertising spread in full color. We also produced 3,000 flyers for direct mailing to time buyers, ad agencies, and others.

This is another example of a rewarding project for the Group Creative Services Department which, far more than the local stations, had the time and money to produce a major and quick response to a great opportunity. And we saved a lot of money by running one ad for five stations, rather than five ads, one for each station.

To be sure, conflicts can arise between the out-of-town Vice President of Creative Services for a Group and the local station Promotion Director with a specialized knowledge of the local community.

However, most such conflicts can be overcome by recognizing the degree of authority of the Group Vice President, and learning to work cooperatively. The local Promotion Director should ensure that the Group Vice President knows all that is possible about the local station's needs and capabilities. The group Vice President must receive input regarding local ad agencies, production companies, and other local resources, local market tastes, and specialized interests and needs.

At the same time, the Group is a resource which allows more time to concentrate on local production efforts and local news and program promotion.

CHAPTER **10**

The Promotion Director as
Manager/Creator *

Broadcast advertising, promotion and publicity represent a unique mixture of business management and creativity. When both mix well and function efficiently, much benefit derives. When an individual Promotion Director can't mix both roles well, many problems can develop.

As a member of the station's management team who supervises creative people and must wear a creative hat, the Promotion Director must be able to function well in both the worlds of administration and imagination.

This Chapter of Part Two explores issues of *conflict, management,* and *stress* that can arise for people who must manage creative efforts, and at the same time be creative managers.

What is creativity?

It is a special combination of experience, preparation, originality, and social values that brings into existence new concepts or ideas.

Since the goals of creativity cannot always be clearly defined, and since they are not always achieved by traditional methods, orderly management of creativity is often difficult.

Here are some observations psychologists and sociologists have made of people deemed to be creative. They will provide the Promotion Director with a better understanding of himself and members of the promotion staff.

> Creative people don't have to be flakey, or nutty. There is no clear correlation between creativity and maturity. Extensive studies *do not* support the claims of some creative people that eccentric behavior is a by-product of the creative process. Some toleration of eccentric behavior may

*Material in this chapter is based primarily on an original draft prepared for this text by Dr. Ray London, President, Human Factor Programs, Ltd., Santa Ana, California.

be necessary now and then, but not if it is disruptive. Creative people can be expected to behave responsibly.

Geniuses aren't always creative. While there seems to be no direct relationship between creativity and academic aptitude (good grades), there is evidence of correlation between creativity and intellectual competence (the ability to observe, reason, and learn). Look for these capabilities in staff members, and provide opportunities for them to grow. It will enhance their creative output.

The successful creative person is not only original, but also acutely aware of the social value—or lack of value—of the creation. Emphasize the positive aspects of tasks. Stress real benefits to the station and its audiences.

Creative persons are neither rigid intellectually, nor are their thinking processes systematic and orderly.

There is a relationship between creative ability and the ability to solve problems. Creative people tend to look at problems from many angles, seeking unique approaches which will work well. Tolerate and even encourage the seeking of fresh approaches and you'll find your staff members responding with imagination.

Creative individuals appear to be more easy-going, more sociable, more self-dependent and more aware than non-creative individuals. They also tend to be self-stimulating, independent, sensitive, goal-directed and capable of giving direction to their life and work situation.

Creativity is basically a learned process, not always a unique natural gift. All people have creative potential. It can be developed in any given work situation. Here are some keys:

• Reduce the potential of ridicule or fear of failure.
• Encourage a certain degree of non-conformity, especially with regard to seeking problem solutions.
• Provide positive motivation to get the job done.
• Help define the problem clearly.
• Encourage examination of a variety of approaches to problem solving.

By effective management of people based on a good understanding of their personality traits and characteristics, the Promotion Director can increase the creativity of the staff and make truly creative individuals effective team members.

CONFLICT ISSUES

Conflict is normal, expected, unavoidable. It is a natural outgrowth of varying needs, motivations and processes. When conflicts are handled appropriately, they can be productive. Benefits can be gained. When conflicts are mis-handled or allowed to become unmanageable, productivity and creativity decrease, and both policy and personnel problems can quickly develop.

Several kinds of conflicts are examined here. The inevitible conflicts between management-oriented and creativity-oriented people frequently beset Promotion Directors. So do conflicts brought about by organizational structures, patterns and procedures; and those brought about by ineffective communication.

Management vs. Creativity Conflicts:

For the Promotion Director who has come to the position via Sales, Accounting, Traffic, or other similar areas, self-management—and the management of others expected to produce creative results—can cause inner conflicts. Managers in these fields are trained to measure productivity from objective and cost-effectiveness perspectives. Success, worth and value are measured in terms of cost, profit and loss. The measure of success is fiscal profit. These, of course, are essential components of the approach of a successful manager. However, in the more productively creative arena of the Promotion Department, they must be blended with less traditional approaches, greater vision, and not-so-easily quantified goals.

On the other hand, the Promotion Director who has risen to a management position because of creative successes may have the opposite problem: learning to set clear, identifiable goals, produce tangible and quantifiable results, and stay within budgets.

For either type of Promotion Director, effective self-management and good management of others requires the following:

• The ability to set short- and long-range goals that have meaning, are easy to recognize and understand, and provide rewards.
• The capacity to assume personal responsibility for tasks. This demands intense identification with productive work, production standards, and time limits.
• The capability of making appropriate and original decisions which conform to rigid time and budget constraints.
• The ability to plan, control and develop other people and their activities.

For the manager, perhaps the key difficulty is in effectively appraising personnel and motivating changes that result in productive work. This involves understanding that individuals differ, and indeed fall across a creativity-management-oriented continuum. Effective management of creative efforts involves recognizing, for example, that some creative individuals work with bursts of energy, while others prefer a steady pace. Some like clear-cut, established ways of doing things, while others become very bored with routine. Some are self-influenced; others are influenced more by others. Some individuals need great praise; others are content just to be treated fairly. Some are motivated by reason; others by emotion. Some need to feel continually included; others are loners. Some tend to be thinkers, planners; others tend to be activists who focus more on action and concrete results.

The successful Promotion Director can assess these traits in him or herself, and in staff members, and organize tasks to capitalize on the strengths of individuals, rather than allow serious conflicts to grow because individuals are expected to perform in ways that are not natural to them.

Conflicts can be avoided by understanding these differences, especially differences between people who are more and those who are less creative, identifying department staff members' positions on the creativity-management continuum and assigning tasks, motivating, and rewarding achievements according to individuals' personal needs and characteristics.

When these personality issues are understood and the Promotion Director can deal appropriately with individual members, conflicts between creativity and management are diminished.

Organizational Conflicts

This category of conflicts includes those spawned by competition and those brought about by rebellion against authority.

Competitive conflicts may be rooted in personality differences, or in misunderstandings. Authority conflicts often have the same roots.

Such conflicts can be very disruptive to efficient and smooth organizational operation. And they tend to multiply if not checked. Time and energy are lost; deadlocks occur; communication among individuals decreases, and employees withdraw and show lower respect for the station and its goals. Eventually, a station may be unable to operate successfully.

All members of the management team, the Promotion Director included, can help lessen organizational conflict by the following means:

• Be sure staff members are fully aware of all rules of acceptable behavior and production; and that they understand the reasons for these rules.
• Seek to minimize such rules when they are, on balance, counterproductive to overall efforts; or help employees find unique and acceptable ways to work within them.
• See that all staff members fully understand station goals, and appreciate their significances.
• Seek areas where individuals and the station have mutual interests, and emphasize them.
• Include staff members in Promotion Department goal-setting, planning, and evaluation of results. Staff members included in plans for change accept change far more readily.
Make plans that are specific and measurable. Employees are more cooperative when they can see where they are going and when they can identify and measure their progress.
Make plans that focus on developing the strengths of the department and the individuals within it, in support of station goals.

A large percentage of conflicts between organizations and individuals, especially those who are creative, are the result of inadequate, unclear job descriptions and expectations. It is extremely important for Promotion Directors to be clear, specific and detailed in defining tasks and stating their expectations. Ambiguity gets in the way of the creative processes. The creative individual needs to have a basic understanding of the scope, responsibilities and power structure of the position. Working relationships, methods of reporting and specific means of performance evaluation should be clearly stated. The expectations should be realistic, achievable, clear and understandable.

Major responsibilities should be clearly explained. Finally, the basic goals, job description, and organizational purpose of an employee's position should be regularly evaluated and adjusted as tasks change and the individual grows in knowledge and capabilities.

Frequently, organizational conflicts are more visible to a trained outside expert than to those within the station. If severe conflicts exist and minimizing them proves difficult, an outside consultant skilled in organizational behavior and interaction should be called in—with the approval of the General Manager—to suggest steps to reduce the conflicts.

Communication Conflicts

Communication conflicts are those which arise because the speaker or writer attempting to deliver a message is vague, too wordy or rambling, unsure of what he or she is trying to convey, or sends conflicting non-verbal messages; and those which arise because the listener or reader receiving the message doesn't really listen to the message being sent, but instead, "hears" a pre-conceived message.

There are some important rules to follow if communication is to be effective:

• Keep messages short and simple. Stick to one idea at a time, and be sure it is understood clearly before going on to the next idea. In written communication, use separate memos for important but unrelated messages or ideas.
• Think a message through completely before attempting to communicate it. Have a clear, precise idea of what must be communicated. Mentally take the place of the listener or reader and see if the message is easily understood.
• Avoid sending conflicting messages, such as a frown or scowl accompanying words of praise or thanks; or belittling expressions delivered along with serious instructions.
• When critical or negative messages are delivered, the sender should use "I" messages identifying his/her perceptions, reactions, or needs; rather than "you" messages casting blame, irrevocably fixing responsibility, or encouraging guilt.
• Finish one thought completely before going on to the next one. Don't let different thoughts or topics become confused with each other.
• During a discussion, periodically review the content and summarize progress of the discussion to that point. Be sure both parties understand what has been said or agreed to at various steps.

• Identify differences in perspective between speaker and listener, and openly acknowledge them, to help eliminate misunderstandings of the "But I thought you meant . . ." variety.

• Listen carefully to what others say, or read carefully what they write, looking at the communication from the other person's point of view. Managers should let information and attitudes flow "up" from employees as well as "down" from the employer.

• Watch for signs of misunderstanding: puzzled looks, blank stares, nodded agreement when it shouldn't be there, or a shaking of the head. All are signs that further discussion or explanation are necessary.

• On complex issues or new topics, do not assume that the person receiving the message has all the necessary background information. Review such information briefly and expand on it where necessary.

MANAGEMENT ISSUES

Major management issues for the Promotion Director involved in supervising creative people include: decision-making, delegation, evaluation, relationships, and rewards.

In these areas, problems can arise when the Promotion Director inadequately handles employee value systems, needs, and motivations; fails to appropriately use group dynamics; displays intolerance; is ambiguous, or makes faulty assumptions about employees.

The effective Promotion Director must handle the management responsibilities listed in the first paragraph above in ways that inspire or motivate individuals, encourage their willingness to take on assigned tasks, and permit effective interaction among employees. Further, the Promotion Director must understand that smooth functioning of the group and its individual members depends on job-task relevancy, acceptance of organizational goals, and individual and group levels of education and experience.

Each of the above management issues is explored here with emphasis on its effects of the management of creative staff efforts.

Decision-Making

A number of factors contribute to effective decision-making. Effective decisions are generally based on:

• Clearly identified problems.
• Realistic appraisals of problems.
• Full evaluation of all possible solutions.
• Availability of sufficient data on both the problem and potential solutions.
• Devising effective means of implementing the final decisions.
• Willingness of those affected by the decision to abide by it; or to help implement a solution.

Management problems, especially with staff members involved in creative work, can arise when subordinates are not included in the decision-making process, yet the decision will be one that directly affects their activities. Including employees who have expertise in the problem area or who will be affected by decisions can help bring about a better decision or solution. It will also ensure willing participation by all in implementing the decision.

There are two basic decision-making patterns. Both apply to broadcast promotion. The first is intuitive; the second is reasoned. When speedy decisions are required, intuition may play a larger role than reasoning. However some decisions demand more time for research and considered analysis. These are called reasoned.

When intuitive decisions must be made, everything possible should be done to have all possible information bearing on the decision at hand, and to set aside non-rational biases. In such cases it is best to carefully follow the basic problem-solving format, good for both kinds of decisions:

- Identify the problem.
- Clarify the goals of a good solution.
- Obtain all available information.
- Generate various solutions.
- Evaluate each potential solution, and select the most appropriate.
- Establish an implementation plan.
- Reevaluate both the decision and the implementation plan.

When these steps are followed, and advice of appropriate staff members contributes to the final decision and problem solution, conflicts are minimized.

Delegation

Most Promotion Directors have more to do than they can possibly accomplish alone. Therefore they must depend on others at the station. Some have one or two assistants. Some have staffs ranging up to 10–15 people. Effective delegation of tasks is essential in each case.

Promotion Directors often rationalize doing a job themselves, rather than delegating, because "the employee can't handle the task," or "I want the job done right," or "it would take more time to explain it than to do it myself," or "I just want to keep my hand in." These, however, are only rationalizations.

The real reasons Promotion Directors don't delegate when they should are:

- They know how to do the task well, themselves. (That's no reason not to delegate, when other things need to be done.)
- They lack confidence in their subordinates. (Employee competence and self-confidence are not built by taking tasks away from them.)
- They think they can do it better. (Again, not enough reason to do the job personally. Let staff members improve their skills. The Promotion Director should build competence by reviewing the work of others with

positive criticism.) (Besides, maybe they can't always do it better; they just think they can!)

• Vocational work (typing, producing, writing, editing, etc.) provides them with instant reward feedback. Effective delegation involves learning to get rewards from other kinds of work: planning, supervision, evaluation, and coordination.

• They lack knowledge of what is involved in effective delegation.

The keys to effective delegation are:

• Know the staff well and choose the right person to delegate to.
• Explain precisely what must be done, and provide criteria by which the subordinate can evaluate his/her work.
• Build in check-points so work in progress can be guided or corrected.
• Mentally view employees as the sources of solutions rather than as the causes of problems.
• Coach employees by telling them where to go for help, research, or assistance.
• Establish clear goals so the employee will know when the job is done.
• Do not delegate major decisions.

In addition, of course, the Promotion Director must develop confidence in staff members' abilities, must encourage employee self-confidence, and learn to gain satisfaction from supervisory and managerial tasks as well as vocational ones.

Evaluation

Most people who have worked for someone else or have been judged by others have experienced evaluation difficulties.

Some creative people refuse to be part of evaluation processes, feeling that no one can evaluate them or their work but themselves. Such attitudes, of course, naively ignore the realities of working for others.

Effective evaluations of employees and their work are invaluable. They serve as a basis for compensation and promotion, as well as provide convenient benchmarks for recognizing progress and identifying employee problems and frustrations.

Evaluation or appraisal processes should start with clear Promotion Department job descriptions. They must be precise, not vague. Each must provide adequate definitions of tasks to be performed, and set goals for each task. This applies to individual special tasks as well as the employee's job as a whole.

With the job description as a yardstick, it is much easier to measure employee accomplishments and progress.

However, with more subjective creative efforts such as advertising copy, promo production, and choice of artwork for publications, objective criteria by which to measure success are more elusive. Encouraging employee self-criticism is often a valuable exercise. Regular meetings with staff members involved in creative work to review and discuss what they have done forces constructive self-evaluation, learning, and employee growth.

Peer evaluation sessions, where several staff members involved in various creative enterprises evaluate and discuss the effectiveness of each others work can have a similar effect.

One television network advertising executive recently revealed that he holds every finished ad produced by his department up to peer evaluation and discussion as a means of refining and improving the ad until all possible objections which higher management might later raise will either have been eliminated, or he will have appropriate counter-arguments prepared. Along the way, a constantly stimulating learning and self-improvement environment is created for the executive and his staff.

Relationships

The working relationships a Promotion Director has to maintain with promotion staff members and others at the station must depend in part on the various individuals' needs, and their levels of maturity at a given moment on a particular task. "Maturity" is defined as the ability of the employee to set high obtainable goals and accept responsibility. It also assumes an adequate level of education or experience to do the job.

In discussing relationships, "high task-oriented behavior" refers to strong direction and communication from the manager with relatively little input by the staff member. In contrast, "high relationship-oriented behavior" involves a high level of interchange between manager and employee.

Starting with these definitions, it is possible to identify several stages of relationships between a Promotion Director and those performing promotion-related tasks.

The "high-task, low-relationship" stage is most suited to the employee with a low level of maturity, as defined above. As the employee's maturity increases, the next leadership stage for a manager is the "high-task, high-relationship" phase, which still features clear cut, explicit direction and authority from the manager but now permits a significant level of interaction between manager and employee.

Next, with a good personal relationship established and the employee's maturity level further increased, comes the "low-task, high-relationship" phase. The employee now demonstrates considerable initiative and self-direction, but maintains close contact and personal relationship with the Promotion Director for guidance when necessary.

The final phase is "low-task, low relationship." At this stage, the employee is very much on his or her own, and, in fact, accomplishes the best work that way.

This is a good progression to use with individuals involved in creative work. But it is important to begin working with each staff member at the level that is most individually appropriate, given the staff member's level of maturity, and to move the employee along to the next stage as soon as appropriate, or as job responsibilities change. An unhappy staff member might be a sign that the wrong manager-employee relationship exists. Conflicts and decreased efficiency can result.

Rewards

Effective leadership rests as much on the ability to motivate others as on any other single trait. Fear, threats and punishments have proved over centuries of trial and error and recent psychological study to be less effective motivators than effective rewards.

Rewards are an essential part of the work situation. Different people are motivated by different kinds of rewards. For some, a quiet pat on the back and an occasional "Good job!" are sufficient. For others, the appropriate reward is public recognition—perhaps a formal dinner, a plaque, or an internal news release. Still others prefer money or promotion.

Individuals involved in creative work often look for a reward of increased meaningful responsibilities, and appropriate recognition. A Promotion Director must carefully evaluate each employee and be certain that appropriate rewards reinforce successful accomplishments at regular intervals.

To be effective, rewards must be individualized. Not everyone can be treated the same, although all members of the same organization must be treated equally. To give everyone a $25. raise rewards no one for individual accomplishment. But everyone who achieves a significant accomplishment should receive an appropriate reward. Give the $25. raises to each individual when they are earned; but don't overlook the other, subtler rewards such as "thank you's," public recognition, and letters of commendation.

Rewards become goals in themselves. Employees will work extra hard to earn that letter, bonus, extra day off, increased responsibility, raise or promotion, if they know that it is the reward for their extra effort.

STRESS ISSUES

Stress is an integral and important fact of human existence. It is a powerful part of complicated bodily motivational and defense mechanisms. Stress can push an individual to achieve more, encourage a person to avoid direct contact with unnecessary danger, and prevent over-exertion.

But too much stress can have disasterous consequences. Psychologists and sociologists believe that as much as 70% of all illnesses—including heart disease, cancer, stroke, and gastrointestinal problems—are stress-related.

Promotion Directors face many challenges, demands, expectations, and constant deadlines. Rewards include personal satisfaction, social recognition, sense of accomplishment, and financial gain. But there are also negative aspects to the job: frustration, heavy demands, hectic schedules, long hours, value conflicts, and high levels of competition.

When job-related stresses are added to personal and family stress situations (moving, divorce, marriage, death-in-the-family, and even birthdays and Christmas) the physical toll on an individual can begin to show up as any of a wide range of symptoms, from allergies and colds to insomnia, drug or alcohol abuse, ulcers, high blood pressure, or more serious physical problems.

Stress first becomes a negative force when it reaches the point of interfering with maximum functioning—that is, when the individual becomes controlled or victimized by stress's symptoms. The time to begin taking counteractive measures is long before the first symptoms appear.

Since the Promotion Director knows in advance that the profession tends to be stressful, and since modern-day life inevitably produces additional stresses, it is best to develop habits that counteract the effects of too much stress buildup. And the Promotion Director should monitor stress build-up in staff members and help them manage stress when necessary.

The following techniques help:

- Take breaks. Once in the morning and once in the afternoon take at least ten minutes to perform some task that is totally unrelated to the job or other stressful activities. Call the family. Read the sports page. Daydream. Go for a brief walk. Vary these break activities from day to day.
- Reduce the number of business lunches. Several days each week use the lunch hour to have a non-business lunch with friends, take a walk, visit a museum, or stop by a library. When business lunches are continually necessary, hold the business conversation *after* the meal.
- Reorganize the daily schedule. Allow time for involvement in a variety of activities throughout the day. This is rarely a problem for the Promotion Director but sometimes a problem for promotion staff members with more limited sets of tasks.
- Do relaxing exercises at the desk. One excellent exercise involves repeatedly relaxing and tensing muscles. Each relaxation lowers the tension level in the body. Three or four tension-relaxation cycles at a time, two or three times a day should produce beneficial results.
- Avoid taking work home. Compartmentalize professional and home lives and keep them separate.
- Get regular sleep, a proper diet, and follow good health habits. (Eat breakfasts, don't snack, don't smoke, drink moderately, and keep body weight within acceptable limits.)

Finally, people who have an awareness of stress, can recognize stressful situations from their symptoms (tight stomach or chest muscles, headaches, sweaty palms), and who can pause for a moment and say to themselves, "Hey, this is a stressful situation. Relax a little," are better off than those who cannot. The key here is to recognize situations over which one has little or no control, and not to let them cause tension; while taking action to solve those problems that are controllable.

SUMMARY

This brief review of conflict, management and stress as they are likely to affect the performance of the Promotion Director are all of special significance because of the unique creative-manager dichotomy that divides not only the kinds of work but also the approaches to promotion work into two distinctly opposite spheres of human personality. The vast majority of Promotion Directors and advertising, promotion and publicity professionals have found some balance between the two extremes that enables constructive performance and enjoyable careers.

Part Three

The Basics of
Broadcast Promotion

There are certain basic skills and areas of knowledge in which broadcast promotion professionals must have—or quickly develop—a higher level of expertise in order to perform well on the job. Chief among them are:

- An understanding of *broadcast ratings,* and how they can serve various promotion needs.
- A knowledge of *research techniques,* what can, and what cannot be accomplished by a station.
- *Budget Planning* capability.
- A solid grounding in the basic *techniques of motivation,* and how broadcasters apply them.
- A mastery of *advertising,* including the characteristics of various media and how they can best be used.
- An understanding of *media selection and buying* processes.
- An ability to achieve maximum effects and results by using the station's own *on-air promotion.*
- The skills of effectively generating *publicity* for the station.
- A thorough knowledge of various *station promotion* efforts, other than on-air.
- The ability to produce effective *sales promotion* materials and campaigns.

These are the subjects of this Third Part of *Broadcast Advertising and Promotion.* Every Promotion Director of every radio and television station needs a good understanding of each of these topics. No campaign is truly effective without a skillful coordination of all the elements listed above.

CHAPTER 11

Research & Ratings *

WHAT RESEARCH CAN DO

Broadcasting is becoming an increasingly competitive business. More and more, managers must make tough decisions about how to build and maintain an audience. With increased competition has come an increased need for audience research to aid in the decision-making process. Managers at all levels who understand the strengths and weaknesses of research information, and the ways in which that information can be used, will be more successful in helping the station meet that competition. The information in this chapter is designed to help those in broadcast promotion understand and use audience research.

Simply stated, audience research is a systematic means for collecting and reporting objective, reliable information about the audience.

More importantly, audience research is a tool. Its effective use depends on knowing its capabilities. Although a carefully conceived and executed study can be of great value to management, some managers feel uncomfortable dealing with research. As a result, they may completely ignore it, or they may let research dictate a certain course of action. Neither of these responses is appropriate.

Research can never be a substitute for the judgment and intuition of an experienced manager. Research can, however, aid management in making decisions. The American Marketing Association lists four broad functions research can serve:

*The material on Research in this chapter is excerpted from a booklet entitled "Audience Research" available from the National Association of Broadcasters, and written by Professor James Webster, Ohio State University. It has been edited for inclusion in this text, and integrated with material from a booklet from the Broadcast Ratings Council called "Understanding Broadcast Ratings."

• It can resolve differences of opinion among equally competent members of management as to what the facts really are.
• It can help management assign a weight or order of importance to a set of known factors.
• It can disclose relationships among facts that were previously thought to be unrelated.
• On occasion it can uncover things that no one had thought of before.

Viewed in this light, research is neither a thing to be feared, nor is it something to ignore. It is simply a way to provide managers with information that can help them make "better" decisions.

Determining just when research is needed is primarily a matter of judgment. The more you know about research, the easier that judgment becomes. Here are some of the areas in which research can be useful to station management.

Basic Marketing Data

Any station should have basic data on the market it serves, for its own guidance in program planning in advertising and promotion, and to satisfy the needs of advertisers. The characteristics of the market, its demographic composition (i.e., age, sex, race, income levels, etc.), its buying and living habits, and so on, are often available from existing sources like census data or trade publications. A manager should periodically challenge the adequacy of these kinds of data, though, for they change constantly. A specially commissioned survey might produce information that more nearly matches the station's coverage area, that is more up to date, or that better answers advertisers' questions.

Promotion Planning

Assessing the nature of your audience, and how it compares with the competition's audience, is one of the most important functions of research. Since broadcast media do not deal in a tangible product, as the print media do, they must turn to research to document whom they reach. Ratings services like Arbitron and A.C. Nielsen survey most markets at regular intervals. These firms will, for a fee, provide subscribing stations with information on the size, age and sex of station audiences during various times of the day and week. These kinds of data can also be analyzed to identify station reach, frequency and patterns of audience flow. Such information can offer Promotion Directors important insights as they make decisions about advertising and promotion scheduling.

Sales Promotion

Research findings can often help to uncover new advertisers and protect present accounts. Sales presentations can and do use the kind of audience information already described. New types of audience data, however, are becoming increasingly important to advertisers who for example, now want to know more about audience incomes, lifestyles and buying habits.

In the final analysis, an advertiser's interest centers on the way a medium can reach a market for his or her particular product or service. As a result, any research indicating that the station's audience includes an advertiser's clientele is valuable. Ideally, research could demonstrate how many users of product X listen to station Y or watch program Z. The cost of gathering such information on a local level, however, must be weighed against its value as a sales tool.

Using research to promote a station is perfectly legitimate. In fact, the use of research for promotional purposes has become one of the media's effective selling tools. Millions of dollars are spent on such research every year, much of it quite sophisticated.

But a word of caution about the promotional applications of research is in order. Sometimes people who would never condone questionable practices when seeking facts that will affect their own businesses, relax their requirements, perhaps subconsciously, when they are eager for promotional research to show them in a good light. Sooner or later, such "facts" catch up with them.

The solution is to remember the true purpose of research: to find unbiased information, rather than to prove a point. Approach the use of research with the idea that it should show you the truth, whether favorable or unfavorable. If facts are unfavorable, the research can be even more valuable, for it may show where corrective action is needed.

Identifying Trends

Effective managers will establish certain goals and objectives for their station. Repeat surveys can often help to monitor progress toward those goals by identifying specific trends. Have the characteristics of the audience changed? Has the share of audience increased? Has the station's image changed? Has an advertiser's clientele deteriorated? Have audience tastes changed? Keeping track of these trends will allow a station to exploit its strengths and set quickly to remedy its weaknesses.

These are just a few of the ways in which research can help managers to be more effective. Doing research, of course, is not always necessary or even advisable. To be of real value, the time and money invested in research must pay dividends. A station's resources are easily wasted on ill-conceived studies that produce inaccurate, irrelevant or trivial information.

The last chapter in this Part concentrates on what factors management should consider when deciding when and how to do research.

DOING RESEARCH

Research is not the answer to all management problems. Deciding when research can be useful is primarily a matter of judgment. There are, however, a number of questions to ask that will help decide when to do research, and subsequently, who should conduct the research project.

Is Research Needed?

The best way to find out whether research is really needed is to set down the questions you have in writing. What problems and decisions confront the station? What kinds of information could help make those decisions: From those questions, develop a brief list of research objectives. Write the objectives down in layman's language and discuss them with other people at the station. Do not, at this point, be concerned with exactly how relevant research would be conducted. Simply try to develop a clear and complete list of informational needs.

Once there is a satisfactory list of research objectives, review each one by asking the following questions.

- How will this information be used? What decisions will be made or what actions will be taken on the basis of the findings?
- Is this information important enough to justify the time and expense of doing a study?

Answering these questions may be difficult, but good research-planning requires weighing the costs of research against the usefulness of research information.

If this orderly analysis still indicates that certain facts are needed, don't plunge into an original research project until information already available has been investigated. The use of existing data is called *secondary research*. This information might be contained in station files, or in the local library. Ask knowledgeable people. Don't ignore competing media. Many newspapers, for instance, publish market studies, available for the asking.

Among the more conventional sources of information are trade organizations, which may sponsor research, as well as various reference works and periodicals. A few of these sources are listed below.

Industry Organizations

- National Associations of Broadcasters (1771 N. Street, N.W., Washington, DC 20036)
- Radio Advertising Bureau (485 Lexington Ave., New York, NY 10017)
- Television Bureau of Advertising (1345 Avenue of the Americas, New York, NY 10019)
- National Cable Television Association (918 16th Street, N.W., Washington, DC 20006)

Reference Works

- Broadcasting/Cable Yearbook (Broadcasting Publications, Inc., 1735 DeSales Street, N.W., Washington, DC 20036)
- Television Factbook (Television Digest, Inc., 1836 Jefferson Place, N.W., Washington, DC 20036)

• Standard Rate and Data Service (5201 Old Orchard Road, Skokie, IL 60076)
• Survey of Buying Power (Sales and Marketing Management, 733 Third Avenue, New York, NY 10017)
• Statistical Abstract of the United States (Business Division, Bureau of the Census, Washington, DC 20233)

Periodicals

• *Broadcasting* (Broadcasting Publications, Inc., 1735 DeSales Street, N.W., Washington, DC 20036)
• *Billboard* (9000 Sunset Boulevard, Los Angeles, CA 90069)
• *Media Decisions* (342 Madison Avenue, New York, NY 10017)
• *Variety* (154 West 46th Street, New York, NY 10036
• *Journal of Advertising Research* (Advertising Research Foundation, 3 East 54th Street, New York, NY 10022)
• *Journal of Marketing Research* (American Marketing Association, 222 South Riverside Plaza, Suite 606, Chicago IL 60606)
• *Journal of Broadcasting* (Executive Secretary, Broadcast Education Association, 1771 N Street, N.W., Washington, DC 20036)
• *Adweek* (514 Shatto Place, Los Angeles, CA 90020)
• *Advertising Age* (740 Rush Street, Chicago, IL, 60611)
• *Radio & Records* (1930 Century Park W., L.A., CA 90067)

Certainly, some informational requirements need little investigation to demonstrate that original research is necessary. Such information usually bears these earmarks: it is strictly local; it applies primarily to the station; it must be current.

Doing It Yourself

If the information needed can only be provided by original, custom research, you must decide if you can do the research yourself, or whether you need to enlist the services of a professional researcher.

The advisability of undertaking the research on your own depends greatly on the difficulty of the problem before you. First, consider the research questions. It's one thing to describe what people think or how they behave and quite another to explain why they are that way or what will make them change. Second, consider the complexity of the research method and analysis needed to answer your questions. A simple telephone survey or "focus group" research (see page 89) might be within your capabilities, but anything more demanding is best left to a professional. In making decisions about doing the research yourself, consider the following points.

Time. Research which is hastily conceived and executed may contain serious flaws which make it worse than no research at all. Doing it yourself, particularly at the beginning, will probably take more time than if you had it done professionally. Can the decisions to be made wait until the research is completed? Sometimes it is smarter for management to act quickly and take a risk than to wait for assurance from research.

Expertise. Do you personally have the time and expertise to plan and supervise the research? Do you have other personnel capable of performing it? If the decisions to be made on the basis of research are of great importance, it might be foolish not to use a professional.

Cost. Don't think that because you do the research yourself it's not going to cost something. For many surveys it is necessary to pay part-time interviewers. Even if your own employees can do the interviewing, it will cost in time lost from other duties. Additionally, someone will have to tabulate, analyze and write up the results.

Objectivity and Credibility. Aside from competence, you may need the objectivity and credibility that an outside professional can impart to the research. For external applications, such as selling an important national advertiser, consider whether your own efforts will be adequate and, more importantly, believable. Remember that media conducted research, even when expertly handled, can be suspect when used promotionally. Even for internal use, if you or others in the organization have strong biases, an outsider can be more objective.

Aside for these general considerations, there are certain types of research which should not be undertaken without professional research involvement.

Advertising Effectiveness. Research that assesses the impact of advertising on consumer knowledge, attitudes and behavior requires considerable technical know-how. Understanding the relationship between exposure to advertising and subsequent purchase behavior involves complex theoretical and methodological questions. It may seem perfectly natural to ask, "What led you to buy that?" or "What type of advertising helps you most?" but the validity of such simple approaches is often questionable because the respondent may not be aware of the answers on a conscious level.

Motivation Research. This type of research tries to explain what motivates people to act as they do. While this is certainly an important research question, it again requires the training of a behavioral scientist. Certainly you can ask people their reasons for doing many things, but don't expect to get complete explanations using simple survey techniques. Focus group research can help you get some idea of underlying motivations, but remember, this approach requires a skillful moderator.

Longitudinal Studies. Measuring changes over time in people's product-purchase behavior, program preferences and media use can offer valuable information. The best way to study these trends is with a series of surveys. Such longitudinal studies require comparability across each survey in the series, with respect to sample, method and timing. While you can approximate a longitudinal study by asking people to report changes in their behaviors or preferences, this is clearly a less satisfactory way to identify trends. True longitudinal studies demand careful planning and oversight that are best left to a specialist.

Ratings. Ratings research, of course, estimates how many people are using a given station at a given time. It is clearly the most visible and widely used kind of broadcast audience research. There are, however, at least two reasons why ratings research is best left to the services which specialize in them or to other experienced research organizations. First, while it seems simple, the accurate measurement of audience size is a highly technical matter. One only needs to read the hearings of Congressional investigations into ratings to become aware of the intricacies and pitfalls. NAB is active in the effort to police the ratings through the Broadcast Ratings Council, which audits the operations of the major ratings services. Second, the foremost use of ratings is as a selling tool. Even if a station succeeded in doing accurate ratings research, such station-generated data would, understandably, be regarded with some suspicion by advertisers.

Bearing all these cautions in mind, there are still many research projects that you can undertake on your own. Certainly audience research encompasses much more than just ratings. If you are interested in doing research yourself, NAB publishes a workbook on conducting audience surveys that can help you learn more about the specifics.

Using Professional Researchers

There are times when the use of a professional research firm is essential. The project may be more extensive or technical than you can handle. You may need the objectivity that only a disinterested third party can provide, such as in making an important sales presentation based on research. You may be considering a substantial investment, and you must have full confidence in the findings.

Finding a Research Firm. There are a great many firms in the business of providing custom-research services. To find one capable of handling your research needs, begin by talking to the station sales representative or other station managers in non-competitive markets. Network affiliates should also consider talking to the network's research department. These informal contacts may lead to a research company that has performed well for other broadcasters, or help steer clear of organizations which have proven unsatisfactory.

Don't be reluctant to consider some of the larger, well-known research companies. These firms can often design a study to meet your needs and your budget. Major ratings services are usually equipped to do specialized market studies, particularly dealing with station reach, frequency and audience flow.

Locate research firms by consulting research directories. *Broadcasting/Cable Yearbook* and *TV Factbook* both have sections that list various research companies and include a brief description of the services they offer. In addition to these sources, review the advertising pages of publications like the *Journal of Advertising Research* or the *Journal of Marketing Research.*

Many universities now have schools or departments that specialize in the study of radio and television. Their faculties may include excellent researchers who offer their services on a consulting basis. Marketing departments can also be a source of research expertise.

Some researchers, commercial or academic, offer counsel aside from conducting entire research projects. When a difficult research problem arises, seek their advice. Expect to pay a fee. Some organizations will perform any one phase of the work. It may be desirable, for instance, to have an expert design the sample, or write the questionnaire, or conduct the field work, or do all the tabulations. Usually, it is the interviewing that is handled by an outside firm.

Selecting a Research Firm. It's a good idea to talk to more than one research company. Use the station's list of research objectives as a basis for conversation. Be as specific about the station's informational needs as possible. Giving the research company a clear idea of what is wanted will allow it to develop a study that is more responsive to the station's needs.

Do the following to make an initial evaluation of the research firms you contact.

- Obtain a description of the firm.
- Obtain references.
- Obtain a list of clients, and if possible non-confidential reports they have produced.
- Insist on a written research proposal, including a statement of the problem, research objectives, sampling procedures, research methods, what the station will receive, cost quotations and time estimates.
- Evaluate the honesty, objectivity, experience and professional competence of the firm. You don't need to be a researcher yourself to do this.

Reviewing Research Specifications

Once a research firm capable of doing the job has been identified, carefully review specific aspects of the research before committing to a contract. There are certain things to look for, and questions to ask, in evaluating the research proposal:

Sample Size. The quality of information gathered in any kind of survey research is critically dependent upon the sample. How large a sample will the study have? While there are no hard and fast rules, a sample size of 200 to 500 people is usually needed to produce an acceptable level of accuracy. If the researcher proposes using a sample that is considerably smaller or larger, ask why?

Sample Type. Even very large samples can produce misleading results if they are selected in a way that fails to represent the population being studied. The best protection against drawing a biased sample is using probability or random sampling. There are several types of probability samples, for example, *systematic random samples, area samples, cluster samples* and *stratified samples.* If the sample in the study does not seem to be a probability sample, ask. Be suspicious of samples labeled *quota, judgment,* or *convenience.* These are non-probability samples and the research company should have a very compelling justification for using them.

Response Rates. No research company can be expected to successfully measure everyone selected in the initial sample. Some people will be unavailable or refuse to cooperate. The response rate, or percentage of people in the original sample who are actually included in the final tabulation, has an important bearing on the reliability of survey results. Response rates vary according to the type of survey done. Mail surveys tend to be low (e.g. 20% and up) and telephone or face-to-face surveys tend to be higher (e.g. 50% and up). The higher the response rate, the more confidence you can have in the results. Low response rates can be improved by repeat mailings or frequent callbacks. Ask the research company how many callbacks they will make (it should be three or more) and what response rate they can guarantee. Be sure you understand their answer. Some firms will report completed interviews as a percentage of the people they managed to contact. This is not the same as the percentage of the original sample and it can make response rates appear much higher.

Telephone Surveys. Telephones are a popular information-gathering device in audience research, but they present some unique problems. If a telephone survey is being considered, ask what sampling frame the researcher will use. If the answer is the telephone directory, ask how people with unlisted numbers will be contacted. Random digit dialing or plus-one techniques can overcome the problem. Remember, not everyone has a telephone. Ask how many people in your area fall into this category, and whether their omission will represent a serious bias. Find out when the telephone interviewing will take place. If calls are only made from nine to five on weekdays, the survey will inevitably under-represent working people.

Quality Controls. Many studies look fine on paper, but are poorly executed in the field. This is most often a problem during the process of interviewing. Find out whether the research firm's personnel will conduct the interviews or whether the work will be done by another firm. If the latter is the case, ask about the interviewer's qualifications. Find out what quality controls will be used to monitor the interviewing. Will some of the people who were supposedly interviewed be contacted to determine if an interviewer actually spoke to them? If focus group research is being considered, ask if the station will be able to monitor the sessions.

Questionnaire Design. Most companies will not submit a complete questionnaire with the proposal because they consider questionnaire design part of the job. If an original questionnaire is to be used, find out how it will be pretested. If a questionnaire is available, review it, bearing in mind the considerations discussed in the section on measurement. If you have questions about the reason for certain wordings or sequencing, don't hesitate to ask for an explanation.

Screening Questions. Some questionnaires contain instructions to interviewers or items designed to screen out certain types of people from further questionining. You may be interested only in people of certain ages or with certain listening habits. Zip codes are sometimes used to screen out people living in certain geographic areas. There is nothing wrong with screening questions as long as you realize what they do. They narrow the focus of the research by redefining the population being studied. If certain areas of the market have been eliminated by using selected zip codes, generalizations about the entire market cannot be made. Make sure the rationale behind any kind of screening device is understood.

Researcher or Consultant. There is a difference between the role of a researcher and the role of a consultant. Research the station buys may provide a good deal of data which the station is left to interpret on its own. Find out whether the research report will include analysis and recommendations that go beyond the numbers. It may be worthwhile to enlist the researcher as a consultant to discuss the findings and suggest a plan of action. The additional charge for these services can make an important difference in how effectively the information can be applied.

Finally, remember, that audience research is a tool—not a cure-all. No matter how sophisticated and skillfully executed, it is no better than the person who uses it. The more the Promotion Director knows about research, the more he or she becomes involved in the research process, the more adept he or she will be at using audience research to the station's advantage.

RESEARCH METHODS

Suppose you have concluded that certain information about the audience would be valuable to you. If that information is not already available from trade associations, the government or other sources, you will have to collect that information through original research. There are a number of research methods used to gather new information. Three of the most common methods are surveys, focus groups and experiments.

Surveys

A survey is a research method used for collecting factual information about some population or market segment. Survey research allows you to:

- Elicit accurate information because questions are asked in a carefully worded and systematic way,
- Use samples to avoid going to every member of the population at obviously higher, often prohibitive costs.
- Analyze responses from large numbers of people by reducing these to meaningful statistics.

The survey is probably the most widely used method of audience research. There are three basic types of surveys.

1. *Telephone surveys* gather information through interviews conducted over the telephone. In recent years, this approach has gained in popularity because it offers a number of important advantages over other survey techniques.

- It is more economical than face-to-face interviewing. Because contact is made over the phone, travel expenses can be cut to a minimum.
- Selection of a sample is relatively easy. With this technique, a telephone directory is often an appropriate sampling frame.

• Interviewing, even of a nationwide sample, is relatively easy because it can be done from a centralized location. Additionally, this allows management to supervise and control the interview process more effectively.
• It is the fastest method. Data become available as soon as interviews are completed. Some research firms even enter peoples' responses directly into a computer, further speeding the process.

Despite these advantages, there are certain disadvantages of which you should be aware.

• Telephone interviews have to be short. People generally don't like being tied up on the phone for long periods of time. This may prevent you from gathering all the information you need.
• Not all types of questions can be asked over the phone. Some questions depend on people sorting cards or reviewing visual materials. These are obviously inappropriate for conventional telephone techniques. Additionally, respondents may be suspicious of the interviewer's motives—for example, believing the interviewer is really a salesperson. Accurate answers to specific questions about income and buying habits can be difficult to obtain unless questionnaires are carefully constructed.
• Not everyone has a telephone. Samples, therefore, may under-represent certain segments of the population like lower income groups or people living in the country. The telephone company can usually tell you the percentage of homes in your market with telephones. If you are interested in replies from specific groups who tend not to have phones, this may require an alternative survey approach. Furthermore, some regions, like urban areas, may have a high percentage of unlisted numbers. Again, this can introduce bias into the sample. To overcome the problem of unlisted numbers, some researchers use *random digit dialing,* where new telephone numbers are created, or *plus-one* techniques, where the number one is added to each phone number in the sample. Either approach will, by chance, draw in those with unlisted numbers. Unfortunately, they will also generate non-working or commercial numbers.

Unless telephone ownership bears significantly on the subject under study, telephone interviews will generally produce information comparable to other types of surveys. Further, innovations in telephone interviewing may eventually overcome some of the limitations in this technique. For example, telephones used in conjunction with two-way cable systems might allow researchers to present visual materials needed for some lines of questioning.

In *face-to-face surveys* a personal interview is conducted with the respondent at his or her home or place of work. Face-to-face surveys have a number of advantages.

• They offer the greatest flexibility in questioning methods. Visuals may be used for aided recall or multiple-choice questions. The interviewer or the respondent may record replies, whichever is most appropriate. The face-to-face situation, unlike the telephone interview, lends itself to questioning in greater depth and detail.

• The interview can be extensive, thus providing a great amount of information from a single survey.
• A sample can be designed that is fully representative of the entire population under study.
• The sample can be more selective in its coverage when the need is to survey a specific area, race, or other group.

Face-to-face surveys, however, suffer from some important disadvantages.

• The cost of this approach is usually higher than other kinds of surveys. Therefore, you must weigh its expense against the value of the information you seek.
• Successful personal interviews require a skilled interviewer. If interviewers are not well trained, they may inadvertantly bias a person's answers. Furthermore, since interviews are conducted in the field, it is harder for management to supervise the interview process.
• Contacting all the people in the sample is more exacting and time consuming.

The increased costs and time associated with face-to-face surveys have, in recent years, resulted in a decrease in their popularity.

Mail surveys are the third basic type of survey research. With this approach, questionnaires are simply mailed to people in the sample. It has a variety of advantages.

• It is easy to handle since there are no interviewers to train or manage.
• There is no interviewer bias.
• The cost is low. This can be deceptive, however, for low rates of return may require large mail-outs of questionnaires to get a large enough final or "in-tab" sample.
• Sample selection is easy, since prepared mailing lists can be used.
• Wide geographic coverage is possible when necessary.
• More thoughtful and candid replies may be given since people can respond at their own pace without an interviewer present.

Mail surveys, however, have a number of serious disadvantages.

• Sampling is limited to the available mailing lists (although letters can be addressed to "occupant" or "householder," but with less effectiveness).
• The usual low rate of return (25% is common) may bias the results. Those who don't respond may be different from those who do, and when non-respondents represent 50 or 75% of the population, distortion can be serious. The rate of return can be increased, even up to 80% or more by using monetary inducements or other devices. These, of course, will raise survey costs.
• Questionnaire length must be held to a minimum, usually no more than a page or two.
• Questions must be relatively simple. Open-end questions can be disappointing since there is no opportunity to probe for meaningful replies.

Further, there is no way to prevent replies from being influenced by subsequent questions since the respondent can read ahead before replying.
• There is no way to know whether the person addressed is the one actually replying.
• Results are obtained slowly. More than one mailing is often required to improve rate of return.

Telephone, face-to-face and mail surveys are the basic research methods used in survey work. These methods, however, are not mutually exclusive. Sophisticated survey research may include elements of all three information gathering techniques.

Arbitron Radio, for example, uses a combination of these methods to produce ratings data. After Arbitron draws a probability sample of telephone households, a letter is mailed to selected households notifying them of the selection. An interviewer then calls these homes to ask for their cooperation. If respondents agree, a diary is mailed to them. Additionally, in certain areas with large ethnic populations, interviewers will personally visit households in order to place diaries and maintain interest in diary-keeping.

Ratings data generated from a system of meters also constitute a kind of survey research. Here, however, measurement is accomplished using an electronic device rather than a diary or more conventional questionnaire.

Focus Groups

Unlike surveys, focus group research does not rely on elaborate sampling procedures, nor does it quantify peoples' responses for further statistical analysis. Instead, a small group of eight to ten people, selected on the basis of some common characteristic, is brought together for an in-depth discussion of a specific topic (e.g. a radio station's format, or personalities, or a program concept). These discussions, which may last an hour or more, are led by a moderator whose job it is to elicit peoples' perceptions and attitudes about the topic being discussed.

As a research method, focus groups have a number of advantages.

• Results are quickly and easily obtained.
• They are a relatively inexpensive method for gathering research information.
• The user of this research can become directly involved by observing the discussions as they take place. Further, the results of focus group research are presented as edited transcripts or selected quotations, rather than statistical summaries which may be harder to understand.
• Focus groups are relatively unstructured and flexible. A skilled moderator can probe and explore a number of areas, often uncovering unexpected reactions and providing new insights into the audience.

As with other research methods, focus groups have disadvantages which must also be considered.

· Results are based on very small, non-random samples. As a consequence, people in the focus groups may not be representative of the total audience. To avoid the possibility of a "bad" group biasing the results, at least three different group sessions should be conducted on the same topic. Even so, generalizing the reactions of a focus group to an entire population is risky business.

· Members of a focus group are not independent of one another. What one person says may sway or inhibit equally valid comments.

· The conduct and interpretation of focus group research is greatly affected by the skill of the moderator. A poorly moderated session can produce very misleading results.

The principal value of focus group research is its ability to reveal detailed and often unanticipated audience characteristics and reactions. Focus groups, however, are best thought of as an exploratory research technique. They can suggest new directions in programming and new avenues for information gathering. Because of their disadvantages, major changes in personnel or programming should not be made solely on the basis of focus group research.

Experiments

Experiments are the last research method to be discussed in this guide. Ordinarily, broadcasters will not encounter experimental research. It is important to mention, however, because it provides a sharp contrast to survey research.

An experiment is a research method in which the researcher can manipulate a particular variable to discover its effect on another variable. It is unequalled among research methods in its ability to find cause and effect relationships.

To illustrate, let's consider a question that has occupied researchers for over a decade; "Does watching violence on TV *cause* people to be more aggressive?" To answer this, we might conduct a survey which measured these two variables (i.e. watching violence and aggressive behavior). However, even if we found a relationship—for example, people who watch violence on TV are more aggressive than people who don't—we couldn't say that viewing caused the aggression. It might be that people who were already aggressive liked to watch violent programs.

An experiment, on the other hand, could manipulate the presumed cause of aggression by showing one group of people a violent program and another, equivalent group, a non-violent program. If the people who saw the violence became more aggressive while the other group was unchanged, then we would have evidence of a cause-and-effect relationship.

Experiments can be useful in copy or program testing by answering questions like: "Does one wording of a commercial cause people to remember product characteristics better than another wording?" or "Does adding a laugh track to a comedy cause people to enjoy it more than the same program without a laugh track?" Unfortunately, experiments must often take place under unusual or atypical circumstances. So, while experimental results can be very useful, they should be generalized to the "real world" with caution.

UNDERSTANDING BROADCAST RATINGS*

Broadcasting was a $15 billion industry in 1980. That figure is growing by more than one billion a year. One pervasive element in all aspects of broadcasting is the audience rating. Ratings largely determine what programs live or die, where advertisers place commercials, what rates will be charged, the market value of broadcast stations, which network is in the ascendency or descendency and the career fate of many broadcast executives. When evaluating industry stocks, Wall Street analysts watch ratings trends more closely than earnings statements because *profits follow ratings.*

Even in the world of non-commercial or public broadcasting, ratings are increasingly important. As government support of public broadcasting tapers off in the fiscally conservative climate of the '80s, the need for greater income from the public at large and from corporate underwriters inevitably translates into an important need for ratings information at the least, and at most, for higher ratings for programming. More viewers and listeners mean more contributions from members, and from corporations which want to benefit by their association with public broadcasting before the widest possible audiences.

Why do ratings exist?

Broadcast programs, commercials and promotion spots reach their audience without any transaction record such as a paid subscription, or a newstand purchase, or a box office ticket sale. Listeners and viewers have free choice in turning on their receivers and in switching from channel to channel to suit their tastes and mood of the moment.

Pioneer radio advertisers decided they must have some measurement of the size of this intangible audience. They inaugurated the Cooperative Analysis of Broadcasting (CAB) in 1930 with telephone recall surveys conducted by Crossley. In 1934 a group of magazine publishers, who believed the CAB overstated radio audiences, commissioned C. E. Hooper to start a second service using coincidental telephone calls. Broadcasters soon discovered in ratings a valuable audience feedback mechanism to help them in better serving the public's changing tastes in entertainment fare. As a result, broadcasting has flourished in attracting audience and advertisers because it has available a continuous flow of reliable, actionable data on audience behavior unmatched by other media.

Ratings reports on broadcast audience size and composition are produced by a small group of private independent research firms. The ratings companies underwrite and provide syndicated services conducted on a regular basis with

*This section is adapted from material prepared by the Broadcast Ratings Council (BRC). It is available separately in pamphlet form from the BRC, and is reprinted here with the BRC's permission. Copyright 1978. Pamphlet author Hugh Beville, Jr., BRC's Executive Director, is currently completing a definitive reference book on broadcast ratings which gives the subject in-depth study that advanced students and professionals may wish to pursue. To be published by Hastings House.

common results for all subscribers. The services establish their own procedures and policies, after consulting broadcast and advertiser and agency users. A preponderant share of the costs is borne by the broadcast media because ratings are an important management tool and because buyers expect media data at minimum cost.

From the initial effort 50 years ago, the syndicated ratings field has developed into today's $75 million business. Approximately 1.5 million households in the U.S. annually supply data for ratings purposes. This represents the most extensive form of commercial survey research in this nation.

Ratings Characteristics

The basic methodologies in use today are four types:

· Instantaneous electronic meters.
· Diaries kept by respondents for one week.
· Telephone interviews using recall questions.
· Telephone interviews conducted coincidentally with the broadcast.

Fundamentally, the temporal aspects of broadcasting make measurement easier and more accurate than in the print field. The fact that a program's audience is assembled at a precise point in time is a critical factor. No memory element is involved in surveys using meters or coincidental telephone calls. Diary and daily recall measurement require limited reliance on memory. TV viewing and radio listening are, for most people, habitual and keyed closely to a respondent's living, driving and working patterns. This contributes to accurate recall.

Measurement services fall into four media categories: Network TV—Local TV—Network Radio—Local Radio. The research problems differ and so do the methodologies.

Television Ratings. Most widely known of rating services is the Nielsen Television Index (NTI). NTI employs meters for household data and diaries for measurement of persons viewing on a national basis. There are, however, two highly competitive and widely used local market TV services. Both employ household diaries in over 200 TV market areas covering the nation, plus meter panels in several major metro areas. One is produced by Arbitron (a subsidiary of Control Data Corp.) and the other by A. C. Nielsen, Inc.

Radio Ratings. In radio, as in TV, there is only one network measurement service—in this case RADAR, conducted by Statistical Research, Inc., employing a unique form of telephone recall. Local radio diary ratings are turned out by Arbitron (in somewhat fewer markets and on a more limited frequency than for TV) and by two new services (BURKE and TRAC-7) which entered the field in the fall of 1978. Two on-going services (MEDIASTAT and RAM) consider themselves supplementary to Arbitron, at this time.

In-home vs. Out-of-home. Television ratings are confined to in-home measurements (which excludes viewing on millions of TVs in hotels, motels, restaurants, bars, waiting rooms, dormitories, hospitals, clubs, as well as on portable sets out-of-home). Radio, because of its significant out-of-home audience, puts emphasis on the listening of individuals, wherever it may be done— in cars, shops, restaurants, etc., as well as at home.

One new form of measurement being pioneered in the 80s by A. C. Nielsen focuses on "rooms using television," attempting to measure television viewing in hotel and motel rooms, college and military dormitories. Initial experiments have shown that audience figures may rise as much as 9% during the entire day and 25% during late evening time periods.

Ratings Are Approximations. A primary fact which must never be forgotten by any ratings user is that these survey figures *are merely estimates, i.e., approximations,* and in many cases very rough ones at that. This fact does not negate their value as important evidence about past audience behavior and as a basis for future projections and decisions. Nevertheless, every rating estimate carries with it a set of limitations.

All Ratings Are Not Equally Dependable. Some ratings are more dependable than others and it's only with professional knowledge that one can make the necessary distinctions. Unfortunately, when specific ratings (with their attendant errors) are projected into number of households and persons in various demographic groups, they imply an accuracy which is decidedly unwarranted.

Deviations and trends in ratings which are strictly of a chance nature, are magnified into seemingly important differences.

The processing of ratings by computer for analytical purposes has increased this danger. A prudent approach is that used by one veteran agency media executive who accepts no rating change as actionable without confirmation from another service or a subsequent report.

Ratings Measure Quantity, Not Quality. Broadcast ratings are quantitative measurements of audience behavior. As such, they mirror peoples' likes and dislikes for programs as they are presented at a particular time in a specific competitive environment. The term "rating" is something of a misnomer because no qualitative aspect is involved. The most popular program is not necessarily the "best" program, or even a "good" program. It is merely the program which, in the area surveyed, reached the largest estimated audience by virtue of its appeal, its promotion, its placement in the weekly schedule, its particular competition (or lack thereof). Qualitative measures are obtained by research other than ratings.

Ratings Measure Performance, Not Opinion. Broadcast ratings, unlike opinion polls, attempt to measure actual activity by viewers and listeners. Do not compare them to political polling which seeks to predict future behavior (action at the polling place) using assumptions as to who will vote, etc.; or to opinion measurement where respondents' knowledge may be meager and their disposition wavery. Under these circumstances question wording can often seriously influence results.

WHAT ARE RATINGS? THE BASIC ELEMENTS

Before going any further, some basic definitions are required. The following are generally expressed in television terms. TV examples are used for simplicity. Radio ratings' nomenclature and definitions are similar except that they are based on measurement of *people* listening—the household base is not employed at all.

A *rating* is the percent of all television households or of all people within a demographic group in the survey area who view a specific program or station.

HUT (Households Using Television) is the percent of all television households in the area surveyed with one or more sets in use. It is the sum of all program ratings for each time period. (This assumes a household viewing only one program. Where two or more programs are viewed simultaneously on multiple sets, the sum of ratings will exceed HUT because the household is tallied only once.)

Share is the percent of households using television (HUT) tuned to a specific program or station during a given time period.

If any two of these figures are known, the third can be derived. It's conventional to ignore all percent/decimal references, though these are implied. Let's assume a rating of 18 and a HUT of 60:

That means that of all the TV households in the market area, 60% are watching TV (HUT). And of all those households in the market area, 18% are watching a specific program (rating.) But suppose you need to know what percentage of the homes *watching television* are watching that particular program (*share* of the audience). Simply divide the rating (18) by the HUT (60):

$$\text{Share} = \frac{\text{Rating}}{\text{HUT}} \quad (\frac{18}{60} = 30)$$

Similarly:

$$\text{Rating} = \text{Share} \times \text{HUT} \quad (30 \times 60 = 18)$$

And:

$$\text{HUT} = \frac{\text{Rating}}{\text{Share}} \quad (\frac{18}{30} = 60)$$

Ratings Projections

The base number of TV households in a given market area or survey is called the "universe" for that survey. Multiplying the universe by the rating yields the actual number of "households delivered."

For example, the January 1978 national universe was estimated at 72,900,000 television households. A program with a 20 rating reached 20% of these, or 14,580,000 households.

Similarly, the New York market in 1978 was estimated to have 6,524,000 households in the ADI (Area of Dominant Influence as defined by Arbitron) area. A 20 rating in New York would have delivered 1,305,000 ADI households (6,524,000 × .20).

Definitions of Audience

Meter generated network ratings are generally "average audience"—that is, the rating during the average minute of programming. The number of different households that tune in a program over its duration is, of course, larger and is called the "total audience." It is used primarily by the rare single-program sponsor and for reporting audiences involving major national events. The "average quarter hour rating" is the major market product of diary surveys where a minimum of five-minute viewing or listening within a specific quarter hour is credited to that quarter hour. Combinations of these quarter-hour audiences produce "average quarter hour" figures for various time periods.

HUT Levels and Radio Usage Patterns

HUT levels are generally in the 20 to 30% range in daytime hours (10 A.M.–4 P.M.); 30–60% in "early fringe" time (4–8 P.M.), and 55–65% in prime time (7–11 P.M.) On most nights viewing peaks between 9–10 P.M., and drops off sharply at 11 P.M. Ratings services can provide specific information for hourly and seasonal variations from year to year.

In radio, with measurement focused on (a) individual listeners and (b) total listening, the major components are: (1) in home, (2) auto, and (3) all other. 1978 estimates by RADAR showed highest total audience levels in the 7–9 A.M. time period. The total of nearly 60 million listeners included approximately 45 million in the home, 10 million in autos and 5 million in the "all other" category. The 4–6 P.M. time period is the second highest, averaging just under 40 million listeners, more nearly evenly divided between home, auto and "other".

These morning and evening peak listening hours for radio are frequently refered to as "drive time" in major commuting cities. Even though in each case the majority of listeners are in homes, auto listening is at its highest levels during these times.

Share

The "share of audience" measures each station's or each network's portion of the total viewing or listening pie in a given time period. The share is a relatively stable figure, not highly subject to seasonal, daily or other factors which influence the rating. *Therefore the share is the best measure of program trends.* Similarly, since it is based on a 100% figure for each time period, it provides a rough comparison of program popularity of shows in different time periods. An early evening network show, for example, would generally have a lower rating than most prime time programs because it is televised in a lower viewing time period. Yet if its share of audience in this time period is relatively high (30 or above) it might be renewed; while prime time shows with larger audiences (higher ratings) but *lower shares* may be cancelled.

Even though "share" is the best quantitative measure of popularity provided by ratings surveys, it does not measure inherent program strength because each program operates in a different competitive climate. To eliminate such variables additional (non-rating) research is needed. In radio, station share figures are generally used for overall comparative purposes.

Cost Per Thousand (CPM)

Costs per thousand (CPMs) are computed by dividing the advertiser's cost per commercial by the average number of projected homes (or viewers or listeners) in thousands viewing or listening to the program carrying the commercial.

If a 30-second commercial in a TV show delivering a 20 rating nationally (14,580,000 households) costs $50,000, the cost per thousand households would be $3.43, as calculated below:

$$\frac{\text{Cost}}{\text{Homes (000)}} = \text{Cost per thousand households}$$

Or:

$$\frac{\$50,000}{14,580} = \$3.43$$

In making such computations, the Promotion Director must be certain not to compare unlike figures. Cost per thousand *households* for TV cannot be compared to cost per thousand *individual listeners* for radio, or *individual readers* of magazines or newspapers, or cost per thousand *impressions* generated by outdoor advertising.

Gross Rating Points (GRPs)

The crudest measure of advertising impact is "Gross Rating Points" (GRPs). GRPs are merely a sum of all rating points achieved (or sought) in a given market area for a particular time span. But most advertisers want more detail than simply "tonnage," even when this is refined to target demographic groups.

GRPs (or gross impressions) tell nothing about the number of different people (or households) exposed (*reach*), or how many times each of these people is exposed (*frequency*). Various combinations produce the same total—6 times 6 equals 36, but so does 4 times 9 and 3 times 12. Therefore, a schedule delivering 30,000 projected gross impressions could be reaching 30,000 people one time each or 10,000 different people three times each. This brings us to *cumulative ratings,* the basis for reach and frequency analysis.

Cumulative (CUME) Ratings: Reach and Frequency

Average minute or average quarter-hour ratings are only the basic elements in audience measurement. Advertisers, including broadcast promotion directors, want to know what net percentage of households (or members of a specific target audience for which a goal may have been set) are reached by a schedule of announcements or on-air promos. Advertisers may want to know these figures for schedules ranging from a few days to many weeks. Promotion directors placing messages about programs on their own—or someone else's—air are more usually concerned with a one-week schedule of promos or broadcast ads.

The measurement employed here is the Cumulative (CUME) Rating. The CUME eliminates duplicated exposure, and nets the audience down to an unduplicated basis. It provides a rating figure in which a viewing household (or person) counts only once, no matter how many times the household or person may have viewed the announcement.

The following illustration may help explain the concept:

A radio station Promotion Director buys a 30-second commercial on four different programs, each on a different station, with these rating results:

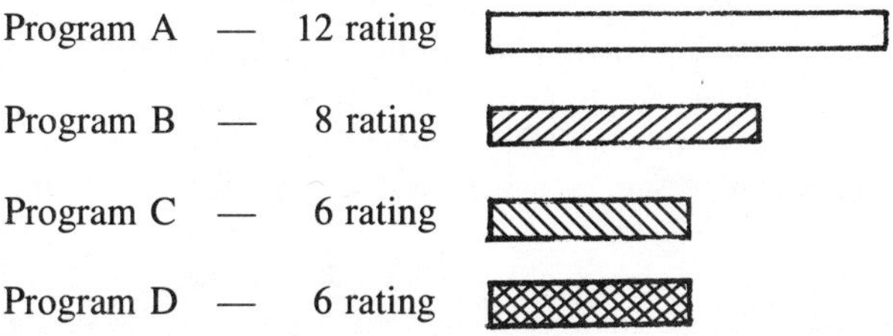

Program A   —   12 rating

Program B   —   8 rating

Program C   —   6 rating

Program D   —   6 rating

The Promotion Director has purchased 32 Gross Rating Points (GRPs). However, he needs to know his unduplicated reach, i.e., the net audience reached one or more times. Rating analysis in effect, by successfully eliminating Program B, C, & D viewers who have watched Program A, etc., produces the unduplicated (or CUME) audience of 20, as shown below:

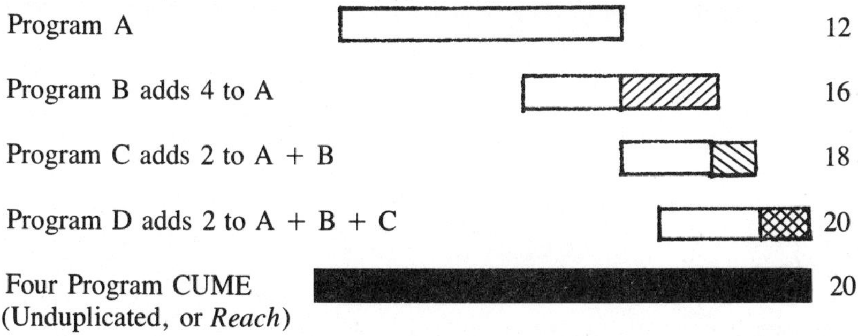

Program A   12

Program B adds 4 to A   16

Program C adds 2 to A + B   18

Program D adds 2 to A + B + C   20

Four Program CUME   20
(Unduplicated, or *Reach*)

Since all duplication has been eliminated by this analysis we have a net reach (CUME) figure from which to compute average frequency of exposure. That is determined by dividing the GRP (32) by the CUME (20), as shown:

$$\text{Frequency} = \frac{\text{GRP}}{\text{CUME}} \text{ or } \frac{32}{20} = 1.6$$

The average viewer has been exposed to our hypothetical radio station Promotion Director's 30-second commercial 1.6 times.

Further Reach and Frequency Analysis

Advertisers may set a minimum frequency for an effective campaign. In the above example, further analysis may reveal that only 10 of the 20 viewers were exposed to two or more commercials—8 representing two exposures and two representing 3. If the Promotion Director believed his commercial objective required two exposures, total target rating points become 10 with 22 exposures or 2.2 exposures per target rating point.

The above type of analysis can be performed for any individual program over a four-week period (assuming meter data are available). For example, this analysis produces a net duplicated audience for a news show (on a weekly or four-week basis) or a half-hour comedy (over four weeks). With diary data such analysis must be limited to one week or estimated by statistical extrapolation.

Reach and frequency data cannot be determined from a standard ratings book. Special reports or analysis are needed, keyed, of course, to the particular rating technique and service available. Here's where ratings and media analysts or station research experts play an essential role in assisting the Promotion Director.

In radio, CUME concepts are of greater significance than in television. CUME combinations of different stations with diverse program formats make significant contributions to advertisers' radio reach. Radio CUMEs estimated by random duplication formulae have proven acceptable and are widely used.

Basic Elements in Ratings Reports

Geographic Area Surveyed. Today virtually all ratings surveys aim to be projectible—i.e. the rating (program viewing or listening percentage determined by the survey) is projected to the population (universe) estimated to be contained in the survey area. The universes used for projection must be defined geographically. Each local market survey is generally reported on three separate geographic areas:

Metro Area. Generally those counties comprising the Standard Metropolitan Stastical Area as defined by the U.S. Office of Federal Statistical Policy and Standards.

ADI or DMA Areas. The Area of Dominant Influence (ADI) as defined by Arbitron and the Designated Market Area (DMA) as defined by Nielsen are essentially equivalent. For a given market the ADI/DMA represents the counties in which the aggregate audience for the stations assigned to the market exceed that of any other market's stations. This measurement device means all

U.S. counties can be grouped into some 200 discrete, non-duplicated areas. This has received widespread acceptance by advertising and governmental bodies for non-broadcast purposes. Major companies use these areas to allocate advertising and marketing budgets; the FCC uses ADIs ranking markets.

Total Areas. These are more extensive geographic areas comprising counties which together represent at least 95 to 98% of all the audience of stations in the market. Different rules are used to define radio areas, but the effort is similar: to achieve a prescribed area for purpose of projecting the people ratings used in radio measurement.

Demographics Surveyed

Whereas households are TV's basic measurement element, demographic breakdowns have assumed a dominant role in recent years, and are of special interest to advertisers and Promotion Directors alike.

In radio, ratings surveys are basically limited to reporting on the listening of individuals. Demographic categories are changed somewhat from year to year to reflect marketing needs of advertisers and agencies. The typical television report involves about 20 different age/sex categories ranging from "All Persons, two years and older" to "Girl Teens (12–17)" and "Working Women." Radio report groups are constructed slightly differently.

Time Periods Surveyed and Reported

With meters, diaries and recall surveys, it is possible to develop ratings data for 24 hours of each day of the week. Generally viewing/listening is so low between 1–6 A.M. that no data are reported, but there are exceptions. Certain groupings of time periods (*day-parts*) are widely used for reporting of averages for comparative and trend purposes. Examples of these are:

> For TV: Early Morning (7–9 A.M.)
> Early Fringe (4:30–6 P.M.)
> Prime Time (7:30–11 P.M.)
> For Radio: Morning Drive Time (6–10 A.M.)
> Afternoon Drive Time (3–7 P.M.)

Ratings Reports

TV meter services supply household ratings daily. These are periodically summarized and "wedded" to demographic viewing data from concurrently conducted diary surveys. NTI puts out national TV bi-weekly pocket pieces (not all with demographics), while local meter services provide weekly household reports and monthly complete reports.

TV diary services provide printed books (and computer tapes) for each four-week survey period. Three—in November, February and May—are known as *"sweeps"* because all markets are measured. Radio's diary reporting is less frequent with only one sweep in April/May. Major markets have more frequent TV and radio reports than smaller markets.

Potential Bias and Variability in Ratings

Again it is stressed that *ratings are estimates!* And when you use rating information in an ad you must be careful to qualify it. Problems in achieving accuracy include response errors (forgetting, lying, or incorrect reporting), conditioning effects (people who don't respond), the sampling frame used, and the statistical error associated with the sample results.

Sample Frame. Whereas ratings actually seek to produce estimates which are projectable to all radio- or television-owning households, a convenient list of such households for any area in the U.S. does not exist. If it did, such a household list would be an ideal "sample frame." Lacking such a list, most early radio and TV ratings used the latest telephone directory as a frame. Telephone recall, telephone coincidental and diary surveys all relied on samples of listed telephone households to represent all TV or radio households. This raised problems: many phones are unlisted, and others have no phone—either for economic reasons, moves, or personal choice. In recent years, Nielsen, Arbitron and Arbitron Radio have adopted "random digit dialing" techniques which enable them effectively to reach unlisted numbers in markets with high numbers of unlisted phones.

On the other hand, meter household samples come from carefully drawn probability samples of *all* households and are not subject to the problems of using telephone lists.

Statistical Sampling Error. Leaving aside sample frame problems, all estimates based upon sample surveys contain a characteristic known as sampling error. Unlike other potential errors referred to, sampling error—for a sample drawn so that each unit has a known chance of selection—can be readily computed. This universally accepted statistical measure of sample error is known as *Standard Error*.

With the aid of the theory of probability, Standard Error enables one to calculate the probabilities of sampling errors for ratings of various magnitude. The formulae for such computations appear in ratings books.

Basically, when using a probability sample and a fixed design, statistical error for ratings is a function of sample sizes. It is not determined by the size of the market or universe measured. For example, it takes a sample of 1,200 households to measure the San Francisco market with the same precision as 1,200 households used in the national Nielsen ratings.

If a sample is drawn on a probability basis, mathematics can determine the size of the statistical error. Assume that one is surveying a metropolitan area with 500 diaries to obtain estimated TV household ratings. The survey may show program XYZ with a rating of 21 (21% of all households in the sample reported viewing the program). A different sample drawn in the same way during the same week might report a 19 rating for the same program; and a third might report a 22. Let's assume that in reality the true rating was 20.

The individual sample findings were all within the margin of error to be expected under these circumstances. Any one of the figures (21, 19, 22) would be as good an estimate as any other.

The expected variability range for a rating of 21 would be from 19 to 23 in 67% of such samples; in 33% the rating would probably be below 19 or above 23. There is a 95% probability that the true value would be between 17 and 25.

The important thing to remember is that when program XYZ's 21 rating is compared with others it must be recognized that this is indeed an *estimate*, not a precise number. And when the next rating report shows program XYZ at 24, it is no guarantee that its audience has gained in size even though a number comparison shows households up by a substantial number.

Increasing the size of a sample will decrease the size of the Standard Error. However the changes are not proportional. For most sampling plans, to reduce Standard Error by 50%, the sample size must be quadrupled.

Relative Standard Error. Relative Standard Error is the ratio of the estimated Standard Error of a rating to the size of the rating itself. For example, a rating of 10 with an estimated Standard Error of 3 has a relative Standard Error of 30%. Since Standard Errors vary with the size of the rating or audience estimate involved, the Relative Standard Error is, for comparative purposes, a more meaningful measure of the reliability of audience estimates.

In any ratings report, the Relative Standard Error figures will vary widely. Household HUT figures and station ratings figures for broad day-parts will have the lowest Standard Error (and therefore be the most reliable statistically). On the other hand, individual quarterhour program ratings for small demographic groups such as Teen Girls, Children 6–11 or Females 15–24 will have significantly larger Relative Standard Errors. In general, high ratings have smaller Relative Standard Errors than low ratings in the same demographic column.

The reliability of various audience estimates in any rating report can differ greatly. Therefore, a user who treats all numbers as equally reliable is poorly equipped to use these numbers in making decisions. One should know the degree of confidence associated with an estimate before accepting it.

The Broadcast Ratings Council requires accredited television rating services to provide threshold values of Relative Standard Error (RSE) at column heads throughout their reports. This simple "on-the-page" evaluation tool can aid the Promotion Director in assessing the effect of sample size on the reliability of audience estimates.

Ratings Accuracy

Perhaps the most significant test of ratings accuracy is the conformation of trends by various rating services using dissimilar techniques and vastly different sample sizes. In the 1977–78 broadcast season, for example, when the National NTI service (1,200 meters) showed the ABC network leaping from third to first place in prime time, the Arbitron and Nielsen diary services (with a million diaries) showed exactly the same trend in markets throughout the nation.

Uses of Ratings

Ratings have become indispensible to networks and stations in making program decisions, pricing and sales decisions, and promotion decisions.

TV Stations. Network-owned and -affiliated TV station use of ratings is centered on sales activities because these stations have a limited number of hours to program for themselves. Independent stations, of course, have to compete strenuously to keep audiences in the face of network competition, so they need extensive rating analysis for programming decisions. They have learned how to counter-program network offerings with sports, movies, specials, news and off-network re-runs by strongly appealing to specific demographic groups.

Network affiliates are very concerned with the ratings of their news operations which are good revenue producers—very costly and highly competitive—and with "early fringe" (the time between 4:30 and 8 P.M.), including the so-called "access time" of 7:30–8 P.M. Here each local TV station slugs it out with its rivals. The market's taste for movies, off-network series and news—as well as the demographic and living patterns of the area—all impact on rating trends. Shrewd analysis of the audience can pay dividends.

For the Promotion Director, ratings are invaluable guides to certain audience promotion activities. They can indicate where to place on-air promotional announcements on TV stations to reach similar audiences, and indicate which shows might be saved with an additional promotional push. Rating information can help the Promotion Director develop a media plan—a mix of advertising, on-air promotion, and other promotion efforts incorporating radio ads for TV stations, TV ads for radio stations, print ads, outdoor advertising, and many other tools.

And they are indispensable in sales promotion activities. Letting potential advertisers know various program audience characteristics helps attract the right advertiser to the right schedule on the station.

Radio Stations. Outside of medium to large markets, ratings are less important in radio than TV. Most radio stations lack a regular service and many others are covered only once or twice a year by Arbitron. Where available, however, ratings are valuable guides to assess program format as related to demographic groups. In addition to average quarter-hour ratings, station daypart CUME ratings in age/sex categories are indispensible to selling radio time. Data systems such as Telmar and Marketron provide reach and frequency estimates for combinations of availabilities on two or more stations. In addition, they calculate GRPs and measures of cost efficiency.

Summary

For the station Promotion Director who has learned about ratings, a world of opportunities opens up—especially for effective use of on-air promotion and for campaign planning. But it must always be remembered that ratings are estimates, subject to variation and error, and should be used with care and responsibility.

GLOSSARY OF RESEARCH TERMS

The definitions below cover the research terms you will encounter most frequently in dealing with audience research. Aside from its value as a reference, perusal of the entire glossary should prove instructive on methodology itself. The definitions have been presented as non-technically as possible.

Aided Recall. Questions that help the respondent remember by prompting him with lists or other materials. ("Which of the radio announcers on this list have you ever heard on the air?")

Area sample. A kind of probability sample designed so that respondents are selected from previously designated geographic areas.

Audience. The people who read, listen, view or are otherwise exposed to a mass communications medium or a specific message.

Audience flow. A type of audience study in which one examines the duplicated or shared audience for pairs of programs scheduled at different times.

Audience measurement. Research to determine the number and/or kinds of people in the audience of communications media.

Audience research. Any systematic means of collecting and reporting objective, reliable information about the audience.

Bias. The difference between the results obtained from a sample and the actual conditions, due to influences other than sampling error. Among various causes of bias are faulty wording of questions, the way the interviewer asks a question or reports an answer, the appearance of the interviewer (such as a white interviewing a black and vice versa), learning the identity of the survey sponsor, failure of some respondents to answer, incorrect responses, errors in processing data, and conscious or unconscious attempts by respondents to upgrade their social or cultural level.

Breakdown. (see "Cross-tabulation.")

Call-back. An additional attempt to find a respondent drawn for the sample but not available for an interview when first called upon.

Call-out research. A type of telephone survey in which a sample of people who are known to be station listeners are questioned about music preferences. Such research often involves playing the "hook" or most important phrase of a song to trigger recall and reactions.

Camouflage. Anything used in a questionnaire to conceal its sponsor, ultimate purpose, or center of interest in order to reduce bias. For instance, asking for opinions on several radio stations, not just yours.

Closed-end questions. A question allowing only a limited number of answers, all of which are specified. ("Would you say that as a newscaster Bill Jones is very good, fairly good, or not too good?")

Cluster sample. A kind of probability sample designed so that groups of respondents are selected rather than immediately identifying individuals. For instance, to sample a large city, you might first randomly select city blocks, then housing units within those blocks, then finally interview individuals within those units.

Codes. Numbers or symbols used to designate replies on a questionnaire, to facilitate data analysis.

Coding. The classification of responses on a questionnaire, schedule, or diary, according to specified rules, to facilitate their tabulation and analysis. As part of this step, code numbers or letters may be assigned to categories of responses.

Coincidental measurement. A measurement of behavior at the time it is taking place, thus not depending on memory. ("Were you listening to the radio when the phone rang?")

Conditional question. Question to be asked only if a certain reply is given to a preceding question. ("Do you own a car?" If yes, ask: "Does it have a radio?")

Convenience sample. A type of non-probability sample in which respondents are selected because they happen to be readily available to the researcher.

Cross-tabulation. A way to analyze or present results by constructing a table in which the responses to one question are paired with those to another question or variable.

Cume. (see "Reach")

Data processing. Coding, editing, and tabulating information, either by hand or by machine.

Depth interview. An interview that goes below the surface by intensive probing questions and discussion.

Demographics. A category of variables frequently used in audience research. They include such audience characteristics as age, sex, income, education and occupation.

Diary. A form or booklet in which a sample of respondents is asked to keep a record of things they do (such as radio listening, television viewing, or food purchases).

Experiment. A study in which the researcher manipulates one or more variables (called independent variables) to discover their effect on another variable (called the dependent variable).

Field work. The gathering of primary data from a public through interviewing or observation.

Flash cards. Lists or statements on a card or sheet for the interviewer to show the respondent in connection with a question.

Focus group. A research technique in which a small group of people (usually six to twelve) have an informal, in-depth discussion of some subject, under the guidance of a moderator.

Frequency. 1) The number of times within some specified period of time when an individual or household is in the audience for a particular station or program. This information can determine the "frequency" with which they see a particular ad. 2) The number of people who are assigned a certain value on a particular variable.

Frequency distribution. The number of people who are assigned a particular value on a given variable over the range of values that the variable assumes. A frequency distribution can be presented as a table or graph.

Image. A pattern of attitudes and information about a company, institution, product, station or person.

Indirect questioning. Questions to obtain views or behavior by asking about related views or behaviors. ("How would you say most people around here would feel about a low-income housing project being built in the neighborhood?")

Interval measurement. A level of measurement in which the numbers assigned to objects are based on a scale with equal intervals and an arbitrary zero point. A Farenheit thermometer, for example, measures temperature in equal degree units. The zero point, however, is arbitrary and does not indicate an absence of temperature. (see "Measurement.")

Interviewer. A person who asks questions of others in a survey, using questionnaire or guide, following a predesignated plan.

Interviewer bias. Any influence upon responses which the interviewer causes, knowingly or otherwise, through his own attitudes, actions or appearance.

Judgment sample. A sample designed so that resondents are selected by non-probability techniques, that is, allowing human judgment.

Longitudinal study. A series of comparable surveys useful in identifying trends and changes over time.

Mean. A statistic used for summarizing the most typical value a variable assumes. In its most basic form, it is a simple arithmetic average.

Measurement. The process of assigning numbers to objects (often people) according to some rule of assignment.

Median. A kind of average defined as that point in a distribution where half the values are higher and half the values are lower.

Meter. A device that monitors television set usage and stores that information for subsequent retrieval.

Mode. A kind of average defined as that value in a distribution which occurs most frequently.

Mortality. The rate of failure, for various reasons, in completing interviews according to the sample plan.

Nominal measurement. A level of measurement in which the numbers assigned to objects simply differentiate the categories that comprise a variable. Sex, for example, is comprised of male and female. Other nominal variables include race, occupation, county of residence, etc. (see "measurement.")

Non-directive probe. An interviewing technique to obtain further comment in response to an open-end question without suggesting anything. ("Is that right?", "How do you mean that?")

Non-probability sample. A kind of sample created in such a way that not every member of the population it represents had an equal or known chance of being included. (see "Convenience Sample," "Judgment Sample," and "Quota Sample.")

Normal distribution. A kind of frequency distribution which, if graphed, would appear as a symmetrical, bell-shaped curve.

Open-end question. A question that allows complete freedom in the reply, no alternative specified. ("Why is XYZ your favorite station?")

Ordinal measurement. A level of measurement in which the numbers assigned to objects reflect a ranking of the categories that comprise a variable. Social class, defined as upper, middle and lower, is an example of an ordinal variable. (see "Measurement.")

Panel. A group of people who are surveyed over time, continuously or periodically, rather than only once. (see "Longitudinal Study")

Precoding. Assignment of numbers or symbols to predetermined responses on a questionnaire before the field work is done, to facilitate marking and tabulating responses.

Pretest. A trial run of a questionnaire or other instrument, in an informal or formal interview, to test workability and understandability.

Primary data. Data collected through original research, because it is not otherwise available.

Population. The total universe or group under study, from which the sample is drawn.

Probability sample. A sample based on the principles of probability, in which every member of the population being sampled has a known, usually equal, probability of being selected. The odds, rather than judgment, rule the selection of respondents. The sampling units must be drawn from a frame (such as a list of names or a map of a city); selection must be mechanical, usually employing random numbers. Also called a random sample.

Psychographics. A category of variables which draw distinctions among people on the basis of their psychological characteristics.

Qualitative ratings. A term used to describe a wide range of audience reactions to specific programs. Qualitative ratings can include viewer or listener assessments of how entertaining, informative, unique or useful a program was, as opposed to more conventional ratings that report the size and demographic composition of program audiences.

Questionnaire. A form designed for the orderly asking of questions and recording of answers in an interview. Sometimes called a schedule or instrument.

Quota sample. A type of non-probability sample in which predetermined quotas of various types of respondents are assigned to the interviewers to fill.

Random digit dialing. A technique used in telephone surveys, whereby telephone numbers are generated in a random manner as opposed to being drawn from a directory. Random digit dialing is used to overcome the problem of sample bias caused by unlisted telephone numbers.

Random numbers. A list of numbers that have been selected randomly, that is, each being independent of the position of any other, as if "drawn from a hat." Used in sample designing, such as selecting interviewing locations or creating a list of random telephone numbers.

Random sample. (see "Probability Sample.")

Range. A simple measure of variability defined as a difference between the highest and lowest values in a distribution.

Rating. The size of a radio or television audience, usually expressed as a percentage of the total possible audience. There are many types of ratings and ways of computing them.

Rating scale. A device through which respondents can express degrees or intensity of feeling, such as a line of markings (vertical or horizontal), a list of consecutive numbers or letters, or a selection of adjectives or phrases (e.g. excellent, good, fair, or poor).

Ratio measurement. A level of measurement in which the numbers assigned to objects are based on a scale with equal intervals and an absolute zero point. Age, income, and time spent using radio or television are examples of variables typically measured at a ratio level. (see "Measurement.")

Reach. The number of individuals or households estimated to be in a certain station's audience at least once during some specified period of time. Also called cumulative or unduplicated audience.

Respondent. The person interviewed in a survey, usually speaking for himself or herself but sometimes also for others in the family.

Response error. The difference between the response as actually recorded and the "true" response. This can arise from interviewer bias or from misunderstanding of the question by the respondent.

Roster recall. An interviewing method in which the respondent is aided in recalling his radio or television exposure by a list or roster of stations and programs, usually by time periods. (Also called "Aided Recall.")

Sample. A relatively small group, selected so as to be representative of a population, that can be questioned or observed and thereby provide estimates of the characteristics, opinions and behavior of the entire population.

Sampling distribution. A kind of frequency distribution that would result from recording sample statistics (e.g. means) from a very large number of probability samples.

Sampling error. The difference between the results from the sample and the results that would be obtained from a complete census, inherent in the statistical processes of sampling. This margin of error does not imply a mistake. For probability samples, this error is calculable, based on sample size and variability in the results.

Screening questions. A kind of question designed to identify respondents as appropriate for further questioning or inclusion in the sample.

Secondary research. Analyzing existing sources of data and information collected for purposes other than the present one.

Self-administered questionnaire. A form on which the respondent, not an interviewer, writes replies. Used in mail surveys.

Share. The percentage of the radio or television audience in a given area that is in the audience of a program, station, or network at a specific time. The base of the percentage is the households or individuals (whichever are being measured) using radio or television at the specific time.

Standard deviation. A measure of variability determined by a mathematical formula.

Standard error. The standard deviation of a sampling distribution. Useful in estimating the accuracy of saple results.

Stratified sample. A kind of probability sample in which homogeneous subsets or strata of the population are identified for selection on a probability (random) basis.

Structured interview. An interview in which the interviewer is required to follow the question wording and their order exactly. (see "Unstructured Interview.")

Subsample. A portion or breakdown of a sample, e.g. teenage males, households with other $10,000 income, etc.

Systematic random sample. A kind of probability sample in which respondents are selected by taking every Nth house or name from a list, such as every third, or tenth, etc.

Universe. (see "Population")

Unaided recall. The response to a question which depends on the respondents memory, without any aid. ("What are the names of radio announcers that you can recall having heard?")

Unstructured interview. An interview in which the interviewer is allowed to word questions as seems most appropriate during the interview, provided he stays on the subject. (see "Structured Interview.")

Validation. Re-interviewing a subsample for the respondents in a survey (usually 5 to 15 percent) to verify the competence and honesty of the interviewers.

Variability. The extent to which people or things differ from one another with respect to a particular characteristic or variable. Variability can be measured by the range, variance and standard deviation.

Variable. Any well-defined characteristic, trait or attribute that differs from person to person. (see "Demographics" and "Psychographics.")

Variance. A measure of variability determined by a mathematical formula.

CHAPTER 12

Budget Planning *

A well-prepared, well-administered budget is critical to the Promotion Director. It is an excellent planning tool for achieving pre-stated goals. More simply, it helps the Promotion Director and the rest of station management know what the Promotion Department hopes to do.

It provides a checks-and-balances system to measure the success or failure of efforts, and to show progress toward goals.

It creates a sense of tangible values in an area of highly subjective intangibles. More directly, it gives the Promotion Director the answer to the General Manager's question, "How can it cost that much . . . it's only a couple of pieces of art?"

It shows what achieving one additional rating point can cost in promotion dollars.

And it shows the impact last-minute changes can have on a budget. Or, as one promotion pundit said, "I can show the GM what it's going to cost the Promotion Department if they change that background to blue at this late date!"

BUDGET PLANNING

The first step in the budget process is to sit down with the General Manager and set priorities, or goals, for the year. Then, when the GM later wants to cut the budget, the Promotion Director can ask which goals must be sacrificed, or crippled.

*This chapter is based on a booklet called "Creatively Servicing the Budget," written for BPA's membership by Dennis Fitch, Director of Advertising, West Coast, ABC-TV, Los Angeles. It has been revised and edited for inclusion in this text.

Highly detailed budgets allow room for nit-picking. So budget categories are therefore usually generalized. Frequently used categories in promotion include: administration, consumer advertising, on-air promotion, publicity, trade advertising, and sales promotion. Consumer and trade advertising might be broken down further into radio, TV, newspaper, magazine, and production costs associated with each.

Next, design a weekly flow chart plotting Promotion Department activities during the budget period: introduction of a new anchorman, three ratings periods, a local festival, etc. Under each, plot the things necessary to support the activity. Show clearly how each element supports and necessarily reinforces the other within each project. Provide project cost breakdowns and totals. The only proper way a budget can be cut is with a complete understanding by others in management of the consequences of the cuts. Those consequences must be clear. It is essential to know exactly what programs and day parts offer the greatest dollar potential for the station. Determine the cost per rating point value of each program and each day part of the schedule. The formula for doing that for TV is:

- Divide the spot cost during a show by its rating. This gives the cost per point.
- Multiply the cost per point by the rating points a given show totals.
- Multiply that number by the number of spots available in the show. That gives the show's revenue *potential*.
- Multiply that number by the percentage of spots actually sold out on a regular basis, and subtract any applicable commissions. That gives the show's revenue value to the station on a daily basis.
- Multiply that number by the number of days a week, month, or years the show airs to get those figures.

Comparing the results for various programs will show which are the most— and least—approachable for budget cutting. And it will provide information on where budgets should be strengthened in the planning process.

A very important tip in managing any budget is to learn to say ''NO!'' to non-priorities. $200. here and $400. there add up quickly. If something has not been planned for, it probably is not essential. Question carefully before spending money on it.

BUDGET MANAGEMENT

Budgets can be a problem. There is either not enough money, or too much at the wrong time, and somebody always wants a ''complete report'' by yesterday. The fact is, however, that managing a budget is almost as vital a part of the Promotion Director's job as writing copy or editing a spot. Broadcasting is now such a competitative business that controlling the bottom line is more essential to success than ever before.

Of course, Promotion Directors—like everyone else—would like a bottomless pit from which to draw funds. One rarely has such a luxury. The idea is to develop a budget system that gives as much control and information as possible with the least amount of time and input. The pages ahead show how to do just that.

Budget Management System

Developing any system first calls for a clear delineation of needs. It also demands a delineation of the exact needs of the station's controller, as well as a good understanding of the demands on—and of—the General Manager. It does no good to have a perfect system that will not generate a report that is needed every quarter; or to have a system so cleverly devised that it can provide reams of useless information. What follows is one system, designed to satisfy one station's needs. It was prepared by Dennis Fitch, Promotion Director of KRON-TV San Francisco, California, for use by his department. While other stations' needs may differ in detail, they will be similar in the areas they cover and the system outlined is easily applicable.

In addition to the GM and Controller, the Promotion Director should understand the selling of the station. How is time sold? Is the late news sold alone, or as part of a package that includes much less desirable product? How are revenue reports submitted? Is it by individual program areas? Or broad day parts?

It is essential for a Promotion Director to know how much is being spent in media, in production, and in other areas generally. Specifically, it is useful to know what is being spent for production and media purchase by various program areas such as news, access, late night movies, children's programming, specials, sports programs, movies, etc.

It is not uncommon for such research to disclose that the station is spending a large amount of dollars to promote an area which will not generate a significant amount of revenue. This is not a problem if the station makes a conscious commitment to do it anyway. Promotion of important public service programming might be an example. But it is a serious mis-application of the promotion budget if it just "happens" without anyone being cognizant of the facts.

With a well-devised system, the Promotion Director can also pick out suppliers who consistently underestimate costs, and can give the controller a complete list of monies to be accrued at the end of a billing period. All of these should be available to the Promotion Director without requiring a great amount of additional effort. The effort should be in setting up the system, not maintaining it.

The following pages outline a simplistic approach to a manual and a machine system. The machine can be a word processor if there is no access to a computer. A mini-computer is preferable because it requires less effort to maintain the system. The word processor may not be designed for handling budgets, but most have various programs available which will sort and do limited math functions.

If the station has a computer system, the Promotion Department may be able to get a program specifically for the department's use. If not, both word processors and mini-computers are reasonable to rent.

One person in the Department should be assigned to handle the daily maintenance of the budget, whether it is manual or by machine.

Basically, the computerized system consists of three parts:

- The Purchase Order
- The Type of Expense
- The Program Area for which an expense was incurred.

Purchase Order. The purchase order is simply a method of getting all the information down on paper when the decision is made to commit to an expense. It can be issued for an expense that will be incurred tomorrow, or in five months. There are definite considerations to take into account for effective use of purchase orders. These are detailed in the discussion of the manual system.

Type of Expense. This refers to media, production, and "other." The latter can include anything the Promotion Director needs to have included. The former are usually broken down into newspaper, TV GUIDE, magazines, radio (for TV), TV (for radio), outdoor, transit, specialties, and the corresponding production costs for each.

Program Area. This section can be set up as individual programs, or in day-parts as needed to match the revenue reports from the Sales Department.

No system is any good if it is not maintained daily or weekly. The details required make it nearly impossible to sit down once a month and enter information without making massive mistakes. It also defeats the major advantage of any good budget system—having up-to-date information every day. The Promotion Director must be able to avoid staying up all night adding up figures to

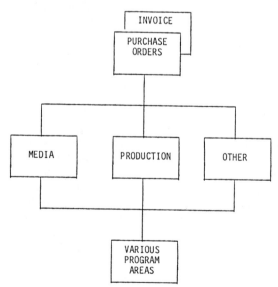

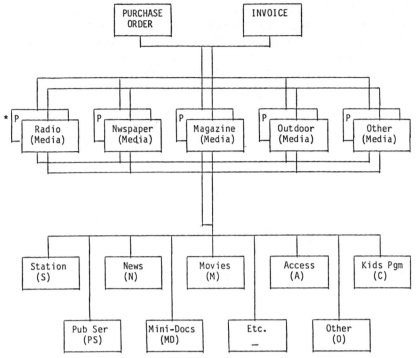

*"P"= Production for corresponding media.

see "how much you can cut," or to answer the GM's question, "How much did that thing cost us?"

THE MANUAL SYSTEM

The manual system for controlling promotion costs consists of four forms:

- Purchase Order
- Purchase Order Ledger
- Account Ledger
- Program Ledger.

The first is generally considered as an authorization to a vendor to provide some service and expect payment. It can also be used to control most expenses.

To make it useful for promotion purposes, three concessions are required on the part of station management.

First, the Promotion Department must be issued a pre-assigned set of numbers. Preferably the PO's can be pre-numbered in the printing process. This greatly reduces the chance of clerical error.

Second, the Promotion Director should be authorized to sign PO's within whatever parameters the General Manager decides. At many companies a dollar amount is set. Within this figure, the Promotion Director may authorize PO's. Above this amount, it must be signed by the GM or Station Manager. In other companies, the dollar amount is not as important as the type of expense the department head is authorized to approve. One company lets department heads authorize PO's for any reasonable amount except for purchasing capital equipment. This provision saves time in handling small ($500. or under) amounts.

The third concession concerns automatic accruals. When a PO is issued, the amount should automatically be accrued from month to month or from quarter to quarter until the bill is received. Therefore, if a $500. PO is issued in January and the bill does not arrive until March, the expense must be charged against the January budget. When a PO is issued, the money has been spent . . . unless the PO is cancelled. These three considerations are important. Without them, the Promotion Director will spend too much time getting PO numbers or waiting for someone to return from lunch, or a business trip, to sign them.[1]

All Purchase Orders must contain at least the following information:

- Vendor's Name and Address
- Date of Issue
- PO Number
- Amount (estimated, then actual)
- Account Number or Name.

Additionally, they should have the Program Area and the Budget Period. The Program Area was discussed earlier. The Budget Period is either a month or a quarter, in which the expense is to be recorded. Whether quarter or month depends entirely on the accounting system at the station. This allows the Promotion Director to issue a PO in one month (or quarter) for a project which is budgeted in another. This mythical PO might look something like this:

large logo	WXXX-TV/FM 0000 First There, CA 94109	PURCHASE ORDER NO. 123456

VENDORS NAME " ADDRESS CITY, STATE, ZIP		DATE: January 1, 1982 ACCOUNT NUMBER: 1-A-2000 BUDGET PERIOD: February PGM AREA: N	
Important	Quantity	Description	Amount
Invoices will not be paid without the P.O. Number.	-----	Photo retouching of news people.	1,000.00

[1] At some stations certain PO's, for continual usage of certain products or services for a very long period of time from the same source, are issued on a 'Til Forbid basis.

The above PO was issued on January 1st, but the amount will be charged against the February budget. It is a *news promotion expense* and the account number identifies it as a *TV Guide* production cost.

On the following pages are examples of the ledgers for PO's, Accounts and Programs.

The *Purchase Order Ledger* is simply a numeric listing of all PO's. It contains most of the information on the PO itself (i.e. the Issue Date, Vendor, P.O Number, Account Number, Amount, Program Area and Budget Period), It is the one place where all PO's are listed and can be traced using their number. When the invoice is received and the PO is completed, a checkmark is made next to the PO number. At the end of the budget period, it is a simple matter to determine which PO's are outstanding and need to be accrued. Simply hunt for the ones without a check mark.

It should already be obvious that this is a very simple system for keeping track of budgets. It does, however, require meticulous attention to detail and consistent effort to make it effective. Someone other than the Promotion Director in the Promotion Department should be assigned to keep track of PO's, invoices, et. al. It should be someone who can devote some time each day to keeping records up-to-date.

For the sake of example, this text uses a greatly simplified Account Number List. At KRON-TV/San Francisco, for example, the Promotion Department uses about 45 seperate accounts. Primarily, accounts are needed for various

Purchase Order Ledger   187

January 1981

	Issue Date	Vendor	P.O. Number	Amount	Account Number	Program Area	Job Number Individual	
1	1-3	ABC Co.	123456 ✓	1,000	2005	N/mD		1
2	1-3	DEF Co	123457 ✓	950	2000	N/mD		2
3	1-3	GHI Co	123458	35	3000	C		3
4	1-3	ABC Co	123459 ✓	140	2005	A		4
5	1-4	TV Guide	123460	4,250	1000	N/mD		5
6	1-6	Animatics	123461 ✓	15,000	2100	S		6
7	1-7	JKL Ltd.	123462	775	2015	S		7
8	1-7	JKL Ltd	123463	2000	2015	S		8
9	1-8	XYZ Co	123464	25,000	1015	S		9
10	1-8	TV Guide	123465	4,250	1000	m		10
11	1-9	DEF Co.	123466	860	2000	m		11
12	1-14	WHO Ltd.	123467	55,000	1005	N-m-A-S		12
13	1-14	GHI Co.	123468	460	3000	N		13
14	1-14	PhotoPrint	123469	50	4000	—		14
15	1-16	ABC Co	123470	3450	2005	N		15
16	1-17	Animatics (2nd Q)	123471	20,000	2100	S		16
17	1-18	~~Box~~ Void	123472					17
18	1-18	Post Edit Co	123473	3,300	2100	A		18
19	1-18	CutRate Video	123474	1,150	2100	mD		19
20	1-18	Prop Rental Inc.	123475 ✓	400	2100	mD		20
21								21

Account Ledger – TV Guide
1st Qtr   # 100

Prepared By ___ Initials ___ Date ___
Approved By ___

P.O. Issue Date	Vendor	(1) P.O. Number	(2) P.O. Amt.	(3) P6m Area	(4) Invoice Date Rec'd	(5) Invoice Number	(6) Par Tial / Invoice Amt	(7) Budget Totals	(8) Adjustment +(-)	(9) Line #	(10)	(11)
1	1-4	TVG (Issue 2-2)	123460	4,250	N/MD			3:11	$10,000		
2	1-8	TVG (Issue 2-9)	123465	4,250	MD				4,250		
3									9,500		
4											
5											

On this page are entries which correspond to those shown on lines 5, 10 and 12 of the PO Ledger. The numbers referred to are located at the extreme left of the paper. The PO Issue Date, Vendor, PO Number, PO Amount and Program Area information has been transferred. The only additional item is the Budget Totals (column 7). The total budget available is shown within the column heading. There is $10,000 available in TV Guide and $100,000 available in Radio. Underneath, a running total is kept so the Prom. Dir. can check spending at a glance. On the TV Guide ledger, there are two entries for $4,250. The total budget is $10,000 and $8,500 is already committed. There is $1500 left to spend. In radio, there is have $45,000 left to spend. The columns labeled Invoice Date Rec'd, Invoice Number, Partial Bill, Invoice Amount, Adjustment and Line # have no entries. This indicates that the invoices (bills) for the PO's have not yet been received.

Account Ledger – Radio
1st Qtr   # 1005

Prepared By ___ Initials ___ Date ___
Approved By ___

P.O. Issue Date	Vendor	(1) P.O. Number	(2) P.O. Amt.	(3) P6m Area	(4) Invoice Date Rec'd	(5) Invoice Number	(6) Par Tial / Invoice Amt	(7) Budget Totals	(8) Adjustment +(-)	(9) Line #	(10)	(11)
1	1-14	WHO Ltd	123467	55,000	N-Mar-3-MD			Bill	100,000		
2									55,000		
3											
4											
5											
6											

Account Ledger - TV Guido Production
2000
1st Qtr.

P.O. Issue Date	Vendor	P.O. Number	P.O. Amt.	P6M Area	Invoice Date Recd	Invoice Number	⟨✓⟩ Partial Bill	Invoice Amt	Budget Totals + (-)	Adjustment + (-)	Line #	10	11
									2500				
1-3	DEF Co.	123457	950	W/MD	1-20	A3004		1000	950	50.✓	6		
—	The Pass-up Group	—	—	0	1-5	none		250	1,200				
—	Cinemike Stats Inc	—	—	MD	1-6	679/416		95	1,298				
—	David Weist	—	—	C	1-7	none			1,598				
1-9	DEF Co	123446	800	M		—		800	2,458				
—	—	—	—	—					3,508		1		

In these examples, the PO information is again entered in the appropriate columns. There is new information in the invoice columns which were blank on the previous page. This simply indicates that bills have been received. In the Vendor column there are also some triangular marks. They indicate the PO is completed. A bill has been received for the entire job or service. These PO's need not be accrued. If you look back on the PO Ledger, you will see that a check mark has also been entered in the PO # column next to completed PO's. If you carry the check back to the PO Ledger, you only need consult one list to make an accrual at the end of a billing period.

Account Ledger - Radio Production
2005
1st Qtr.

P.O. Issue Date	Vendor	P.O. Number	P.O. Amt	P6M Area	Invoice Date Recd	Invoice Number	⟨✓⟩ Partial Bill	Invoice Amt.	Budget Totals + (-)	Adjustment + (-)	Line #	10	11
									$5,000.				
1-3	ABC Co.	123456	$1,000	W/MD	1-10	4744		985.✓	$1,000.✓	(15-)	4		
1-3	ABC Co.	123459	140	A	1-16	5135		645.✓	1,144.✓	303.	5		
—	Hearye Sound	—	—	MD	1-4	34210		632.25	1,772.25		1		
—	—	—	—	—		—			1,257.25				
—	—	—	—	—					2,250.25		2		
1-16	ABC Co.	123470	340	N		—			5,790.25				

media, corresponding production, and a few other accounts: administration, supplies, sales promotion, etc.

Sample Account Numbers:

1000 *TV Guide*	2005 Radio Production
1005 Radio	2010 Newspaper Production
1010 Newspaper	2015 Outdoor/Transit Production
1015 Outdoor/Transit	2020 Trade Publication Production
1020 Trade Publications	2025 Magazine Production
1025 Magazine	2030 Co-op Advertising Produc-
1030 Co-op Advertising	tion
1035 Other	2035 Other Production
2000 *TV Guide* Production	2100 On-Air Promo Production

After the information from the purchase Order has been entered on the ledger below, it is next entered on the Account Ledger There will be an account ledger for every account with which the Promotion Department deals. On the preceding pages are examples using PO's from the PO ledger.

Referring back to the previous page, you will note that an invoice was received on January 20th for $1,000. This matched the PO# 123457, issued to the DEF Company. The original PO was for $950, but the bill was for $1000. Since the Budget Totals column reflects $950, an adjustment must be made. The Adjustment column is next to the Budget Totals column for just this reason. Next to the $950 entry is $50 and a notation in the Line # column of "6." This indicates that $50 is added to the Budget column on line #6. If you look at line #6, you see $2,508. This is exactly $50 more than the previous total. Now the budget total is up to date.

If the invoice had been less than the estimate on the PO, the difference would have been deducted from the Budget Totals column. An example of this can be seen on line 1 of the Radio Production sheet. There a $985 bill was matched to a PO for $1000. The $15 difference reduced the running total. The reduction is indicated on line #4.

Invoice numbers are on the Account Ledgers to make it easy to find invoice entries if some payment problem or question arises. The date it was received is also handy when a supplier calls and asks if his check is in the mail.

Lines 2, 3 and 4 of the TV Guide Production Ledger show invoice entries without a corresponding PO. Frequently expenses are incurred which have not been PO'd for one reason or another. Obviously, these must be recorded too if the budget is to be managed. You should make every effort to issue a PO for as many expenses as you anticipate.

On the next page are two Account Ledgers for On-Air Production. One is the 1st Quarter and the other is the 2nd Quarter. Compare the Second Quarter sheet with line 16 on the Purchase Order Ledger. There you see the notation "2nd Q" next to the vendor's name. This indicates that the $20,000 will be paid out of your 2nd Quarter budget and not the 1st Quarter's. If bills are

Account Ledger – On-Air Production # 2100
1st Qtr '81

P.O. Issue Date	Vendor	P.O. Number	P.O. Amt.	PGM Area	Invoice Date Rec'd	Invoice Number	Partial Bill	Invoice Amt.	Budget Totals	Adjustments +(-)	Line #
									50,000		
1-6	Animatics	123461	15,000	S	1-6	57324	✓	5,000	15,000		
1-13	Post Editco	123473	3,300	A	1-8	57360	Ⓟ	11,000	18,300		
1-13	Animatics	123461	1,150	m/o	1-25	7V-910		300	19,300	1,000 #	6.1
1-18	Cat Rate Video	123474	400	m/o				—	20,450		5
1-18	Prop Rental Inc	123475	—						20,850	(100)	
									20,750		

Prepared By / Approved By — Initials / Date

Account Ledger – On-Air Production # 2100
2nd Qtr '81

P.O. Issue Date	Vendor	P.O. Number	P.O. Amt.	Pgm Area	Invoice Date Rec'd	Invoice Number	Partial Bill	Invoice Amt	Budget Totals	Adjustments +(-)	Line #
									50,000		
1-17	Animatics	123471	20,000	S					20,000		

Prepared By / Approved By — Initials / Date

Program Ledger — Mini-Doco

	P.O. #	TV Guide #1000	Radio #1005	Newspaper #1010	TV Guide Production #2000	Radio Production #2005	Music Production #2010	On-Air #2100
P.O. DATE (Service)								
1	1-3	123456 (Shared)						
2	1-3	123457 (Shared)						
3	1-4	123460 (" ")	$2,000					
4	1-18	123474				$500		$1,150
5	1-18	123475				$600		$400
6	1-6	I. # 679141C (Overnite)			$99.-			
7	1-4	Harry's Sound		$6,000				
8	1-14	WHO Ltd (Shared)				$635.25		
9								
10		Totals	$2,000	$6,000	—	$99.-	$1,735.25	$1,550
11								
12								
13								

Prepared By | Initials | Date
Approved By | |

The Program Ledger is the final step in the process. Information for this sheet is extrapolated from the Account Ledgers and occasionally from media plans or actual invoices. The results allow the Prom. Dir. to track the dollars spent against the various program areas.

The first entry (PO# 123456) was a shared expense. If you check the PO Ledger, you'll see the production bill was for both news and mini-docs. It has been estimated that the cost could be split between the two areas. Check the next two PO's to see which program area(s) shared expenses with mini-docs. The entry on line #6 is for an invoice that was not PO'd. The original entry can be found on the Account Ledger for TV Guide production.

If the Program Ledger is updated weekly, it is an easy task to arrive at totals at the end of your billing period. The information is useful as a summary. It is also useful in projecting budgets and in answering the eternal question, "what have you done to improve the ratings of _____?"

received during the 1st Quarter against that PO, the payment will be charged against the 2nd Quarter. This stops a lot of juggling.

On line #1 of the 1st Qtr ledger there is another checkmark in the Partial Bill column. In the same column on line #3, a checkmark appears with a circle around it. The first indicates that a bill has been received, but there are more to come which will apply to that PO (#1234611). The PO was for $15,000, but this partial bill is only for $5,000. The circled check on line 3 indicates that this is also a partial bill, but it is the final bill. With this $11,000, the total billed is $16,000. Since the PO was for $15,000, the $1,000 overage is added to the Budget Totals column on line #3. There may be cases where the billing will take place in 5 or 6 installments. For convenience, the PO number has been re-entered, but not the PO Issue Date, on the same line as the partial bill.

This is not difficult, but it is tedious. Once it becomes habit, it doesn't take long if done on a daily basis.

MINI-COMPUTER OR WORD PROCESSING SYSTEMS

Following are three flow charts which visualize the handling of the Creative Services budget by computer. The charts are not actual computer program flow charts.

If there is access to a computer and a programmer at the station, the Promotion Director should run, not walk, and beg assistance. A word processor, with "sort" and "math" packages available, can easily do the work outlined. Most word processor manufacturers have field representatives that can help. If not, learn to do it yourself. The time spent (it will be a fair amount) setting up a program or series of programs to handle the budget will pay off handsomely in useful information.

The simple system on the following pages is based on the same basic files as used in the manual system. They are: 1) Purchase Order Ledger, 2) Account Ledger and 3) Program Ledgers. A key to having an accurate system is to allow the machine to do the work. Enter information only once. Check the entry immediately for accuracy and then let the program draw what it needs from the verified entry. The less humans mess with it, the better.

Refer to "Entering A Purchase Order." The six information items entered from the PO are only entered once on the Purchase Order Ledger. (They are in bold type.) A "sort" program then selects all the information for that PO and puts it in the correct Account Ledger. The program should be devised to automatically keep a cumulative total of expenditures for each Account Ledger. (Budget Totals) If this is confusing, refer back to an Account Ledger form in the manual section. After this, the program sorts on the same Purchase Order Ledger, but this time by Program Area and duplicates the information on the Program Ledger. Again, you might want to refer back to a Program Ledger in the manual section.

So far, it is very simple. You enter the information from the PO just one time and the machine extrapolates what is needed for both the Account and Program ledgers. Obviously, if one enters the info wrong and doesn't correct it, errors will result.

Regardless of efforts to use PO's for most expenditures, there will be bills that were not PO'd. For invoices that do not have a matching purchase order, everything said about entering PO's equally applies. Devise a program that requires entry of information only once. "Sort" programs can transfer that data to both the Account Ledger and the Program ledger.

The only difference between the PO entries and Invoice entries is that the invoices do not have a general ledger. They go straight onto an Account Ledger. Depending upon your system, you may find it easier to have an invoice ledger which allows entry of 20 or 30 invoices at once. Then let the machine go to work sorting into Account and Program Ledgers. The schematics illustrating the above follow:

The system gets slightly more tricky when it comes to matching the Invoice with the correct PO. On the following page is a simple approach. It is by no means complete, but it gives the basic information needed.

The first problem is identifying invoices that have an outstanding PO. Many vendors keep forgetting to put the PO on their bill. Delay payment to consistent offenders and then send them a hand written note explaining that with "our computers" it delays payment if a PO is not shown on the bill. Most of them begin to get the message and start putting PO #'s on their invoices.

When entering the PO's invoice, safety checks are necessary. Enter the PO#, the Account #, the Invoice Amount, the Invoice # (if any), the Date received, and whether or not the invoice completes the PO. If not, it is a partial billing. (We'll come back to partial billings.)

The program should be so devised to compare the PO # and the Account # with PO's outstanding in the Purchase Order Ledger. If the PO # is not in the PO Ledger, or the PO # in the Ledger is assigned to a different Account number, something is wrong. This is the time to find out and correct it. Most of the time it will be a simple typo. If everything is right, the program should pick up the the Program Area and Vendor listings from the Purchase Order Ledger and match them up with the four other bits of data entered with the invoice. All of this is now sorted by Account #.

Next, the program "sorts" on the PO number and adds the new information to the Account Ledger, matching it up with the Purchase Order information previously entered on the Account Ledger. (At this point, it may again help to look at an Account Ledger in the manual section.) What is now in the Account Ledger is: PO Date, Vendor, PO Number, Program Area, Invoice Data Received, Invoice Number, Invoice Amount and Partial or Final Billing.

If this invoice only represents partial billing and more invoices can be expected against this Purchase Order, the system stops. It cannot update any amounts because all the information is not in, and the estimate filled when the PO was first entered is presumed still in effect.

If it is a final billing (most cases), that information should be sent back to the Purchase Order Ledger and entered with the original PO #. This step makes it very easy to extrapolate outstanding PO's at the end of a quarter or a month when the controller wants to close the books. All that is needed is to hand in a list of PO's to be accrued.

ENTERING A PURCHASE ORDER

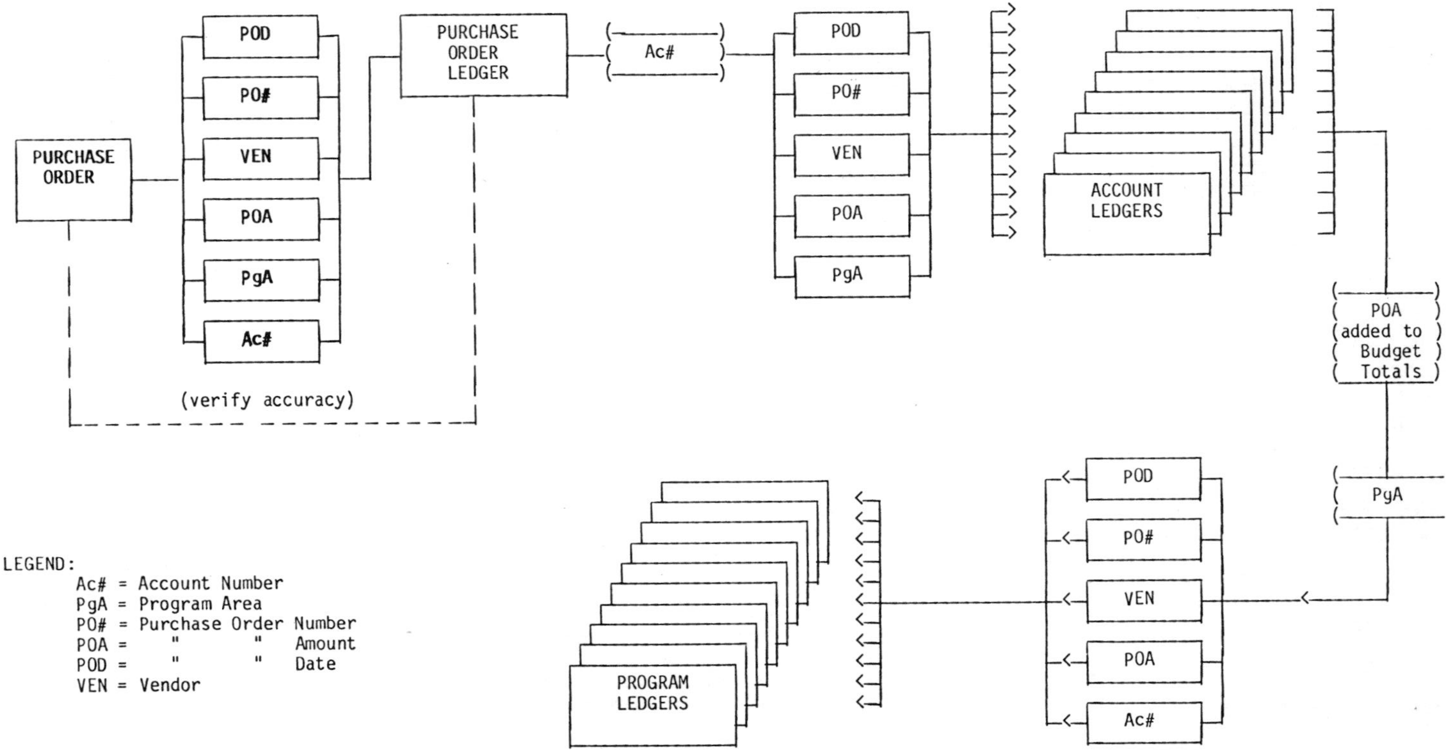

LEGEND:

Ac#	=	Account Number
PgA	=	Program Area
PO#	=	Purchase Order Number
POA	= " "	Amount
POD	= " "	Date
VEN	=	Vendor

PURCHASE ORDER

POD PO# VEN POA PgA Ac#

(verify accuracy)

PURCHASE ORDER LEDGER

Ac#

POD PO# VEN POA PgA

ACCOUNT LEDGERS

POA added to Budget Totals

PgA

POD PO# VEN POA Ac#

PROGRAM LEDGERS

123

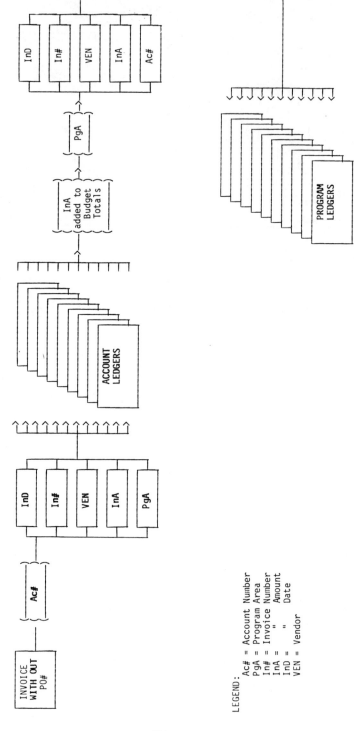

ENTERING AN INVOICE WITH *NO* MATCHING PURCHASE ORDER

LEGEND:
Ac# = Account Number
PgA = Program Area
In# = Invoice Number
InA = " Amount
InD = " Date
VEN = Vendor

124

MATCHING AN INVOICE WITH A PURCHASE ORDER

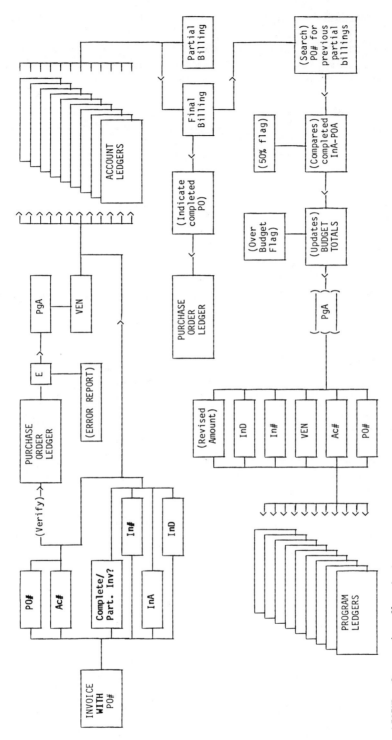

LEGEND: See previous flow charts.

Next the program must search the Account Ledgers for other Invoices filed against this PO. There may have been 4 or 5 other invoices that were partials. If so, those amounts must be added to the final invoice to arrive at a total actual figure.

This actual figure is now compared to the PO amount. If the invoice amount is greater than the PO amount, the *difference* must be added to the Budget Totals as an adjustment. If the invoice amount is less than the PO amount, the difference must be subtracted from the running total. It is helpful to incorporate flagging devices at this point. One will print out all the invoices that exceed the PO estimate by 50% or more. This report makes it easy to spot Vendors who underbid and overcharge, or your own tendency to underestimate actual costs.

The other flag is a comparison of the cumulative budget total with a fixed amount entered on each Account Ledger. If the running total exceeds the amount entered for the entire Account, the computer will call it to the operator's attention.

After all this sorting and comparing is completed, the information is shunted onto the Program Ledger. Here it is a much simpler process. The program "sorts" on the Program Area to get to the correct Program Ledger. Then the PO # is found and the actual invoice total (shown on the sheet as "Revised Amount") is substituted for the PO estimate. A simple program that totals the expenses in the Program Ledger by Account Number and also as a grand total is recommended. Again, look at the Program Ledger sheet in the manual section.

Once such a program is set up and running, the Promotion Director will be able to quickly and easily generate the following reports:

- Purchase Orders Issued
- Purchase Orders Outstanding
- Purchase Orders Completed
- The above three for any Account
  (i.e., TV Production, Radio, Radio Production, etc.)
- Vendors
- Vendors with Outstanding PO's
- Vendors whose invoices exceed estimates
- Total Media Expenditures
- Total Production Expenditures
- Total Media by Program Area
- Total Production by Program Area

The Promotion Director who likes lists can easily develop more. However, it is quite possible to get tons of meaningless information. There is plenty of that around already. What is needed is the correct information, when the Promotion Director needs it, to make intelligent decisions—or essential budget reports—in an increasingly difficult marketplace.

This budget information system helps achieve that goal.

CHAPTER 13

Motivational Techniques *

The most important goals of a Promotion Director involve motivating people. One major goal is motivating viewers or listeners to tune in to a specific station or program. Another very important goal is motivating advertisers to spend money with the station. And still another goal is to get the press to take notice—preferably favorable—of station programming.

To achieve these and most other goals, the Promotion Director must be able to write powerful or subtly persuasive motivating copy. And he must be able to construct visual and sound images which, together with copy, stimulate and move people to desired action.

In writing copy and combining it with visual or sound elements to make an advertisement, promo, or sales piece, the Promotion Director's most important tool is a thorough understanding of motivational techniques—the so-called "secret" ways to make people act.

Why are they called "secret?"

Very few viewers or listeners know why they *really* do or don't choose a particular station or program. That's because their decisions are based on unconscious, emotional motivations as well as conscious rational reasons. In many instances decisions are entirely motivated by the subconscious rather than the conscious mind.

People can't say why they prefer a radio or TV station or program any more than they can explain why, for example, they prefer Marlboro cigarettes. Marlboro smokers will say they like the taste. They simply aren't aware of the hidden motivations that influence them.

*This chapter is based on the writings and Seminar presentations of Jon Beacher, Senior Vice President of Reymer & Gersin Associates, a marketing research firm based in Southfield, Michigan.

They were captured by the psychological powers of the "macho" individualistic "Marlboro" cowboy. He's a hero figure among children who are in puberty—the ages when most people begin smoking. Eager to prove their freedom and sexuality, they associate with a masculine, sexy man who roams the fields, always alone. He appeals to teenagers eager to escape from the control of their parents' homes.

Just as hidden motivations influence decisions to buy most products, so they affect peoples' choices of broadcast stations, programs, personalities and formats. Before examining examples of effective and ineffective motivation in broadcasting, it is important to understand how motivation works.

THE MOTIVATION PROCESS

An advertisement or promo is a force which motivates people to move through a series of steps. The process begins when a viewer or listener recognizes he or she has a problem with the current program or station. The problem can be one the viewer/listener encounters without "assistance," or one the Promotion Director helps him find. (See Motivation Process chart.)

To solve the problem, the person uses a mixture of reason and emotion.

In the rational stage, the viewer/listener becomes aware of other stations, acquires information about each station's physical characteristics: how it looks or sounds, its personalities, format, programs, broadcast times, reception quality, and channel number or dial position.

In the concurrent emotional stage, the viewer/listener develops emotional feelings about the nature of the station or program and its characteristics. Which station or program will best fulfill his or her emotional needs? Which has an image most consistent with his or her own self-image? Which is perceived as helpful in solving a personal problem?

For radio stations, both rational and emotional decisions center on station format and personalities. For television stations, decisions are made more on a program-by-program basis. However, since local and network news programs lead viewers into the evening prime time viewing period, special emphasis is given to both personalities and the "look" of news programs.

Local stations often hire market research firms to study viewer needs and preferences, likes and dislikes. News Directors want to know which newscasters viewers can most easily identify, how they feel emotionally about each, and which ones viewers like or identify with. They want to know how viewers "feel" about the news set, the use of a "mini-cam," live remotes, news graphics, and every other element of the newscast.

Once the News Director knows answers to these questions, news programming and personalities can be adjusted to satisfy audience needs and preferences. And the Promotion Director can base advertising and promotion on those same needs.

Most network-affiliated local television stations use news programming as

MOTIVATION PROCESS CHART

PROBLEM STAGE—Viewer/Listener recognizes a problem with current station or program; looks for alternatives.

RATIONAL STAGE—Viewer/Listener becomes aware of other stations and programs; seeks information on physical characteristics of each.

EMOTIONAL STAGE—Viewer/Listener develops emotional feelings about the nature of other stations, programs; subconsciously seeks satisfaction, identification.

BEHAVIORAL STAGE—Viewer/Listener chooses "favorite" station or program, and watches or listens to it.

EVALUATION STAGE—Viewer/Listener determines whether or not there is a difference between what he/she is doing, and what he/she thinks should be done.

IF THE ANSWER IS "NO" . . .	HABIT CYCLE is formed
IF THE ANSWER IS "YES" . . .	PROBLEM CYCLE is formed

a key to their local identity; so motivational research and use of motivational techniques usually focus on news program elements and audiences.

In the behavioral stage, the viewer/listener chooses a particular program or station and watches or listens to it. The *reasons* behind the behavior, as noted above, are a mixture of reason and emotion. Even highly educated people who have trained themselves to use reason and logic in decision-making are subject to motivational techniques. A conscious decision by such a person to want to be thought of as a rational, intelligent person governed by reason is usually very much an emotional decision. It represents an effort to establish a self-image, and that conscious effort is rooted in some inner need.

After the behavioral stage comes the evaluation stage, in which the viewer/listener constantly compares his or her current activity to what he or she thinks should be done. A viewer watching a particular television program might be perfectly satisfied; or might feel uneasy for some reason. The program might be dull. Its stars or storyline might be displeasing for any of a variety of reasons. Or the conflict might be that the program does not offer enough justification for watching television at all, as opposed to reading, doing housework or chores, or engaging in other entertaining or intellectual activity.

A radio listener's taste in music might change; his or her need for news or talk show information might increase; or the lure of a contest prize might touch on a particular need.

If the viewer/listener is satisfied, if the answer to the question "Is there a difference between what I *am doing* and what I *should be doing?*" is "No," then the viewing or listening continues. A "habit cycle" is formed: "I never miss '60 Minutes!'" "I always watch 'Laverne and Shirley'." "Channel 4's News is my favorite!" "KXXX is the only good rock music station in town!" These are typical statements of people locked in a "habit cycle."

On the other hand, if the viewer/listener is *not* satisfied, if the answer to the question, "Is there a difference between what I *am doing* and what I *should be doing?*" is "Yes, there is!", then the person returns to the problem stage and begins to look for alternatives.

USING THE MOTIVATIONAL STAGE TO ATTRACT AUDIENCES

To succeed, ads or promos must *move* someone through all the stages. But often they fail to do this. They stop at the rational stage. They give the potential audience information about what the program is like, and tell when and where it can be seen or heard, but they fail to persuade. They do not move people to the next step, the *emotional stage,* by promising emotional benefits or evoking emotional images.

For example, consider the average TV promo used to promote a program such as the TV game show "Tic Tac Dough." Like most promos, it might typically show amusing scenes from old programs, followed by an announcer who says, "Join the fun with 'Tic Tac Dough,' tomorrow at 7 here on Channel 5."

The promo merely shows what the product looks like, and reminds viewers when and where to find it.

An ad agency certainly wouldn't use this technique to sell Crest Toothpaste. If it did, the commercial would merely show what a tube of Crest looks like, followed by an announcer saying "See what Crest looks like? Buy some tomorrow at your local store."

It is not enough to inform people about a product . . . *or programming!* They must be *persuaded* by being made to feel emotions. As with Crest and Marlboro, so it is true with radio and television stations and programs.

The people at Crest don't sell toothpaste by just showing the product. They show people using it and fulfilling an important need—taking good care of their children by preventing cavities. Other brands of toothpaste fulfill other needs. One brand whitens teeth. Another freshens breath. Whiter teeth and fresher breath might not be considered major needs—that is, not until the commercials and ads clearly drive home the point that a successful love life may depend upon these assets. And for many, a successful love life is a major need.

Now consider ways to encourage viewing of "Tic Tac Dough" using emotional appeals. If the principal competition is a situation comedy, the Promotion Director might advertise and promote "Tic Tac Dough" as being a more intelligent show to watch, playing on the viewer's guilt or need to feel educated. Rather than program clips, a promo might feature a viewer at home sharing some thoughts with fellow TV viewers:

> VIEWER: "Now when I watch TV at 7:30, I don't waste my time. I'm learning something. I watch 'Tic Tac Dough.' You see, it's the only show on at 7:30 that challenges my intelligence. It lets me play along. And it's amazing what you can learn by watching every night."
>
> ANNOUNCER TAG OVER PROGRAM CLIP:
> "If *you* think *real* fun is watching a show that's brain-tickling as well as rib-tickling, switch to 'Tic Tac Dough.' It's the smart show for people who think thinking can be fun! Weeknights at 7:30, here on 5."

This promo conveys information about the program by showing a brief sample of it and presenting viewer comments. But it goes a major step further. It conveys emotional appeals. Instead of putting all the attention on the program, it concentrates on a need the program can satisfy. It shows a viewer using the program to derive appealing benefits: knowledge *and* fun. An ad headline or slogan for the show might be: "Tickle your funnybone . . . *and* your brain!"

BENEFITS WHICH MOTIVATE AUDIENCES

What types of emotional benefits do people want in their lives? Psychologists studying peoples' behavior have identified various motivators. These are benefits, or things which people want to have or to achieve, and which they will act to acquire. Jon Beacher of the Southfield, Michigan-based motivational research firm, Reymer & Gersin, has compiled the following relatively short list of "things people, including you, I, *and* radio and television audiences, want from life." People want to be:

- Loved by others, and good at loving others.
- Popular and admired.
- Better than others, successful.
- Smarter, more intelligent.
- Comfortable and secure, both physically and mentally.
- Good looking, sexy.
- Older if we're young; younger if we're old.
- Amused ad not bored.
- Similar to the majority, but different enough to be considered an individual.
- Rich and thrifty.
- In tempo with the latest trends, or the first to do something.
- Creative, imaginative, innovative.

- Treated fairly and honestly.
- Lazy, whenever it can be justified.

Effective motivation promises one or more of these benefits because they help people solve problems in their lives by filling needs. All viewers or listeners use radio and television to help solve many of their problems. At any given time, each person chooses the station or program that solves a particular problem or fills a need best. (Of course, people's problems and needs differ, and change continually.)

The following, again from Jon Beacher at Reymer & Gersin, is a partial list of problems people can solve by listening to radio or watching television. The broadcast media can help people to:

- Relax, unwind, escape from problems and unpleasantness.
- Prevent loneliness by providing company.
- Ease boredom, give something to do to pass the time.
- Encourage social interaction, put people in touch with others, introduce them to others, see if others share their views, give them something to talk about.
- Avoid danger, protect, and reassure that nothing is going to hurt them.
- Do what is popular with friends or family, respond to peer group pressure.
- Feel warmth, love, companionship.
- Create a romantic mood.
- Fantasize, feel excitement, enjoy being frightened.
- Be cheerful, laugh, overcome depression.
- Gain social prestige, impress other people with what they know, do something fashionable or impress people with their choice of stations or programs.
- Be intellectually stimulated, learn, improve their understanding in order to benefit themselves and others.
- Feel creative, excell in life, feel like they are improving themselves.
- Understand how to live better, see how other people solve problems, know other people have similar problems.
- Wake them up, or put them to sleep.

Ads and promos will motivate people if they promise to solve their specific problems. The challenge for the Promotion Director is to match the characteristics and qualities of a particular program, station, or personality to one or more emotional appeals, and through doing so, to show how problems can be solved.

For example, one newscast in a particular market might have an important "product benefit:" it shows a lot more film than the other newscasts. How might this be promoted? One might create a promo that shows scene after scene of news film, quickly and excitingly edited to a lively music track. The only words in the promo come at the end, and state: "Channel 6 News has more film. A *lot* more film!"

This promo would be attention-getting. It would be fun to produce. It would convey information about the news programming and highlight the difference between this news and the competition. It might even win graphics awards for its design and execution. But it fails to promise a true viewer benefit. "More film" is not one of the benefits people want to get out of their lives. It is not on the above list of benefits. Nor is "lack of newsfilm" on the list of problems people want solved.

The same promotion spot—scene after scene of news film edited to a lively music track—would offer a benefit if the announcer's voice-over the visuals said, "Because Channel 6 News has more film, you'll see more. And that will make you smarter." Or, the announcer might say, "Because Channel 6 News has more news film, it really gives you something to talk about." Being smarter and having exciting things to talk about are things people want, and for which they often turn to broadcasting.

Here's another example—this time a television commercial actually used by a radio station. It conveys information, but provides no explicit benefit:

"The Newsman Who Works Hard" Promo

VIDEO: Scenes of WXXX Radio's newsman, John Smith, at work in the newsroom.

AUDIO: Announcer's voice over film:
"On WXXX Radio, you get John Smith, with the total news update. John's a no-nonsense newsman with sixteen years experience. He's been in the middle of things around New York, New Jersey and Connecticut. Political wrongs, national crises, local conflicts. He stays on top of the world, because he knows this world is changing. And that's why so many people are changing to John Smith, weekdays, on WXXX Radio."

This promo fails to promise any benefits. It spends all its time bragging about the newsman. But all the information given about him could promise social prestige by saying, "If you like being more up on the news than ordinary people, you'll like listening to newsman John Smith. He knows more, so you'll know more!"

News-related examples such as those above are of special significance to Promotion Directors because news is such an important part of programming. It provides a substantial amount of station income, and consumes an equally large share of the advertising and promotion budget. The industry trend for a number of years has been to actively seek news reporters and—more importantly—anchorpersons who have appealing personality characteristics and who perform well on-air together as a team.

A News Director who has found such personalities or assembled such a team will want to trumpet it loudly in print ads and with on-air promotion announcements and radio or TV spots. The Promotion Director's job is to fashion such advertising and promotion materials into campaigns that link the personalities, teams, and even the specialized, ultra-modern equipment they use to gather and broadcast the news, to benefits for the viewer or listener.

The personalities, the "happy" news team, the new "mini-cam," or the new helicopter will not attract audiences by themselves. It is the audience benefits of those attributes, characteristics, personalities and pieces of hardware supply that must be the focus of ad and promo copy that works.

Many local television stations rely heavily on feature film packages, and on daytime or prime-time talk shows. These programs, too, must promise benefits.

Just showing the guests on tomorrow afternoon's "John Davidson Show," or tomorrow night's "Merv Griffin Show," is not as effective as letting audiences know what a particular guest will have to say that has some meaning, interest or value to them.

"John's guests will include fashion designer Calvin Klein, and actor Robert Conrad," is informative. As promo copy it describes the program. But it lacks appeals to the program's largely female mid-afternoon audience. Better copy might be: "Fashion designer Calvin Klein gives you an advance peek at the jeans you'll be wearing next season; and actor Robert Conrad reveals what he looks for in a well-dressed woman." This copy appeals in several ways. It will attract people who are style-conscious, those who want to be the first to know about something new, and women who want to appear more attractive to men. All three appeals are important and strong motivators.

In promoting feature movies, first analyze the film. What are its appeals? Does it have a legendary star? Lavish sets and costumes? A story line that touches on basic human emotions? Memorable music? If so, relate one or more of these elements to the preceding lists of things people want from life and the ways television can help achieve them. Copy in an ad or promo which simply announces the star and title and bills the film as a movie "classic" will not motivate effectively *unless* the title strikes emotional chords ("Earthquake!"), the stars make the heart throb (Robert Redford), or the Program Director has put the film on for film buffs ("Casablanca").

THE BEHAVIORAL AND EVALUATION STAGES

In the diagram of the motivation process, it is shown that motivation requires both the presentation of information *and* the promise of benefit. Only if both steps occur will the ad or promotion succeed in causing viewers or listeners to enter the *behavioral stage.*

Now they sample the station or programming to see if the ad or promo was correct about the benefits promised. If they are satisfied they'll soon become regular listeners or viewers. As time passes, they'll no longer think about "why" they originally became a regular fan. Day in and day out they will, without consciously thinking about it, select the same station or program. A habit is formed. On the diagram of the motivational process, this is the *habit cycle* of the evaluation stage.

For instance, radio listeners may "choose" their station without any forethought: it automatically comes on each morning when the clock radio awakens them; or when they turn on the pre-tuned car radio. Their habits do nothing to encourage them to change stations.

TV viewers may arrive home from work at 6 o'clock and, without thinking, turn their sets on to the same channel's newscast day after day. Or they may lazily "choose" a program by watching a lead-in program (the one that was on just before it) and not bothering to change channels. They just "flow" into the show that follows.

These habits are fine—in fact, the ideal—for station WXXX. But what about the competition? How can the Promotion Director of station WYYY in the same town break their habits and capture them as viewers or listeners of WYYY?

MAKING THE AUDIENCE PERCEIVE A PROBLEM

To break audience habits, a Promotion Director must make the members of the audience perceive problems with their current behavior. Ads and promos can create dissonance—that is, a lack of consistency between what the person knows is the right thing to do, and what the person is currently doing. Once a person experiences this dissonance, he'll change his behavior so it is in harmony with his opinions, beliefs, and needs.

One key to success with this technique is to make a person think about his or her viewing/listening habit in a negative way. Another is to present a positive alternative to the current habit. Combining both is especially effective.

This need to make the person recognize a problem is very evident in most national television commercials. A typical spot begins with a woman discovering "ring around the collar" or "dandruff on your black dress." The same technique can be used in broadcast advertising and promotion spots. Here's an example from a promo used successfully by WXIA-TV (Channel 11) in Atlanta, Georgia. The station wanted to break habits of viewers watching a competing news program on Channel 5.

Promo Copy:

OLDER WOMAN: I don't choose my TV newscast. Mike Douglas does. You see, every day I watch the "Mike Douglas Show" on Channel 5. Then right after his show is done, I just leave it on the same channel for news. Not because I think their news is best—but because that's the channel I already have on. But you know, lately I've been thinking that's not the best way to choose a newscast. In fact, for all I know, maybe the news on Channel 11 is better. So now I'm going to see which one is best. After all, if I'm going to watch the news, I might as well make sure I'm watching the best.

This promo makes the viewer recognize a problem. It points out that this type of behavior—lazily flowing into a newscast—is inconsistent with the viewer's belief that she should watch the best newscast. This dissonance causes viewers to change their behavior and sample Channel 11's news.

Of course, the key to changing viewer or listener behavior is to know the nature of the behavior patterns that must be changed. Research of audience patterns can show where the problems lie.

For example, a Promotion Director may discover his radio station has a good share of the total audience listening at homes, but a poor share of the people listening in cars. Further research might reveal that they aren't listening simply because they haven't preset one of the car radio's push buttons to the station. If the station was on a pre-set button, they would listen regularly. Finally, research might disclose that the station seems to have its greatest appeal to male listeners who have a "classy" self-image of themselves, and would be motivated to listen to a "classy" station. Now the Promotion Director's job seems clear. Print, outdoor and broadcast ads and promos should depict a well-dressed, suave listener in a very classy car. An announcer's voice might say, "How can you tell if a man has 'class'? By looking at the first button on his car radio. If you touch the first button and it is WZZZ, you've got a man with a 'touch of class.' "

The campaign will be successful if the research was accurate, and if the ads and promos are placed where they can reach the right people. Outdoor ads to catch drivers, and TV commercials around News and sports programs would reach the right audience.

The Promotable Difference

There is one important way advertisers decide what it is about their product that should be emphasized in an ad or commercial—or for broadcasters, in a promo. They look for something that is unique or different about their product, program, or personalities. Something that sets it apart from the competition. That "something" should also satisfy a need or be a benefit of importance.

The main purpose of all toothpastes is to keep the mouth relatively clean and prevent cavities. The manufacturer who first added an ingredient that "freshens the breath" had something unique and promotable. After all, breath odor is a more immediate and noticeable problem than tooth decay, and a problem that is related to some very basic daily needs: getting along with others, impressing the opposite sex, not offending people.

But soon many toothpaste manufacturers had picked up on that theme. So when one added "teeth whitener," it acquired a new "promotable difference."

The same principle applies in broadcasting. First, the Promotion Director examines the programming to be advertised and compares it with what is on competing stations. What are the differences? Make a list. Then decide what kinds of people might be attracted to the things in the programming that set it apart from the competition. These people become the "target audience" for advertising and promotion. Finally, fashion ads and promos with appeals related to those differences and place them where the target audience might see them.

For instance, if station WXXX-TV's news program features the only female anchorperson in town, she might be considered a promotable difference. To whom might she appeal? Audience research might show that she has appeal to women who identify with her success and to men who find her attractive. But, research reveals, men don't watch her because they don't realize a woman can be as professional an anchorperson as a man. She can, however, still be featured in promos and ads. Several copy approaches might be used, depending on where ads and promos will be placed.

Copy which highlights her professional abilities will call attention to her in a way that reinforces what female viewers want to identify with—and still not alienate viewers who might be offended if her role was shown as offering a "woman's perspective." At the same time it would encourage viewing by males who want to watch her because she is attractive, but might feel that they should be watching a "more professional male" in the anchor role. A good slogan to satisfy both audiences might be, "With Shirley Jones, WXXX-TV has a professional edge!"

However, spots which show Shirley Jones as a mother and homemaker— spots designed to reinforce the identification many female viewers feel—might also reinforce mens' negative feelings. Such spots have value—when placed appropriately in the schedule, next to programs heavily viewed by women and not men; or when ads are run in sections of the newspaper which women read most: feature and food sections.

The Promotion Director in both cases is capitalizing on a promotable difference, using appeals, and carefully considering the audience. The promotable difference is carefully analyzed to discover what appeals it might hold for potential audiences—and what negative appeals might be generated. Advertising and promotion are shaped and placed accordingly.

POSITIONING

Many broadcast research specialists call the process of identifying and capitalizing upon the promotable difference "positioning."

"Positioning" means discovering what unique position a program or station format holds relative to the competition, and promoting it. It can also involve changing programming so that it has a unique position relative to the competition.

To illustrate from the example above, station WXXX-TV's news has the "female anchor position" relative to competing news programs, and a "news position" relative to competing non-news programs. A competing station airing an "I Love Lucy" re-run has the "situation comedy position." A competing news program with no female anchorperson but with a larger staff of reporters and more "live mini-cam" reports might be said to have the "Action News position."

Like promotable differences, however, positioning is of little consequence if the position selected does not relate to a viewer or listener need; if it does not have appeal to the viewer because it can help solve a problem; or if adequate research has not been undertaken to ensure that there is an audience need for the position, or difference.

These three ads appeared in Atlanta newspapers in succession. What was Channel 11's goal? How did the station Promotion Director appeal to newspaper readers to get them to try his station's news? What did he have to know about his audience in order to design ads like these and be sure they would be effective?

DEVELOPING AWARENESS OF MOTIVE APPEALS

A Promotion Director succeeds or fails largely because of success or failure in motivating potential audiences and advertisers. Continuing study of ads and commercial practices and results is a useful way to increase awareness of audience motivation.

Several techniques are effective in raising one's consciousness about the "secret" ways audiences are motivated.

First, pay close attention to all print and broadcast advertising, commercials and promotion announcements—both broadcast and for commercial products. With advertising, examine which appeals are being used (there are often more than one.) With ads that especially attract your attention, examine what in that ad appeals to you. Look for the "problems" advertisers inject to entice you to sample the product in your search for a solution. In broadcast promotion ads and promos, determine what elements of the program are being used to attract particular kinds of audiences. Recognize to whom messages are directed.

Second, talk to friends about commercials and promotion announcements as you watch them on television and listen to them on the radio. Discuss whether or not messages appeal to you and your friends in the same ways. The differences you find will help you isolate specific appeals upon which commercial and promotional messages are based. Question your friends in depth about the reasons they watch certain television programs and listen to certain radio stations. Learn what causes them to make their choices.

Finally, participate in classroom (or group) discussion about how the following television programs and radio station formats might be made to seem appealing to the audiences described:

1. A Monday–Friday 6 P.M. re-run of "I Love Lucy," opposite news programs on other major stations. You are looking for the largest possible general audience.
2. The first-run release of a 2-hour film about a black female stunt pilot who overcomes the injuries sustained in a plane crash to fly again, before she can happily marry the man she loves. Starring Diahann Carroll and Brock Peters. Shown in prime-time, 9–11 P.M. opposite Monday Night Football.
3. A three-hour morning radio program, on during "drive-time," featuring two personalities with a humorous, upbeat approach. The program concentrates on traffic information, notes about community activities, weather, bulletins, and news and sports. No guests, no listener phone calls, relatively little music. Research reveals that potential audiences are housewives and automobile commuters.
4. An all-news radio station, in a market where there is an all-talk radio station that is about 50% news. You decide what the audience is, and how to advertise and promote to that audience.
5. An all-talk radio station in a market that also has an all-news station. Again, you determine the audiences and approaches.
6. A 9–10 A.M. all-talk local television program with two local media personalities as hosts (one white male, one black female.) Every show has at least two guests, typically, someone plugging a book and a person with "how-to-do-it" information (cooking, household repairs, exercising, etc.). Research reveals an audience that is predominantly middle-income, female. The producer wants to add lower income viewers and adjusts some of the guests accordingly.

These are the kinds of problems Promotion Directors face on a continuing basis. Of course, you can open a guide to local TV or radio programming and structure countless more situations of your own for further discussion.

CHAPTER **14**

Advertising *

Earlier in this book advertising was defined as "time or space purchased or traded for by the station to put forth its message exactly as the Promotion Director intends it."

The principal advantages of advertising are:

• The Promotion Director has complete control of the words (copy) and overall design of the message.
• The Promotion Director determines exactly where the message will appear, and in what size or length it will be presented.
• It can reach relatively large numbers of people at a reasonable cost per person (usually measured as "cost per thousand" people.)

To capitalize on these advantages, the Promotion Director must know the characteristics of the various advertising media, how to write and design effective ads for each, how to place ads in each medium to achieve the strongest effect, and how to choose the right mix of advertising media to achieve the station's goals.

This section covers characteristics, style, creative concepts and placement considerations for print and outdoor advertising, and looks at the advertising agency as a potential resource.

PRINT ADVERTISING CHARACTERISTICS

Broadcast Promotion Directors usually place print advertising in newspapers, trade publications, local magazines, regional issues of national maga-

*Information on media characteristics and ad placement in this chapter was prepared with advice and consultation from Los Angeles-based media buyer Terri Brady.

zines, and *TV Guide Magazine* (primarily used by TV stations.) Following are characteristics of each.

Newspapers

Most cities and towns, or markets, are served by at least one newspaper. It may be published weekly, daily including Sunday, or daily excluding Sunday. Major markets may have two or three daily papers. Within each major market area there are usually smaller towns and communities served by local papers—often weeklies or bi-weeklies. The major metropolitan market paper serves the entire market, while the smaller papers emphasize news of the smaller local community in which it circulates. These smaller neighborhood papers often have more impact in select areas and should be a part of newspaper campaigns.

Newspapers are distributed via newsstands, home delivery and mail. Coverage and circulation information is usually reported in a circulation statement issued by the newspaper, and most large papers report this information to an auditing firm which in turn publishes it in a standardized form and certifies to its validity. Generally, newspaper circulation is reported by county, by retail trading area, and by "outside" market (areas beyond the major metropolitan market or core city and immediate suburbs.)

Although a newspaper may serve an entire market, its circulation does not necessarily include all of the market and its various homes and neighborhoods. Actual newspaper circulation varies greatly from market to market, depending on the strength and popularity of the individual paper, as well as the presence and effectiveness of other news media.

Newspaper readership is not measured on a regular, industry-wide basis. Major publishers may commission readership surveys to their particular specifications, but for the majority of newspapers there are no standardized surveys regularly reporting readership habits, patterns and demographics.

Readership studies and qualitative information (what kinds of people are actually reading the papers) are more readily available for major newspaper supplements such as Sunday magazine and television sections. Such sections usually appeal to more desirable kinds of audiences from an advertiser's point-of-view, and therefore produce audience characteristics that are more merchandisable than those of run-of-the-paper (ROP) readership.

Occasionally an advertiser or trade association will commission surveys of ad readership in newspapers. Sometimes such surveys are made available publicly and provide information about the newspaper's effectiveness in terms of size and position. The best known research organization in newspaper readership measurement is Starch INRA Hooper (Starch).

When buying newspaper space, the advertiser usually wants to relate a target audience to an editorial section of the paper having a connection with the product being advertised. Thus, similar advertisers are frequently clustered together (i.e., supermarket ads in the food section, ladies wear ads in the womens' section, automotive ads in the sports section, and, of course, television and radio station ads on the TV/radio pages).

Sometimes, however, the Promotion Director may want a particular ad to appear in a section of the paper likely to be read by a specific kind of newspaper reader, rather than in the TV/radio section. An ad for a sports special or a broadcast sports contest may be especially effective in the sports section. The assumption is that sports fans who watch TV will know of the program from promos or TV listings. Thus an ad in the sports section of the newspaper may attract sports fans who are not regular viewers or listeners.

Likewise, an ad for a documentary on local crime might have special impact in the local news section where crimes are regularly reported. Again, such an ad is more likely to reach non-viewer/listeners. Those who are regular viewers or listeners can be counted on to see or hear promotion spots or newspaper listings. At the least, they will browse through the listings page of the paper and will see an ad there. Non-regular audiences cannot be counted on to do so.

Ad size and dimensions are the Promotion Director's decision, although the newspaper may specify certain minimums. The choice of ad size generally relates to creative considerations and to the degree of prominence that is desired and/or affordable. However, numerous readership studies indicate that full-page ads attract only 10–15% more readers than half-page ads, yet cost considerably more. Further, a full-page newspaper ad—and in may cases, even a half-page ad—cannot appear on the same page as TV listings, so the effectiveness of having an ad immediately adjacent to the listings on the same page might be lost.

On the other hand, boldly designed full-page ads do signify a message of special importance to the newspaper browser.

When a request for precise position for an ad outside the radio/TV section is made, the newspaper may charge a premimum rate; or it may decline to accept such a request.

The space an ad occupies in a newspaper is called "display space." Display space is measured by the column inch, or by the agate line, and by column width. A 2-column, 4-inch ad is two columns wide and four inches deep. It occupies 8-column inches of newspaper space. The "agate line", or "line" as it is usually called, is 1/14th inch. Fourteen "lines" equal one inch. A 112-line ad, therefore, might be one column wide and eight inches deep; or it might be two columns wide and four inches deep. Or it might even be three columns wide and 2.7 inches deep. So ad space descriptions must always specify both depth in terms of lines or inches and width in terms of columns, while the total amount of space an ad occupies might be referred to simply in terms of column inches.

The correct ways of expressing ad size, using the example above, are: 56 x 2 (written), and "56 on 2" (spoken). This ad is 112 lines (eight inches) total, divided over two columns of newspaper space.

It should be remembered that the term "line" stands for "agate line" and has no relation to the number of actual printed lines which might appear in the newspaper.

Many newspapers restrict advertising to minimum depths, depending on the ad's width, but requirements vary from newspaper to newspaper and each must be checked to determine its policies.

Larger spaces in newspapers are measured as fractions of a page—quarter, half, three-quarters, and full pages, for example. Page size and number of columns vary by paper, but in most newspapers, columns are two inches wide.

Most newspapers have two rate structures. One is for national business usually placed by an advertising agency. The other is a local rate which is non-commissionable and available to non-national advertisers. Some newspapers have flat rates not subject to discounts. But many papers offer volume discounts with declining rates based on the amount of lineage run during a 12-month period. Most papers require contract commitments in advance to qualify the advertiser for annual discounts. Others will let the advertiser accumulate lineage over a year's time, and will charge at whatever discount rate is earned, or charge a penalty if a pre-set amount of lineage is not reached.

Certain sections or supplements published by the paper may have separate rate cards: Sunday supplements, TV magazines, and special entertainment or home-living magazines often fall into this category. The higher rates are charged because of better readership demographics.

Promotion Directors at television and radio stations most frequently advertise in TV/Radio sections, Sunday TV supplements, and on sports pages for sports programming. Other sections of the newspaper are only used when reaching a particular specialized audience is essential, or when it is necessary to reach community or business leaders or others who might be too busy to watch television or listen to radio and who might therefore miss an ad on the TV/Radio page.

A newspaper's circulation figures do not tell how many people read an advertisement. In fact, combined information from a number of sources indicates that between 25% and 50% of the number of people who receive a paper actually notice an ad, and only 10–20% actually read most of the ad. The variations are factors of the ad's size and design. More people notice and read larger ads than smaller ones.

AD READERSHIP ESTIMATES BY AD SIZE

	WOMEN		MEN	
SIZE OF AD	NOTED AD	READ MOST OF AD	NOTED AD	READ MOST OF AD
Spread (2 pages)	55%	25%	34%	11%
1 Page (2,400 lines)	50%	19%	31%	11%
3/4 Page (1,800 lines)	43%	13%	32%	9%
1/2 Page (1,200 lines)	33%	11%	27%	8%
1/4 Page (600 lines)	29%	10%	24%	8%
1/8 Page (300 lines)	25%	9%	16%	6%

(Estimates, as reported by the Radio Advertising Bureau, were averaged from 32 Starch INRA Hooper surveys taken between 1970 and 1976.)

The Newspaper Advertising Bureau points out that ad design factors can increase the percentage of ad readers significantly, as can the addition of one color, which increases readership by as much as 70%, while only increasing the cost of the ad by about 17%.

Magazines

Magazines fall into two categories: *consumer*, and *trade*.

Consumer magazines include those which are available to the general public through subscription and newsstand sales.

Most consumer magazines are classified by editorial content. Only a minority describe their contents as "general." Editorial specialization results in audience specialization. Although the editorial subject matter of some magazines is broader in appeal than others, certain characteristics of lifestyle, interest and socio-economic status are common to readers of each one.

Most magazines publish weekly or monthly. The major magazines are distributed for national circulation, but most national magazines have regional editions for local or regional advertising. This means that an advertiser in Washington, D.C., for instance, can place an ad in *Time Magazine*'s regional edition—which is distributed in the Washington-Baltimore area—and pay a much lower ad rate than an advertiser whose ad appears in all *Time* editions across the nation.

General national consumer magazines sometimes used by broadcast Promotion Directors include *Newsweek, Time, Sports Illustrated, Reader's Digest,* and *Life*.

In most larger cities, the "city magazine" might be an important part of the overall ad plan for a radio or television station. These magazines tend to reach active, involved members of the community, a higher socio-economic group that includes decision makers, advertising agency people, business and government leaders, and potential clients. *Los Angeles, Baltimore, San Francisco, Pittsburgh* and *New York* magazines and *The Washingtonian* are examples.

The other group, trade publications, are those which circulate to particular sectors of industry or specific professions on a paid or non-paid basis. Trade journals are used for the most part by advertisers in related industries and occupations. They are of interest to broadcasters in two ways.

First, they enable broadcasters to reach very specialized groups of people in specific professions about specific kinds of programming, or with messages tailored just for people in specific trades or occupations.

Second, and more importantly, the broadcasting and advertising trade press (publications such as *Broadcasting Magazine, Variety, Standard Rate and Data, Advertising Age, Back Stage, Radio & Records, Adweek, Television/Radio Age,* and *Madison Avenue*) enable radio and television stations to reach media buyers with ads designed to call attention to ratings and other station successes and help influence decisions to place advertising on the station.

As just one example, *Marketing & Media Decisions* magazine's current circulation of 32,000 includes approximately 11,000 copies to media-buying decisions-makers at companies advertising in more than one geographic market, and over 13,000 people at ad agencies serving these major spenders.

In the years ahead, station interest in trade publication advertising is expected to grow. Broadcasters are feeling an increasing need to identify their properties, their markets, their call-letters and their significant ratings success nationally with trade publication readers.

Here are several factors leading to this growing interest:

• National media dollars, spurred by an avalanche of new brands and rising media rates, offer an increasingly attractive incentive. It is common today for a television station in a medium-sized market to take in several million dollars in advertising placed by national media buyers at advertising agencies. A radio station can take in a million dollars or more. A recent estimate is that national media buyers spent more than 7 billion dollars with local radio and television stations in 1978.

• Stations are increasingly recognizing that the growing thousands of marketing directors and brand managers, in collaboration with their advertising agencies, who are involved in media-buying decision-making—including choice of markets—cannot be ignored. They work together, are exceptionally busy, and often can only be effectively reached via the advertising trade press.

• Station and group identification has been minimized in national selling for a number of years. Rating points and available time have been the strongest factors in the sale of advertising time. Now there is new competition, more need to explain station, group and network values than ever before. Since the decision to purchase advertising time on one of three stations in a given market might be very close, consistent trade advertising by one could help tip the balance.

Because of the importance of trade advertising, a list of key advertising and marketing publications featuring frequency of circulation, reader targets (the people for whom the publications are designed), and a brief description of the editorial content of each is included as an appendix.

There are a few consumer magazines which carry advertising that is such an integral part of the editorial content that they may be regarded as both consumer *and* trade publications. Some examples are *Architectural Digest, Modern Photography* and *TV Guide*.

It should be noted here that placing magazine ads usually requires a long lead time—much longer than newspaper. If you use magazines, plan way ahead.

TV Guide

TV Guide is the nation's largest circulation magazine. It reaches a sizeable percentage of TV homes in most major cities, and has a strong reputation for the accuracy of its listings and information. It is heavily relied upon by viewers seeking program information, so it is a very important advertising vehicle for TV station Promotion Directors.

TV Guide is very amenable to trade arrangements with TV stations, by which station ads in the magazine are compensated for by air time for commercials for *TV Guide*. This makes it a particularly important "buy" because it frees up station advertising money for use with other media (radio, newspapers and outdoor.)

Ad sizes most frequently used in *TV Guide* are full-page, half-page (vertical or horizontal), and quarter-page. One and two-thirds page ads are also common.

John W. Brown, Promotion Art Director of *TV Guide Magazine*, listed the following specifications for *TV Guide* ads at a recent industry seminar:

- The program section of the book is printed on 38-lb. ground wood stock.
- An 85-line screen is mandatory for all half-tone artwork. Because this paper is naturally absorbant, a 100-line screen chokes up, or becomes a blotted mess; and a 65-line screen falls apart, or does not present detail well.
- Reproducible (repro) copy should be a lined or screened unmounted velox.
- Ads must be submitted in a form that can be pasted directly on the layout pages as the magazine is being made.
- Don't let cutout lines show around peoples' heads, sections of copy, headlines, or other artwork.
- Do not use press type in making ads because it is affected by heat and humidity and peels or flecks in transit. This is especially true of white type on a black background.
- Copy subject to possible last-minute change should be separate and freestanding in the ad, not worked into other art. Also, reverse type should be avoided in such instances.
- Art in photographic film form, either positive or negative, is unacceptable. The magazine needs reflective art, black and white, on opaque paper.

OUTDOOR ADVERTISING CHARACTERISTICS

While most people think of outdoor advertising as "billboards"—a concept that reverts to bygone days when oversized handbills were tacked on any available boards, including the sides of barns, stores and houses—today "outdoor" generally refers to advertising messages on uniform structures owned by outdoor companies, situated on land or property leased by these companies.

Major outdoor companies today include: Foster & Kleiser, Gannett Outdoor, Independent Outdoor, Eller, TDI/Winston, Donnelly Advertising, and General Outdoor.

The definition above *excludes* signs on the premises of businesses identified by the signs. But it does include painted bulletins, posters of various sizes, transit ads, bus shelters and benches, subway ads and vehicle advertising.

Painted Bulletins

These are the largest and certainly one of the most dramatic forms of outdoor advertising. They are usually located in busy, high traffic locations in cities or along interstate highways and freeways.

Generally the size of a "paint" is 14' by 48'. Some companies now offer an even grander size—20' by 60'. A relatively small number of permanent boards are even larger.

The artwork is prepared by the advertiser—in this case the broadcast Promotion Director or the station's ad agency—and sent to the outdoor company where skilled artists transform the small piece of art into a huge mural. Detail is amazingly accurate, and the end result closely resembles the original artwork. The mural units are trucked to the display site and assembled on huge steel sections. The advertiser is usually permitted to change copy two or three times a year.

Painted bulletins are normally illuminated at night, and glittering examples of the latest state of the art in terms of design can always be seen in the largest sizes along Hollywood's famed Sunset Strip, where motion picture and record companies advertise their latest productions.

Painted bulletins have several advantages over smaller "posters".

• They can be read from great distances and so are favorites for freeway and highway locations where they can attract motorists' attention from far away.

• The art can be extremely intricate and displayed in a much larger-than-life way. Imagine a news anchorman's face 12-feet tall.

• Special extensions such as lighting effects, neon tubing, free-standing letters, stick-out sections, glitter, and day-glo colors can be added—at additional cost.

As advantageous as this type of advertising is, a station normally cannot afford more than a few in the advertising effort because of the considerably higher cost over other forms of outdoor advertising.

The normal display period for a painted bulletin is 60 days in one location. They are often sold as 4-month "rotates," the message being rotated from one location to another at the end of each 60-day display period. This precludes an advertiser from locking up single prime locations for indefinite or long periods of time, unless the location is a "permanent."

Posters

This is the most common form of outdoor advertising. Posters are found in cities and along highways in most parts of the nation. Numerous types of posters are available. The largest size is a 30-sheet "bleed" size displayed on a 12' by 25' panel. The smallest size to fit this panel is a 24-sheet poster (actually comprised of 10 sheets of poster paper fitted together, rather than the 24-sheets used years ago. By tradition, the size is still referred to as 24-sheet.) A display this size covers about 8'8" by 19'6" of available space on the billboard panel, leaving a white border around the message area.

Unlike painted bulletins which are hand-painted by outdoor advertising company artists, posters are furnished by the client. Production involves: flat-tone silk screening for small quantities; posterized silk screening for cost savings; flat-tone silk screening combined with half-tone photos; and any flat tone with four color photos. Besides silk-screening, other types of poster printing include lithography. Printing is done by a printing company and the client has the posters delivered to the outdoor display company. The amount of white border allowed is determined by the advertiser. Larger poster sizes using minimum borders, or none at all in the case of "bleeds," are more expensive to print. And, aesthetically, the white space may or may not be desirable, depending on the board's design.

Most 24- and 30-sheet poster boards are illuminated at night, giving nighttime effectiveness.

Smaller 8-sheet size posters are becoming increasingly popular in many parts of the United States. For example, in Los Angeles, several years ago there were none. By 1980 there were more than 7,000 8-sheet locations. Their chief advantage is that the small size permits the purchase of more units for the same amount of money, compared to the larger 24- and 30-sheet sizes. The major disadvantage is that most 8-sheet locations are not illuminated at night, so poster effectiveness is limited to daylight hours. Unlike the 30-sheet size panel which accommodates three basic poster sizes, the 8-sheet only accepts one poster size on its 5' by 11' panel.

A two-sheet poster is the typical size for horizontal displays used in subway advertising, though smaller one-sheet sizes are also available. Rail commuters in the Eastern United States are very familiar with these units, which can accommodate longer amounts of copy for readers who may have to wait for trains.

Posters are usually bought in groups, called "showings," by the month. A 100 gross rating point (GRP) showing package provides enough panels to deliver in one week a number of exposure opportunities equal to 100% of the market's population. For example, in a city or market area with a population of 100,000 people, a 100 GRP-package would indicate that the locations of the particular advertiser's panels should theoretically expose his message to 100,000 passersby, or vehicle drivers and occupants, in one day.

The authenticity of these impact figures in various markets around the nation is verified regularly by measurement of traffic past 100,000 billboards by the Traffic Audit Bureau (TAB). TAB publishes a semiannual *Buyers Guide to Outdoor Advertising* containing rates, allotments, special pricing and discount information for all outdoor advertising companies.

Transit Advertising—Buses

Advertising on buses includes signage on both the outside and inside of the bus.

The workhorse of the industry is the "King" panel, usually on the driver's side of the bus. It is the largest of any of the framed transit panels, measuring

These variations of bus posters and displays, courtesy of TDI, A Winston Network Company—one of the nation's largest outdoor advertising companies—shows some of the variety of bus signage available in different cities.

Interior bus cards are also available in a variety of sizes, and can include tear-off take-along sheets, as shown in this illustration, also provided by TDI.

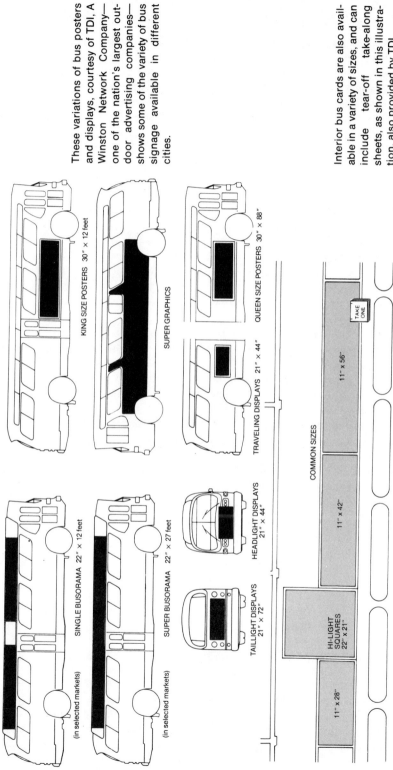

(in selected markets)

SINGLE BUSORAMA 22" × 12 feet

(in selected markets)

SUPER BUSORAMA 22" × 27 feet

KING SIZE POSTERS 30" × 12 feet

SUPER GRAPHICS

QUEEN SIZE POSTERS 30" × 88"

TRAVELING DISPLAYS 21" × 44"

TAILLIGHT DISPLAYS
21" × 72"

HEADLIGHT DISPLAYS
21" × 44"

COMMON SIZES

TAKE ONE

11" × 56"

11" × 42"

HI-LIGHT
SQUARES
22" × 21"

11" × 28"

2½′ by 12′. The next largest size, the "Queen", measures 21″ by 88″ and is located on the entrance side of the bus. "Taillights" are located on the rear of the bus and measure 21″ by 70″. Finally, some buses carry "headlights" on the front which measure 21″ by 44″. Some newer bus designs prevent use of some of these posters, so transit advertising in each individual market should be explored carefully before plans are made for a campaign using bus advertising.

The "King" posters are considered by the transit advertising industry to be the approximate equivalent of a 30-second on-air promotion announcement or commercial. The "Tails" are likened to a 60-second spot because drivers behind a bus have significantly longer exposure to the advertisers message. And the "Headlights" are considered the equal of a 10-second television commercial. While the "King" unit is the most expensive because a much larger area of the bus is being used, many advertisers prefer the "Tails" as the premium advertising unit.

Some buses carry large illuminated "Bus-O-Rama" signs across the top. Still another type of bus ad involves applying the design directly onto the side of the vehicle with a vinyl application, usually covering the entire bus side. Both kinds are considered effective, but are expensive and many clients use them sparingly.

Interior "car cards" inside buses and subway cars have been in use since before the turn of the century, when they took the form of handbills fastened to the interior walls and suspended from the ceilings by strings and hooks. By 1869, panels and frames were introduced. Along with painting on the sides or barns and buildings, car cards were the earliest forms of outdoor and transit advertising.

Some advertisers overlook car cards, or consider them an afterthought. But since the average bus ride today is 25 to 30 minutes, research has shown that these smaller 11″ by 20″ cards are, very effective, giving the rider something to read to pass the time. Up to 60 words of copy can be used on such posters, far more than can be put on exterior panels. This makes them more valuable for several specific kinds of messages. Personality endorsements, institutional messages, and group photographs are examples.

Other Vehicle and Outdoor Advertising

"Beetleboards". This is the name of an enterprising company formed in the 1970s on a national basis which made the Volkswagen "bug" an advertising medium. The company recruits VW owners and pays them to allow their cars to carry advertising messages, usually for at least a year. When the showing is completed the owner can opt for a new ad, or the company will repaint the car back to normal. "Beetleboards" are most common on college campuses. The artwork is frequently innovative and covers the entire vehicle.

Airport Advertising. Island displays, dioramas, illuminated showcases, and other forms are available to advertisers who want to reach a decidedly up-scale audience—the air traveller and his or her family and friends. Some broadcast stations use airport displays to call attention to their news programs for arriving out-of-towners.

Commuter Trains. Similar to bus advertising, commuter train advertising includes both interior posters of various sizes, and platform posters in stations. Platform-waiting time and train-riding time permit longer-than-usual messages by the advertiser.

Taxi Advertising. For center-city marketing, rooftop and rear postings on taxicabs are available in most major cities. Backlighted signs are not uncommon and extend the effectiveness into evening hours.

Bus Shelter and Bus Benches. This type of advertising has been common for many years, usually carrying ads for local restaurants, funeral parlors, hardware stores, and similar establishments. It has had limited effectiveness since

Chart # 1 **LEGIBILITY OF LETTERING**

This is a guide for outdoor advertising letter size and readability. It assumes that simple type styles and proper spacing and color contrast will be used. Guidelines courtesy of Foster & Kleiser, an outdoor advertising firm representing metropolitan markets throughout the United States.

HEIGHT OF LETTER	WILL READ AT....
2 feet	840 feet
1 foot	420 feet
6 inches	210 feet
3 inches	105 feet
1 inch	35 feet

Chart # 2 **OUTDOOR POSTER SIZES**

	24-SHEET	30-SHEET	BLEED
COPY AREA (length)	19'6"	21'7"	21'7"*
COPY AREA (height)	8'8"	9'7"	9'7"*
TOP & BOTTOM BLANKING	10½"	5" (double these figures for amount of blanking needed for both top & bottom.)	5"
END BLANKING	19"	6½" (double these figures for amount of blanking needed for both ends.)	6½"
FRAME WIDTH	11"	11"	11"

*The 'live area' is identical to the 30-sheet poster. The bleed is achieved by adding colored blanking paper to the basic 21'7" x 9'7" area. Blanking must be supplied by the station purchasing the outdoor space, to ensure proper color match. Courtesy of Foster & Kleiser.

Additional examples of exterior and interior transit advertising and posters at subway and train stations; and an example of transit bench advertising.

KNX's "Why" board is a "bleed." The "When" is a "King" bus poster.

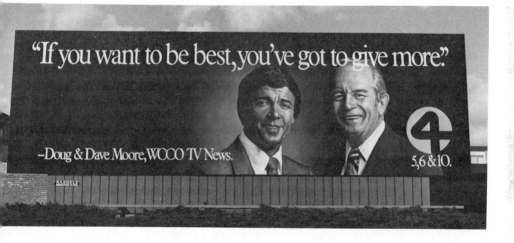

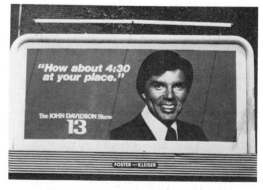

John Davidson is pictured on a standard 24-sheet poster display, while WCCO-TV shows off its anchormen on a large painted bulletin.

Strength, boldness and imagination characterize these outdoor ads by WSOC and WSOC-FM. The billboards showing the station's dial position on a car radio make it easier for listeners to remember where to find the station. The WSOC-FM board uses extensions to simulate a country fence, reinforcing the station's country-music format.

people are often standing in front of the shelters or sitting on the advertising message, obscuring the view of passing pedestrians and motorists. However, sleek new bus shelters with illuminated panels in some markets are changing bus stop advertising to more of a priority in promotional campaigns.

Outdoor Advertising Demographics and Effectiveness.

In general, outdoor advertising delivers preferred demographics for many broadcast advertisers: young out-of-doors, mobile, up-scale people. Billboards are particularly effective for radio stations trying to reach people with radios in their cars. Main commuter arteries make ideal locations.

According to the Institute of Outdoor Advertising, a showing equal to 50 gross rating points (GRPs) reaches 50% of a market's population within one week. Within two weeks, however, the reach is 92%. Within three weeks it is 97%, and at the end of four weeks nearly 100% of a market's population will theoretically have been exposed to at least one billboard. In fact, each person will have seen the posting approximately 14.7 times.

The Institute of Outdoor Advertising stresses these advantages:

- Outdoor advertising delivers the lowest cost per thousand in audience reach of any national advertising medium.
- It has high selectivity, allowing locations near supermarkets, shopping centers, car dealers, fairgrounds, on highways, etc. Messages can be delivered near the "point-of-purchase." In the case of radio stations, this means drivers with car radios; in the case of television, locations on commuter routes can be reminders of news and other programming for drivers on their way home.
- Outdoor reaches people on the go, in their cars listening to the radio, travelling, shopping, looking for things to do.
- Standardized outdoor advertising—the only kind offered by most major outdoor firms—is neat, attractive, and governed by industry codes and local laws and ordinances.

· Using few words, it has high visual impact and can effectively deliver a strong single theme, title, logo or slogan.

Impact research by the Outdoor Institute indicates that outdoor advertising generates strong recall (24% of people questioned recall the message). This compares with 10% recall for a radio commercial, 11% for television, and 12% for magazines. Boldness and brevity have strong impact.

Eye-movement measurements during simulated driving recall experiments show that 66% of people driving by billboards actually notice them; 58% can later recognize the boards, and 39% can recall their messages. 38% glance at boards twice in passing. And the average person looks at a billboard for 1.1 seconds while driving by. This last measurement has implications for outdoor advertising design which will be covered in the next section.

Outdoor Advertising Design

There are four basic rules to keep in mind when planning the design of outdoor ads—especially painted boards, posters, and exterior transit ads which people don't have much time to read:

· Limit boards to one idea only.
· Use large, bold, simple graphics.
· Use legible, readable typefaces. Avoid frills and serifs.
· Have good color contrast.

Artwork and copy must work together to support the single idea presented. The following guidelines help improve a board's effectiveness and impact:

· Use strong colors. Even a small amount, such as a touch of bright red or orange can be very effective in drawing attention.
· Black and white boards can work well if the creative idea is good. A touch of a single bright color added to a black and white board can have astonishing impact unequalled by many full-color boards.
· Keep the number of words to an absolute minimum, and test boards by seeing how many words you can read at different speeds and distances. A general rule-of-thumb is 4–8 words per board for large billboards.
· Keep sentences extremely short and simple. They should be uncomplicated, easily readable. Some examples from broadcast billboards around the nation: "We're All Soul." "You Gotta Hear It." "Dial a Smile." "Gives Good Music."
· Closeups of faces get attention effectively. Avoid letting them get lost in, or be overpowered by, the background.
· Avoid lapping words over graphics. If they don't stand alone they can easily get lost.
· In showing off personalities, be sure they look attractive. Use color behind a head, especially if the head is in black and white. Otherwise the anchorperson might look like a convict in a wanted poster.
· Outline or shadow words to help them stand out, and to add dimension and perspective.

- Extensions from the top or sides of the board can help call attention to faces, words, special features.
- Embellishments help draw interest. Reflectors that glitter, inflatable additions, and more are available.
- Metallics and day-glo paint can be used for special emphasis on call letters, channel numbers, logos, dial positions, program titles, and other important elements.
- Powerful adjectives make short sentences or phrases strong, attention-getting and effective, as in: "Incredible Music, Incredible Information." Or, "Makes Marvelous Music."

Outdoor advertising has come a long way since the original "bill" postings on fences, painted ads on the sides of barns, and leaflets hanging in streetcars. Sophisticated research coupled with a vast improvement in utilizing this larger-than-life medium makes outdoor, in all its forms, something for a Promotion Director to consider in a media plan. The type of outdoor used depends on budget, the availability of trade arrangements, the peculiarities of a given market, the demographic target of a campaign, the overall concept and objective of the campaign, and the personal tastes of the station's ad agency, the Promotion Director, and the General Manager.

BROADCAST ADVERTISING CHARACTERISTICS

The characteristics of television and radio as advertising mediums are important to the Promotion Director for two reasons. First, as part of a campaign, the Promotion Director might want to use other radio or television stations to reach the public. And secondly, the Promotion Director uses the station's own air as a major part of any campaign. While the traditional term for using a station's own air is "on-air promotion," many stations are beginning to call it "broadcast advertising," reflecting the importance they place on it.

In the first instance, a radio station is most likely to advertise on television stations; and television stations are most likely to advertise on radio stations. In some cases, public television and radio stations purchase time or acquire public service time on their commercial counterparts.

In the instance of on-air promotion, station Promotion Directors need to be experts in examining their own schedules and placing well designed promotion announcements with the same precision they would use in making buys on other stations; or that advertising agencys use in placing commercials.

This section of the text will focus on the characteristics of other radio and TV stations as advertising media. On-air promotion is the subject of a separate section. However, these same characteristics apply to a station's use of its own air time to promote its own programs.

Radio

The average market receives many radio signals. These may be stations licensed to the home market, and they may include stations located in adjacent markets or metropolitan centers. In any case, the radio audience is fragmented. However, few radio stations try to program for the total potential audience. Stations in small markets that receive limited radio service may program for a wider variety of tastes, but the typical station format is specialized; programming is consistent and tends to draw a particular segment of the market. As a consequence, the radio advertiser may zero in on a particular target group. This is one of the medium's greatest advantages.

Commercial time is sold primarily in units of :60-seconds and :30-seconds. Announcements of :10, :15 and :20-seconds may also be available, but are not used extensively.

As opposed to print ads which are thought of as single, one-time insertions, radio time purchases are usually made in multiple spots. The radio audience tunes in and out. All listeners do not listen at once. Multiple spot purchases are necessary, therefore, to accumulate audience. Schedules are structured generally by the week, with discounts and package plans usually relating to weekly use.

The determination of how many spots should be purchased is based on penetration goals (how many listeners are to be reached), how quickly they are to be achieved, and on the repetition or frequency requirements of the promotion.

Major radio markets are measured at least four times a year by Arbitron, the major radio ratings research organization. There are other survey organizations operating in local markets with varying regularity which will perform special audience measurements as ordered by local stations and station ownership groups. Arbitron, too, has a wide variety of special research services for individual stations.

Arbitron reports audiences by daypart, week, sex, age groups, length of listening, in-or-out of home, etc. More in-depth audience breakouts are availble through AID, an Arbitron service. Broadcasters can order periodic qualitative studies of local radio audiences, for example, which report specific consumer habits or assorted individual family characteristics.

Advertising rates on radio stations may be steady, fixed rates; or they may be discounted at declining levels of weekly, monthly or annual frequency. This means that as the number of spots placed on a station increases during the discount period, the lower the cost of each spot becomes. Rates usually vary by daypart. Higher rates are assigned to portions of the day (dayparts) drawing larger listening audiences. For example, stations which attract commuters in vehicles may have audience peaks during morning and afternoon rush-hour traffic periods and may charge their highest rates for advertisers between 6:00-10:00 A.M. and 4–7:00 P.M.

Some stations have separate rate cards for national and local advertisers. Other stations use only a single rate card for both. In recent years, many stations have adopted the "grid system," with variable rates for the same time periods. This system permits a station to quote from whichever grid it choses in order to adjust to current market demands and conserve inventory.

Most radio stations offer package plans with cost advantages to encourage the use of all dayparts. These plans are intended to stimulate sales. They also serve to equalize availability, controlling domination of prime time by advertisers who will pay premium rates. Many stations have separate rates for pre-emptible or run-of-schedule buys. The pre-emptible schedule carries no guarantee of delivery, so the buyer of pre-emptible time must be prepared for the possible effect when purchased radio advertising does not run.

In addition to the advantage of being a targetable medium (the advertiser can easily select stations that reach the specific audiences desired), radio intrudes on the listener. It reaches people wherever they are and whatever else they might be doing at the time—driving, at the beach or involved in sports or recreational activities, while shopping, even while drifting off to sleep. Newspapers and magazines, on the other hand, require the physical efforts of reading and concentrated attention.

Continuing the comparison with print advertising, however, the radio message is a fleeting one, while the print ad can be kept, studied, re-read, or referred to for specific information. In fact, it is possible to design "clip-out" ads, encouraging the reader to keep an ad for future reference.

Television

There are approximately 780 commercial television stations in the United States.* Most major cities have stations affiliated with each of the three commercial television networks (ABC, CBS and NBC). Many cities also have independent stations not affiliated with the major networks.

Spot announcements on commercial television stations are bought as adjacencies to specific programs, or as spots within programs. Commercial units are primarily :10, :20, :30 and :60 seconds. The :30-second spot is the most common.

The building of a schedule of television spots is based on the advertiser's predetermined coverage goal of a target audience and the desired frequency for reaching that audience. TV schedules are usually structured on a weekly basis. A schedule of spots purchased on a station is called a "flight." "Flight" length, or number of weeks, is determined by the advertiser's overall campaign objectives. Retail advertisers may plan schedules in terms of days rather than weeks. Such advertisers with short-run flights tend to use vertical scheduling—that is, may place commercials as often in the schedule as possible through the course of the day—to achieve projected viewership goals. Horizontal scheduling of spots refers to placement of commercial material at specific times in the schedule day after day to reach specific pre-determined audiences with frequency.

The selection of TV time is also often subject to judgmental factors. The nature or appeal of an adjacent program is of prime concern. Much is known about program audiences. The advertiser who can match the characteristics of the people he is trying to reach to the characteristics of television viewers of specific programs or times of the day will make an especially significant impact.

*Television Digest's 1980 "Television Factbook."

Audiences are reported in terms of *households* and *viewers,* and in percentages or points (ratings), by sex and age group, as detailed earlier in the section on ratings. Reach and frequency levels for specific ad schedules are measurable through Nielsen and Arbitron.

TV rates are seldom routine quotations from a rate card. Changing inventories relating to supply and demand, plus competitive factors, cause the station and the advertiser to negotiate rates on each ad-buying occasion. High-volume buyers, usually representing multiple advertisers, negotiate rates annually in anticipation of a large annual investment. The advertiser who does not have precise requirements for the scheduling of spots may buy at pre-emptible rates (run-of-station, or ROS) with a substantial savings over the cost for guaranteed time. These, too, are negotiated on each buying occasion. Since such buys are, in effect, "potluck," it is difficult to judge their value in advance.

ADVERTISING DESIGN

Designing effective advertising, whether print, outdoor or broadcast, is not a random exercise in coupling words and visual images. There are specific goals to be accomplished, approaches to use, and generally accepted styles to follow Many examples of broadcast station ads in various media are included in this section to illustrate principles discussed in the text.

Ad Goals

These "goals" are things a Promotion Director must be sure each ad accomplishes.

Capture Attention. An advertisement or commercial is of little value and serves little purpose if it does not first capture the attention of its audience, or reader. Here are some attention-getting principles:

- Separate advertising message from surrounding material.
- A print ad smaller than full-page is competing with other advertising and/or editorial material on the same page for reader attention.
- A strong border, or effective use of white or black space surrounding the copy and artwork helps isolate the ad from other material on the page and focuses attention on it.
- Similarly, a radio or TV commercial is frequently clustered with other commercials, public service and promotional materials in a station break or within programming. With radio material, a characteristic sound effect, or theme music, can help the listener separate your material from that which preceded and that which follows it. On television, couple the sound with a recognizable video image—something that is familiar, such as themed animation or a logo; or something that is unusual, such as an extreme close-up. Don't start copy in the first second of the spot, where it might get clipped off as the spot is put on the air; but don't delay it longer than two or three seconds, or the viewer at home might lose interest.

NewsCenter4

Tonight we'll show you who really controls state government.

Is it our elected officials, or the highly paid lobbyists and special-interest groups the politicians depend on for their survival?

Find out all this week at 6 PM on Channel 4 as Doug Kriegel investigates "The Lobbyists."

You'll see if $15 million of your tax dollars is really being spent in your best interests.

"The Lobbyists"
with Doug Kriegel

4 N KNBC
All this week at 6PM

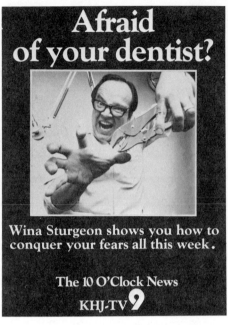

Afraid of your dentist?

Wina Sturgeon shows you how to conquer your fears all this week.

The 10 O'Clock News
KHJ-TV 9

"ONCE YOU'RE IN HERE, YOU STOP BEING A WOMAN"

Life in a women's prison is a world without men. And some of the women inmates don't miss them at all. Join reporter Jackie Nedell as she investigates homosexu- ality in prison in Part Three of her Special Series, *DROWNING IN MY TEARS*, tonight at 5:30 and 12:30 on ACTION NEWS.

36 ◢ WPCO-TV

Each of these three ads demonstrates principles of how to capture attention. Separation: the "Newscenter 4" ad uses white space. The "dentist" ad uses black space, and the "Once you're in here" ad uses a rule.

Boldness: "Newscenter 4" uses an intriguing, strong, single illustration. "Dentist" uses large, simple headline type, and a simple but compelling illustration.

Organization: All three ads keep headlines, body copy, illustrations and logos separate, easily distinguishable, quick and easy to find. "Dentist" uses the head to lead to the illustration. "Newscenter 4," however, relies on the illustration to bring the reader to the ad.

Simplicity: all three ads are simple in structure. In each the headline and illustration support each other. Each is trying to get just one idea across.

Present Material Boldly. Strong, simple, large lettering in a headline, or a large, strong, forceful illustration will draw the reader's eye to the print or outdoor ad. These same qualities should apply to visual material used in TV spots and sound effects or music at the start of radio commercials.

Organize Material. In an effective print ad, headline, artwork and body copy must be arranged so that one leads the eye to the next, and so that each further reveals the ad's message to the reader. One of these elements should be allowed to totally dominate the ad. White space can be used to lead the eye from one element to the next. In television spots, show what you are talking about. Audio should always support or explain video, or further its meaning.

Keep It Simple. Overcrowding print and outdoor ads with art and copy should be avoided. Each ad should be based on one major idea. Keep headlines short, and body copy brief and to the point. Illustrations should be simple: don't show three or four people when one will do. Picture only one object that makes the point you want made. Simplicity gets attention by enabling quick comprehension. The ad telegraphs to the reader that information will be easy and quick to encompass and comprehend.

Much the Same Is True for Radio and Television Spots. But because the viewer/listener, unlike the print ad reader, can't go back and "re-read" the advertising material, the dictum of sticking to one major idea is even more important. Encapsulate the idea in the opening words of copy; explain it in the words that follow, and with sound or visual images.

Arouse Interest. Once an ad has attracted the reader, listener, or viewer's notice, it must arouse interest. The most effective way is to refer to problems the audience needs to have solved, or benefits to be gained (see ealier section on motivational processes.) Headline, opening words in a broadcast ad, body copy, and illustration or visual or sound material should all relate to reader needs, problems, or concerns. In addition, there are several techniques which can help involve the target audience in the material in a print or broadcast ad:

  • *Ask a question.* A simple, brief question in a headline or as opening copy in a broadcast ad involves the subject by soliciting a response. The subject's mind becomes actively engaged with the ad message. When an ad asks questions, however, it should either answer them or provide a source where the answer can be found (the program or station being advertised) to prevent frustration with the ad.

  • *Use the well-liked.* A popular personality, a warm remembrance (mom, apple pie, grandma, etc.) a happy moment (wedding ring or scene, graduation, new baby, etc.) all help maintain interest. Testimonial ads by TV or movie stars are classic examples. So are the scenes of touching moments at home with the children or loving looks between people in love, because the audience or reader wants to be a part of such scenes and vicariously enjoy them.

  • *Appeal to the senses.* Strong, pleasant appeals to the senses of sight, smell, touch, hearing or taste through strong wording, or impressive visuals also help hold interest. Words can describe sensual experiences with precision and evoke sensual images at the same time: "velvet" and "sandpaper" describe textures. "Marshmallow", "oily" and "granite" describe consistencies. Colors and shapes have visual impressions which can be evoked with precise words: "violet," "crimson," "triangular," "round" and "pointed." For strong visual images which appeal to the senses, think of a close-up of a steaming apple pie (smell and taste); a man with a jackhammer (hearing); a fingernail on a blackboard (irritating sound); a beautiful rose (sight and smell); or a pile of goose-feathers (touch).

• *Appeal to the emotions.* Picture or describe a person, object or occurrence which calls to mind particular experiences with which the audience can identify. Such images clearly form a mental picture of a larger experience by association and are powerful attention getters as well as interest holders. Photographs or artwork of prison bars or a rat in a corner of a prison cell; a close-up of two men holding hands; a lonely grandmother in a rocking chair on a front porch, doing nothing; or a hungry child's pleading, upturned face are all examples. So are the wedding kiss; an athlete at the moment of victory; a happy child at play; or an attractive couple on the beach.

Present Information Clearly. Every ad presents some kinds of information. Broadcast ads need to identify program or station format, where programming can be found (channel number or dial position), and at what time. They must also contain persuasive or motivating information relating programs to audience interests, needs or problems. The presentation of such information must be as effective as possible. The following important principles help. Copywriters, designers and promotion producers should keep them in mind.

• *Establish a campaign identity.* Seasonal or program-group themes are used by most stations. So is a design format for station or program ads. Some theme examples: "Lookin' Good Together" (CBS-TV Network, Fall Season campaign, 1980); "More to News on Action News," (a news ad theme used in 1978 by WOWT-TV, Omaha, Nebraska); "Good Television, Good Business," (a sales promotion or development theme used by the PBS Network and many public TV stations for several years in the late 70s and early 80s); and "You've Got It All, on WMAL" (an on-air theme carried into print and TV advertising by AM radio Station WMAL in Washington, D.C.).

Establishment of a campaign theme helps the ad reader or broadcast ad audience to recognize that promotional or station advertising material is involved; and may instantly identify what station the program is on. Through repetition in print and on-air, it becomes memorable and helps establish an image of the station as a resource for a particular kind of programming (news, contry music, general entertainment, etc.)

• *Stick to a single idea.* Complex ads which try to convey several different, unrelated ideas are more difficult for the reader to struggle through, harder to remember, and may be confusing. If a number of facts are to be presented, find one single thought that embraces them all. Stress that overall idea and use facts to support it. Eliminate any which don't fit.

BUYING A NEW CAR?

Congratulations. But you've got a lot to think about. Things like handling, performance, safety, reliability, and even the quality of the paint job. But how do you decide?

Channel 4's Bob Mayer has all the important facts and figures. Don't miss his *Behind the Wheel* report tonight and every Friday night at 6 and 11.

4 WTVJ
SOUTH FLORIDA

Each of these ads displays principles of arousing interest. One uses the headline to ask a question designed to arouse interest of many car-buying viewers (all buy cars sooner or later). "An Ounce of Prevention" clearly appeals to the emotions, as well as the "well-liked"—a young child. "The Muppet Show" ad prominently displays two very popular television "stars."

LESLIE CRANE has a 24-hour-a-day job. As a busy, young homemaker, she considers the health and well-being of her family an important responsibility. KATU can't solve all of the Crane's health problems, but through regular medical features and special reports, CHANNEL TWO NEWS can provide Leslie's family with tips on good health care and when to see the family doctor.

There's more to news than headlines.

We Work for You.
CHANNEL TWO NEWS KATU abc 2

AN OUNCE OF PREVENTION.

THE MUPPET SHOW

THURSDAYS 7:30 PM

4 KOMO TV

• *Let one element dominate.* In print ads, of space or weight given to the headline, illustration, and block of body copy, let one of these three clearly dominate. In TV news and program ads, the illustration usually dominates. Body copy is almost always subservient to the other two elements. Don't let it have the same amount of space, or weight, as the other two. Giving equal weight to all three, or two of three, can cause the reader to be confused about how to approach the ad. The eye doesn't know where to go first, and so may go to some other ad on the page—one which is easier to grasp quickly. The generally accepted approach is to use the illustration to bring the eye to the ad and direct it to the secondary element, the headline. The headline then directs attention to the relatively small block of body copy by arousing interest or curiosity.

• *Use an organized approach.* Present information in a way that builds idea upon idea. Answer questions immediately after they have been asked. If news in announced, immediately give the story behind it. If a command is given, tell why it should be obeyed. Start with a basic idea and expand upon it with a brief explanation or illustration. Use lists of benefits, each set off with a hyphen, asterisk or sound/visual effect. Make it easy to follow orderly, logical thought progression.

• *Be direct.* The ad should immediately convey to the audience what is being advertised, and what benefits are involved, needs addressed, or problems solved. A straightforward approach is generally more effective than an approach which obscures the ad's message or intent. Use direct address forms, with or without the word "you." Be specific and concrete by giving examples, statistics, reasons, illustrations. In on-air material show—or let listeners hear—actual program material, or benefits related to watching or listening.

• *Be brief.* Use as few words as possible. The smaller space a print ad occupies, or the shorter an on-air message, the more concise the copy must be. In print, 10–12 words might be acceptable for a headline in a full-page newspaper ad, but 3–5 words should be considered maximum in a half-page or quarter-page *TV Guide* ad. Body copy in the larger ad might run several paragraphs—perhaps 200 words in 3–5 brief paragraphs at the most. But in the smaller ad, copy should be limited to 15–25 words, if it is necessary at all. Short, powerful words are useful in conveying ideas quickly and involving audience emotions. Some examples of frequently used words:

Free	You	Here	Save
New	Your	Try	First
Easy	Learn	Now	Hot
Fast	Earn	Check	Hoax
Offer	Facts	Gain	Deadly
Cut	End	Profit	Keep
Compare	Put	Live	Laugh
Quick	Improve(d)	Go	
Stop	Get	Come	

Notice how many of these words are related to possible audience benefits: Free, Easy, Earn, Gain, Save, and Deadly are just a few.

Certain standard words or phrases can be useful shorthand for broadcast advertising audiences:

"Premiere" means the program (usually a film) is not new, but that it has never been seen on TV before."

"All-New" means "not re-runs."

"Marathon" implies continuous programming of a similar type, i.e., several series episodes aired back-to-back; or several feature films with the same star or director.

"Special" means that a program is not part of a series.

In print advertising, brevity also means short paragraphs. Never include more than one simple, brief thought in each paragraph. Keep the number of words to a minimum and the length of sentences short. Complex sentences are to be avoided whenever possible. Two or three short sentences are easier to read and understand quickly than one long one.

In on-air advertising and promotion, the same rules apply. Short sentences are even more important, because the viewer or listener cannot "re-read" a sentence to figure out what was said. The meaning must be accurately conveyed with the first hearing.

• *Use appropriate language.* Avoid scientific jargon, business-related terms, or pedantic, polysyllabic words. Remember that for most television programming, the range of level of education of the potential viewer is great—from grade-school dropouts through advanced college degree holders. Yet an attempt must be made to speak to them all. If a specific ad is directed at a narrow audience, as in a trade magazine ad or a broadcast ad or promo designed for reaching a particular audience (i.e., after *Wall $treet Week* on public television, or a radio program aimed at a specific minority group), some jargon may be appropriate. The word "cume" may mean little to the average reader. But in a trade ad for a station in *Broadcasting Magazine,* it has the very specific meaning of "cumulative audience" rating figures.

Ad language should be friendly, rather than stilted or formal. Direct address ("You," "Your,") or implied direct address usually associated with commands (You "Watch this special, tonight at 8.") are frequent. They involve the audience in the communication. Short sentences, a positive tone (emphasizing what *should be done* rather than what should not be done), and emphasis on audience needs all help make ad language friendly.

Induce a Response. In the presentation of information in a broadcast ad, the advertiser's intentions are usually to get the audience to sample the programming, or, if a trade ad, to get the potential client or agency to buy time on the station. These are the most common responses broadcast ads seek to induce.

Audience building and sales promotion (trade) ads both rely heavily on motivational processes outlined earlier. In addition, however, both must tell readers exactly how to respond.

In an audience-building ad, that means clear and precise tune-in information. For television programs, the day, time and channel number are critical and should always be in larger type than body copy, bold enough to be seen instantly, and separated from the body copy for extra emphasis. Sometimes the words "Tonight" or "Today" are in a type size almost as large—or larger—than the headline. One of these words might even *be* the headline, if immediacy is of crucial significance—often the case with news and documentary programs. In areas where broadcast stations are heavily carried on cable television systems, station call letters may also be important if cable systems carry the station on a channel number different from the broadcast channel.

Radio station ads must prominently display the call letters and dial position where programming can be found. If particular programs are being advertised rather than station format, program times must also be boldly displayed.

Trade press advertising designed to increase sales must clearly indicate where the advertising agency or potential client should go to buy time on the station. This usually involves plainly listing the station's national sales representative, its address, phone number, and in some cases, a contact's name. For material designed for local distribution, the local sales staff's phone number and address are a must.

Be Truthful and Ethical

The Advertising Federation of America, the Advertising Association of the West, and the Association of Better Business Bureaus have devised an Advertising Code of American Business. It includes the following principles. They are important to a Promotion Director, not only because of their ethical implications, but also because false or misleading advertising by a station will inevitably breed audience mistrust and even hostility.

• *Truth.* Advertising shall tell the truth, and shall reveal significant facts, the concealment of which would mislead the public.
• *Responsibility.* Advertising agencies and advertisers shall be willing to provide substantiation of claims made.
• *Taste and Decency.* Advertising shall be free of statements, illustrations or implications which are offensive to good taste and public decency.
• *Disparagement.* Advertising shall offer merchandise or service on its merits, and refrain from attacking competition unfairly or disparaging their products, services or methods of doing business.
• *Bait Advertising.* Advertising shall offer only merchandise or services which are readily available for purchase at the advertised price.
• *Guarantees and Warranties.* Advertising of both shall be explicit, and shall clearly and conspicuously disclose the nature, extent and manner of satisfaction to the purchaser.

• *Price Claims.* Ads shall avoid price or savings claims which are false or misleading, or which offer no provable bargains, savings or advantages.
• *Unprovable Claims.* Ads shall not use exaggerated or unprovable claims.
• *Testimonials.* Ads with testimonials shall reflect witnesses who reflect a real and honest choice.

As a general rule, program advertising which fixes on a significant advantage or viewer/listener benefit in a positive way, or trade ads which focus on provable ratings or demographic advantages, will comply with these principles.

Summary

Here is a summary of the goals of broadcast advertising:
Capture Attention.

• Separate ad message from surrounding material.
• Present material boldly
• Organize material.
• Keep it simple.

Arouse Interest.

• Ask a question.
• Use the well-liked approach.
• Appeal to the senses.
• Appeal to the emotions.

Present Information Clearly.

• Establish a campaign identity.
• Stick to a single idea.
• Let one element dominate.
• Use an organized approach.
• Be direct.
• Be brief.
• Use appropriate language.

Induce a Response.

• Use motive appeals.
• Provide bold tune-in information.
• Provide sales contacts.

Be Truthful and Ethical.

• Be truthful and accurate.
• Keep material tasteful.
• Don't disparage the competition.
• Don't make unwarranted or unprovable claims.

Advertising Approaches

Broadcast advertisers have found that there are several generally effective approaches to use in a successful ad. Sometimes they are used singly (remember the caution to stick to one main idea in an ad); occasionally they may be combined.

Here are the most common approaches:

New Program. The emphasis here is on "new." If the program or personality is new, or the approach is a very different one from most other station or broadcast programming, this might be what is selected as the main approach for the advertising. Words and phrases such as "All New," "Premiere," and "First Time on TV" would highlight both the headline and the copy. For on-going programs, changes in format, cast, hosts, news personnel, or other elements can point to a "new program" approach for your ads.

Program Description. For television, a story line, plot description, or definition of the kind of news stories to receive emphasis in a news or documentary program fall into this category. For very popular programs, this approach might be all that is needed. The viewer is already predisposed to watch. Reinforce this disposition with specific information about tonight's show. For radio stations, format descriptions, and information about special programming, contests and personalities are grouped in this category.

Program Benefits. For audience-building ads, this approach should answer such questions as, "What can this program do for the viewer?" Storyline, personalities, and other aspects are secondary. In trade press or sales promotion ads, the "program benefit" ad might call attention to how well the program delivers certain kinds of audiences to perspective clients; or may call to mind other benefits of being associated with the program.

Program Type. "From the producers who brought you 'M*A*S*H' comes this new series . . ." is one form a "program type" approach ad can take. This approach calls for audience recognition of other programming; or, as its principle appeal, classifies a program in a recognizable category: entertainment, news, documentary, educational, etc. Other sub-categories of this approach are the evening line-up ad showing various programs to be aired during one particular span of time; the sales promotion ad which links programs with similar demographics; or the themed news ad which displays past and upcoming special news features.

Problem-Solving. This is the kind of ad that presents the audience with a relevant problem, and shows how watching or listening to the station can solve the problem. In the world of commercials it might well be refered to as the "Ring Around the Collar" approach. It is useful in promoting special news features ("Learn how to protect yourself on the streets at night. Watch News 4 this week,") and in bringing about changes in viewer/listener habits ("Are 'Captain Sagebrush' cartoons good TV for your children?") Problem-solving ads are closely related to program-benefit ads.

Testimonials. This approach features a person, either well known or typical, making a positive statement about the qualities, value or characteristics of a program or station. A typical viewer might tell how she benefited from Channel 7's recent news feature; a mother might explain how the TV game show at 7:30 made her smarter; the movie star might be shown watching public television; and the baseball star might tell how he gets his sports news first on the local all-news radio station. All are examples. Using a popular figure for a testimonial places in the ad a person whom people feel they can trust, and whom they like. Use of an "average" or typical person (housewife, mail carrier, truck driver, stock broker, clerk, etc.) trades on ad readers' tendencies to identify with the job and/or socio-economic status of the person giving testimony. In either case, the message is more believable than if it comes from a non-seen anonymous announcer's voice, or an unidentified copywriter.

Case History. Usually similar to the problem-solving approach, the case history is a mini-story of success generally told in narrative form. Here's a tongue-in-cheek example from a hypothetical on-air news promo:

> *ANNOUNCER:* (Voice over corresponding scenes)
> "The first time Bob went out on a date with Susan, it was clear she was bored. He took juggling lessons. That didn't work. He memorized and recited poems. She was unimpressed. He dressed outrageously. 'Ho-hum.' Then he started watching Channel 9's 'Eyewitness News.' His conversation became informed. Now Susan calls Bob for dates . . . when he's not already booked. 'Eyewitness News' makes you someone worth knowing . . . well!"

How To Do It. This approach by-passes the problem and goes directly to a detailed solution, often in step-by-step format. A public television development (sales promotion) flyer using this approach might have illustrated copy which reads:

Four Steps to Increased Prestige

Step One: Underwrite 'The American Drama' series on public television station WXXX. (You get credit on-screen before and after each program.)

Step Two: Support the program with an advertising budget.

Step Three: Inform all your employees, clients and corporate friends about your company's support of public television.

Step Four: Smile when you receive the increased loyalty of your staff, the plaudits from critics, and the letters of thanks from upscale viewers across America!

Result:

The next time they see your company name on a product ad, they'll remember your concern for good television.

These are some of the traditional and effective approaches broadcast advertisers use in designing program, format, image and sales promotion ads for print and broadcast media campaigns, and for on-air promotion.

Ad Headline Goals

It is difficult to overstate the importance of effective headlines for advertisements, or the opening seconds of broadcast ad or promo copy. Here are four goals for headlines and promo copy opens for the writer to keep in mind:

Help Select the Ad's Audience. An ad headline which reads "Your First Look at Tonight's News" draws the attention of:

(a) People who are interested in news.
(b) People who want to watch news.
(c) People to whom today's news is important.
(d) People who want to be the first to get the news.

These are the people the station wants to reach with its advertising message. They might be different from the people who would respond to a headline such as "The Most Experienced News Team," or, "News With Real Meaning For You." And these headlines select audiences very different than those attracted by specific content-oriented headlines such as, "Rape Crisis in L.A.—See It Tonight," or "The Used-Car Rip-off—Tonight on News 7." Each ad has an intended audience to reach. The ad's headline must alert those people that the ad contains information for them, in particular.

Present the Central Idea Clearly. Generally, the most direct, straightforward, simple ads work best. Estimates are that up to 60% of newspaper or magazine readers do not *read* ads—they only take notice of them. That usually means a quick scan of the illustration and the headline with little or no attention paid to the body copy. Putting the main point clearly and simply in the headline ensures that the message will reach more people. In a trade or sales promotion ad, the key sales point should be clear in the headline. In on-air promotion, the opening sentence of copy should make the main point clearly.

Stimulate the Ad's Audience to Look Further. Since many print ad readers are only ad "noters," and since people watching television or listening to the radio have many potential distractions, especially during commercial breaks when promotion messages occur, there should be some element in an ad headline or in the opening seconds of promo copy to pique curiosity, arouse interest, or otherwise stimulate people to go beyond the headline or opening statement and read the rest of the ad or watch/listen to the rest of the promo. Specific ideas on attracting attention and holding interest through use of motivational techniques were discussed earlier in this text. In brief, the headline or opening copy must be written with a clearly defined target audience in mind, and must be based on specific concerns, interests or needs of that audience. The headline must contain some basic audience appeal.

Support the Artwork. Ad headlines should help make artwork or photography in a print ad immediately understandable. In promos or broadcast ads for television, opening copy (the headline's counterpart) should explain opening video. Advertising graphics are often dominant, highly unusual, startling, or otherwise attention-getting. They usually need explanation. Rely on the headline or opening copy to make the visual material clear and give it meaning.

For example, a photo of the station's chief anchorperson at a typewriter in the newsroom takes on a particular meaning when the headline reads: "Bill Jones Writes His Own Copy, With You in Mind." How different the meaning if the headline with the same picture read: "Bill Jones Brings You Years of Experience." Or, "Bill Jones Covers News In Person."

Ad Headline Approaches

There are a number of specific approaches the ad headline writer can use. The approach may depend on the general approach of the ad as discussed above; or it may dictate the body copy approach, if the headline is written first. Here are 12 common ad headline approaches:

· Specific Fact	· Testimonial
· News	· Comparison
· Command	· Prediction
· Statistics	· Teaser
· Reason Why	· Slogan
· Question	· Title

Specific Fact. A simple statement of a factual nature which achieves the objectives of audience selection, main-point presentation, and stimulation— where there is artwork support for it—comprises the first approach. Examples: "You'll Hear it First—On KXXX Newsradio," or "Bullets vs. Kings—Live, Tonight at 8 PM."

News. Often a statement of fact, this kind of approach is special because it imparts news. Examples: "John Smith joins TV-8 Sports," or " 'Laverne and Shirley' Moves to Wednesday Nights at 8."

Command. This headline approach tells the ad reader to do something. Examples: "Hear it First on the News Machine—Radio 98," or "When It's Happening, Be There with News 7!"

Statistics. Such headlines, particular favorites in sales promotion ads or sales flyers, work best when there is meaningful and quantifiable information to impart that is a crucial part of the message. "More People Watch TV 11 News than Any Other Channel" is not a statistical head; it is a statement of fact told in a comparative way. But, "The Score: TV 11 News—38%; All Other News Combined—29%" is statistical. So is "Murder in N.Y. Up 120%— Special Reports Nightly on News 7". And so is "3 Out of 5 Radio Listeners in Twin Cities Get Their News From Us!"

Reason Why. This approach to headline writing is appealing because the head or opening copy tells the audience what information the rest of the copy will provide. Examples: "Three Reasons Why News 4 is #1," or "Here's Why Bob Smith is Iowa's Best Anchorman:". Note that a common element in a "reason why" headline or opening sentence of copy is the word "why," when it promises further explanation.

Question. A question, when related to a storyline, plot development, or a viewer/listener need, is often an effective way to draw audience interest by arousing curiosity. Here are several randomly selected from ads in issues of *TV Guide:* "After Her Dirty 'Dallas' Dealings, What's Kristen Up to Now?'' (From an ad for "Knot's Landing.'') "Aliens. We Have the Ability to Hear Them. Now Can We Find Them?'' (from an ad for "Cosmos.'') "Can Billie Expose a Deadly Coverup?'' (From an ad for "Lou Grant''). "How Do They Look Today?'' (Coupled with a photo of the Mouseketeers, this ad was for "The Mouseketeers Reunion.'')

Testimonial. Whether the headline and ad are based on comments by a viewer, listener, star, or expert in some field related to the program, the fact that the comment is coming from someone other than the station helps influence potential audiences. In broadcast and movie advertising, comments from critics are common forms of testimonial ads. The form is recognizable to the reader when in print becasue of quotation marks around the headline, and because a photo of the person quoted is usually used. Besides being a non-biased source, the person giving the testimonial draws interest because ad audiences want to see, hear or read what well-known people have to say. In this kind of ad, the person giving the testimonial should be identified. Print ads can use captioned photos or an attribution line beneath the headline. Radio copy should have the

This ad attracts attention with a startling headline. It arouses interest with a question. And it stimulates viewing WSB-TV's Action News by promising security, personal safety.

This radio station ad evokes basic emotions to attract attention: an illustration of an attractive male, and a slogan headline that titilates. For whom was this ad designed? And with what probable rationale?

These three ads from two successive KNX Newsradio Campaigns are direct and indirect testimonial ads designed to create listener identification with the station.

personality give his or her name in the first or second sentence. TV spots can use a lower third screen superimposition of the person's name, occupation, title, or whatever is necessary for effective identification.

Comparison. Words such as "better than," "more than," "more often," and "earlier" typify this headline approach. It is especially suitable for sales promotion because the target audience for the ad—people who make media buys—is comparing stations and the relative merits of competing programs, personalities, and rating demographics. Comparative ad headlines for audience-building is appropriate when similar programs are competing head-to-head. Local news is a good example. Direct references to competition are usually undesirable. They serve to remind potential audiences of the competition, and can offend people who like the competition. But indirect references are common and can be effective. Example: "NewsCenter 4—More Reporters, More Features Than Any Other Local News."

Prediction. These headlines tell the audience what to expect, what to look forward to from the station or the program. They usually refer to a specific benefit. One recent broadcast news ad predicted "The More You Watch, The More You'll Know." A situation comedy ad predicted "You'll Laugh Like Crazy." And a news feature ad predicted, "This Could Happen To You," referring to an illustration of a mugging.

Teaser. This type of headline does exactly that; it teases the reader into reading the copy, or teases the viewer/listener into sticking with the promotion spot. It must arouse sufficient curiosity to ensure that the reader will want to learn more. Such heads can be cryptic statements such as "Race Against Death" (advertising a dramatic show); or single words, such as "Outrageous," "Hilarious," or "Astounding." They can try to lure the reader into the plot, as in

Do you know who?

Fill in the correct name(s) and score yourself in this important evaluation of current events:

1. _____is police chief for the City of Los Angeles.
2. _____is Chairman of the L.A. County Board of Supervisors.
3. _____are the co-authors of Proposition 13.
4. _____is Secretary of State for California.
5. _____is the judge involved in desegregation plans for the L.A. Unified School District.
6. _____is the out-spoken former U.S. Ambassador to the United Nations.
7. _____ousted Howard Miller and is now President of the L.A. City Schools Board of Education.
8. _____is the youngest U.S. Open Tennis champion. Resident of Palos Verdes.
9. _____is the field goal specialist for the Los Angeles Rams.
10. _____are two of the four co-hosts for "60 Minutes."
11. _____has hosted the "Tonight" show for 17 years.
12. _____is the former Playboy centerfold now married to tennis star Jimmy Connors.
13. _____is the country star famous for his recording of "Georgia On My Mind."
14. _____is the injured coach of the Los Angeles Lakers.

15. _____is the new owner of the Forum, Kings, Lakers.
16. _____is the mayor of San Diego.
17. _____is the conductor of the L.A. Philharmonic.
18. _____is the head of CalTrans.
19. _____is the Prime Minister of England.
20. _____is head of the U.S. Department of Energy.
21. _____won the 1979 World Series.
22. _____is the President of Egypt.
23. _____is the Chair-man of Chrysler Corporation.
24. _____is the "Queen of Disco."
25. _____is the "frog" star on The Muppets.

Add up your correct score by comparing your answers with those listed upside down at the bottom of this page. If you got 20-25 right you really know who's who in current events. If you got 17-19 right you're above average. 16 right is an average score. If you scored less than 16 you won't exactly be the who's who expert at the next cocktail party you attend.

Want to improve your score? Listen to KNX Newsradio. We bring you the Who, What, Where, When, and Why of the World every day!

(ANSWERS AS OF 12-5-79)

A "teaser" campaign run by KNX Newsradio in magazine ads in 1979 presented a series of "questionnaires" for magazine readers. Other ads asked sports and national news questions.

KNX NEWSRADIO 10.70

1. Daryl Gates 2. Baxter Ward 3. Jarvis-Gann 4. March Fong Eu 5. Paul Egly 6. Andrew Young 7. Roberta Weintraub 8. Tracy Austin 9. Frank Corral 10. Rather, Safer, Reasoner, Wallace 11. Johnny Carson 12. Patti McGuire 13. Willie Nelson 14. Jack McKinney 15. Jerry Buss 16. Pete Wilson 17. Carlo/Maria Giulini 18. Adriana Gianturco 19. Margaret Thatcher 20. Charles Duncan 21. Pittsburgh Pirates 22. Anwar Sadat 23. Lee Iacocca 24. Donna Summers 25. Kermit

---

"Hot Bodies for Sale?" (a show about characters who steal recently dead bodies for organ transplants), or merely arouse curiosity: "No Christmas This Year," advertising a program called "The Year Without Santa Claus." Teaser headlines are among the most common used by Promotion Directors.

Slogan. Slogan headlines are especially useful in establishing the identity of a news team, or as an umbrella head for several shows, featuring the station's slogan. To be effective as headlines, the slogan should embody one central point which is related to a viewer benefit, and which is simply and clearly phrased. Examples: "News 9—News worth Watching!" "See It First—On News 5." "Beautiful Music, All the Time." And, "All News, All Talk, All the Time!"

Title. Many ads, especially small space ads in *TV Guide* or similar small format publications, feature just a program title as the headline. This is very effective when the program is popular, or if the show bears the name of a major star who is its biggest attraction. In such cases, body copy is very brief and in the form of a sub-head. One example: the headline is "Eight Is Enough," a series title. The sub-head is "Tom's Out of a Job! Does Nicholas Have a Plan to Save the Family?"

Ad Headline Length

There are three rules-of-thumb about ad headline length:

• First, use as many words as necessary to accomplish the headline's objective, based on the approach which has been chosen.

• Second, generally stay within a 5–15 word limit.
• Third, in small space ads, such as quarter-page ads in *TV Guide,* limit the number of words in the headline to 1–4.

As with all other sets of rules, there is one additional unspoken dictum: any of the preceding rules may be broken if there is a sound creative reason for doing so.

BROADCAST ADS FOR DISCUSSION

The following pages contain a number of typical station ads for news and programming. As you examine each ad, ask the following questions:

Ad Goals

1. What has been done to get my attention?
2. What in the ad is designed to interest me? If not me, whom is the ad designed to interest?
3. Does it present information clearly? Do I quickly know what the program is about? What the ad is trying to say? What day, time and channel the program is on? (Or what radio station and dial position?)
4. Does the ad use motive appeals?
5. Does the ad stick to a single idea? Does the design let one element dominate?
6. Is the copy as brief as it could be?

Ad Approaches

1. Which of the ad approaches discussed earlier does each ad use?
2. Do some have combined approaches?
3. Can you think of an approach that might have been better for program?

Ad Headline Goals

1. Does each ad help select its audience?
2. Is the central idea of the ad clear? What is it?
3. Does the headline stimulate you to read further?
4. Are the headline and artwork supportive of each other?

Ad Headline Approaches

1. Which of the approaches discussed earlier does each ad take?
2. Do any use more than one approach?
3. For each ad, think of at least one other approach that might have been used effectively.

These newspaper and magazine ads are grouped in several broad categories. First are ads for news program special reports. These are among the most frequent ads station Promotion Directors must prepare. They are especially important during rating periods when many stations place extra effort in preparing news special reports that will attract attention.

The second group of four ads are for news personalities. Each represents a slightly different approach to advertising the newsperson. Discuss each, and relate them to ad approaches and ad headline approaches discussed earlier in the chapter.

The third group of ads advertise the station, its programming, its news product, or its sound. Again, relate each to the approaches listed on the preceding pages.

Finally, there are two sets of ads designed for the relatively small space available in *TV Guide Magazine*. Notice how they maintain a campaign look, or identity; and how they are extremely simple, emphasizing topic or title. What else is done to make each of these ads capture attention and interest?

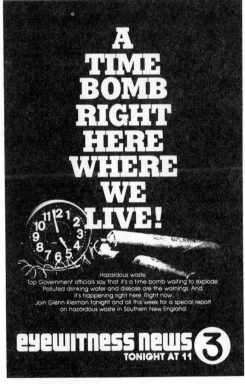
NEWS PROGRAM SPECIAL REPORTS

NEWS PERSONALITIES

STATION/PROGRAMMING

NEWS PRODUCT/SOUND

TV GUIDE SETS

CHAPTER 15

Media Selection and Buying *

Once the Promotion Director knows the programs that need advertising, promotion and publicity attention, has a good basis of ratings and research information on which to build a campaign, and is familiar with applicable budgetary considerations, decisions about which media to buy, and how much of each should contribute to the media mix must be made.

The common trait shared by all media is exposure to the public. But building a media plan entails more than counting exposures. The differences and distinctions among media are great. The same evaluation criteria cannot be applied to them all. The Promotion Director must look at how each is used, its image, the response it evokes, the dimensions and characteristics of each.

Also, the Promotion Director has to consider the message that is being delivered, the audience that must be reached with a particular message, the station effort in terms of money and staff time that is possible, and the potential mix of paid advertising, on-air promotion, station promotion activities, and publicity for any given campaign, large or small.

THE MESSAGE

The station's message is usually designed to build audiences or promote sales (or development support). However there are other kinds of messages that are important. So the Promotion Director's first step in the media selec-

---

*This Chapter is based on original material provided by Linda Nix, Promotion Director, WYES-TV, New Orleans, and by Los Angeles-based media buyer Terri Brady.

tion/buying process is to assemble all the facts about a proposed campaign by answering the following questions:

What is to be advertised?

Image? Format? A program? A personality? Coverage of a special event? A facilities change? An award? A contest or gimmick? The nature of the campaign acts as an important qualifier assessing the appropriateness of the various media.

Image building messages can relate to a station's news programming, minority-related program, or can be designed to make the community feel the station is a valuable resource in a general way or a number of specific ways: a resource for good childrens' programs; superb entertainment; traffic and school-closing information; various kinds of music. Image messages are frequently designed to reach specific audiences, such as minority groups or business and government leaders. Such messages are highly targetable—that is, they can be placed in media with limited but specific reach.

Other more general image messages, such as the kind that promote the station as "an important part of the community" require transmission on media with broader reach.

Format, program and personality messages must sometimes be specifically targeted to special interest groups, and sometimes put before the general public at large.

The key is to examine each principle message of each small or large campaign, make a list of the groups—large and small—the station wants to reach with the message, and identify media that can deliver those groups efficiently.

What is the Creative Thrust?

Does a certain campaign lend itself to all media? Is the campaign theme flashy, or laid back? Does it entail short, punchy copy, or require extensive copy? Is it simple, or detailed and complex?

A campaign begins with a station need, followed by a creative concept and its execution, followed in turn by implementation. If there is thoughtful material to be presented for audiences to ponder and digest, billboards might not be the right medium. If there are lists of program air dates to remember, radio or television might be less effective than print ads which can be torn out and saved. If there is strong visual impact, large illustrations or TV spots might contribute the most.

The Promotion Director must examine the creative needs of the campaign and the creative possibilities inherent in each medium under consideration.

THE AUDIENCE

What is the Audience?

This question is closely related to considerations about the station's message. Is it necessary to reach everyone? Or are there smaller, key market segments that are more important to the station's need and the campaign's goals than others? Is the target a hard-to-reach group, or is it comprised of a large generalized audience or existing fans?

In speaking of "target audiences" and "general audiences" consideration is given to the physical characteristics of each, including location, size of audience, sex, race, and many other factors.

But another important set of audience characteristics revolve around awareness of the station's message. A Promotion Director needs to know the "mind-set" of an audience. Is it unaware of the station's message? Or subconsciously aware? Or partially aware? Or fully aware? To which of these levels of awareness does a Promotion Director want to move the audience? Audience research, as discussed earlier, is the only way to make these determinations with certainty, and research must be done both before and after campaigns to measure effectiveness.

Since different media have different kinds of impact, and the size and strength of a campaign affects overall audience impact and resulting awareness, the station's goals in these areas are important media selection factors.

Target Audiences

A target audience might be one easily defined by such things as race, age group, special interest or problem, or other rather narrowly and easily defined characteristics which do not require extensive research to discover.

However, sometimes target audiences consist of less well-defined groups evenly dispersed in age, geography or, in fact, in every possible way except for one unique determining factor. For example, deaf people are an easily targeted, or well-defined target audience; they can be reached through associations, schools, doctors, and organizations in the community concerned with those suffering complete hearing loss. But the hearing-impaired are clearly a less easily targeted group—they, too, come in all ages, races and places. But more often than not they don't belong to organizations, associations or schools. The are a larger, harder-to-reach target group. Distinctions on how to reach both kinds of target audiences are suggested in the media selections charts.

General Audiences

A general audience is undefined, except by very broad, general categories. If the term "general audience" is limited to less than the total potential audience for a station's message, it encompasses such groups as males, females, families with the children, people who live in the suburbs, people who live in the central city, non-smokers, etc.

Though these audiences are still general in the sense that it might be impossible to reach them through targeting specific messages in uniquely targetable media (such as direct mail or personal contact), if it is possible to identify a large sub-category of the total potential audience, even that information might provide some clues to media selection.

Here is a hypothetical example of how a total audience might be broken down progressively to a clearly defined target audience, to show distinctions:

- General Audience: All potential viewers/listeners.
- Loosely Defined General Audience: Non-smokers (majority of the population).
- Less Well-defined Target Audience: People who would like to stop smoking.
- Clearly Defined Target Audience: People actively trying to stop smoking by belonging to groups or attending non-smoking clinics.

Here is another example:

- General Audience: All potential viewers/listeners.
- Loosely Defined General Audience: Blacks.
- Less Well-defined Target Audience: Upper middle class black professionals.
- Clearly Defined Target Audience: Ministers of predominantly black churches.

GOALS AND TIMETABLES

What is the station's objective, or goal?

A change of image? Building or strengthening a particular demographic? Community goodwill? Countering a competitive campaign thrust? Increasing audiences in a certain time block? Building total audience? Increasing sales of station time? Raising volunteers for a station project?

Different goals may suggest specific media to reach specific kinds of people.

What is the timetable?

Is there a specific period of time in which the objective must be met? Does the objective require immediate reaction to the campaign? Is the objective limited in scope, or a phase of a larger, long-range plan with various steps along the way?

Some media can be used with relatively little advance notice, such as a station's own air time, or purchased time on a radio station. Magazine ads, on the other hand, can require as much as two or three months lead time.

And some media—outdoor advertising, for example—permit a message to remain in the public eye for a considerable period of time for one price; while others, such as newspaper and broadcast ads, are fleeting.

BUDGETS

What is the budget?

Ideally, the budget will be realistically determined by the importance of the promotion campaign and the returns expected. All too often the media planner must work with an arbitrary budget that does not relate to local media costs, and virtually dictates the media plan without regard for media criteria such as previously discussed. The Promotion Director should avoid this arbitrary approach. Budgets for campaigns should be based on expected returns from investments. Sales and Promotion Departments can work together to predetermine the amount of media exposure needed to create desired goals—for example, a 10% increase in prime-time access program audiences, and the amount of increased revenue the higher audience levels will generate. This will provide dollar figures from which promotion campaign and media planning expenditures can be calculated.

Reaching audiences with the station's message involves expenditures of staff time as well as money. Some media are high in cost, and relatively low in expenditure of staff time. Others are the reverse—inexpensive, but time-consuming. And there is a wide range between the two extremes. Each station Promotion Director should examine various media and promotion approaches in the market and classify them as *cost-intensive* or *labor-intensive*.

Cost-intensive

These things, on balance, are usually more costly in terms of money, as compared to the cost of staff time involved:

Radio Advertising	Outdoor Advertising
TV Advertising	Direct Mail (Large mailings and/or
Newspaper Advertising	expensive pieces)
TV Guide Advertising	Posters
Magazine and Supplement Advertising	Premiums, or Giveaways

Of course, trade or barter arrangements with any of the above advertising media can shift them to the labor-intensive category.

Labor-intensive

These are the things which consume larger amounts of staff time and cost relatively smaller amounts of money. They frequently are not direct and identifiable items that show up in a budget. A press release, for example, is an invaluable and often-used tool. Yet in a budget, paper, postage, typewriter ribbons and staff time are not listed under a budget-item called "press releases." In fact, not all the Publicity Manager's time is spent writing releases.

Here are some of the many labor-intensive media a Promotion Director might select:

Target Releases
General Releases
Contact with Special Interest
   Groups & Agencies
Personal Contact with Business
   and Community Leaders
Speakers

Personal Appearances by Station
   Staff
On-Air Promotion
Special Station Events (Parties,
   booths at fairs, etc.)
Involvement in Community Events
Promotion Stunts

For Public Broadcasters:

Station Program Guide Magazines
TV Public Service Announcements (PSAs)
Radio PSAs

(Note: Schedule listings (or logs) are not included above in the media selection charts because it is presumed that they are a basic essential and are produced regularly by all TV and many radio stations.)

GROUP SIZE

Both the size of the community and the size of various special interest groups or target audiences in the market can affect media selection.

The size and location of a station's market can have an affect on whether a media is cost- or labor-intensive, or both. For example, in a small New England town, it might be very inexpensive to send a direct mailing to local Hispanic groups. The effort would also require very little staff time. The problem would become progressively more cost- and labor-intensive in a larger Northeastern town, a small Southwestern town, or a large Southwestern city, such as San Diego, where the same effort might be both labor- and cost-intensive.

A large group, or target audience requires more station effort than a small group. However, the definitions of "large" and "small" vary as they impact on a Promotion Department's budget and staff size. When Linda Nix, was Public Information Director of public station WDCN-TV in Nashville, she developed a series of media selection charts, calling 10,000 people the "psychological break point" between large and small groups in Nashville. Her Public Information Department, however, consisted of only one full-time person with some part-time and volunteer assistance.

Use of the media selection charts on pages 190–191 calls for each station to assess its own budget and staff limitations and to determine for its own market what the dividing line is between large and small groups.

MEDIA CHARACTERISTICS—SUMMARY

Despite any benefits one advertising medium may enjoy over any others, a mix of several or all media is most desirable. Rarely will a limited campaign budget permit a total effort, however. The Promotion Director planning media buys and usage must recognize that the use of even two media can create an inter-action that makes each medium more effective. Put simply, one plus one *can* equal three.

In the process of selecting and rejecting media, the planner should make a thoughtful comparison between the nature of the promotion and the nature of the media, as stated earlier. Start by studying the involvement of the audience. Learn what each target audience's principal media exposures are: Do they read newspapers? Which ones? Do they listen to the radio? Which stations? Are they mobile? Do they travel by cars or public transportation? What magaazines do they read? Which television shows are they likely to watch? To which forms of media do they pay the most attention?

All this information can be supplied by ad agencies, research organizations, and the various media themselves, as well as consumer and research organizations specializing in specific target audience preference—especially large minority groups.

The following are general observations about key advertising media:

Newspapers

It's current news. It's today! Notice the dominance of retail ads touting "today's" sales. Notice, too, that the great majority of broadcast ads promote "tonight's" programs. Newspapers feature the clustering of product categories by section—the food section, travel, sports, TV/radio. Consider if the choice of a section should be because: that is where the ad is expected to be . . . where people will look; or because that is where the competition is; or that is where the ad will perform best for a particular program. Answers may differ with different objectives and different target audiences.

Magazines

In general, magazines mean feature material and/or pictures. They invite leisure readerhip. They may be kept around the house for as long as a week or a month, depending on the frequency of publication. Presumably, then, this improves the odds for better ad readership. Is the ad one that can wait that long? Is the topic one that requires the extra copy that leisure reading permits? Appearance is significant in magazine advertising, where national product ads may be rich in color and the production of some of the nation's finest commercial photographers, copywriters, and designers. Can the station's ad compete or dominate in this environment? Or will it make the station look cheap?

Outdoor

How do people see, or use it? It's certainly not voluntary, but outdoor advertising's limitations are also its advantages. Consider the repetitive exposures likely with strategic locations—on the way home from work, for example, or while commuting to work in an auto. An outdoor ad at its best is an uncomplicated and notable message, conveyed very quickly. Notice who the heavy users of outdoor advertising are: political candidates or issues which rely on quick and repeated name or "yes"/"no" recognition; special events such as plays, fairs, sporting events or exhibits which need to get across the "when" and "where" information for limited-run engagements; auto manufacturers, cigarettes, liquor and soft-drink companies which need reinforcement of package indentification, or image building centering around a slogan. These categories are comparable to television personalities—especially news team members, new television series, and station formats or news slogans. Outdoor can play an important supportive role with other media because it can trigger recall of a more elaborate message in another medium, and through recall, provide valuable reinforcement.

Radio and Television

Their relationship to a campaign must take into account the inherent entertainment, informational or other emotional and intellectual values. The audience is voluntary; there is a receptiveness the advertiser must try to sustain. Since the commercial message cannot be physically retained like a newspaper or magazine, its recall is essential, and repetition through frequency is essential to generate recall. In short, in both media a strong, brief, uncomplicated message must be repeated often to be remembered, and it must not be offensive.

Timing

How soon should the station's campaign goals be achieved? The media planner must consider the time that is needed—a day, weeks, or months—to accumulate the market penetration the campaign's goals call for; plus the time that is needed to build sufficient frequency (repetition of audience exposure) to motivate the response the campaign's goals require.

Audience studies for individual media provide some possible conclusions. The planner then measures these possibilities against campaign objectives. One very practical influence on timing is tied to the closing time for submitting material to each medium. Two days is common for daily papers, radio and television. But in radio and TV this lead time is drastically affected by a limited supply of "inventory," or available positions for commercials. Actual lead time for clearing radio and TV availabilities can be erratic and lengthy. For newspaper supplements and magazines, closing time may be a matter of weeks; and monthly magazines usually have closing dates two or more months prior to publication. Outdoor advertising may vary from 15–45 days prior, but actual availability of space on boards may prolong the lead time needed.

So, clearly, it is not always possible to begin a major multimedia campaign with short lead time. The best bet when time is short is to couple newspaper ads with on-air promotion, and utilize space reserved for existing trade arrangements with local radio or television stations to supplement the exposure. As the available start-up time increases, *TV Guide,* Sunday Supplements, and additional radio and TV buys can be made.

Cost

The factor of cost, as discussed earlier, is often the first consideration. It sometimes even dictates media selection, prompting normal evaluation of media options. A limited budget should not discourage the consideration of various media. It is always useful to weigh the contributions each medium can make to a particular campaign before ruling it out simply on the basis of cost. There are gauges of cost efficiency to consider:

Cost per thousand. This is a measure of how much it costs to make impressions on each thousand people, or households. Referred to as CPM, the figure is calculated by dividing the cost of placing an advertising message by the number of people reached by the message and multiplying by 1,000.

$$\frac{\text{Cost}}{\text{Reach}} \times 1,000$$

For example, if a single radio commercial costs $200 and is estimated to reach 175,000 listeners, the CPM is $1.14.

$$\frac{\$200 \text{ (cost)}}{175,000 \text{ (reach)}} \times 1,000 = 1.14$$

In making such estimates, it is important not to confuse cost-per-thousand figures for individuals and for households. There are more than one individual watching or listening in each household. Comparisons between media must be made on an individual vs. individual basis; or an impression vs. impression basis; or a household vs. household basis.

Other measures, similarly derived, include Cost Per Rating Point (useful in comparing radio stations, or TV stations), Cost Per Impression, Cost per Unduplicated Impression, and Cost per Percent of Market.

These comparison devices can help a media buyer compare media of the same classification—that is, radio vs. radio, television station vs. television station, or newspaper vs. newspaper, etc. Applying the same cost efficiency standards to all media is not always practical.

The end result of the various steps in planning will be the selection of the media types needed for a particular advertising campaign—that is, broadcast, print, outdoor—singly or in a mix. The plan will describe the length of time involved in the campaign, and will show how the advertising weight will be distributed over that period—equally from beginning to end, front-loaded (heaviest advertising near the beginning of the campaign), in waves, or in some other pattern. The plan will estimate the audience requirements (the number of people who must be reached), the frequency with which they must be reached, and will specify how the reach will be achieved by each of the media involved. The budget will allot specific dollar amounts to each medium, based on the "flight" (length and quantity of exposure) in each.

The buying process which starts at this point is really only the fulfillment of these plans.

MAKING THE BUY

The actual buying process means applying the same considerations studied during the planning stages to the media competing for the buy. The buyer must bear the campaign requirements in mind throughout the screening of options.

The buyer should draw on all syndicated and local research sources which can add to an effective knowledge of audience projections and delivery profiles for various local media. Signs of audience growth, declines and shifts that may affect local media should also be noted. This requires constantly being aware of what is happening with newspapers, radio and television stations, local magazines and supplements, commuting habits and other factors affecting the various media in a local market.

For each medium the buyer seriously considers, its strengths should be clearly identified and compared from outlet to outlet. Then buy the strengths needed in a cost-competitive way.

If possible, the buyer should encourage long-range planning to take advantage of the most attractive buying opportunities in the market. Seasonal special rates, discounts for regular or long-term buys, and special opportunities are all ways to stretch the ad dollars.

The buyer should inform the media representatives of the station's goals and expectations so that the media representatives can make constructive recommendations. They want your repeat business, so they want to see that your station's buys work as well for you as possible.

Trade opportunities may exist with other media. The Promotion Director should know station policies and legal factors involved, as well as the trade possibilities and policies with all other major media outlets. There are no hard and fast rules governing the value of what is to be exchanged when a TV or radio station exchanges time for time on another broadcast station, or exchanges time for outdoor or print ad space. This is a highly negotiable field, and each occasion will entail different terms and a different method of appraising the benefits derived from a trade. But even where trade possibilities exist, the Promotion Director should evaluate them by applying sound media criteria and station needs and goals in order to negotiate the best possible deal—or, perhaps, make a determination not to trade at all.

Media Selection Charts

To use the charts which follow:

(a) List a campaign's goals.
(b) Classify the audiences which should be reached to achieve the station's goals. (Target or General; Easily Defined, Less-well Defined, Loosely Defined, or Undefined).
(c) Make a determination whether the groups to be reached are large or small, based on the staff effort needed to reach them.
(d) Beneath those designations on the charts are listed the effective media

MEDIA SELECTION
TARGET AUDIENCES

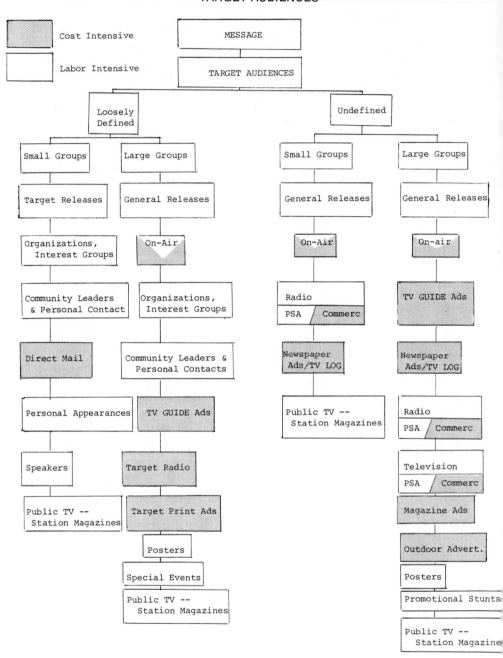

MEDIA SELECTION
GENERAL AUDIENCES

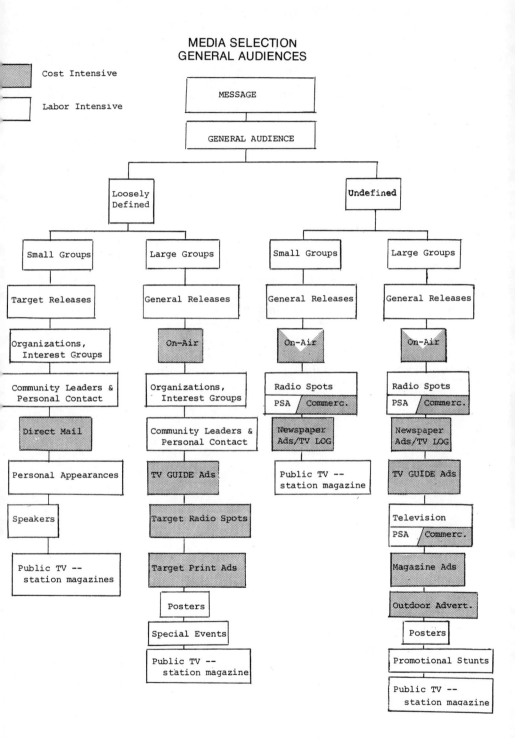

that might be selected for a given campaign. Cost-intensive media are shaded; labor intensive media are not. Media selections can then be made based on available budget and staff size.

If a budget has not been determined for a campaign or project, these charts can be useful guides to the media to be used—and the Promotion Director can select appropriate media without budget considerations, so as to come up with the most effective campaign money can buy. Then, if the budget needs to be cut back, the chart enables a quick overview of cost-intensive areas that can be reduced and labor-intensive efforts which can be increased.

MEDIA BUYING: SUMMARY

The decisions of media buyers, including experienced Promotion Directors, are subject to many challenges. But, as a leading media buyer in Los Angeles, Terri Brady, pointed out, "The buyer is on solid ground if his knowledge of the campaign and planning requirements is complete, and if he or she has considered all appraisal standards before making the final decisions. There are always points for debate in unscientific decisions; and in the end, the buyer's best answers are logic and practical experience."

This advice for media buyers serves well for broadcast station Promotion Directors functioning on their own in selecting the right mixture of media and promotion techniques for a campaign.

CHAPTER 16

On-Air Promotion

On-air promotion is defined most simply as a broadcast station's use of its own air time to inform and attract audiences for programming, to create community awareness of the station, its policies, programs and needs, and to create or reinforce the station's image in the community.

Most radio and television stations consider on-air promotion their most effective audience communication device. Here is what some experts have had to say:

"On-air promotion is the single most cost-effective audience-building tool we have."—Jerry Rowe, Former NBC-TV VP of Advertising.

"The viewer doesn't stumble into a choice of programs. He has to make a conscious decision about what to watch. And on-air promos help him do it!"—Sy Cowles, ABC-TV On-Air Promotion.

"All media can contribute to the size of a rating. But a television station's own air is the single most important avenue for audience-building."—Hal Cranton, former VP of Advertising, Sales Promotion & Publicity for MCA-TV.

"On-Air promotion establishes the identity of the station. It is important that the station's image be positive and professional, for with it comes public support."—Blaine Baggett, former PBS Network Director of Creative Services.

"On-air promotion is the cheapest, most efficient way to increase viewing frequency."—Karen Farr, Director of Research, WNET-TV/New York.

"Nothing else works as well. All other forms of advertising and publicity can only be supplemental."—Bill McLain, Promotion Director, KSTW-TV/Seattle.

CHARACTERISTICS OF ON-AIR PROMOTION

Audience Building

Audience-building is the most important job of on-air promotion. It does this by informing viewers and listeners which program is on next, or later in the day, or tomorrow, or the day after. For interested audiences, just knowing about the program can cause the decision to tune in.

Others may think they are not interested in an upcoming program or special feature until a skillfully produced persuasive promo peaks their interest, arouses their curiosity, or promises a benefit that encourages them to watch or listen.

Still others are led through a particular part of the day or evening on one station, encouraged by on-air promotion to stay-tuned, their attention continually directed to what is coming up next, or soon.

The techniques of informing and persuading audiences have been discussed earlier under the section on "Motivational Techniques." Specifics as they apply to on-air promos are discussed in the pages ahead.

Station Image

For the audience, on-air promotion gives the station its "personality" or image . . . it's own distinct, memorable look and sound, and its relationship to the community. This helps the listener or viewer remember the station in a positive way.

Typical image spots may summarize types of station programming in areas of entertainment, film presentations, news and public affairs, education, cultural presentations, and contests.

When on-air promotion has a strong look and/or sound coordinated with print ads, ads in other broadcast media, outdoor ads, publicity, and other campaign elements, an "umbrella" theme is established in people's minds. This theme helps people identify the station's messages and differentiate them from those of the competition. And a theme is vital in establishing the station as a credible and valuable information and/or entertainment resource in the community.

All the station's other advertising, publicity and promotion efforts reinforce the on-air theme; and it reinforces them. The station becomes easier to find, easier to remember, easier to like.

Independent promotion package expert Bob Klein, an industry expert on station image, summed it up at a BPA seminar: "Your station is like a big electronic garage sale; it's got a lot of rooms—now you need a roof over its head. Your station has got to add up to something. A great image breeds viewer loyalty, if the public likes and believes what you tell them the station adds up to!"

Station Goals, Needs

Especially true for non-commercial broadcast stations, effective on-air promotion creates a positive climate for appeals for funds, volunteers, and other resources. It can be a prime means of letting the audience know the differences between public and commercial broadcasting. It can help mold audience, community, and legislative opinion about non-commercial broadcasting issues.

Informed, educated audiences are less likely to complain and criticize; more likely to offer positive support.

Commercial broadcasters' goals are profit and community service. The medium can be used to promote itself to potential advertisers, directly or indirectly—directly through messages about the medium's effectiveness; indirectly through a strong image coordinated with sales promotion efforts. And, there is strong public relations value in using on-air to let the public know about the station's services to the community.

This all sounds like an awesome burden for the limited amount of on-air promo time a station has. But one program promotion spot, if carefully conceived, written, produced and placed, can accomplish many—if not all—of the above . . . and can do it in less than :30 seconds.

Answering the Arguments

While most enlightened General Managers have come to recognize the importance and tremendous potential of on-air promotion, there are some who resist its effective implementation. There are two principal reasons, and several excuses given to cover those reasons.

The real reasons some stations don't give effective support to strong on-air promotion efforts are:

• At some commercial stations, management is reluctant to "give away" air time to itself that could be sold to clients for real dollars. Instead of an effective schedule of promos, they air commercials.

• At some public stations, management learned not to depend on on-air promotion efforts in the 50's and 60's when PTV and public radio audiences were miniscule. All station effort had to go into reaching out with other media or publicity to bring in new audiences.

Here are the excuses given for not using on-air effectively:

"We're Only Talking To Ourselves". When a Promotion Director encounters this argument for lack of attention to on-air, he or she should turn it around and use it as the strongest argument *for* a major on-air commitment. Bill McLain, on-air expert and Promotion Director for more than 20 years at KSTW-TV/Seattle, put it this way:

"To reach viewers the very best place to go is the 'point of purchase' . . . in the retail trade it's where most goods are sold, because the customer is right there looking at the wares on display.

"To reach that captive audience, your viewers, you have to 'buy' time on your own station. You have to 'purchase' your own commercials . . . on-air promotion spots. Nothing else works as well. All other forms of advertising can only be supplemental. For example, in my market (Seattle/Tacoma), *TV Guide* has a reach of only 300,000 homes. The most popular newspaper doesn't even go to 50% of the population. But nearly everyone has a TV set, and with a modest schedule of promos I can out-deliver any other medium."

According to PBS Network Creative Services Director Blaine Baggett, the point has not been lost in public TV either, with its rapidly growing audiences. "Last year (1978)," he pointed out at a recent promotion conference, "our national audiences rose by 11%. Likewise, the value of our on-air promotion rose by that same 11%."

At any television station, the Promotion Director can compare the number of people likely to "notice" an ad in a major daily paper with the number of viewers tuned in during the station breaks where promos are scheduled and come up with impressive comparisons. And, TV promos have the added impact of sound and motion.

Radio stations, of course, usually have smaller audiences during many parts of the day than television stations. However, there are more opportunities during a broadcast day for radio stations to promote their own personalities, contests, and formats. And, in some markets, commuter drive-time audiences on key stations can rival TV audiences.

So stations may be "talking to themselves," that is, talking to the people who already watch or listen, but on-air promotion is still reaching people who might not otherwise watch or listen to the programming being promoted.

Perhaps most important, it is increasing the *frequency* with which people view or listen to the station. Increased frequency translates into increased exposure to additional promotion announcements, and increased identification with or loyalty to the station, its programs and its news efforts.

"On-air Promotion is Too Expensive and Time-Consuming". If the Promotion Director's job is to increase audiences, where better way is time and money spent than in the most effective means of achieving that goal? The station has an advantage over producers of commercials by having production facilities and staff in-house. The station is its own complete production facility.

However, more and more stations are going out-of-house to highly specialized production companies and commercial animation houses for more elaborate on-air materials. Why? Because of the positive effect high quality, visually appealing, attractive materials have on viewers. It can be costly, so stations look for ways to beat the high costs.

Some join with stations in other communities to pay for production of similar materials and share production costs. Some buy existing packages developed for other markets. Since the material has already been produced, costs are lower. It may be economical to plan a minimum amount of materials to be produced out-of-house which can serve a maximum number of station needs:

Animated IDs which, with only minor changes, double as promo "wraparounds" or program openings; News special report or feature animation that doubles for news promotion use, and more.

One good answer to the "it's too expensive to go outside" argument from a General Manager is, "Well, let's check with some production companies and see how much it really will cost." The Promotion Director then plans one or more of the above cost-saving production procedures and is able to show how a significant amount of outside production can be combined with inside production at reasonable costs.

"We Need All Our Air Time for Paid Commercials". This argument, fortunately declining in use by most General Managers, is regarded by most experienced broadcast executives as poor, shortsighted judgment. Again in the words of Bill McLain, "The astute broadcaster knows that share-of-audience and share-of-revenue are indivisible. To be a winner in the TV battle for ratings, a broadcaster must present the best programming possible, schedule it at the best time possible, *let viewers (or listeners) know about it,* and *stimulate them to watch it!* Once the station is convinced on-air is the way to sell, it simply cannot afford to run its own commercials (promos) only in unsold time periods. The General Manager and the Promotion Director must sit down and negotiate the 'purchase' of spot inventory for promos in fixed positions that only the GM can preempt."

Broadcast promotion expert Dave Course, in his book *Stroking Themselves: The Double ESP System For Enlarging TV Audiences,* proposes the following pertinent formula:

Programs *plus promotion* = Acceptance
Acceptance = Ratings
Ratings = Sales
Sales = Money
Money = New Programs and *More Promotion*
New Programs plus More Promotion = More acceptance
Etc., ad infinitum!

In short, a successful station which has clients knocking down the doors to buy commercial time will not remain successful unless it reserves *some* of its *best* commercial air time for its own promotion announcements.

Station Commitment to On-air

The first commitment must be management's recognition that on-air promotion is the most cost-effective means of reaching potential viewers or listeners, and therefore the most valuable tool of the Promotion or Public Information Department. With that must come recognition that poorly made promos are worse than non-productive. They are counterproductive. They cause audiences to decide *not* to watch or listen to programming they might have otherwise enjoyed or benefited from. And poorly written and produced promotion gives a negative impression of the station and its production capabilities.

On-air promotion is cost effective, but it is not free. Personnel, facilities and effective coordination cost time and money.

Budget. An important budget item in this area is a qualified staff member to concentrate solely on on-air promotion. Whatever is necessary should be spent in a given market to attract an individual with production background, an understanding of the equipment and its potential, good copy and script-writing abilities, and the kind of personality that will enable productive relationships with many others at the station (producers, directors, graphics, traffic, technicians, etc.).

If production time costs are billed back to the Promotion Department, they must rank as a high budget priority. The section on resources below gives an idea of what is involved.

A third important budget element is money for outside animation. A station's "look" can receive a tremendous shot in the arm—which can last for a year or more with only minor modifications—with the expenditure of a modest sum for professional animation of logo, promo beds, presentation and program opens and closes, and similar materials. For radio stations, some of the work can probably be done in house for on-air promotion, but the Promotion Director should have budget items for musical arrangements, jingles, and video material for broadcast advertising.

Costs can range from $1,000 for :10 seconds of animation, to as much as $1,000 per second for very advanced, slick techniques. But for $10,000 to $20,000 nationally known graphic animation houses can supply many coordinated and useful on-air elements for television use. Good resources also exist in a growing number of local communities. The Promotion Director should inquire about them, and build a library of samples from each.

For television stations, vidifont or other electronic, computerized titling equipment, and ¾″ cassette equipment for screenings and even on-air playback of promos are useful when 2″ videotape facilities are limited. (These items might be included in the engineering department's budget.) More recently, 1″ videotape equipment which makes slow motion and freeze-frame effects possible, and which allows single frame or frame-by-frame editing (a great time saver) has become less expensive and an invaluable on-air tool.

Budgets should also include:

Adequate allowances for in-house and/or outside artwork for film, videotape, animation and slide use.

Money for outside film or videotape production work for special campaigns or for those times when the promotional need is great but the station's facilities are tied up by other departments.

Money for props, scenery, and special effects.

Money for outside talent and/or announcers for special promo needs. (The station announcers are not always the perfect voices.)

Expenses for some remote tape or film work. Costs will vary widely in different locales.

Personnel. In the ideal situation, one person (or more) handles all on-air promotion production and scheduling. There are many who feel that on-air is so important that the Promotion Director should take on these responsibilities, and delegate advertising, publicity and other forms of promotion to staff members. On the other hand, many Promotion Directors—particularly those with adequate staffs—prefer to hire someone more explicitly qualified to produce, write copy for air use, and perform the many on-air functions. These Promotion Directors see their own roles as administrative. They set policies, determine budgets, and encourage, supervise and coordinate the work of all the promotion staffers.

But whether it is the Promotion Director or a subordinate staff member handling on-air, the Director must recognize that on-air promotion is usually more important to audience-building responsibilities than advertising, publicity, or other promotion efforts. So the job should be in the hands of one totally capable person, not spread arbitrarily around the department or the station.

If responsibilities at a station rest in different departments without close coordination—for example, if production of promos is done by program producers in the Program Department; scheduling of promos is done by traffic personnel; and design of advertising and publicity are the Promotion Director's responsibility—then the Promotion Director must take the initiative to see that communication among all concerned is effective and that there is coordination of effort. Many stations with this kind of problem have instituted weekly "creative" or "coordinating" meetings attended by all concerned.

Facilities. Let's look at access to facilities, or simply, commitment to *time*. A station must recognize that effective on-air promotion requires substantial commitments to various kinds of equipment use time:

- Regular production time for local promos (those not produced by a program's production staff, network or outside firm) can easily involve an entire day or evening a week—often more. Movie promos, syndicated program promos, and promos for news features must all be turned out on a regular basis.
- For many stations (especially public TV) regular time to record network promo feeds or adapt network promos to the local station's "look" is critical. This can involve re-editing, inserting material into promo "donuts," changing music and voice-over announcements, adding local day/time supers, and other similar alterations.
- For TV stations which make heavy use of radio advertising through purchase or trades, production time for finished radio spots can be important.
- In addition, large blocks of time are regularly needed to produce (or adapt) preview programs and other presentation materials for clients, agencies, and the press. This time is usually needed prior to Fall Season and Winter "New Season" kickoffs, and prior to auctions and fund-raising drives at public stations.
- At radio stations, heavy production efforts often precede major remotes and important contests.

To re-emphasize, TV stations with limited 2″ VT playback facilities should investigate 1″ or ¾″ VT equipment for promo playback in station breaks. The dollar investments (under $15,000 for ¾″, under $75,000 for 1″) can pay off handsomely in increased effectiveness of the station's on-air promo scheduling. Public TV stations in more than 25 cities, including Boston, New York and Los Angeles, now run most station break material in these smaller formats.

Finally, the capability of quick production, storage and recall of attractive typefaces makes some form of computerized character generator an essential on-air tool at any size station. It enables a station to take advantage, on short notice, of many otherwise unavailable opportunities stemming from last minute program changes, network schedule revisions, or news events and coverage. Even station logos can be pre-programmed into type fonts.

Technological advances in these and other facilities for improved on-air promotion are being developed so quickly that the person in charge of on-air promotion has a responsibility to the station to keep appraised and informed of all new technology and its possible benefit to the station's promotional needs.

On-Air Promotion Limitations

It Can't Work Alone. Alone, on-air promotion can rarely achieve dramatic results. That's because it can't directly reach non-viewers (though it does reach them *indirectly* by word-of-mouth.) On-air promotion works best when coordinated with effective advertising, publicity, and off-air promotion efforts in a consistent campaign.

It Can't Make Winners of Losers. People can be led to bad programming once. Maybe, sometimes, they can be brought back a second or third time. But if the product is consistently bad, or unwanted, the best on-air promotion in the world will eventually fail to generate audience support.

It Can't Work If It's Bad. No station can bring viewers or listeners to programs if its promos are badly written and badly produced. If they are dull, uninteresting, confusing, if they fail to sufficiently inform about program content, fail to use effective persuasive or motivational techniques, or fail to provide effective tune-in information, they are a waste of time and money.

To be effective, a promo must give a clear idea of what the program is about, offer a good reason to watch or listen, and tell the viewer or listener where, when and at what time he can see or hear the program.

On-Air Promo Styles—Television

What kind of promos work best for various kinds of programs? First, let's look at some of the options available. Then we'll look at the situations on-air promotion people face and list the most common and successful approaches.

Voice Over Credits. TV networks discovered years ago that putting an announcer's voice over the closing credits of programs greatly increased the inventory of available promotion time. By catching viewers before they've had a chance to switch channels, they had a better chance of holding them. Now, networks and local stations use VOC announcements first to promote upcoming shows, then later programs the same evening, and finally, on occasion, programs with similar audience appeal later in the week.

Commercial network affiliates must be alert to block out network VOCs for programs they aren't carrying. All networks provide timing for when their VOC announcements will occur.

VOC copy, usually :10–:20 seconds long, must be terse in order to promote two or three programs quickly. Copy usually includes a strong, positive reference to a star, a character, or an unusual storyline. Specific information about program content is very important. "Playmate Magazine tries to get LaVerne and Shirley to pose nude, next" is effective. "Stay tuned for fun on 'Laverne and Shirley' " is not.

Whenever possible, VOCs should be pre-recorded on audio tape. This allows the best possible delivery, with no errors and plenty of enthusiasm. The On-air Promotion Manager should personally supervise all VOC recording sessions and coax the right inflections, tone and enthusiasm from the announcer for every spot. These announcements are not to be taken lightly. They are a very important element in the station's effort to maintain and build audiences.

Voice over Slide(s). It's best to use film or videotape for promos. Moving pictures capture attention better than still ones in most instances. But often equipment, production, or schedule time aren't available. Then the slide and announcer technique can be used.

These on-air promotion slides are used with announcer voice-over copy to promote station programs in five or ten second spots between programs. Film and videotape promos on TV and audiotape spots on radio are also on-air promotion.

KNXT-TV
SATURDAY, NOV. 14, 1981

THE FOLLOWING STATION ID'S AIR BEGINNING 11:30 PM, LOG LINES 36100
THROUGH 54000:

SLIDE   ANNOUNCER COPY

ID/"TWO ON THE TOWN"   HOW TO DRESS SEXY...MONDAY AT 7:30.

ID/"ROCKFORD FILES"   STEPHANIE POWERS GUEST STARS MONDAY AT THREE.

ID/"BARNEY MILLER"   A FAT BURGLER ARRESTED...MONDAY AT FOUR.

VOICE OVER CREDIT ANNOUNCEMENTS

LOG LINE	PROGRAM	LENGTH	COPY
02950	"DUSTY'S"	:11	LATER TONIGHT, LEONARD NIMOY TAKES YOU INTO THE FUTURE WITH "JOURNEYS THROUGH SPACE AND TIME." "IN SEARCH OF...", TONIGHT AT SEVEN.
14750	"TWO WITH YOU"	:11	LATER TONIGHT, CATCH THE ACTION. CATCH FEVER, ON "DANCE FEVER" WITH DENNY TERRIO AND GUEST STAR, PHYLLIS DILLER, TONIGHT AT SEVEN-THIRTY.
30450	"DANCE FEVER"	:11	STAY TUNED NOW FOR DELIGHTFUL ENTERTAINMENT WITH "MICKEY AND THE BEANSTALK," AND "DUMBO," AS "WALT DISNEY PRESENTS," COMING UP NEXT.
35800	LATE NEWS	:10	STAY TUNED NOW FOR "BARNABY JONES," FOLLOWED BY DAVID JANNSEN IN "WARNING SHOT," THE CHANNEL TWO SATURDAY NIGHT MOVIE SPECIAL. NEXT.

The above is a condensed version of the announcer station ID and voice-over-credit copy used in one day on KNXT-TV, Channel Two, in Los Angeles, California. ID copy is timed at two to three seconds. Voice-over-credit copy lasts longer, usually nine to fifteen seconds. The log line references indicate where on the station's operational log the particular item is found, to help the station break director and announcer avoid putting a particular piece of copy on the air at the wrong time. Under the "program" heading is listed the program which is ending, and over the credits of which the announcement is to be read live by the announcer. Usually, each of these announcements is on a separate sheet, inserted in an announcer's Copy Book which contains all live announcer material for the entire day.

Again, the voice should be pre-recorded to avoid dull delivery and error. If the spot is to be longer than :10 seconds, more than one slide should be used to add visual variety. As a general rule, a slide whould be on the screen at least :04 seconds to make a good, solid impression; and no more than :10 seconds before it loses audience attention. Simple two-slide promos can be made by keeping the same art for slide #2 but adding day, time and channel information. Or the second slide can be visually different. However, the day, time and channel information must be on the last slide the audience will see in all such promos. Otherwise it will be hard to remember.

If the spot is a shared ID (that is, a program title slide with station identification information as well as day and time information) it will probably be used for only a few seconds. Make sure the visual is very simple and bold; and that written information is as short as possible.

The FCC does not require audio and visual station identification on all station breaks. If the channel number, call letters and city of license are on the slide, the announcer can make reference to the program the slide is promoting.

Program Clip Promos

This is probably the most common promo production style, or technique. The On-air Promotion Manager previews locally produced, syndicated, or specially acquired programs and picks out several scenes. These are pieced together in a meaningful sequence, and copy is written for the announcer's voice over the start, middle, or end of the promo (or all three) to flesh out the story or program content. Some critical things to remember:

- Rarely can one clip be as effective as two, three or four. Clips from several scenes enable the promo to show more characters, more action, more stars, more locations. Audiences receive a broader glimpse of the program. The promo producer must resist the temptation to try and tell the whole story with one scene. It can't be done in most cases. . . . To show off an actor's ability, pick out a two-to-ten word segment that shows him at his best. In building suspense, it takes too much time to show the car careening around corners on two wheels; pick out the two or three seconds just before an obvious crash . . . but don't show the crash. Don't give away too much action.
- Rarely—if ever—can one scene from a show—or two or three scenes— tell the audience what that show is about without an announcer's voice-over. The announcer *must* place scenes in context, provide some background information, and tease the viewer about the outcome. The program producer who also produces the promo might be too close to the show. In producing the promo, he may make assumptions that are not warranted. To interest a viewer, program content must be made explcit. Rarely in a program does a host, personality or character sum up in a few words what the relevance of the program is to the audience. That must be done in the copy for the announcer's voice over.

• In selecting film clips, the On-air Promotion Manger should refer to the section of this book on motivational techniques, and to the section on tips on promo production, to know what will attract attention and hold interest. Movement, star value, close-ups, excitement and action are key elements. But a promo should be balanced. Material should be varied. Don't rely on all zooms, pans, close-ups, or stars.

Original Production

When there is no access to program footage or tape—and sometimes when there is—the promo producer may need to go into the studio or the field to produce a promo from scratch. There are as many options as the creative imagination of the producer, the program content and the subject matter allow. Here are some of the obvious:

Personalities. Use the program host, in studio or on location. This is especially effective if the on-camera program host has a strong personality, good delivery, warmth and charisma. Frequent appearances by a host in promos can help establish him or her strongly in viewers' minds. Many stations use this kind of promo with news program personalities ranging from anchorpersons to sports and weather people. Community service programs, interview and discussion programs, and live programs also rely heavily on this technique. If the personality is a good writer, he or she can write the spots personally. The promotion producer should review them for essential information (themes, title, tune-in information), but when the talent does the bulk of the writing, the delivery gets an unexpected boost.

Graphics. If hosts, program clips, and studio or outside production are not possible, perhaps there is access to photos or artwork relating to the program. Or the resources of the station's design department may be recruited. Zooms, pans, tilts and supers used with photos or art cards in the studio can add movement and life to an otherwise static spot. The addition of music and/or sound effects behind the announcer's voice can give the spot the look and feel of being a part of a fascinating program.

This type of spot can illustrate problems to be discussed on a talk show, or present cartoon images of guests and stars. But because it takes time to prepare the material, planning must be begun well in advance to research and find, or produce artwork.

Episodic Promos

Specifics always sell better than generalities. That is an advertising, promotion and publicity maxim. Thus, the episodic promo—which tells the viewer exactly what is on an upcoming episode of a series—is better than a generic spot about the series in general.

Most things a Promotion Director might want to accomplish with a generic spot can be done in an episodic spot. If exposure is needed for the host, use him or her on camera. If it is important to tell what the whole series is about, develop a slogan that sums it up and use that at the beginning or end of episodic promos. If the intent is to sum up accomplishments of a documentary-type series or community service program, do so in the episodic with a few quick clips and very tightly written copy at the beginning of the promo before going into this week's topic. The viewer needs specific information that will help justify his program choice. Tell who the star is, what the topic is, and how watching this particular program can benefit the viewer in some way. The specifics are important.

Generic Promos

Some experts argue that generic promos are a waste of time altogether. Others hold that generic program promos can be useful in establishing a program image, explaining a series' premise, or preparing an audience for a new series. One thing is certain: the best generic spots are those which are specific about program content. Clips or scenes from earlier programs are most effective, as are lists of upcoming topics. If you can't give the viewers a specific reason to watch next week's show, give them good reason to check the listings or the show itself by showing the kinds of things that have been on the program in the recent past, and that they are likely to see.

Still, the generally accepted maxim is that if only a generic promo exists for a program, promote some other program with an episodic spot.

Station Image Promos

Promos which are designed to establish an image for the station in the community as "The One to Watch," or "We're 4 You," or "3 For All," are often developed with musical themes, elaborate animation, and top-quality film or tape production. Typical or recognizable scenes from around the community are often part of these promos.

The principal use of such spots by stations with large, active or competitive news departments is to establish a climate of public acceptance for their news. Independent stations, on the other hand, sometimes use such image material to position themselves as "The Movie Station," or the local sports team's broadcast home.

Such spots achieve their goals most effectively when scheduled close to or adjacent to the kind of programming they are trying to build a climate for. They work as reinforcement for the people who have tuned in to that programming. So the community image promo might be scheduled during or following news, community service programs and local documentaries. The image is strongly inforced. "We are the home of the Washington Bullets" promos might be scheduled during sports sections of newscasts, or around other sporting events to drive home the point to sports fans.

Placement of such promos in other parts of the schedule is more effective when the image is supported by advertising in other media, such as newspapers and billboards, as part of a campaign.

In any case, use of such spots should be relatively rare, if they displace specific or episodic program promos which are designed to attract viewers to specific programs.

THE USES

News Promos

For most commercial network and many independent stations, promotion of news programs is a primary concern. News promos fall into three broad categories: personalities, slogans and features.

News Personality Promos. These feature one or more members of the news team and highlight their strengths, humanize them, or summarize their achievements. Such spots are particularly effective with a news team which has strong, promotable personalities, or which is in first place in the ratings and wants to solidify its position by keeping its popular people visable.

Different successful approaches have ranged from showing anchor, news and weather persons and reporters at home, to showing how they prepare their stories, to describing their extensive experience and background, to showing how well they relate to each other as friends and as a team.

In preparing this kind of promo, it is important to work closely with the news persons involved. Respect for their concerns about privacy is important. So is avoiding approaches which might seem to ridicule or make fun of them. Humorous promos are possible, but very delicate to execute. They require the complete cooperation of the subject, and excellent writing.

Placing heavy emphasis on news team members has helped many stations improve their news ratings. But there is a danger, too. Once newspeople become "superstars" through excessive promotion, the station has to pay higher salaries, and can be in real trouble if a "superstar" leaves for another local station—or another market.

The personality approach is most successful when it works to establish the new newsperson as an authority, when it adds to his or her credibility, when it convinces audiences that these are the people best equipped to learn about what is happening in the world around them and interpret it in meaningful ways for the viewing audience.

News Slogan Promos. Slogan promos generally revolve around a theme that sums up what the station's news team is trying to accomplish; or that encapsulates the team's strengths; or that describes how a particular news team accomplishes its work. The slogans might often be news program titles as well. "Eyewitness News," "Action News," and "Newscenter" are examples. "Award-winning News," "News for People Like You," "Cleveland's Number One News," "First with the News," and "Channel 4 News Covers It All" are subtitle slogans.

In all cases, video and copy on promos should illustrate the title or subtitle slogan by showing examples of the slogan in effect. Many stations use a "Minicam," or "Action Cam" slogan if they are the first to use such equipment. The same applies for "Eye In The Sky" or "Skywatch" slogans when the station acquires a helicopter. These lose their edge when the competition acquires the same capability, but at first they are examples of the advertising maxim of promoting the significant difference the station has that makes it better.

Slogan promos frequently revolve around news team personalities or features, but should be consistent in illustrating the slogan.

News Feature Promos. News promotion spots which promote special indepth feature stories on particular topics are considered the most solid and successful promos in the long run. They give viewers what they need most: concrete reasons to watch the news on a given station each night. If the feature continues more than one night, each night's promotion should be different and specific. Tell viewers what they will see *tonight!* These spots can use actual footage from the feature, or highlight the topic or problem, or be specially made by the reporter, usually on location or any combination of the three. The key is to make a connection between the topic and the audience, or a segment of the audience. Over a period of time, such features should cover topics of interest to everyone in the viewing area.

By using reporters or anchorpersons on-camera in feature promos, the station can retain some of the value of a personality promo. By tagging feature promos with a slogan, the station can capture some of the title or slogan which means so much to the News Director. Yet the information in the promo will still be specific and of immediate relevance to part or all of the audiences which see it.

Movie Promos

Whether for an isolated movie or part of a heavy movie schedule, the best promotion is made from clips from the film. In writing and editing movie promos, *sell the show's strength!*

First, do some research. Who are the stars? Was the music memorable? Was the director famous? Was the plot unusual? What did the critics have to say? Did it win any major awards?

Then tailor the promo to the film's strengths and audience appeals. If the stars were big, pick clips which show them. If the music was superb, let the viewer see/hear clips from the track. If the director was famous or if this film is one of his noteworthy achievements, say so right up front in the copy, and show a scene that epitomizes directorial brilliance. If it's the plot that needs highlighting, don't rely on a single :20 or :30 second clip to sum up the whole story. Use announcer copy to set the scene and evoke audience interest in the outcome—or, if it is a popular rerun, remind viewers of their favorite scenes.

When animated opens and closes for movie series promos must be produced, keep the animated material very short. In a :30-second spot, :03 seconds is all that is needed to let the audience know this a promo for your "PM Movie." Spend most of the time in the spot on the specifics of the film to be promoted. Remember to leave the last :04–:05 seconds for title/day/time information at the end.

Movie series titles have particular promotional value if they incorporate the day-part time that movies air; or if they point to the kind of films to be shown. "Prime Time Movie," "The Late Show," and "Saturday Matinee" are examples of the former. These reinforce the position of films in the regular schedule in viewers' minds. "Hollywood Musicals," "Horror Classics," and "The Golden Age of Film" are examples of the latter, and help audience with particular film preferences find those movies that appeal to them.

Live Sports

Promos for sporting events present a challenge when live telecasts preclude use of actual game footage.

The first and most popular solution is to turn to tape or film from a previous similar event and use clips edited together in an exciting, stimulating way. Show runs, points or goals being scored, fumbles or errors (by the opposition), and moments of jubilation or the thrills of victory. Use the station's sportcaster for voice-over. The teams playing or the sports leagues involved can supply footage.

A second popular approach is to have players, coaches or participants tape or film "personality" promos. Even the "play-by-play" announcers might be used to tape promos.

A third approach involves taping "man-in-the-street" comments of anticipation about the upcoming match and editing them together into a fast-paced commentary on the game.

Yet another possibility is to show the field or playing arena in preparation. A great public television tennis promo started with a close-up of the white lines being laid out on the court. The announcer voice-over copy began, "They're getting the court ready now. . . ." A mood of expectation and anticipation was set.

Live Events

Live coverage of local public, community or entertainment events can present a challenge. As with sports, the options include using participants, public figures, or entertainers if they are available to record spots; using material from a previous similar event; or showing preparations.

Promos can also help set the stage by presenting the issue or problem to be discussed at a public meeting to be televised; or summarizing happenings to date in an on-going local activity. As always, involve the viewers with a clear presentation of the significance to them of what the station is going to televise. Give them a reason to watch.

Talking Head Shows

Interviews and discussion program promos can be dull. Avoid dullness by picking out controversial statements and using brief clips of them. Use the announcer's voice-over to place the remarks in context, provide necessary background information, and supply viewer motivation.

Better yet, use still photos with camera movement, or film or tape to show the problem to be discussed. A promo which shows a program host saying "Tomorrow night on 'Peoria PM,' we'll examine the possibility of chemical wastes in our city," is not as effective as one which shows pictures while the announcer's voice over says, "This is Love Canal in New York State. The people who lived here had to move away because they and their children were being poisoned. It could happen to you, here, in Peoria, tomorrow! Find out more . . . tomorrow night at 7:30 on 'Peoria PM.'"

Even though it is a talk show, the promo doesn't have to promote the guests. If they are audience-attracting names (Jimmy Stewart, Dolly Parton, Ralph Nader, the governor of the state, or an acquitted ax-murderer), use them. If they are not, promote the topic. Little-known guests' fields of expertise are more important than their names.

Talking head shows can also be promoted effectively by a precise, tightly scripted, well-written talking-head promo by the program host. This only works well if the host is well-known, popular, articulate, or warm and easy-going on camera. Public television has used this technique with "Wall Street Week" promos starring Louis Rukeyser . . . who writes and delivers his own copy flawlessly and with a sense of humor. The humor always underscores the topic.

Finally, the studio-produced promo with simple props can be effective. If the show is a discussion on oil shortages and distribution in the U.S., little model oil company tank trucks (available in most toy and drug stores) manipulated around a map of the U.S. by a disembodied hand wearing a big diamond pinky ring could be very powerful in conveying the show's idea to the viewer. A program on ineffective education might use a child's alphabet building blocks to spell—or mispell—the show's title or topic. The variations are endless; the creative potential limitless; and the production budgets low. And the effect can be much greater than mere talking heads. Look for inexpensive but symbolic props, and stick to close-ups.

Syndicated Series

Situation comedies and game shows are often stripped—aired five nights a week in the same time period, usually 4:30–6 PM and 7:30–8 PM. Regular production of promos for each night's shows can be prohibitive in terms of available staff and production time at the station. Also, air time might be hard to find to telecast promos for all those programs. One suggestion is to pick only one or two shows a week to promote on-air with episodic promos. Pick a funny or exciting scene which gives the audience the main idea of the night's plot, but doesn't give away the outcome.

A second approach is to find a unique way to position the show. In the section on motivation earlier in this text, the example was used of station WXIA-TV/Atlanta's promotion of an access program as suitable for family viewing and togetherness. Promos showed typical viewers getting together as a family to watch the show after dinner. The togetherness appeal was based on audience research to determine what kind of program viewers wanted in that time period—and what kind of things they wanted from the program. The program content was of less concern to the promotion staff than the viewers' needs. They were able to increase audiences significantly.

The secrets of this success are simple to state, but require a lot of hard work and research data to accomplish:

- Know what the audience wants, or needs.
- Provide programming that fits those audience needs.
- Promote how the station's programming fills those needs.
- Stress the differences between the station's programming and what is on the competition through this emphasis on "audience need" satisfaction.

ON-AIR PROMO PRODUCTION—TELEVISION

The following steps lead the promo writer/producer through the process of actually constructing a promotion spot that will effectively attract viewers. Each is examined in detail.

- Get their attention!
- Give them a reason to watch.
- Provide clear tune-in information.
- Let writing style help convey the message.
- Help the viewer remember.
- Things to avoid.
- Watch television promos.

Get Their Attention!

This is a "must." Do it, and do it quickly. After watching a TV program, the viewer has a strong inclination to divert attention elsewhere: to TV listings, to friends, to that phone call that needs to be made, to taking dishes to the kitchen or going to the bathroom.

The first *five seconds* of a promo can stop any of this distracting action and keep viewer attention on the TV screen . . . and the station's message.

Following are things a promo writer/producer can do singly, or in combination, to enliven those first five seconds and help hold attention to the promo. Psychologists call them "factors of attention." Woven through a promo, they can help keep attention throughout, but the first five seconds are the critical ones.

The Startling or Unusual! Begin with a stark scene; an elaborate visual or graphic effect; a provocative, stimulating fact or statement; an unexplained sound or visual; strong single words, or brief memorable phrases. Unusual animation can help, too. The key is to present on the screen something that holds attention because it is something the viewer hasn't seen before, and which is compelling enough to arouse curiosity. The responses you want to evoke are "Wow, what's that?" or "Hey, look at that!"

Movement. Begin with a sweeping pan; a rapid zoom; an unusual pan, tilt or dolly; or a moving character or object on the screen. Movement is compelling if it continually reveals more and more of a provocative scene (remember the scene of Scarlett O'Hara walking out among the wounded soldiers in the Atlanta streets in "Gone With The Wind"). Conversely, a similar effect is achieved by zooming in, showing less and less scope but concentrating more and more on one specific detail of a scene, bringing it into focus or crystal clear. Often, of course, the promo producer doesn't create such scenes, but finds and edits them from the program. Again, unusual movement in animation can achieve the same effect.

A Question. A question involves the viewer in the promo. The copy could open with a very short question which has meaning or importance to the viewer. "Is your drinking water safe?" Or, "Is your child really in school today?" Promo copy can either answer the question immediately, let the promo indicate the answer to the question subtly, or tease by making the viewer watch the program for the answer.

The Well-Liked. Opening a promo with a person on-camera (star, host, or spokesperson) whom the viewer respects, likes, admires, is curious about, or with whom the audience can identify. Popular stars and personalities are the best bet. A word of caution, though: it is rarely sufficient for a spokesperson—star or otherwise—to merely say he (or she) likes a program. Have him (or her) give specific reasons why—specific benefits of viewing the particular program.

Appeal to the Senses. A strong, pleasant appeal to the senses—sight, smell, touch, hearing or taste—strongly worded and strongly visualized in the first seconds, can get and hold attention. Show delicious food. Use that sound that brings back pleasant memories (the railroad whistle, cow's 'moo', church bell, baby's laugh, or a loving sigh). Use words that describe with precision and evoke images at the same time—short, powerful words like those listed in the advertising section of the text.

Involvement. Immediately involve the viewer in a piece of very dramatic action from the plot. The daytime soap commercials do this all the time with great success. Follow up with necessary background information on how the plot got to this point, and on principal characters. But that opening zoom-in to a close-up of the terrified woman screaming, or the man hanging from a ledge by his fingertips is plot involvement that a viewer will be hard-pressed to tear him or herself away from. They'll be hooked on the promo.

Give Them a Reason to Watch

As with advertising, this is the real heart of on-air promotion. Return to the section on motivational techniques and re-read it carefully, this time with on-air promos in mind. Pay special attention to the list of things people want to get out of life, and the list of ways television can help fulfill their needs.

Then find ways to work that information into promo copy. Promo copy must promise the viewer something—something relevant, something needed, something useful. It might be laughter; it might be life-saving information; it might be enriching information, or diversion.

Whatever promises are made in the copy, support them by showing brief clips from the program that prove that what you promise will actually be part of the program.

Provide Clear Tune-in Information

Every on-air promotion spot, whether a film, video tape promo, slide or voice-over-credit announcement, must make it *very clear* to the viewer exactly what day and time . . . and on what channel . . . the program can be seen. Call letters are less important than channel numbers, except in areas with heavy cable penetration where various cable companies carry the same station on different channel numbers. In most cases, viewers remember channel numbers because the dial on the TV set points to a number, not call letters.

Always make sure this tune-in information is the *last* thing the viewer sees and hears in a promo. In that way it has the best chance of satisfying the viewer's aroused curiosity, and the best chance of being remembered. Make sure it is bold, uncluttered, and, whenever possible, reinforced by the announcer's voice over.

When preparing copy for announcer's to use, the following format can be used:

"See it (Friday Night) (Tomorrow Night) (Tonight) at 10 PM, (Next,) here on Channel 4."

As announcer copy is placed in a daily copy book, copy can easily be particularized to a given day or part of the day by crossing out the words which don't apply. For example, if the copy which ended as shown above were to air on Friday at 7 PM, it would look like this:

"See it (~~Friday Night~~) (~~Tomorrow Night~~) (Tonight) at 10 PM ~~(next)~~, here on Channel 4."

Rarely should day and time information be permanently recorded on promos. This tag copy comes at the end and is read live so that it can be particularized as shown above.

Let Writing Style Help Convey the Message

Here are some useful tips for on-air promotion copy-writing:

Be Personal and Direct. Speak directly to the viewers as friends. Make extensive use of pronouns "you" and "your" in promo copy. Use direct and rhetorical questions which force the viewers' minds to respond and become involved with the promotional message.

Provide Instant Comprehension. The viewer/listener can't "re-read" a fleeting promotional message. There is no glance-back to the previous line as there is with the printed word. So keep ideas simple, sentences short, construction easy to follow. Use accurate words which mean exactly what they say and are not ambiguous. Avoid technical words, foreign words and phrases, and slang when they might confuse.

Be Original. Avoid trite, over-used and often mis-used words. A copy writer must have a broad vocabulary of short, powerful words. Keep a thesaurus and dictionary at the office desk. Spend a few hours each month reviewing all recent copy, and looking up alternatives for words that have been used too often. Some common over-used words in on-air promotion are:

a) The "see," "watch," "join us," "be with us" group. Possible substitutions include—

"Experience . . ."   "Enter the World of . . ."
"Come to . . ."   "Travel to . . ."
"Be a part of . . ."   "March with. . . ."
"Live the life of . . ."   And many more.

Let the nature of the program dictate the kind of involvement viewer might have with it.

b) The "explore," "discover," "examine" group. Try "probe" if it hasn't been used too often. "Unravel" and "unlock" might be appropriate for programs with a mystery. Again, let the program content help.

c) The "exciting," "fantastic," "fabulous" group. Viewers are told that most TV programs are "exciting." They don't always believe it any more. If that word is used, the promo should show something really exciting as proof. Further, something should actually be highly unusual, wonderous, or existing in fantasy to be labeled "fantastic"; and fabled in story and legend to accurately be called "fabulous." When tempted to use the word "fabulous," test it by seeing if "fabled" will fit in its place. If so, "fabulous" can be used. If not, don't!

Angle the Copy. Use language appropriate to the program being promoted and the audience being sought. Slang may be appropriate in some cases. Many segments of society have their own special languages. Truckers and CBers have their language. Concert and symphony goers have their language. Businessmen and government officials have their own languages. And these languages are constantly changing. When a program has a special appeal to a unique group, key words can be used to signal them that they should pay special attention to the promo, and the program. Seek out a member of the group you want to reach, or someone from the program's production or writing team, and ask advice. The extra time it takes will pay off handsomely in more effective audience-attracting copy.

Be Objective. Don't overpraise a program in promo copy unless it can clearly be shown why such praise is justified. Use words of others—critics or reviewers—to describe how extraordinarily good the program is. A third party will be perceived as impartial and believeable. And the station's credibility won't be on the line. Instead, describe productions accurately, positively, even enthusiastically. "A *powerful* performance . . ." is safer than "A *brilliant* performance . . ."

Be Vivid and Impressive. Arouse the viewer's senses with imagery. Use words, phrases and scenes in the promo and its copy to create images which appeal to the senses of touch (texture), smell, sight, taste and hearing. Close-ups of texture, of human faces registering emotion; sounds which have emotional contexts (brakes squealing, a creaking door, a telephone ringing, an ambulance siren); and action words which add vividness and excitement to promo copy style.

Use Parallel Language and Structure. Orderly progression or development of ideas in a clearly recognizable, structured way helps viewers follow and understand copy. Repeating key words can help.

> "An evening of stars . . . of music . . . of comedy.
> An evening you've long waited for!
> An evening you'll long remember!
> An evening of live TV from the Grand Ole Opry . . . here, on Channel 12!" (At least they'll remember that it's on in the evening.)

Use Surprise, Conflict, Suspense. In copy and choice of video material, cause the viewer to wonder what the outcome of a scene or plot or interview will be. Show opposing forces—they exist in even the most mundane programs. Hint at things the viewer will see which are unexpected. Hint at possible outcomes—without revealing the real outcome. Questions can create mystery and suspense. Soap opera promotion has long used this approach: "Will Marsha have an abortion? Or will Bruce marry her to give her unborn child a father? And who is the real father? Tune in Tomorrow. . . ."

Be Informal. Promo copy is for the spoken language, not the written. Use contractions. Use short sentences and simple sentence construction. These help both the announcer and the viewer/listener. Always, *always* read copy aloud to be sure no-one's going to stumble on too much formality, big words, confusing construction, misplaced modifiers, and the like.

Use Present Tense. Things are more urgent, exciting, and immediate to the audience if they happen in the present tense. "Johnny's guests tonight *are* . . ." (not "will be . . ."); "Next week our news team tracks down rats in city housing projects . . ." (not "will track down . . .").

Help the Audience Remember

Five elements of writing style are particularly important in helping audiences remember spoken messages. Incorporate these into the important elements of promo copy.

Repetition. This is most important with day, time and channel tune-in information. If possible, put it in a promo twice . . . once early in the copy, and again at the very end. Also, consider the value of repeating other key elements (especially in longer spots). Stars' names, major issues and startling facts are all good possibilities for repetition.

Restatement. Consider saying the same thing a different way, especially if dealing with a difficult concept or unfamiliar words. In the concise writing of promos restatement most often appears in the use of synonyms . . . single words which have the same meaning. Restatement not only aids the memory, but can be a bit of help in aiding comprehension.

Controlled Pauses. A pause isolates a word, thought or idea from the rest of the copy. Standing alone, words gain significance, are awaited with anticipation, often are anticipated by the audience, which means members of the audience are involved with the promo. Words set off by pauses are perceived as having greater significance. For most announcers, as series of dots (.....) serve to indicate a pause. Dashes (—) can serve the same purpose. Find out which the station's announcers prefer, and use them.

Memorable Quotations. Aphorisms, maxims, adages, slogans—tersely phrased statements of truth, principle, folk wisdom, or common knowledge (especially if familiar)—help audiences remember. Because of their familiarity and connotations they can convey broad meaning in a fewer number of words.

The Last Words. The last things an announcer says in a promotional announcement stand the best chance of being remembered. Similarly, the last visual image or sound image will stay with the audience. Ninety percent of the time those last things should be the program title, day, and air time. If there is a key phrase or slogan that sums up what a show is about, let it precede title, day and air time, *in that order!* It is generally best to further reinforce the day and time by showing *and* saying both at the end of the promo.

Things to Avoid

Negatives. Tell viewers and listeners what a program *is,* not what it is *not.* Don't apologize for, or even mention a program's weaknesses. Find and dwell on its strengths. If it has none, consider not promoting it!

Unintended Duplication. Be sure to factor out identical words in successive sentences (unless deliberately used for effect as with parallel structure). Reading copy aloud helps to discover that the words "great" or "special" have been used three times in four sentences.

"Who," "Which," "What," "That". When these words introduce sentence-extending phrases or clauses, they will probably make the sentence too long—or unclear. End the sentence and start a new one. "These are superb musicians who play the great music of the Seventies which you'll thrill to hear again" is bad. Get rid of "who" and "which" and you've got: "These are superb musicians. They thrive on music of the Seventies . . . Music you'll thrill to hear again." (Notice, the meaning-broadening word "thrive" replaces the more mundane "play", and the word "music" is deliberately repeated for emphasis.)

Anticipatory Construction. Don't begin sentences with phrases such as, "In the interest of . . ." and "In order to . . ." (both simply mean "to"); "To begin with . . ." or "In the first place . . ." (neither of which is necessary, but both of which could be replaced by "First, . . ."); "On the occasion of . . .", and similar sentence-lengthening, do-little groups of words. They rarely add anything, and destroy conciseness.

In-house Humor. Jokes relating to the television business, goings-on around the station, or humor which depends on a special knowledge of unusual words or phrases will miss most of the audience. It will seem clumsy, vague, or incomprehensible.

Dull Program Segments. Never use one long, dull, uninterrupted program segment as a promo, with simply a tune-in tag line. Add copy to explain the context and increase the excitement of the scene if its the only one available. Use more scenes than one, especially if that one scene is longer than :15 seconds.

Falsification. Don't falsify or fabricate program content. Don't deliberately give a false impression about a program. Don't use specious (seeming true but actually deceptive) reasoning. These things create ill-will with audiences. They are inevitably counter-productive to station efforts in the long run.

The Clever Ending. The funny one-liner, or punch line at the end of a joke, used to end a spot leaving the audience laughing can be destructive. Build humor into the spot . . . make it an integral part of the scenes chosen and the copy that is written . . . but *always* end the spot with information the audience *must* remember: title, day and air-time.

Mis-use of Emotional Appeals. Don't use emotional appeals when there is no evidence to support them. Don't appeal to hatred, bigotry, or intolerance in any way that reinforces these feelings in audiences. Television is a very powerful tool. In producing promos, you will be reaching the minds of thousands, even millions of people. All kinds of people, from the intelligent to the ignorant to the unstable. What you put on the screen is intended to evoke responses from these people. Make sure the responses you evoke are those you intend . . . watching, listening, and/or responsible action.

Watch Television Promos

Watch the competition. Be aware of the competition's campaigns, promo styles, copy techniques, slogans, and scheduling. There's a lot to learn . . . even if it's bad. Regularly sample their promos in various parts of the day and evening. Sample on-air promotion when travelling to other cities. Jot down good ideas. They may be useful later. Knowing what the competition is up to makes it possible to develop counteracting strategies and tactics.

Watch your own station! View your own promos at home for several kinds of input: Is the approach designed at the station and in the editing room effective on the home screen? Do the station's promos work well next to each other? Are they effectively scheduled?

Here is a list of questions to ask about each promo—yours and the competition's:

- Did it catch my attention at the start? How? Why?
- Did it make me want to watch the program? Why? Why not?
- If not, what *would* have made me want to watch that program?
- Did *it* contain solid information about the program's content?
- Did I lose interest in the promo before it was finished? Why?

- Is the program promoted too far in advance of its air-time to remember it?
- Do promos flow well on each break?
- Do I remember the title/day/time a few seconds later?
- How could I have done it better?

Keep a note pad near the TV for criticisms and ideas. Review them regularly. Look for good, original, non-trite words in copy written by others. Keep a list so you can call on those words when necessary in your own writing.

RADIO ON-AIR PROMOTION—SUMMARY

David Milberg, Director of Operations at WBBM/CBS Newsradio, Chicago, provides these summarized guidelines for radio station on-air promotion:

Tools Available

The basic production tool available for radio is audio tape (reel-to-reel, one-track cartridge, and cassette). In addition, turntables for playing records are also used.

Various effects and production short-cuts can be achieved by using cartridges and reels to mix down to the final product. Where multi-track reel-to-reel equipment is available, even more sophistication is possible. Cassettes should be used only for remote recordings, but are generally not used in the studio in any other way for the final on-air spot.

How Do Promos Get Scheduled

Generally, this is done by instructions, either from the Promotion Manager or the Program Director, to the station's Traffic Director (or person in charge of preparing the station's logs).

Typically, because of the unavailabilities of time, many stations schedule their promos and PSA's in light sales periods (nights, overnights, and weekends). However, this is not desirable. The optimum situation is to schedule at least one promo per hour. If inventory availabilities and other time constraints make this impractical during certain day-parts, an alternative is to work a promotion message into the legal I.D.'s aired on the hour and half-hour.

On-Air Promos Other Than Contests

These generally involve promotion of: 1) station personalities; 2) programs; and 3) special station sponsored events that are not broadcast (e.g. a station sponsored rock concert or charity activity).

It is important to note the importance of "live ad-lib" type promos here. These are generally put in small binders for 3x5 index cards and placed near the announcer's microphone in the broadcast studio. These allow for the instantaneous placement of promos on the air when "last-minute" programming decisions are made. They also are helpful to the announcers as segues between various other program elements.

Separately, it is also possible to work promos into specific programs such as news, to highlight the effectiveness of the station's news staff by inviting listeners to participate in news coverage by submitting newstips on fast-breaking stories they witness. Some stations offer cash awards for newstips; others do not.

Guidelines for On-Air Promos Other Than Contests

Whether they are pre-recorded or live, all promos should end, if possible, with the station's call letters (and frequency if this is part of the station's logo . . . e.g. WBBM NEWSRADIO 78, WLW RADIO 7, WLS MUSICRADIO 89, etc.) The reason for this is that good programming dictates that station call-letters get aired as much as possible (that way listeners are certain what station they are tuned to when they are responding to research questionnaires and diaries from ratings research services). Also, in the case of recorded promos, it is an automatic cue to announcers and technicians (at stations that are not "combo" operations) that the promo is over.

For Stations which have a sister TV or AM or FM station with the identical call letters, it is important to make the station's identification clearly separate from the others. For example, WBBM TV, WBBM NEWSRADIO 78, WBBM FM 96.

If possible, when the Promotion Director (or whoever is in charge of securing station jingle packages) orders new station jingles, try to make sure that the package includes instrumental beds with the station's musical signature that can be used for promos. This will give the station an integrated sound and first-class image.

PROMO PRODUCTION

Actual production of promotion spots may be done by the Promotion Director, or an assistant in charge of on-air promotion activities. At small television stations and many radio stations, the actual production of spots might be the responsibility of the program producer, working with guidelines or a script from the Promotion Director.

In either case, a brief review of the elements necessary to ensure good production will provide a valuable check list to make sure the production job is accomplished effectively and efficiently.

The promo producer has available all the same tools used by a producer of programs: a TV or radio studio; remote locations with film, television mini-cameras, and microphones and audio tape recorders; a control room; video and audio tape machines; one or more announcers; music; graphics; editing facilities; animation and sound effects; and qualified station technical and production personnel.

The use of elements listed above may depend on the time frame involved—a rush-job may reduce the options available—and the budget. In all cases, however, certain procedures are standard.

Plan Fully

Once the script is prepared, make a list of all special promo requirements: props, music, animation, sets, graphics, announcers, sound effects, etc.

Then take the list to a *production meeting* with key station people who will be involved in the spot's production. Usually the station will assign a director to the job. The director will know who else should be called into the meeting: supervising engineer, facilities scheduler, graphics personnel and scenic designers are some of the possibilities.

All elements important to the promo's production should be discussed during the production meeting. These include studio or location requirements such as number of cameras, lights and mikes; announcer cue-cards; props and sets; and manpower. Also cover special requirements such as costumes, make-up, and special effects. Exterior locations should be thoroughly discussed, even visited in advance with the director and crew-chief.

Studio Use

There are advantages to producing promos in the studio rather than on location. Delays because of bad weather can be avoided, and all equipment and personnel are easily at hand, should changes be required from the original plan. Time is not lost in travelling to and from a site, and lighting can remain constant. Extraneous sound such as street and airplane noises can be avoided.

Remote Locations

On the other hand, using remote locations can give a sense of reality to taped or filmed material. Elaborate set construction costs can be avoided, and a wide range of backgrounds can provide important atmosphere. Remote locations are especially useful for promos involving special news series and public affairs programs relating to the local community. Spots can show the police in action, or the family in need, or the place in question. This specificity contributes to the effectiveness of the promo.

Remote locations require some special considerations not usually associated with studio production.

- Check the weather carefully and continuously in advance.
- Are special clearances needed to film or tape at the chosen site?
- Is an engineering survey necessary to ensure availability of power and other technical requirements?
- Is the station's remote truck (for video) or film crew available when they are needed?

Mike Ahern and Carol Krause work so well together they're making my life miserable. I'm responsible for the ratings of our news team.

How can I get anyone to watch my people when Mike and Carol are on?

What's more

there's almost a chemistry between them.

If you watch them I'll lose my job. ...Think of the wife and kids.

I'll have to give back the key to the executive washroom.

PROMO STORY BOARD prepared by Channel 8 in preparation for production of an originally produced generic promo for its news. The storyboard is an invaluable planning tool, whether produced by an ad agency to give the station-client an exact idea of the audio and video in a proposed promotion spot; or prepared by the station's on-air promotion writer-producer (usually with the help of the Design Department) to show others in station management and the promo director exactly what should be done, from scene to scene.

You're not listening.

I mean, how can you knock all those years of experience in Central Indiana Mike has . . . his community perspective.

And Carol . . . . a working anchor and reporter producing health documentaries.

The two of them are so likeable I can't stand it.

So what if they're the best?

Watch Mike and Carol at 6 & 10 on 8.

Storyboards do not have to be elaborate. Even rough sketches can convey the relationships of people to objects on the screen, and show the kind of close-ups, medium or long shots desired. The more accurate the rendering, however, the more precisely the promo planner will be able to convey specific ideas and visuals to others; and the greater the chance that the resulting promotion spot will be what he or she had in mind.

- Are parking and meals readily available to the production unit?
- Will crowds of onlookers be a problem? Can they be controlled, or will extra security precautions be necessary?

Remote location videotaping has become more common with the advent in recent years of the mini-cam, or small, portable TV camera and video tape recording equipment. At a 1978 National Association of Broadcasters Convention workshop, results of a survey of BPA's membership revealed that many promotion people now use mini-cams for promo production:

KSLY-TV/Spokane, WA—Stephanie Falvey, Promotion Director:
TK-76 mini-cam used to shoot commercials and promos, including station image ID's. Reasons: Flexibility of equipment, quality of picture, ability to achieve effects not possible in the studio.

WSOC-TV/Charlotte, N.C.—Al Batten, Promotion Manager:
Uses ENG to promote station under umbrella concept of "People." Took a syndicated promotion package, customized the words, and shot many people in station service area. The spots are such a hit that when their camera crew pulls into one of the outlying towns to shoot a new promo, they are mobbed by people who want to be on the air.

WMT/Cedar Rapids, IO—Phil Arrington, Promotion Manager:
For the past 2½ years has made extensive use of their electronic field production capabilities in promos, as well as commercials and program production. Production department has EFP equipment dedicated to promo and commercial production only.

WRAL-TV/Raleigh, N.C.—Vara J. Bell, On-Air Promotion Coordinator:
Edits nearly all promos on EFP, even though must transfer program footage to ¾" tape to edit. "It's the only way to fly!"

KOAM-TV/Pittsburg, KA—Becky Kinnard, Promotion Director:
The 114th market, they still have a TK 76 for commercials, promotion and community affairs use. "It enables us to do a better job of promoting."

KTVY/Oklahoma City, OK—Jim Whittaker, Promotion Manager:
Lots of uses for ENG equipment include recent use for a full sales presentation piece on the city and the station. Uses cameras in conjunction with mini-mobile unit equipment with 1" VT recorder.

WSBT-TV/South Bend, IN—Justin Meacham, Promotion Manager:
Used ENG for "seasons greetings" spots of staff members in their offices; plus used to promote sister radio station on TV.

The TV Control Room

TV Control room technology is advancing at such a rapid state that many students now in college working with equipment dating from the 60's and 70's will find an amazing array of un-dreamed-of technical possibilities. A few among them include: frame-compressors which can reduce a full screen image to any desired size and place it anywhere on the screen; video art computers which can quickly "build" elaborate artwork, images or cartoons on the screen and animate them; and computer storage capabilities to pre-store effects, type, and graphics for later use by instant retrieval.

Engineers and graphic designers can be very creative people, especially when it comes to exploring the limits and capabilities of this new video equipment.

To fully comprehend the possibilities available in the control room, it is important to schedule experimental time, if the budget allows, to learn what the equipment will do. The time will not be wasted. It will pay dividends in more effective audience building through more attention-getting promos. Each time a new piece of equipment is added to the control room, spend some time experimenting with it, along with a director, technician and graphics person— even if the only time available is after the station's late night sign-off.

Videotape vs. Film

Both have advantages and disadvantages for the promo producer. Tape's most important advantage is instant playback. A second advantage is ease of editing. Film, on the other hand, provides greater depth of focus and some optical effects not easily available on tape.

Videotape allows easy experimentation with slow motion, stop action, and frame-by-frame editing. Multi-track audio capabilities on many tape machines make audio-track mixing (i.e., announcer's voice, music treacks and sound from the tape) easy. Tape also gives the "live-action" feel of actually "being there."

Determinations of whether film or tape are to be used must take all these factors into consideration. Again, consultation with the director will be invaluable in making the determination.

The Announcer

The announcer who reads promo copy can be just as important as the copy, itself. A superb delivery can make average copy enticing; poor delivery has often rendered brilliant copy impotent.

If possible, and if the budget allows, the promo producer should find just the right voice for each promo. This involves maintaining a library of available announcer voices in the community, with the goal of having access to a wide range of voice types and sounds. A cultured, English accent might be suitable for an intellectual drama; a rich, deep "voice-of-doom" for a serious documentary on an important local issue; and a gentle, sympathetic female or a tender drama or sensitive-issue documentary. Or, for contrast, try using the soft female voice for a serious problem program.

At most television and radio stations, however, the pressures of time and budget restrict the promo producer to station announcers. Again, they will differ in their abilities and capabilities. If it is possible to use whichever ones will work best in a given situation, the producer must know their capabilities well and capitalize on them.

In working with any announcer, especially those who work at the station regularly, here is a list of important courtesies and reminders of professional behavior:

- Read copy aloud before giving it to an announcer to be sure all difficult construction has been removed.
- Provide copy the way the announcer likes it: all capital letters, or caps and lower case? Double-spaced? Wide or narrow columns? phonetic spellings within the body of copy, or at the bottom or top of the page?
- Provide cleanly-typed copy with no typos or scratched out errors.
- Time the copy, and check the timing with the announcer.
- Provide video cues in the left-hand column where appropriate, see that a monitor is available to the announcer for following the video material.
- Provide the announcer the opportunity of hearing directors' commands and sound-on-tape in a headset.
- Rehearse copy with the announcer beforehand. Be sure he or she knows clearly which words need special emphasis, where pauses belong, and the kind of flavor or atmosphere you are looking for.
- Provide coffee or hot chocolate. It helps the announcer loosen up the voice.

If a great deal of promo copy—such as day/time tags—is read live in the form of voice-over-credit announcements, slide promos, or promo identifications, and there is no coffee/tea/hot chocolate-making equipment near or in the announcer's booth, consider it a sound investment for the Promotion Department's budget to buy one, put it there, and encourage its use.

Finally, have periodic talks with the announcing staff to reassure them of the importance to the station of effective delivery of live promo copy over program credits or in station breaks. Remind them that they are not only the sound and image of the station, but that the enthusiasm and skill they put into the copy delivery can add hundreds, even thousands of viewers to the station's programs. That means more dollars in revenue, and a better future for everyone.

Graphics

An area critical to advertising and promotion success is the graphics or design staff. Maintaining a close and positive working relationship with the design staff is essential, particularly at stations where the design activities are carried on outside the promotion department.

These artists provide on-air promotion slides, station IDs, name supers, and—in many cases—station print ads. They are invaluable when sets and props are needed.

The 1980's are a time of radical change for many medium and large market television station design and graphics departments. Traditional techniques of design are undergoing a revolution. Paper, pen, marker and film are giving way to highly sophisticated video graphics equipment. Artists will be able to construct "animated slides" while sitting at a blank table-top attached to a TV monitor. With a stylus, they can call upon a computer to create and store shapes, forms, type styles, lines, colors and symbols; and to place, move or animate them in countless ways.

On-air promotion can receive a tremendous shot in the arm when a station acquires this equipment, and the promo producer should spend a great deal of time with graphics personnel exploring new techniques.

But remember, change brings uncertainty to many individuals, and this graphics revolution may make some designers uncomfortable. Be supportive, be sensitive to their needs, and work with them to create an atmosphere of anticipation and enthusiasm for the new things they will be able to do for the Promotion Department.

Animation

The Promotion Department can spend a lot of money for animation. Why spend any? Because good animation helps call attention to the station's message and helps viewers remember the station. Most large cities have competent animation production firms. Some large stations have their own animation capabilities. From whichever source, the Promotion Director will have to determine which kind of animation best suits station needs and budgets.

Before discussing the types of animation available, remember that other departments may need animation too, and combining their budgets with the Promotion Department's budget may enable the use of better animation production facilities. The News Department may need program openings and teaser animation; the Program Department may need program logos, opens, and closes. Explore the possibilities of all going together at the same time to the same company to pay a lower rate; or of preparing similar materials which can be adapted for various department's uses.

Film Animation. This process is expensive, time-consuming, but can produce animation that is rich in detail, flowing in movement, and realistic. The process requires hand-painting part or all of thousands of different pictures, and photographing each one in sequence.

Video-tape Animation. This process requires taping an action, then editing the tape. A picture, slogan, or logo can thus be ''assembled'' a frame at a time. For instance, Channel 3 could animate it's ''three'' by assembling dozens (or hundreds) of little dots (or cubes, or tiny 3's, or newspeoples' faces) one at a time into the larger ''3'' shape. The finished ''3'' might assemble in as little as :03–:10 seconds, although the editing took hours (30 edits required for each second of screen time). The best way to accomplish this in the editing process is to start with the finished, assembled image and, with the camera and tape machine running, subtract single elements from the image one at a time. Then edit the tape.

Effects Animation. The station has the capability of creating special effects which can seem like animation. Camera and color adjustments, video feedback distortion, and other techniques should be explored with station engineers. Again, scheduling facilities time for experimentation can be useful for learning what can be done inhouse. Be sure to keep notes on how various effects are achieved so that they can be recalled in a hurry when needed in actual promo production.

And remember—equipment and capabilities change at a rapid rate. What is not possible this year might be easy to do next year.

Computerized Video Animation. During the 1970's, computer animation began to offer a wide new range of visual styles that made startling openings, bridges, credits and promos. This mode uses a computer to create, build and imaginatively distort colorful images on the video screen for instant taping. While computer animation lacks the impression of depth that computerized film animation (the type used in the film, *2001,* can give, it compensates with lower costs, shorter production time (a job might be completed in only a few hours), and a splendid array of visual effects.

Computerized Film Animation. Coupling a computer to a film camera for efficient frame-by-frame exposures and pre-planned tiny movement can produce dazzling animation effects. The 1968 movie "2001" represented the first mass public exposure of this technique, and ABC-TV quickly followed by encorporating similar special effects into its network movie openings. Various television stations around the nation used variations of the effect and its decendants for news and movie opens and promo spots. The art has progressed considerably, and though relatively expensive, can capture audience attention very well.

Video Library. The station with frequent need for animated material might want to establish a video library of effects by writing to companies which produce the different kinds of animation listed above and requesting a loan of demonstration tapes, to be dubbed and held for future reference. Even without a video library, an on-air promotion producer should request samples from various animation houses when the need for animation arises. Learn what is

Radio station WHYI 100 FM Stereo in Hollywood, Florida, is promoted exclusively as "Y-100." This animation highlights their station image commercial, used on area TV stations.

available, the quality of a company's work, and get some good ideas along the way.

Music and Sound Effects

Music and sound effects can be used in promos to attract attention, create mood or atmosphere, evoke emotional responses from audiences, and underscore copy points.

There are usually three sources for music and effects: the program, itself; a library of pre-recorded music and sound effects; and originally prepared material.

Program Music. When work must be done in a hurry, this is usually the most efficient approach. Look to the program being promoted. Usually, behind the opening or closing credits, there is music selected by the producer for it's appropriateness to the program. And sound effects (doors creaking, cars squealing, people shrieking, etc.) can be found in the body of the program. Be sure to check with the producer of the program or the station's Program Department to find out if promo rights to the program music exist. They usually do.

Library Music & Effects. Collections of pre-recorded music and sound effects can be purchased for specific uses; or the companies or libraries which sell them can work with the on-air promo producer to find and supply very specific pieces of music or sound effects on an individual basis. The different kinds of music range from classical to country, and from jazz to romantic instrumental. They include very short "stingers" only a few seconds long, up to much longer original compositions.

In most cities, lists of companies providing these services are found in phone book yellow pages under Music Libraries.

Original Music. This category includes music which has been composed especially for Promotion Department use. It is the most costly method of acquiring music, but a radio or television station often needs a series of "jingles" for various station image, news, contest, and/or program promotion use. The following tips on buying a music and jingle package are excerpted from a presentation to a recent BPA Seminar by Bo Donovan of San Diego's Tuesday Productions:

Plan Ahead. Begin to get serious about the production project at least six months before it is scheduled to air. (Three months for radio). Time passes very quickly, and the Promotion Director needs all the time possible to plan and execute each step of a promo campaign.

Select the Production House. Make a list of all known musical production firms, contact each, and request a general presentation of their work. Ask for tapes that reflect the quality of their production, but don't expect to receive samples that are just right for the station's current need. Listen to everyone's tape from start to finish—that perfect sound might be at the end of the tape. Eliminate all firms that don't live up to quality standards, or that have never done radio or TV work before. It's important to look at all firms, including the small and obscure. The least known might be the best, and the least expensive.

Pick finalists. From the three or four best presentations, select two finalists. Ask each of them to visit the station for a personal presentation of their work and a candid discussion of the current project. Schedule different firms on different days; set aside a sufficient amount of time—as much as two hours—and be sure other key people in the project attend the meeting, perhaps including the General Manager.

Questions they should ask you:

- How much are you prepared to spend?
- What are your image and marketing goals?
- What is your target date?
- What are your programming and promotional strengths and weaknesses?
- What are the station's needs in terms of number of individual pieces of music, lengths, and their applications?
- Describe your competition in detail.
- Explain the contents, style and details of your last music/jingle package.

Questions you should ask them:

- What is their production procedure from start to finish?
- What are the terms of the agreement? (Ask for a sample agreement form.)
- What are costs and payment terms?
- What is their production timetable?
- What are their guarantee policies?

Make a final commitment based on the following:

- The quality of their work.
- Their understanding of the station's needs.
- Price. Price is the least important of the three, because without quality and understanding, a low fee might well produce poor quality or ill-suited work that is money wasted. (Caution: Do not buy "bulk." Select for quality and efficiency. The "bulk," or large volume of extra material the station pays for may sit on a shelf unused.)

Final Input and Direction. Once an agreement is signed, it's time for rough demos and concepts on the complete package. Visit the firm's offices or studios for this step. Approve each element and have a complete understanding of their direction, but be flexible. This is a creative production firm. Trust their judgment and let them create.

Final Production. Multi-track recording will now begin. Ask that the station's package be produced in more than one session, especially if five or more seperate cuts are involved. This provides time to reflect on the first stage of the project and add or subtract elements. It gives the creative energies on both sides a chance to relax and reapply themselves.

Let the creators create. Any production company will welcome you to their studios, but you are not being invited to produce. The creation and production of quality motivational music is a highly specialized and technical process. The best work is performed for the client who provides an exciting and cooperative atmosphere. Your presence can cause the producer to be more concerned with playing "host" than producing the package. Judge the product when it arrives at the station and avoid the potentially lethal "Hollywood Flash"—symptoms of which are dim lights, large and loud speakers, lots of knobs, dials and meters, and music that somehow "sounded better in the studio."

Edits and Mixes. If, in fact, you don't attend the studio session, anticipate all the station's needs in detail and ask for every edit or sound mix that will be needed. Quality edits can rarely be made later at the station.

PROMO SCHEDULING

Once promos are written and produced, the voice-over-credit announcements, slide/announcer spots, and film or tape promos must be placed in the schedule in the most effective audience-building ways. Two key principles apply: saturation, and placement. Saturation has to do with the quantity of promotional announcements put in the schedule, and placement pertains to the value of the positions in the schedule where promos are placed.

Saturation. A basic goal in placing a promo in a schedule is to try to air it enough times so that every viewer will see it at least once. No program draws 100% of the viewers in a market at one time. Therefore promos must be placed more often than once to achieve the minimum goal.

But how does the promo scheduler know when the goal has been reached?

The starting point is to know what is meant by the term "gross rating point," or GRP. The GRP, simply defined, is 1% of the total potential audience in the market. It follows that 100 GRPs equal 100% of the total potential audience in the market—the minimum goal for a program promo.

If time permits, though it rarely does, the promotion scheduler can look to ratings books to see what the ratings are for each position in the schedule in which a promo airs, and keep adding promos until the total accumulated rating points equal 100. This is 100% of the potential audience, or 100 GRPs.

To reach every potential viewer twice, keep adding promos until 200 GRPs are reached. For very important promotions such as major specials or the start of new programs, the goal might be 800 or 1000 GRPs. That means each person in the market would see the promo 8, or 10 times.

In fact, about half of the viewers in the market will have seen the promo 10 times, with about 25% seeing it less than 10, and 25% seeing it more than 10 times.

Promotion Expert Dave Course, in his book on on-air promotion, *Stroking Themselves*, explains the practical way to determine the number of spots that will equal 100 GRPs for any station:

> "In a sweep rating book for a similar rating period, under 'day-part averages,' find the total week average rating (Sun.–Sat., Sign-On to Sign-Off. With Arbitron, you'll have to settle for 7 AM–1 AM). That's the rating your spots would get if they were run evenly throughout the week's schedule. Since they're not, deduct a third of that, to compensate for the scarcity of prime-time spots for program commercials. Shared IDs get you into prime time, but this formula applies to full-dress :30's and :60's.
>
> "Let's say the average rating over the total week was a 10. Deduct a third, and you come up with 6 & 2/3s. In order to go around your universe once (100 GRPs), just divide that into 100. The spot will have to run 15 times in availabilities that average 6 & 2/3 rating to pile up the needed 100 gross rating points."

Course further advises that in that situation, no promo should be produced unless there was a certainty of getting it aired 15 times.

And he recommends working closely with traffic personnel to be sure that they completely understand the GRP goal for each promo, since they can be very helpful in getting additional exposures.

In the example Course uses above, with 15 promo placements called for, the promos should only be spread evenly through the week if they are generic in nature, as a news campaign might be. Otherwise, for episodic promos and promos for specials, use of on-air should begin a week in advance and build to a peak on the day of air for a prime time program (or peak the day before for a daytime program.)

This strategy would mean placing one promo seven days in advance, most probably during the same time the program will air. The rest of the schedule would build as follows, to achieve a 200 GRP schedule (30 promo exposures):

> 6 days prior to air—1 time
> 5 days prior to air—1 time
> 4 days prior to air—2 times
> 3 days prior to air—4 times
> 2 days prior to air—6 times
> 1 day prior to air —7 times
> Day of air   —8 times

Using this formula, a station with low ratings may air some promos as many as 50 or more times a week. Some people at the station and a few frequent viewers might complain that it is on the air too much. The truth is, it is not—if the station's goal is to build audiences by letting as many people as possible know about the program. No one watches a station as much as the people employed there, and their families. Their views on the frequency of promos should not be taken into consideration.

Reaching everyone in the potential audience once is rarely enough. Reach is important, but "frequency" is just as important. "Frequency" refers to the number of times a potential viewer is exposed to a promotional message. Other tools besides :30 or :60 second spots are needed to increase the frequency with which a message about a program gets to the potential viewer. Voice-over-credit announcements, slide/announcer and shared ID spots can reinforce promo messages and increase frequency.

Again, to quote from Course's book:

"A station is lucky to average 15 promos per day. That's 5,500 per year. As a ballpark figure, in markets #40-50, let's say an average of 100,000 people were watching each. That's 550 million impressions. Voice-over-credit announcements on 3 or 4 syndicated programs stretch that to over 650 million.

"By getting a provocative message onto every staton ID, and regularly in prime-time, the station can triple the number of impressions to 1,860,000,000. That's nearly *TWO BILLION*."

Placement. Promo placement in the schedule to achieve the GRP goal should not be random. In addition to building the frequency of promos as the day of air approaches, the promotion scheduler must also look for audiences similar to that expected for the program being promoted.

In the ideal situation, the Promotion Department—like an ad agency— would research every program to learn from ratings its comparison (age groups, sex, and other demographic data). But there is rarely time for such on-going research. Instead, promo schedulers must be generally familiar with all program ratings and demographics. That information can come from the station's research staff, from program producers, from the Program Director, the station's ad agency, or other sources; but it has a basis in the Promotion Director's personal familiarity with the station's programs and audience profiles.

Once the audience composition of existing programs in the schedule is known, and the anticipated audience for an upcoming program is surmised (or learned), the promotion scheduler should match up the two. If it is a sports program or feature, promote in around programs men are likely to watch— news, other sports programs, documentaries, war movies. If it is a soap opera, promote it around other soaps, cooking shows, light feature and afternoon talk shows, and other programs likely to have similar audience composition. This way, people most likely to have an interest in the program are the ones exposed to the promotion. Response to promos will be greater, more efficient.

Summary. By combining the saturation and placement strategies, the station builds the frequency of well-placed promotion spots to achieve a predetermined amount promotion exposure to the audience. Promotion scheduling is not hit-and-miss, or random. If the promo-writing and production are good, the result will be increased audiences. (Assuming the program is good.)

CHAPTER 17

Publicity *

For the broadcaster, publicity was defined earlier as free newspaper or magazine space, or air time on another radio or TV station devoted to comment on programs, personalities, staff or activities.

Publicity is usually generated by the station Promotion Director, who keeps the press informed about things the station wants publicized. But publicity may occur as a result of spontaneous comment by members of the press on station programs or personalities. In such cases, the Promotion Director provides additional information and photos for support, or background information that might help to minimize negative comment, or place it in perspective.

Like advertising and on-air promotion, publicity has advantages and disadvantages.

A major disadvantage is that the station does not directly control what is said in print or other public comment. Promotion Dieectors can use press releases, press kits, personal relationships and many other devices and techniques to try to influence what is said by others, but there is no direct control over a free press. This disadvantage is also a major advantage. Because the station does not control what is said, the resulting publicity is highly credible with potential listeners and viewers.

Another advantage of publicity helps to compensate for the risk of occasional negative comment and criticism. For the budget-conscious station, costs of maintaining publicity contacts are lower than costs of buying advertising space, producing TV broadcast and some on-air promotions. But most importantly, the newspaper space or air time gained by publicity is free.

*This chapter was prepared with advice and consultation from Beryl Spector, an officer of the Broadcasters Promotion Association and Public Information Director of public station WMHT-FM/TV, Schenectady, New York.

In actual practice, many stations capitalize on their advertising, promotion and even on-air promotion activities to increase puclicity for the station, and call additional attention to campaigns.

The pages ahead examine basic elements of a broadcast station's publicity and public relations efforts, including materials a station must produce, events a station must sponsor, and the kinds of personal contact that should exist between broadcast stations and members of the press and broadcast media.

PRESS RELATIONS

As spokesperson for the station, it is the Promotion Director's (or Publicity Manager's, Public Relations Manager's, or Press Representative's) responsibility to keep the press informed about station activities and programming. It is the press's job, however, to decide whether what the station has to say is important, relevant or newsworthy. The station can "influence" these decisions by following certain basic tenets of good public relations. Just how well the appropriate member of the Promotion Department knows the press will determine to some degree how much space the station gets, and how often it gets it.

Get to Know the Press

Visit newspapers in the market. Meet the TV and/or radio editor, the arts editor, the city editor, the sports editor, the business editor, the feature editor of each paper. It will take a number of visits and a lot of time initially to get to know all these people, plus columnists and other reporters. But it is worth every bit of time it takes.

In the case of those who must be dealt with most often, get to know them well enough to know their likes, dislikes, needs and interests. Learn what the station can provide to help them (and therefore itself) the most, and in what form information and materials should be provided. Should releases be mailed or handcarried? Do phone call follow-ups help? What formats work best for various kinds of materials?

Investigate the chain of command at each paper. Should everything go through a certain editor? Does he (or she) consider the station as exclusive territory, or can the business editor be dealt with directly when publicizing a financial program; or the "lifestyle" editor when there's a new cooking show; or does the city editor want everything funneled across the city desk?

Know when press contacts are "on deadline" and avoid visiting or calling at that hour. Look for opportunities to meet the press away from the station and their offices. Join the local press club or other similar organizations. Attend occasional press conferences in the community which the station has been asked to cover—there is often opportunity for social contact with the press at such functions.

Once a good working relationship has been established with the press, notes (especially "thank you" notes) and phone calls can replace visits but, whenever possible, hand deliver the really important releases.

Get to Know the Newspapers

Just as important as getting to know the reporters is an understanding of the papers that employ them. Be armed with a thorough knowledge of all newspapers in the market. Read as many as possible each day. Keep an eye out for a series of articles the station might be able to tie into. Check on what the competition is getting into the paper. Be able to congratulate a particular reporter on a well-written feature or article. Subscribe to a clipping service if you can't read all papers often, but remember, a clipping service provides only articles that mention the station. The rest of the paper is just as important in helping to establish that all-important relationship with the press.

Investigate the "slow" news days in the market and take advantage of them. Thanksgiving, Christmas and New Year's Day are traditionally slow days and news geared to break then might get more space. Also, vacation periods for a key reporter, if known, might provide an "opening" in the paper for more of the station's material.

Be Easy To Reach

Accessibility is essential to maintaining good press relationships. Be sure the press have a home phone number of an appropriate station contact for after hours and weekends. Make sure, too, that the station's press contact can be reached at the station at all times, and that a call from a reporter on deadline can get through to that person in a meeting.

If the press contact can't answer an inquiry directly, he or she should be able to get the answer as quickly as possible from the person who can. The General Manager should be available when needed. And make sure that the GM is willing to talk to the press when "the chips are down" as well as when things are "going great." A "no comment" reflects badly on the station in most instances and may give a reporter the impetus to dig deeper.

Supervise Station Press Contacts

When a meeting is arranged between a member of the press and a station executive not skilled at press interviews, make certain that all the necessary homework has been done. The executive to be interviewed should be carefully prepared on the subject matter, and perhaps even given a "devil's advocate" rehearsal of anticipated questions. The press contact can help the interviewee to organize the topic, have a firm grip on the subject, and respond in an orderly fashion. Such preparation can go a long way toward assuring a positive rather than a negative story.

Here's a convenient checklist for Promotion Directors who must hand-hold other station executives through potentially sensitive meetings with the press:

- Decide beforehand on the specific points that are to be communicated, and list them in writing.
- Control the interview by sticking to those points.
- Don't let a reporter put words in the executive's mouth. Be alert for reporters who begin with "Would you say that. . . ." Such statements may end up in quotes if the executive says "yes."
- Don't be evasive. If an answer isn't known, say so and try to get it. If a topic is not to be discussed, say so and give a good reason why.
- Don't be long-winded. Keep answers brief, concise, quotable.
- Don't say "no comment." It reeks of evasion and raises more questions.
- Remain calm. Don't insult or ridicule a reporter.
- Don't be defensive. Stick to positive aspects of the situation.
- Don't rely on anything that is said remaining "off the record."
- Don't cancel an interview once it has been set without good reason.
- If an unknown reporter calls on the phone, use a screening technique such as a call-back to assure his or her authenticity.

Some corporations have instituted the "mock-interview" technique. Executives who need to build skills in dealing with the press are subjected to practice sessions. They learn how to present the company's point of view without stress, embarrassment, or lack of poise. Interviews are recorded on videotape and played back so that the executive can assess the results and learn from the experience.

Be Resourceful

When dealing with more than one paper, look for several angles in a story so that each reporter has something different or exclusive to write about. Keep an eye out for the local angle in a national program and underscore or circle it in red on the station's (or network's) release.

Always be aware of "connections"—where the station's story will tie into another, or where several seemingly unrelated things that are happening can be put together into one neat package.

Be Accurate

Check and double check dates and times of program and spellings of names, etc. If a mistake is found after a release has gone out don't hesitate to admit the mistake by phoning in the correction immediately. Another technique is to publish a "corrections and changes" page in a followup release. This is a very important "must" in maintaining good press relations.

Keep up-to-date mailing lists. Newspapers are constantly getting material sent to former or even deceased staff. They will more than likely toss the material in the "circular" file.

Be Honest

A good working relationship with the press depends to a large degree on the Promotion Director's credibility and reliability as a news source. Don't fudge answers to questions. Be completely factual. If the Promotion Department is doing something "gimmicky"—and much promotion is just that—then call it a gimmick. Earn respect for honesty. The press will usually be delighted to go along with the fun.

Always Follow Through

Be sure to provide all the material promised—the details, biographical information as needed, photos or photo possibilities, etc. Then, remind the reporter about the story but don't badger. There is a difference in approach and a fine line between being persistent and being pushy. Know when to back off.

Remember, the original approach to convince the publication to cover the idea has to be one of the most difficult parts of the assignment. Don't blow it by dropping the ball or throwing roadblocks in the path of the reporter when he or she is carrying out the station's idea!

Notes of appreciation to newspaper reporters and photographers, to their superiors, even to the key editor if appropriate, and to any individuals at the station who cooperated are important. Such courtesies can only help improve cooperation when the next creative story idea comes along.

Reaction

In most cases where a story in the press is negative, the station's best posture is to "take it like a man." Over-reaction to criticism draws more attention to the controversy or negative aspects of the problem. This is especially true of criticism of specific programs.

The best defense against unwarranted "attacks" is a strong, ongoing positive public relations campaign which emphasizes the station's strengths.

Nevertheless, if there must be response to a newspaper, a broadcast station should remember that its own air is a supurb, proven vehicle for reaching people in large numbers. The disadvantage is that the people reached might be different than the ones exposed to the original criticism in print, thereby extending the reach of the negative remarks. On the other hand, reaction by letter to the paper (free) or by purchased ad space (costly) limits the exposure of the controversy to those who are already familiar with it.

If, for example, a newspaper critic blasts a TV station for cluttering its own air time with self-serving promotional announcements, several possibilities exist for the station—it can:

• Do nothing. Ignoring the comment is often the best approach. The critic will go on to other things, having gotten his frustrations off his chest.

• Respond with a reasoned letter or ad in the newspaper about the valuable viewer service that promotion announcements are in letting people know about upcoming programs. Avoid reference to the critic's article. (In no case should a response be irate or attack the newspaper in kind.)
• Respond indirectly with production of a modest schedule of on-air announcements for the station's promos, explaining their value and effectiveness in keeping viewers aware of station programming—again, without mention of the original newspaper criticism.
• A combination of both the direct and the indirect response.

Perhaps the best approach would have been for the station's press rep or Promotion Director to have such close contact with the critic that such an attack could have been foreseen and avoided in the first place.

PRESS RELATIONS SUMMARY

• Give the media good, honest, regular and prompt service.
• Provide factual and accurate information.
• Adhere to deadlines.
• Don't ''double-plant''; an exclusive must be exclusive.
• Maintain the respect and cooperation of station management in dealing with the press. Be a positive influence at interviews.
• Plan a publicity calander, including story ideas and items, possible interviews, photo ideas and layouts, press trips, and other elements; and spread them around equitably among the appropriate local press.
• Don't overwrite or pad copy. Keep it clear and concise.
• Accept press phone calls.
• Return press phone calls promptly.
• Maintain up-to-date mailing lists.
• Don't be talked into ''buying'' an editorial story by placing an ad.
• Don't try to sell a shallow story.
• Know the press and other media well: their personalities, deadlines, and media characteristics.
• Don't complain if nothing ever comes of an idea. Just take it to another paper.
• Don't criticize the end product of an idea, even if it turns out badly.
• Don't ask for a correction unless there is a glaring error.
• Don't promise what can't be delivered.
• Don't expect miracles. The station is competing with others for a limited amount of space.

PRESS MATERIALS.

After personal contact with the press, the backbones of any publicity effort are print and photo materials.

Basic print materials include:

- Press Releases
- Photographs
- Press Kits

- Logs, schedules or listings
- Updates, changes and corrections

Press Releases

Even in a small community, the number of people the station wants to inform about programming and other information is so great that personal contact and phone calls to each media person, ad agency, community and business leader would be an impossible burden.

So, as many other companies and organizations do, broadcasters rely heavily on written press releases. A press release is a brief, straight-forward, simply and attractively presented positive delivery of factual information.

It must be brief because the recipients of press releases generally receive many—sometimes hundreds—each day, and there is little time to wade through pages and pages to discover essential facts.

It must be straight-forward because editors at newspapers and other media are quick to recognize obvious persuasive writing and reject attempts by Promotion Directors to shape their opinions on broadcast programs and matters for them. They look for factual information, and especially the traditional "inverted pyramid" journalistic style of writing.

Releases should be simply and attractively worded. Simplicity is necessary in releases which go to newspaper editors because their readers will have difficulty with unfamiliar words and confusing sentence construction.

Release Format. Members of the press have come to expect a traditional format. Certain rules are more-or-less standard:

Releases should *always* be typewritten. Editors are very busy people, inundated by hundreds of releases a day. To subject them to hand-written releases will cause resentment. More likely, the release won't be read or taken seriously.

- Use $8\frac{1}{2}'' \times 11''$ white paper.
- Type on only one side of the page.
- Leave at least $1\frac{1}{2}''$ margins at the left, right, and bottom of every page; and at the top of all pages beyond the first.
- Start the first page at least ⅓ of the way down the page. (Some suggest beginning at the middle of the sheet of paper.)
- Double or triple space between lines.
- Type "-more-" at the bottom of each page, except the last, for a multipage story.
- Put several number signs (#) at the end of the release, centered, as:

#   #   #

- Number all pages consistently at the top of the sheet, beginning with page 2. Many release writers recommend a key word from the headline be used next to the page number, as this example from a release about a special on animals: ANIMALS—2

• Indent each paragraph at least five, but no more than eight, spaces.

• End each page with a completed sentence or paragraph. This makes it easier for the editor to follow complete thoughts, and avoids incomplete communication if the following or second page of a release has become misplaced.

• Provide release date information at the top of page one of each release. Usually this takes the form, "FOR IMMEDIATE RELEASE," meaning that the editor can use the material at any time, beginning immediately. If, however, it is important that information should be withheld until a certain day or time, the wording might be:

"FOR RELEASE AFTER 9:00 AM, MONDAY, JANUARY 12, 1982."

• At the end of each release (or on page one, if there is room) provide a name and phone number for the reader to contact for more information. This is usually done as:

CONTACT: Barbara Smith
(333)555-1234

or:

FOR MORE INFORMATION: Barbara Smith
(333)555-1234

Release Headlines. Headlines on releases serve two purposes, in this order: first, they should be designed to get the attention and interest of the reader of the release; and second, they may suggest actual headline treatment if the release is picked up in a newspaper.

Because the first purpose is more important than the second, the length (or brevity) of a broadcast station release headline is not as important as the content. Some releases might have short heads:

SMITH NAMED TO WXXX SALES DEPARTMENT

Others might have long headlines:

WXXX FALL SEASON FEATURES 8 NEW SERIES:
MAJOR STARS INCLUDE RICHARD BURTON, DOLLY PARTON,
MARK HAMMILL
———
DEBUT SET FOR OCTOBER 2ND

Since the top third or half of the first page of a release has been left empty of copy, the headline goes in there, with ample room above and below for an editor to try out various heads to conform to the amount of space available in the paper. Since the headline is usually a condensed version of the most important information from the first paragraph, it is sometimes easier to write *after* the first paragraph is composed.

Each line of a headline should be centered on the center of the page, as shown above.

News Release Style. News releases should always follow the basic jour-nalistic "inverted pyramid" style. That is, the lead (or first) paragraph should contain virtually all essential information about *what, who, where, when,* and *why,* referred to as the *five W's.*

Subsequent paragraphs should provide additional information in order of decreasing importance. The least important information should be last.

The inverted pyramid looks like this:

WHAT WHO WHEN WHERE WHY	IMPORTANT DETAILS
(Whatever information	LESSER DETAILS
is essential)	MISC.
	INFO.

The pyramid, of course, gives reference to the importance of information rather than quantity. First paragraphs should always be very short, limited to three to five lines.

The inverted pyramid provides the newspaper editor with essential mate-rial at the start so a judgment can be made on its importance. It also enables the editor to shorten the release to fit into available newspaper space by cutting off paragraphs starting at the end, with assurance that the eliminated material is the least important.

How long should a news release be? Ninety percent of all broadcast station releases should be written according to a rule of *twos:*

· Sentences should be no more than *two* typewritten lines.
· Paragraphs should be no more than *two* sentences.
· Releases should be no more than *two* pages.

There are times when content will dictate longer sentences, paragraphs, and news releases. However, the rule of *twos* provides a goal for the release writer which forces brevity and clarity. Remember, also, that one typewritten line translates into approximately two lines of print in the standard 2″ newspa-per column width. So the rule of *twos* keeps sentences and paragraphs in news-papers to quickly read, easily understood dimensions.

Precision is another essential in news release writing. Any editor working quickly to assemble a paper wants to be able to rely unquestionably on all spelling, address, location, day and time information. If this information is wrong in the release and therefore wrong in the newspaper, it is the newspaper that will get the angry phone calls from readers—not the station. The reader will assume the newspaper was at fault. It doesn't take long for most editors to learn which stations regularly provide unproofed or incorrect information, and to discard those releases. Editors can develop animosity toward the public-ity person, the Promotion Department, and perhaps the entire station, and may form an overall impression of the station as a place that produces shoddy work.

As mentioned earlier, news releases should describe accurately rather than praise extravagantly. Avoid adjectives that make value judgments for those who will read the release. In describing TV and radio programming and personalities, avoid words such as: *lovely, delightful, intelligent, marvelous, divine, wonderful, excellent, superb, exciting,* and other such words which are more the province of critics.

Descriptive words such as *provocative, stimulating, youthful, colorful* and *fast-paced* are good alternatives.

Feature Releases. A feature release is usually not "hard" news. Rather, it focuses on some singular aspect of a program, person, place, event or activity. It provides more information for the reader who might be interested in narrower areas. It gives the editor the option of lengthening a news release with additional information; or running a longer, entirely separate "feature story" on the subject.

There are several types of feature release of particular interest to broadcast publicity writers:

• *Background Feature.* The background feature provides information to the editor on the following kinds of areas:

- Why the program was produced.
- What costs were involved.
- Who started this annual activity.
- When, and why an activity began.
- Previous similar endeavors.
- Research that made a program or activity possible and meaningful.

• *Personality Feature.* The personality feature is a close look at a particular individual associated with the station, a program, or a station event. The approach should involve a human interest angle—what is it that makes this person different, special, or the same as others? How does this person get a difficult or unusual job done? What special character traits does the person bring to the job?

Personality features should avoid the biography described later in this section.

• *Highlight Features.* A highlight feature singles out a particular aspect of the program, event or activity for close scrutiny. Human interest angles are again best. Each program will suggest angles of special interest. Any individual item listed above under "background features" might be singled out for a special release. It differs from the background feature by presenting only one "highlight," rather than a broad spectrum of background information.

All feature releases about radio or television programs or specific station activities are designed to help call attention to those programs or activities. So essential information such as title, day, time, and place should be in a second paragraph where they will not be cut by an editor with only a small space to fill; or where the reader will be sure to see that really important information.

A good approach to use in determining possible feature releases is to look again at the list of those things which motivate human behavior. Find those elements of what must be publicized and prepare feature releases that call special attention to things that people want to get out of life.

Generic Releases. "Generic release" refers to a news release about a program series consisting of more than one episode. This release is often an official announcement of a series that a station will run, and should contain basic information about:

- Series start date and time.
- Series star(s).
- General content (type of programming).
- Sponsors, or underwriters.
- Production team, effort, and locations.

It should not attempt to provide specific information on each program in the series. Appended to a generic release might be one-paragraph descriptions of each program, or a separate news release about each.

Other Specialized Releases. There are several other specialized kinds of releases. The *announcement release* is designed to be the first public notice of a program. Like the generic release, it may be longer than two pages because it contains all available information about the program, including sponsor or underwriter mention. The *follow-up release* is one that follows an announcement or news release and adds or changes additional information. If, for example, an additional personality is added to a program's cast, a follow-up release featuring that information may be picked up by editors. Because readers may not have seen, or editors may not have used, the announcement release, the follow-up must also contain all essential information about the program, such as other stars, day, time, station, and—to a lesser degree—program content. This time, however, the details of content are omitted.

In cases where a program or activity grows considerably in scope following the announcement release, a *wrap-up release* may be advisable. Prepared close to air (or the time of the event), it pulls together the basic information from the announcement release and subsequent follow-up information, providing everything that is known and relevant in one place for editors, readers, and station files.

While not technically a release, a *biography* is an essential kind of background information publicity personnel must regularly prepare. The Promotion Director of a station should always have on hand a "bio" of the General Manager and key on-air personnel. In addition, brief bios for any station personnel who regularly make public appearances (Sales Director, Community Services Director, Promotion Director, News Director) are advisable. They are useful when the person must give a speech, accept an award, or otherwise represent the station; and when a promotion occurs warranting a release to consumer or trade press. Bios of program stars provide feature writers at newspapers information to build their own articles from both the station's "personality feature" and the bio. Finally, it is important to be able to respond quickly to press needs for personal information in the event of unusual occurrences ranging from surprise visits to calamities, tragedies and sudden illness or death.

FOR IMMEDIATE RELEASE:
October 24, 1980

For Further Information
Scott Hunker 444-3332

NEWS RELEASE

"FROM STUDIO 4 IN DOWNTOWN ST. LOUIS...NIGHT MOVES!"
AN INNOVATIVE TELEVISION EXPERIENCE SATURDAY, NOVEMBER 22
ON CHANNEL 4

KMOX-TV brings another first to St. Louis television with the innovative, "Night Moves!" The half-hour variety program is scheduled for broadcast on Saturday, November 22 at 10:30PM on Channel 4.

This "pilot" episode features the unique sound of St. Louis' own "Jasmine." These two gifted musicians combine their talent to open the program with a medley of "The Lady Is A Tramp" and "Tuxedo Junction." "Jasmine" features Carol Schmidt on piano and Michele Isam on sax. The ladies compliment one another with their special blend of harmony in the opening number.

The second segment of "Night Moves" showcases another native of our area, comedian Dan Chopin. Local viewers will appreciate Dan's routine as he takes the audience from "White Castle" to traffic court.

Val and Frank LaFemina, a local husband and wife dance team which has received national television attention, are featured in the third segment of "Night Moves." Val and Frank perform their original choreography to "I May Not Be There When You Want Me But I'm Right On Time."

"Jasmine" ends the evening with their rendition of the Carole Bayer Sager hit, "Movin' Out."

"Night Moves" was recorded before a live audience in KMOX-TV's "Studio 4" and features a "night club" atmosphere, allowing for a valuable "audience reaction" element. The program showcases local talent.

Bobby Day is the host of "Night Moves."

"Night Moves" was produced by Jan Landis and directed by Skip Goodrum.

*   *   *

Ⓚ KMOX-TV ST. LOUIS, MISSOURI 63102 ● ONE MEMORIAL DRIVE (314) 621-2345

This program-oriented news release from KMOX-TV, St. Louis, tells the reader the following things in the first paragraph: a) The program title. b) The station, date, time, and channel number. c)The program is an innovative variety show. d) It is new. e) It is a St. Louis TV first. f) The program's length.

The second paragraph quickly follows with a brief description of the program's content. Further details are added in subsequent paragraphs. There is room at the top for editors to re-write the headline; and release date, station contact, and phone number are evident at the top of the page.

Pre-printed station letterhead helds call attention to the various kinds of press material a station sends out. This set of letterhead from Washington D.C.'s WMAL Radio is an example of what a station needs.

Biographies are most effective when they follow this format:

Begin with an opening paragraph or two to sum up the person's major accomplishments or achievements and state his/her current job position; look for, and include a theme that ties these things together (life dedicated to public service; 40 years in the broadcast business, or, star of many major television dramas over the years); and then go to chronological order to discuss the highlights of the person's life.

This sequence uses a person's strengths to draw interest in his or her life, then presents that life in an easily understood form of organization that shows personal or professional growth.

Release Distribution Patterns. Some stations release stories on an "event" basis, as things happen. Others group stories together into a "press bundle" for mailing weekly, or twice-weekly. Lead time is very important. Make sure that the press is advised well in advance of an event or program so that they will have time to cover it adequately. Important releases close to newspaper deadlines might best be hand-delivered to major papers.

Photographs

Photographs are important to television promotion because they show, visually, what will be seen. They are important to radio promotion because they satisfy public curiosity about the faces behind the voices. There are other important uses for photos, as well.

Photos for the Press. Because photos add interest to a story, newspapers like to use them. But they have very specific needs.

The Head Shot. This is the most common publicity photo used by both radio and TV stations, for consumer or trade press. It is a vertical close-up of a star, personality or staff member. These should be always available for all key station personnel for whom there are biographies on file; and for key stars or hosts of all the station's programs. Copies should be supplied to all daily, weekly, and bi-weekly newspapers in the market area for their files, or for quick use. They should be updated annually with newer photos. These photos are easy for a newspaper to use, because newspaper column width lends itself most readily to vertical photos. Head shots should be crisp, clear pictures of people from just above the middle of the chest up, with a little head room above the top of the head. Plain backgrounds which contrast with the dark or light shade of clothing and hair color are preferred. Props relating to a program might add interest and meaning.

The Mood Shot. Usually a "head shot," the mood photo provides additional elements of interest through dramatic lighting, expression, and sometimes costume, make-up or hair-style to place a performer in a program's context and give the audience an idea of the mood of the program.

The Group Shot. For most press uses, two people—at most three—are all that should be included in a "group" photo. Such photos can show relationships between characters in a dramatic production, or can feature news anchorpeople or program hosts. Again, if possible, vertical shots are preferred. If more than two people are to be photographed, they should be arranged to permit a vertical composition.

When the budget allows, both vertical and horizontal photos should be provided, giving the newspaper the option of using a larger two, three- or four-column space in a different kind of layout.

Format. It is best if the photographer uses a camera which takes negatives larger than 35mm.—2¼ x 2¼ negative size provides sharp, clear photos when enlarged to the 8 x 10″ glossy print size that newspapers prefer to receive. Larger sizes are not necessary, except for color.

Color. Use of color by the press is relatively rare, but consistent and predictable. Possibilities for networks include national magazines such as *Time, Newsweek* and *People* to *TV Guide* covers and features and the covers of newspaper Sunday supplement TV magazines. TV stations compete for the supplement covers. To do so, they must provide exceptionally good quality, crisp, clear color with broad reader interest. The following factors help in providing color that might be used:

Limit color photos to one or two people, in medium to close shots, with some program-related material in the picture. It might be a prop, costume, set piece, or background that gives the photo the special interest, but the focus must be on the personality.

Have the photographer shoot with a camera that produces a 4 x 5″ positive transparency, rather than a negative. These enable the best possible reproduction, especially important to supplements which are printed on low-quality newsprint paper. Offer the newspaper its choice of the original 4 x 5″ transparency, or a color print.

Guarantee the newspaper exclusivity. No paper wants to run a full-color shot on its supplement cover only to discover that an identical shot—in color or black and white—has been used somewhere else. Take several photos to the paper and let the editor choose what he wants.

Meet with the local supplement editors at least once or twice a year to discuss their needs, and when a possible subject for color placement comes along (either from original material the station generates or from a network or syndicator), call the editor and discuss it as a possibility. Don't expect a commitment from the editor, who will want to keep his options open. But look for encouragement.

Cutlines. All photos should be supplied with descriptive cutlines attached. The standard procedure for a station is to type a 3–6 line description of the photo on the bottom half of an 8 x 10″ sheet of paper. The top of the sheet is then taped to the back of the photo, and the sheet folded around the photo so that an editor can fold down the part of the sheet that covers the photo and reveal the caption. (See illustration.)

Cutlines must identify all people in a photo, and provide information about the program, activity, or other involvement they have with the station (promotion, new assignment, etc.) As with releases, photo cutlines for program-related

The following pages contain illustrations of various kinds of television publicity photos, supplied courtesy of the PBS Network.

This photo of Sarah Vaughn is a standard head shot taken during program production to show the star in costume and setting. As all photos should be, this one is in perfect focus, crisp, clear, and with visual interest provided not only by the costume, but the pose as well.

This photo of actor James Grout is a production photo. Though it was posed, it looks as though it is a part of the actual program. This technique adds a dynamic quality to a single person photo, adding to the visual interest, and conveying more of the program content to the potential viewer.

This extremely close head shot from a National Geographic Special also adds interest to the character through the ceremonial garland.

In the case of live programming, the cast may not be together or in costume far enough in advance to provide still photos. One alternative, used here by a PBS "Live From The Met" production, is to use artists renderings of the costuming.

This photo, from the PBS series "Walsh's Animals," shows yet another technique for adding visual interest to a routine head shot. Notice that the photo can easily be used horizontally, or cropped vertically.

Two routine head shots can be combined on one 8 x 10″ glossy to save in printing and postage costs, yet provide newspaper editors with more material, as was done in this publicity still for "The Key to the Universe."

This combination shot, from "The Way It Was," combines principles shown in photos above. Four photos have been grouped together to show sports stars "then" and "now"—and provide action shots.

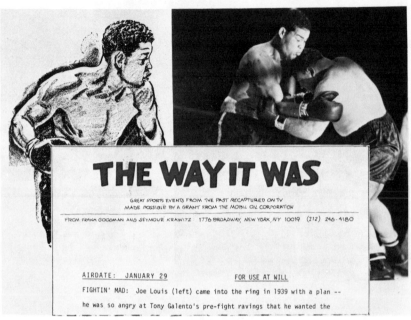

THE WAY IT WAS

GREAT SPORTS EVENTS FROM THE PAST RECAPTURED ON TV
MADE POSSIBLE BY A GRANT FROM THE MOBIL OIL CORPORATION

FROM FRANK GOODMAN AND SEYMOUR KRAWITZ · 1776 BROADWAY, NEW YORK, NY 10019 (212) 246-4180

AIRDATE: JANUARY 29   FOR USE AT WILL

FIGHTIN' MAD: Joe Louis (left) came into the ring in 1939 with a plan --

he was so angry at Tony Galento's pre-fight ravings that he wanted the

This illustration, from "The Way It Was," shows how many stations and producers service photos to the press, with the caption on a separate sheet of
paper, taped to the back and folded over the front.

This photo of artist Georgia O'Keeffe places the subject of the TV documentary in the context of her life (the desert) and her work. It would be highly
suitable for a feature story on the artist which a newspaper might time to
coincide with the TV program.

250

Depth and character involvement add interest to this two-shot from the "Microbes and Men" series. Again, this photo was posed especially for the publicity photographer.

This block of "Studio See" photos provides, on one sheet, a single person photo, a group shot, and the show's logo, the balloon, giving editors a wide choice of material.

This artwork montage of potential Presidential candidates was created for a public television series on the 1980 election. Artwork provides a new way of looking at familiar subjects, thereby creating interest in them, and hopefully in the program. Artwork such as this can also double for press kit covers, on-air slides, and flyers, posters, brochures and ads.

Group shots are best limited to two, three or four subjects. More than that de-emphasises each individual and makes one or two-column reproduction in a newspaper highly unlikely. Group photos are useful when there are feature story possibilities, several major stars, or when several headshots or single-person photos are being provided in addition.

pictures must contain the program's title, air date, and time. Also include the mailing date and the name of the station's publicity contact. Many stations have special paper prepared for cutline use which prominently display's the station's logo and seasonal theme. This helps editors quickly identify a photo's source.

An alternate method of attaching the cutline is to glue it onto the back of the photo. But in no case should cutline information be typed or written on the back of the picture. This can damage the photo on the other side, and make it useless.

Photos as Rewards. Another important station use of photos is as rewards. Pictures which include members of the station's staff or on-air talent should go to these people. The prints are cheap to have made, and the identification with a station activity helps encourage employee loyalty and future cooperation with the Promotion Department.

Copies of photos of station clients and guests involved in station-related activities, such as contests, community promotions, agency-client parties, and other events should go to the people in the photos. Again, it is a public relations effort that pays dividends in increased identification with the station. Here are some possibilities for meaningful reward photos:

- Station staff members, clients and press with visiting stars.
- Clients, ad agency people and media buyers with station sales representatives at station parties or other functions.
- Tour groups visiting the station, pictured with a station lobby display, logo, and/or program host or news person.
- Production personnel on-location in unusual circumstances.
- Well-known community figures who can benefit from being photographed with each other, at station functions.
- Members of the public with station on-air talent at community events. (These might be taken as Polaroid shots and distributed on the spot.)

These kinds of photos can usually be taken with 35mm camera equipment, preferable because of its portability, versatility and because the camera holds more film than other formats. Polaroid pictures provide the advantage of instant distribution, but the disadvantage is small size, with enlargements a complicated process.

Photos as Records. Often it is wise to have a photographer present even if no press or reward use is planned. Photos become a part of station records, with a number of possible subsequent uses.

Award entries for programming, promotion, advertising, and community service activities can be brought to life with meaningful photos as part of the entry. To these ends, Promotion Directors may want to keep on file pictures of unusual production, station guests, program talent, station outdoor advertising, lobby displays, station vehicles, building contruction, and station participation in community events. If the occasion, production or advertising is colorful, color photos should be taken.

A filing system, or photo library of original photographs and pictures which come to the station from networks and syndicators is essential. It enables the

Promotion Director to quickly find specific pictures from among hundreds, perhaps thousands.

These files are invaluable when any kind of historical retrospective of the station's activities is needed.

The Photographer. Photography can come from several sources: the Advertising, Promotion and Publicity Departments; the Graphics Department; the station's staff; or outside the station. The wise rule is to have a principal photographer and a back-up who can be called upon in emergencies.

The first choice is to use the station's Graphics or Art Department, if there is a trained photographer on staff. Station photography should be a part of the person's job description. Scheduling should be done in advance so that photo work does not conflict with other responsibilities.

If an experienced and capable photo hobbiest works for the station in some other capacity, it might be possible to use that person as either principal photogtapher or emergency back-up. Be sure to clear this responsibility with the person's superior, pay standard rates, and avoid a photo work-load that conflicts heavily with primary responsibilities. Many Promotion Directors make photographic experience a requirement in the job description of one of the Department's staff members, reimbursing for film and print costs, and in some cases overtime for time spent at nights in the darkroom.

Another option is to contract with an outside photographer by paying a retainer for a certain number of "shoots" through the year. Such contracts usually stipulate a specific maximum number of sessions beyond which the station pays extra; and guarantee a minimum number of prints per picture ordered, based on average station needs. Extra prints must be paid for separately.

Whoever the photographer is, the promotion or publicity person supervising the photography has the responsibility to work closely alongside to ensure that photos meet station needs. The best procedure is to explain the needs of a particular situation clearly in advance so that it isn't necessary to hover over the photographer's shoulder during a session. Show examples of pictures similar to the ones needed. Samples should be available from the Department's photo files. And, if necessary, critique sessions afterwards by looking at proof sheets to identify good and bad angles, expressions, and framing. A good photographer will quickly learn your needs.

Press Kits

Many stations prepare press kits for programs, special events, or new season kick-offs. The press kit, simply, is a folder containing a number of elements useful to members of the press, or station clients, community leaders, or special interest groups. Press kits can be tailored to the needs of a specific occasion. Typically, a press kit consists of: an attractive folder with a printed cover; one or more releases on the program, event, and/or personalities; one or more photos (at least two—one horizontal and one vertical—are recommended).

Other press kit items might include:

• A letter from the General Manager, program producer, Promotion Director, News Director, Community Service Director, or other appropriate station official or on-air talent. Letters can be used to personalize otherwise identical kits for different kinds of recipients: a letter from the Promotion Director in kits for the press; from the GM in kits for editorial page editors and community leaders; from the Community Services Director in kits for minority group leaders; and a letter from the Sales Director in kits for media buyers and clients.
• Sales promotion flyers.
• Background information sheets on programming.
• Program flyers for community use.
• Bookmarks.
• Program schedules.
• Coverage maps.
• Rate schedules.
• Credit sheets listing all persons involved with a program.
• Feature releases and personality profiles of on-air talent.
• Biographies of talent and key members of production staff.
• Audio tapes. (Kit covers can be ordered which have tuck-in slots for audio-tape cassettes, or special containers can be used.)

Press kit cover design should be bold, simple, attention-getting, and if possible, related to the subject matter inside. Many stations, however, find it useful to have generic station kit covers which can be adapted to specific uses by adding decals, stickers, or over-printing.

The kits serve two purposes: to hold together all relevant material pertaining to a program; and to attract attention to an unusual or important station happening. Imaginative design of kit covers and letterhead for use inside is more important than specially made die-cut or fabric bound covers, but if the money exists in the budget, such extras can be real attention-getters.

Some stations prefer to format kit cover design, using program-related artwork in a pre-determined way to individualize kits for different uses. Other stations prefer to make each kit separate in design. The first technique emphasizes a continuity of effort; the second draws special attention to each program or activity. Pages 256–7 show an example of press kit materials.

Logs, Schedules, or Listings. Though called by different names, for the Promotion Director these are the actually one item which we will refer to as the *program schedule.*

The Program Schedule is the most basic element of a TV station's entire advertising, publicity and promotion effort. It simply lists all the station's programming by days in chronological order.

Schedules are usually provided to newspapers, *TV Guide,* and sometimes ad agencies and community leaders on a weekly basis, usually 3–4 weeks in advance of the week of air, to meet magazine and supplement deadlines. See page 255 for a sample press information sheet.

PROGRAM HIGHLIGHTS FOR THE WEEK OF NOVEMBER 15 THROUGH NOVEMBER 21

SUNDAY, NOVEMBER 15   1:30PM to 3:00PM

THE SUNDAY AFTERNOON MOVIE - "The Warriors." (1955) Errol Flynn stars in this
    costume melodrama of kings, knights and noblemen. (1 hr. 30m)

3:30PM to 4:00PM

USC HILITES - Highlights of the USC game at Washington. Ted Dawson hosts. (30m)

4:30PM to 5:00PM

GREATEST SPORTS LEGENDS - (805) - Owner Frank Whiteley and jockey Jacinto Vasquez
    discuss the career of the racehourse Ruffian. Ruffian so out-classed the other
    fillies that trainer Whiteley decided to run her against male horses. It let
    to the famous and tragic match race between Ruffian and Foolish Pleasure, the
    1975 Kentucky Derby winner. During the race, Ruffian broke a bone in her leg,
    forcing her owners to put her to sleep. (30m)

6:30PM to 7:00PM

THE PEOPLE'S COURT - (145) - "The Case of the Presidential Decision," and "The
    Case of the Bad Bed Buy." Gerard Pick of Santa Monica is suing the Professional
    Air Traffic Controller's Organization because the organization's strike caused
    him to lose potential business; A senior citizen sues because she feels she
    was overcharged for a bed. (30m)

11:45PM to 1:45AM

SUNDAY NIGHT MOVIE - "The Love Machine." (1972) John Phillip Law, Dyan Cannon,
    Patty Duke star. An ambitious young man advances ruthlessly via his sexual
    powers from a six o'clock newscaster to a network president. (2 hrs.)

MONDAY, NOVEMBER 16   10:00PM to 11:30PM

THE KABC-TV MONDAY NIGHT MOVIE - "Shaft." (1971) Richard Roundtree stars as the
    black private eye tracking down the kidnapped daughter of a Harlem kingpin who
    becomes involved in a power struggle between the Mafia and black mobsters.
    (1 hr. 30m)

12:30AM to 2:30AM

THE KABC-TV MONDAY LATE NIGHT MOVIE - "Journey into Darkness." (1969) Robert Reed,
    Patrick McGoohan. Two tales of the unknown: A rich and bored young man devises
    a game in which he condemns to death any who break his unwritten laws; a young
    boy, one of quadruplets, is linked to his brothers and has the power to direct
    them in evil deeds. (2 hrs.)

KABC-TV · 4151 PROSPECT AVENUE · LOS ANGELES · CA 90027 · (213) 663-3311

Under the title "Press Information," KABC-TV in Los Angeles sends out what many
stations call "Highlights." These are synopses of programs the station feels important
or significant. Frequently, programs which are important to the station from a financial or ratings point of view are included, and most of the programs are local rather
than network, because the TV networks send out their own "Highlights" to local market newspapers.

Anatomy of a press kit: This press kit is typical of the effort that might be expended for a major program or series, from a national producer, a television network, or a local station. This kit, for the PBS/CTW series, "The Best of Families," includes the following: 1) Kit cover. 2) Five photos with captions. 3) A 21-page viewers guide to the series, including specially commissioned articles on political and social conditions during the era represented in the programs. 4) A large-sized brochure with information and photos of the families portrayed in the series. 5) Five press releases, including: an announcement release, a program release, a production feature on research that went into making the series accurate, a release on the free offer of American history guides, and a set of bios of the series' cast and staff. 6) A program fact sheet detailing producers, description, broadcast schedule, staff, funding, performers, Board of Advisors, CTW personnel and Board of Trustees. 7) A genealogy chart of the five families portrayed in the series, with photos for quick recognition.

The Best of Families

A major new American television series produced by CTW for Public TV which dramatizes the critical years in the late 19th Century.

The Best of Families
·1977 CTW

a primetime drama series for public broadcasting produced by CTW

FACT SHEET: 'THE BEST OF FAMILIES'

PRODUCER: CTW, creator and producer of "Sesame Street" and "The Electric Company."

DESCRIPTION: The nine hours of primetime adult drama to be broadcast in eight weekly episodes will constitute a social history of the last two decades of the late 19th Century in America.

The series will illustrate how urbanization and technology transformed American society and culture in that period, especially in New York City, which provides the backdrop.

The stories revolve around the lives of three fictional families and a cast of more than 40 family members and friends from differing economic, social and ethnic backgrounds who shared in the life of the city and contributed to its development.

BROADCAST SCHEDULE: A two-hour premiere episode will be broadcast on Thursday, October 27, at 9 p.m. (Eastern time) on the 272 stations of the Public Broadcasting Service. Seven one-hour episodes will be aired weekly in the same time slot with repeats at 4 p.m. and 8 p.m. each Saturday.

PROJECT STAFF:
Series Concept Created By.......Naomi Foner
Executive Producer..............Ethel Winant
Producer........................Gareth Davies
Series Head Writer..............Corinne Jacker
Writers.........................Conrad Bromberg, David Epstein, Roger Hirson, Corinne Jacker, Ernest Kinoy, Loring Mandel
Directors.......................Jack Hofsiss, Glenn Jordan, Peter Levin, Seymour Robbie, Robert Stevens
Associate Producer..............Bob Spitzer

FUNDING: The series is underwritten by the National Endowment for the Humanities, Mobil Corporation, Arthur Vining Davis Foundations, Corporation for Public Broadcasting, Ford Foundation and CTW itself.

October, 1977

ONE LINCOLN PLAZA, N.Y. 10023 / (212) 595-3456 / CABLE: SESAMEST / RCA: 236168 / TWX: (710) 581-2543

6

The Best of Families
·1977 CTW

a primetime drama series for public broadcasting produced by CTW

A New View of 1880-1900

'THE BEST OF FAMILIES': A DRAMATIC
TV RE-CREATION OF A 'REVOLUTIONARY'
ERA THAT TRANSFORMED AMERICAN LIFE

AMERICAN SOCIAL HISTORY UNFOLDS DRAMATICALLY
ON TV'S 'THE BEST OF FAMILIES' OCT. 27 ON PBS

METICULOUS RESEARCH AUTHENTICATES
HISTORICAL DETAILS AND PRODUCTION
VALUES IN TV'S 'BEST OF FAMILIES'

EDUCATORS AND VIEWERS OFFERED
FREE AMERICAN HISTORY GUIDES
FOR TV'S 'BEST OF FAMILIES'

BIOGRAPHICAL SKETCHES: CAST AND STAFF OF 'THE BEST OF FAMILIES'

GUY BOYD (Stephen Rafferty) has appeared on "The Andros Targets" TV a
motion pictures "Between the Lines" and "Strawberry Statement." His
includes the Off-Broadway productions of "Fishing," "Heat" and "Kaspar
in regional presentations of "A View From the Bridge," "Alice in Wonde
the Man," "The Skin of Our Teeth," "The Homecoming" and "Pictures in th

---

The Best of Families

A Genealogy
1880-1900

7

Schedules provide a valuable reference tool for many at the station, as well. Circulation should include all department heads and others on a request/need basis. Because so many people inside and outside the station rely on the schedule, accuracy is vital.

Updates, Changes and Corrections. In spite of the need for accuracy in schedules and releases, errors sometimes occur. More frequently, programming changes are made between the time that schedules are distributed and the week these programs go on the air. Also, additions of stars, guests, and changes in program talent may occur. So every Promotion Department must have a recognized, regular format for announcing these corrections, changes and updates.

Use of pastel-colored paper stock (pink is a frequent choice) helps call attention to these sheets and identifies them as correction or change sheets. They should clearly indicate at the top that changes and corrections are listed below; and should prominently display the weeks involved. Change sheets usually cover a time span of several weeks, since they must update any previously released information. They should be issued on a regular basis—perhaps two or three days a week, and can be mailed in a packet with other materials. All changes, corrections and updates should be in one continuous chronological flow to make it easy for readers to transfer the information to the original schedules.

See page 259 for example.

MAILING LISTS

Promotion Departments must work with other station departments and the station's mail room to develop, maintain, and creatively use a number of different mailing lists for distribution of wide variety of publicity and promotional information. Different lists for different needs help reduce mailing costs by enabling the station to target materials to specific publics. Among a typical station's mailing lists might be:

Press List (TV Editors), Press List (Editorial Pages); Press List (Sports Page Editors); Press List (Regional Magazines); Press List (Womens Page, or Feature Section Editors); Press List (Trade Press); Community Leaders List (including politicians, business leaders, and heads of social, political, business and religious organizations); Lists for various minority groups; Churches (for church bulletins); Key ad agency personnel and media buyers; Major clients; Libraries (for bulletin board postings); Colleges and universities (newspapers, student activity centers, dorms, fraternities and sororities, etc.); Service Organizations (Kiwanis, Junior League, Chambers of Commerce, etc.); Fraternal Organizations (Elks, Masons, American Legion, etc.); High Schools (principals, newspapers); Businesses with company newsletters.

Each Promotion Director in each market, together with the Community Service Director, Sales Director, Program Director, and others at the station, must devise the appropriate set of lists for the particular market area. Once lists are prepared on plates or computerized by the mail room, it is easy for the

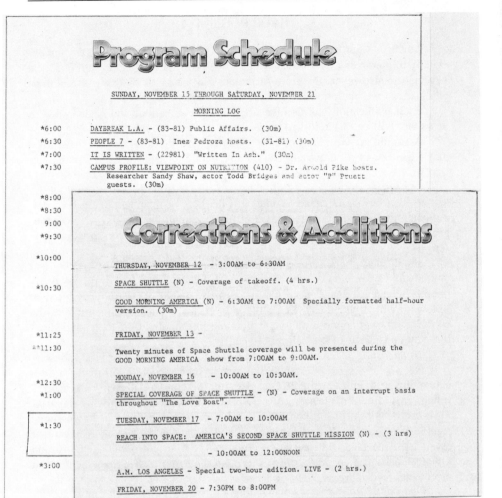

Program Schedule

SUNDAY, NOVEMBER 15 THROUGH SATURDAY, NOVEMBER 21

MORNING LOG

*6:00	DAYBREAK L.A. - (83-81) Public Affairs. (30m)
*6:30	PEOPLE 7 - (83-81) Inez Pedroza hosts. (51-81) (30m)
*7:00	IT IS WRITTEN - (22981) "Written In Ash." (30m)
*7:30	CAMPUS PROFILE: VIEWPOINT ON NUTRITION (410) - Dr. Arnold Pike hosts. Researcher Sandy Shaw, actor Todd Bridges and actor "P" Pruett guests. (30m)
*8:00	
*8:30	
9:00	
*9:30	
*10:00	
*10:30	
*11:25	
*11:30	
*12:30	
*1:00	
*1:30	
*3:00	

Corrections & Additions

THURSDAY, NOVEMBER 12 - 3:00AM to 6:30AM

SPACE SHUTTLE (N) - Coverage of takeoff. (4 hrs.)

GOOD MORNING AMERICA (N) - 6:30AM to 7:00AM Specially formatted half-hour version. (30m)

FRIDAY, NOVEMBER 13 -

Twenty minutes of Space Shuttle coverage will be presented during the GOOD MORNING AMERICA show from 7:00AM to 9:00AM.

MONDAY, NOVEMBER 16 - 10:00AM to 10:30AM.

SPECIAL COVERAGE OF SPACE SHUTTLE - (N) - Coverage on an interrupt basis throughout "The Love Boat".

TUESDAY, NOVEMBER 17 - 7:00AM to 10:00AM

REACH INTO SPACE: AMERICA'S SECOND SPACE SHUTTLE MISSION (N) - (3 hrs)

- 10:00AM to 12:00NOON

A.M. LOS ANGELES - Special two-hour edition. LIVE - (2 hrs.)

FRIDAY, NOVEMBER 20 - 7:30PM to 8:00PM

Under the title "Program Schedule," all TV stations provide the press and *TV Guide Magazine* with a complete rundown of each week's programs about 3–4 weeks in advance of the week of air. Coupled with the schedule is a list of "Corrections & Additions," noting any changes in previously announced programming.

station's Publicity Manager to indicate which lists should receive program releases. Targeting releases so that not every release goes to every group, and so that groups which have specific interests can learn about programs or news features of special interest to them enables the stations to better serve both broad sections of the community as well as narrow special interests, while saving money on distribution.

TRADE PUBLICITY

Much of what has been said earlier about relations with the press applies equally to members of the broadcasting trade press as well as the staffs of local newspapers. However, there are differences in the kinds of news stories trade publications are interested in.

Each publication has its own areas of specialization, and each looks for news that will be of interest to its readers.

A station activity that got a lot of mileage in the local papers—such as a major contest, or an important community public relations activity in conjunction with a local charity—would probably be of no interest to the trades.

The key to getting space in trade magazines is to find some element of the activity that has significance to other broadcasters or members of the advertising community, and base the release of news around that "hook." If possible, gear each release to the editorial requirements of the publication to which it is sent.

Should news be mailed, phoned, or delivered in person? The best bet is a combination of printed release and personal contact—whether in person or by phone. Send the release, give it time to arrive at the trade publication, then follow up with a phone call. Or deliver the release in person. This provides the editor/reporter an opportunity to question you further about the topic; and stress that you consider it of special importance.

Broadcasting magazine is a key news magazine of the broadcast industry. It is the weekly magazine that station management people and broadcast educators turn to to know if the FCC is changing regulations, if courts are making rulings that affect broadcasters, if networks and broadcast institutions are making—or changing—plans, and what local stations are doing that has national significance. Because *Broadcasting* is so widely read at the station management level, it is one place where stations frequently try to get publicity for certain kinds of activities. *Broadcasting* is printed Thursday and Friday nights and reaches its readership Monday or Tuesday, in most cases.

Television/Radio Age is another important trade publication, published biweekly. It differs considerably from *Broadcasting,* placing less emphasis on spot news and more space to detailed coverage of specific issues. Considerable emphasis is placed on commercial production and the buying plans of national advertisers. There are also sections for information about job changes, syndicated programming news, and broadcast-related Wall Street news.

Weekly Variety, Radio and Records, Adweek, Advertising Age, Broadcast Communications, Television Digest, Facts, Figures & Film, Back Stage, Marketing and Media Decisions, and *Madison Avenue* are other publications read by different groups in the broadcast and advertising communities. Except for *Weekly Variety,* few are as useful for publicity as they are for paid station ads designed to reach media buyers and ad agency executives. *Variety* provides thorough news coverage of major network activities, government regulation, personnel transitions and movement, and virtually every other aspect of the film, television, radio and recording industries.

In all cases, station placement of publicity information depends on news value for each publication's readership. Releases tailored to meet a publication's needs and interests stands a good chance of earning space.

PUBLICITY EVENTS

Screenings, press conferences and station parties are all events designed to attract members of the press to the station, where they can receive printed information and personal contact from members of the Promotion Department and others on the station's staff.

Screenings

In their simplest form, screenings provide a chance for critics or reviewers to see television programs in advance. This enables reviews to appear in newspapers prior to, or on the day of air.

It is not possible to make a reviewer like a program. Nor is it desirable to have newspaper critics come to the station to see every program. The time isn't available—either for the television station, or members of the press. However, comfortable environment and congenial atmosphere may influence the critic's mood . . . and that may have an effect on his perception of the program.

It is traditional to preview premieres of new series, major documentaries, special or unusual episodes of on-going series, and major entertainment specials. These are the things audiences are most likely to be interested in, and thus the reviewers most want to see and report on—or critique.

The TV station promotion staff must be aware of the interests of people in many different departments at each local paper. It is possible people at the newspaper other than the TV critic may want to preview a program. All who might be interested should be invited. In many instances, the guest list should include representatives from college papers, and people responsible for in-house or company newsletters at major local corporations, plants, or associations.

Special interest groups with interests related to an upcoming documentary or drama might also be included as a public relations gesture.

Screenings range from the large scale variety, with dozens of interested persons present to the small one-on-one screening for just one newspaper critic. The following tips apply to both, and the range in between:

Provide some form of refreshments. The chances are most of the guests have had to travel—sometimes in rush-hour traffic from across town—to be present. Most stations have no policy against making alcoholic refreshments available. Those that do should have a variety of non-alcoholic beverages, ice, and—at the very least—potato chips, pretzels, peanuts, or something similar. The larger the gathering, the greater the need for catered hors d'oeuvres. Often these can be paid for by a program sponsor or underwriter.

Provide adequate screening facilities and viewing space. Be sure everyone invited can clearly see the picture and hear the sound. Avoid screenings in busy offices, or any place where office noise or interruptions can distract reviewers. Make sure the room is a comfortable temperature. A cold draft or a hot house won't help your relations with the press.

Give attendees at a screening whatever handouts are available in advance of actually showing the program. Allow time for review of the written material. A news release on the program containing a basic description, air date/time and channel is mandatory. If possible, a press kit containing photos, background and pertinent biographical information, plus a cast and production crew list is impressive and can encourage the reviewer to devote more space to the program. Feature releases increase the story potential still further.

Make cast members or key production personnel (producer, director) available, if it is a local production. This person can make a few brief introductory remarks and answer questions after the show is over, giving the reviewer the feeling that he is developing a story on his own—one that might be exclusive.

Some newspaper critics have their own cassette machines for screenings. If at all possible, hand-deliver cassettes to them. This provides an opportunity to discuss publicity materials in person, and answer questions on the spot.

Finally, accept negative reviews with good grace. If a critic's response to viewing a show seems negative, point out some positive element of the show. But don't argue with the critic's judgments on specific points. Not all programs are good. Not all critics are always fair and just—but most usually are. And most programs have some redeeming features. If you're fortunate, the critic will pick up on those in the review.

Press Conferences

Press conferences are usually called when the station has a major news announcement to make. Some examples might be:

A change of station ownership; purchase of land for a new building; a drastic change in programming policy; a change in network affiliation; hiring of a new anchorperson for the news.

Many of the same principles discussed earlier under press relations and press materials apply to the press conference:

- A printed news release with all pertinent facts should be available at the start of the press conference.
- Members of the press who might be interested should be called and invited, with a written reminder sent if there is time. A telegram might be used if the event is of great importance.
- The Promotion Director should brief the principals in the press conference beforehand, letting them know who is coming, and helping them identify the key information that is to be given out.
- The press conference should be held at a place convenient to the majority of members of the press who will be present. This might be the station. Or it might be a hotel or conference office reserved by the station at a more central location. The convenience of the press is paramount. If radio

and TV people will be present, be sure the necessary electrical outlets are available.
• Liquor is rarely served at press conferences, though soft drinks, coffee, pastries or small sandwiches are routine.
• If reporters will be close to deadline and some distance from their papers, be sure enough phones are available for those who will need them.
• Other niceties include ample parking space, coat-check facilities, and seating that makes note-taking easy (i.e., tables and chairs).
• It is always wise to tape-record press conferences so that reporters' quotes can be checked afterwards; so that there is a record of exactly what was said, and so that tapes can be supplied to members of the press who might later request them to verify or add to their quotes.
• Plan in advance who will speak, in what order, and what each person will say. A prepared statement may be read, then questions answered. Normally, the station's top official will do most of the talking.
• The Promotion Director should stay very close to the person holding the press conference, ready to supply additional information, clarifications, specifics, and even help reporters probe further when it would be helpful.
• Press conferences should always start promptly—within a few minutes of the appointed time.
• Normally, photographs are permitted when the station's representative first steps up to speak. TV crews are usually kept to the rear of the group of reporters so camera and lighting equipment does not obstruct communication between hosts and guests.
• Never expect to speak "off the record" at a press conference. Such comments may be made in private interviews. But things said in public are going to be considered "fair game" and may show up in print, even if they are presented "off the record."
• Be sure members of the press have a contact—usually the Promotion Director of chief press representative—whom they can easily reach for follow-up information.

Remember: press conferences are for major announcements that will have an effect on the entire community. They permit the simultaneous release of information to all members of the press—don't forget the station's own News Department—and are most effective when dealing with complicated announcements which might require follow-up questioning.

Parties and Meetings

Station parties are usually for members of the press, community leaders, media buyers, ad agency personnel, and clients—actual and potential. Some parties, such as a TV station's annual Fall Preview Party, are designed for all of these groups. Other parties might center around Sales Department, press, or community relations needs.

Generally, the meeting affects the entire station staff and there are many ideas and suggestions. But the main responsibility for coming up with just the "right kind" of event or party remains the responsibility of the Promotion Director.

Planning such a special event is like having a suit tailor-made. It has to "fit" and has to personify its purpose. Anniversary events take one road; Fall parties demand a slightly different approach; "star" appearances need a twist of their own; launching a new personality has emphasis in other directions; sales meetings, account or agency soirées need a personal touch, and so it goes.

The following includes suggestions from a number of station Promotion Directors, and from "The Seagram Meeting & Convention Organizer," a publication of Seagrams Distillers, New York.

Selecting the Site. The location of the party is a primary key to its success. The location should be chosen with the event's purpose in mind. Fall preview parties, generally the most elaborate events TV stations become involved in, are designed to stimulate excitement among time buyers, clients and the press about the station's new schedule.

Holding them at the station is a way to call attention to local productions, and emphasize the station as a distinct physical entity in the community. It might be the logical site if there has been a recent new addition to the building, a new tower on the premises, a significant renovation, or if there are one or more new sets for important new programs or news which can be shown off to advantage. These parties take advantage of the station's largest studio as a gathering place. They save money, personalize the station, and make it easier for the staff to coordinate audio-visual, signage, and other requirements. Station arranged caterers and bar arrangements save still more money over a hotel site. And decoration limitations imposed by some hotels will not apply. If the station has the outdoor space and the climate promises good weather, rented tents, beach umbrellas, tables and chairs can be set up on a lawn. This is especially effective when the station exterior is imposing, or there is a great view. The darkened interior of a tent or an inside studio can be used for showing excerpts of the new season.

Holding the Fall party at the station every year, however, might become routine for the guests. Unless there is sufficient imagination to use the station location in a fresh and imaginative way each year, it might be wise to breathe new life into the event in alternate years by looking around the community for alternative sites.

Hotels are a logical choice. They provide all the catering, bartending and parking services normally required, and they have easily accessible locations. Working with hotels requires personal negotiations to get the best "deal" possible for space and food, and have as much flexibility possible in decorating and creating an atmosphere. Menus can be altered, extra "screening rooms" added, and special services arranged as needed to support the party's theme.

Country clubs or nearby resort locations might provide adequate facilities and a chic or sports-oriented atmosphere. Other ingenious party locations have included: local art museums, railroad stations, libraries, drive-in theatres, stock-car race tracks, riverboats, 747 airplanes, baseball stadiums and executive dining rooms of large firms.

Former BPA President Clarence Martin of KYTV, Springfield, Missouri, wrote the following on Fall parties for a BPA publication on special events. It displays the considerable imagination and showmanship expected of a Promotion Director year after year:

KYTV will have, in the course of a year, many parties and sales meetings, but the one we put the full station to work on is the Fall Preview Party. In 1973 we bussed the guests to Silver Dollar City, a theme park 35 miles from Springfield, and had coctails and dinner served in an old early 1800's saloon, complete with dancing girls and a multi-media presentation on the new season. Invitations read "Cocktails at a certain location and dinner and entertainment at a surprise location." Guests were given a drink, name tags, and put on buses. Hors d'oeuvres were served on the bus."

The following year we felt we had to top the 1973 party. We used the same busing system, but this time guests were taken to a commercial cave, with the dinner, cocktails and the multi-media show being held underground. Highlight of the show was a marching band that came from the back of the cave, as a surprise feature on the presentation on sports.

In 1975, in search of another unusual location for the dinner and coctail party, we found a bank building under construction, where only the first two floors had been finished. That's where we had our party, but on the fifth floor! Guests were invited to cocktails on the parking lot of the bank and told that dinner and entertainment were to be at a surprise location. When they arrived we put them on the elevator and up to the fifth floor for their surprise party.

We then took over a nearby old vaudeville theatre for the multi-media presentation. We added a live pit-band, a group of 35 singers, college cheerleaders, an actor doing a sketch on Ben Franklin, a girl from a massage parlor and Art James from "The Magnificent Marble Machine." The problem: how to get everybody from the dinner to the presentation without someone going home on you. We decided on a parade.

When dinner was over, we got everybody outside where they were met by a 150-piece marching band, a 35-girl drum corps and a mounted flag patrol. Placards on the new shows were given to the guests to carry. With a police escort, drum corps, marching band and horses, we marched them to the theatre where glasses of cold champagne were waiting.

The presentation was multi-media with rear projection by 12 slide projectors and three sound-on-film projectors, plus all the extra live segments. The close of the show was the 35 singers on stage singing "America the Beautiful," and a huge 30-by-40 foot American flag being lowered behind them. We got the audience on its feet and ready to leave, with tears in many eyes.

What makes a party like this work? Or a simple cocktail party? There are 10 rules we follow at KYTV:

1. Use imagination when picking a theme, place and method of presentation.
2. Allot enough money to do the job in a first class way. Do not cut corners.
3. Get the entire station involved.
4. Invite not only local advertisers and agencies, but also community

leaders, national reps, politicians and the press. Send teasers to arouse curiosity prior to the invitation.

5. Have unannounced surprises, either in the presentation or by guest star appearances.

6. The actual presentation must include more than just material supplied by a network. Local access programming and news are very important additions. Either work them into a network presentation, or use network-supplied material to create an entirely new preview with emphasis where it will help the station most.

7. The preview should be long enough to tell the station's story, but not so long that it drags out or becomes boring—25–40 minutes are guidelines.

8. Limit the cocktails prior to a preview to one hour. Drunks don't make good audiences, and no station ever lost an order just because it closed the bar early at the preview party.

9. Have a rousing way to end the party and get the guests started on the way home. Provide coffee if they've been kept to a late hour and served a lot of liquor.

10. Follow up by sending photos of people enjoying your party to them, along with "thank you" notes for attending. (If it's been a great party, they'll send you "thank you" notes too.)

Martin concludes by emphasizing "We always try to show, in anything we do, that ours is a first class operation. That means from the invitations to the booze and dinner. A station can save a few dollars by cutting corners, but to a businessman who is accustomed to the best, it loses points. Make everything first class, highly imaginative, or don't do it."

Site Determination and Arrangement Checklist

In choosing a party site, here is a checklist of things to look for:

• Be sure the rooms involved are large enough to hold the expected guests.
• Reserve those particular rooms well in advance.
• Choose a site for the reception, if one is to be held.
• Decide on the number of persons per table.
• Approve menus, and arrange food prices with the hotel or caterer.
• Select brands of liquor. (Name brands are more impressive than house brands to guests, but cost more.)
• Decide on the number of bars. (One for each 75 people is usual.)
• Decide on table decorations, usually to help carry out the theme.
• Decide on music for dinner, entertainment and/or dancing. Again, if possible, tie it in with the party's theme.
• Arrange for coat-checking. It is better to have complimentary checking than to have guests worry about paying. They can tip.
• Determine if signs can be hung, where, and what restrictions exist.
• Find out what equipment the hotel (or other location) can provide. At hotels, the following is frequently provided with the space at no extra cost:

easels, rostrum, microphone, and chalkboards. There may be extra charges for slide projectors and screens, if available.

· Arrange for the station (or an outside contractor) to provide slide and videotape projection and playback equipment and screens or monitors.

Room Layout for Audio-Visual Playback

Audience of 25 to 50, use a 50″ x 50″ screen.

Audience of 50 to 75, use a 50″ x 60″ screen.

Audience of 75 to 250, use a 7′ x 7′ screen, or four-six 19″ monitors.

Audience of 250 to 500, use a 10′ x 10′ screen, or four 4′ x 6′ video projection screens.

Audience of 500 to 1,000, use a 12′ x 12′ screen, or six–eight 4′ x 6′ video projection screens.

Audience of over 1,000: screen should be at least 14′ x 14′.

Beverage Consumption Guidelines

To determine the amount of liquor needed:

A. A quart is 32 ounces, a fifth is 25.6 ounces, the most popular size drink is 1½ ounces. Therefore,

B. One quart equals 21 drinks of 1½ ounces.

C. One fifth equals 17 drinks of 1½ ounces.

D. Consumption during a one-hour period will equal an average of three drinks per person, or 14 quarts for every 100 at 1½ ounces per drink.

To determine the amount of mixers needed:

One quart of soda or ginger ale will make six drinks, using a standard 8-ounce highball glass with 1½ ounces of liquor.

About cocktails:

One gallon of Manhattans (128 ounces) serves 32 cocktails, using a average four-ounce cocktail glass. All cocktails can be estimated this way.

Based on a cost of $4.17 per fifth, cocktail parties liquor costs can be estimated as follows:

no. of guests	no. of drinks	no. of bottles 5ths	Qts.	total cost
50	150	9	7	$ 153.
150	450	26	21	442.
500	1,500	88	71	1,496.
800	2,400	141	115	2,397.

· Arrange for water, ash trays, pads, pencils, etc., as necessary.

· Set type of seating: banquet or picnic for meals; schoolroom (with desks or at long tables) or theatre (without writing space) for meetings, screenings, or workshops.

· Decide if gifts will be given out at the door, at tables, or in some other fashion. There are a number of ingenious ways door prizes can be awarded, but the most common are by a drawing, with guests holding numbered tickets they received on entering, or with numbers on the backs or bottoms of chairs.

· Arrange room rates for sepcial guests needing overnight accommodations. This often includes special guest "stars" on tour, or major speakers from another city. Explore the possibility of special room rates because of the station's use of the hotel meeting and banquet facilities.

· Check on whether parking will be complimentary or pay. If parking is not available at the site, it must be arranged nearby, and busing or other transportation arranged to get guests to the party.

· Make necessary arrangements for someone to be at the site to receive equipment, props, and other special deliveries when they are made.

· Make arrangements for help in setting up decorations, equipment, chairs, tables, and other necessary items.

· Be sure deliveries are far enough in advance to allow ample set-up time.

· Determine all applicable union restrictions. (Many hotels have restrictions on setting or moving tables and chairs, plugging in electrical devices, and putting up signs or decorations.)

· Arrange method of payment for hotel or meeting site bills, caterers, and other vendors.

· Determine if car rental, limousine or special taxi services are needed, and contract for them.

· Determine deadline for making final space and meal guarantees, and adhere to them.

· Set a rain date, if the function is totally dependent on good weather out-of-doors. If possible, arrange for a fall-back indoor site and quick transfer of all necessary items.

· Check on other activities at the site at the same time to avoid confusion and conflict. Even nearby events, such as games at a sports arena or performances at a cultural center can cause traffic and parking problems.

· Determine location of head table(s), if needed, and place reserved signs on them. Name cards reserving a specific seating arrangement may be desirable in some cases.

· Always check seating plans for clear visability of speakers, podiums, and audio-visual presentation screens.

· Be sure there is sufficient electrical power at the site for the party's needs.

· Know the location of, or proper contact for, changing heating and air conditioning controls.

· Arrange for rehearsal time, if needed.

· Arrange for dressing rooms, if needed.

· Locate rest rooms; be sure they are nearby or directions clear, and that they are maintained in sanitary condition.

· Designate a dancing area, if it will be a part of the evening's activities.

· Locate the orchestra, and provide platforms if necessary.

· Arrange for aisles in seating areas.

· Determine the color of the linen service, especially at themed events (orange for Halloween, red for Valentine's Day and Independence Day, Green for St. Patrick's Day, etc.)

· Determine if there will be "smoking" and "non-smoking" areas, and

decide where they will be. Be sure they are clearly marked. Plan on 40% of the space for smokers, 60% for non-smokers, and be prepared to have a "middle ground" that is flexible in case one or the other area must be enlarged.
• If a piano is needed, be sure it is reserved, is there, tuned, and in good condition.
• Arrange to have paging systems (at hotels or similar locations) turned off. Make other paging arrangements with the site people. A message board outside the party area might be arranged, if necessary. This is especially useful at all-day meetings.
• Check on the sound-proofing of rooms, and activities scheduled in adjacent rooms. Many meetings, parties and A/V presentations have been disturbed by distracting activity in adjoining rooms.
• Determine in advance tipping policies with the hotel, restaurant, or site officials. Proper tipping is important. It provides good insurance for fine service at a later date. Put tips in envelopes with person's name outside. Include a note of thanks when deserved. Send a copy to the owner or manager. Those who may be deserving of tips include:

Doormen	Waiters	Houseman
Parking Attendants	Bartenders	Headwaiter
Bell Captain	Wine Stewards	Maitre D'
Telephone Supervisor	Mail Room Supervisor	Banquet Manager
Housekeeping Supervisor	Chambermaids	Service Bar Manager
Front Office Manager	Chief Engineer	Sound Man

The owner or manager of the site can offer the best advice on tipping at a given location.
• Determine if wine is to be served or made available to all tables, or available only by request, with each table picking up the tab for its own wine.
• Determine bar service, length of time open, and whether it will be an "open bar" (the station pays) or a "cash bar" (guests pay.)
• Check elevators for prompt service. If they are slow, it may be necessary to arrange staggered arrival and departure times.
• Establish procedures for preventing gate-crashing. At small functions, someone who knows all the invited guests might remain at the entranceway. At larger events, invitations might be required, but it is still advisable to keep knowledgeable station officials at the entrance during times when most people arrive. Better to have a quick decision on someone who forgot his invitation, than to embarrass an important client or member of the press.

Promotion, Publicity and Advertising Checklist

The following checklist covers those things a Promotion Director often needs to do to see that the right people are present, and that media coverage in maximum:

• Set up mailing list for invitations, and for publicity about the event.
• Determine if mailings will be by the station or an outside agency.
• Determine dates for invitations and other pre-event mailings to take place. Remember that mail delivery time varies widely, and that people make plans well in advance . . . but if an invitation arrives too far in advance it might be lost or forgotten. An invitation one month in advance, with a reminder two weeks in advance, is a good idea.
• Determine if an advance press release is needed, and when.
• Determine if a press conference is warranted, with key speakers or major out-of-town guests or stars. Decide on its location and time in relation to the party or event. It is usually best held prior to the event, in a separate room away from invited guests and the curious.
• Arrange for coverage in the trade press, usually by releases, follow-up photos, and invitations to key trade press representatives.
• Arrange for coverage in home-town papers, and—if possible—on radio and/or television stations. This is often possible if there are important, newsworthy guests or speakers, or highly unusual activities. KYTV's parade, mentioned earlier, might have been such an opportunity.
• Have photographs with cutlines of all the principals available for the press in advance.
• Develop a press kit, if necessary—especially if the party is for a new program season or a major new program series.
• Arrange for local photographic coverage before and during the event.
• Determine if a principal will autograph photos for guests, where, and in what location—and for how long. Discuss this with the principal in advance.
• Develop all pre-printed materials, usually with a specific theme and graphic look. Depending on the event, these might include:

Invitations	Program books
Registration forms	Program for the evening's events
Direction signs	Name badges for guests & staff
Logos for rostroms	Name signs for panelists or speakers
Registration signs	Meeting room signs
Welcome signs	Program signs
Theme signs or banners	

These materials may be produced in-house if the station has a large print shop, or contracted for outside.
• Arrange for a registration area for meetings. It should be in an easily accessible area and provide enough personnel to prevent long waits in line.
• Arrange for a message center, and a communications center. Often these are in a meeting headquarters room, near the center of activity for easy, quick access and use—but private to avoid constant interruption by registrants or guests.
• Arrange for a press room if it is a meeting which might attract significant numbers of the press and generate news. Typewriters, paper, pens, phones, and a person in charge who knows where to get quick answers

for the press are essentials. It is a central point for the distribution of press or news releases generated by the meeting.

(NOTE: Press rooms, message centers, communications centers and registration areas are usually not required for parties, but only for meetings which run one day or more.)

• Develop a list of persons attending the event for station and press use, and for guest reference.

• Plan follow-up releases on activities and the remarks of major speakers. If possible, prepare these in advance.

• Have prints made of photos of party guests. Supply copies to key people who can influence decisions that affect the station, and use photos as rewards for staff members who contribute the the party's success. For meetings and conventions, photos may be made available to registrants by the photographer for a fee.

Registration Procedures for Meetings & Parties

Parties usually require only that invitations be shown at the entrance. Meetings, however, frequently require a more careful registration of attendees, especially if there are important handouts for each person present, or if registration fees are required.

• At parties, if name tags are to be worn, lay them out on a long table outside the entranceway in alphabetical order. Have guests ask for them by name. Be sure the table is supervised to discourage gate-crashers.

• At meetings, be sure the registration area is large enough to quickly accommodate arriving guests. Have plenty of help, with extra people ready to pitch in if needed.

• Have name tags or badges pre-typed as much as possible.

• Have a special area for on-site registrations, which take more time.

• Color code name badges to distinguish between different categories of guests, if that is important. Typical coding provides different colors for: station staff, clients and agency people, and press. The staff designation can include special guests, speakers, and station-contracted vendors.

• The following supplies are frequently needed on site and should be kept on hand in a meeting headquarters room or behind the registration desks:

paper clips	scissors	felt pens
ash trays	pins	ball point pens
rubber bands	rulers	pencils
waste baskets	tape measures	storage cartons
staplers & staples	a tool kit	letter openers
adhesive tape	typewriters	index cards
masking tape	typewriter ribbons	pencil sharpeners
scotch tape	carbon paper	station letterhead
lined pads	phone message pads	& envelopes
petty cash slips	file folders	labels
receipt slips	in-out box	matches
date stamp	numbered stamp	scissors & knife
dictionary		

- Be sure large, clear signs point the way to the registration area. Also have a map of the meeting area displayed there.
- Arrange for telephone service in the registration area.
- Clarify all payment procedures with those assisting with registration.

Handling Celebrities, Guest Speakers, and VIPs

Station parties, station-sponsored meetings and conventions have celebrities, guest speakers and VIPs. Here is a checklist for their care and feeding:

- Issue special invitations or personal letters of invitation. Send them out as far in advance as possible to avoid schedule conflicts.
- Determine if overnight rooms or suites are necessary, and reserve them well in advance. Also, determine who is to pay for them—the station or the guest, and be sure this is clear to the guest.
- Arrange for a welcome note and either flowers or a basket of fruit to be in the room when the guest arrives.
- Assign a responsible person to greet and accompany the guest, if the Promotion Director cannot handle this task personally. This person should expedite baggage and transportation from the airport, and satisfy any reasonable needs or requests of the guest. (See section on Star Tours.)
- Request reference or biographical material on each special guest well in advance, and use it for programs and introductions, as well as in preparing press releases and a press biography. Also ask for photos.
- Arrange for honorium payment in advance, and pay on site or by mail later, as per arrangement.
- Determine special preferences of key guests regarding food, liquor, shows, etc.
- Get a copy of the guest speakers' remarks in advance if possible. Make them available to the press afterwards.
- Determine if a reception line is to be held, at what time, and in what location. Be sure the guest knows about it. Guide the guest to the right location at the appointed time.
- Be sure someone is assigned to cover the doors during guest's speeches to curtail extraneous noise from outside.
- Determine if a ''Question & Answer'' session is to be held after guests' remarks; arrange for floor microphones if the assemblage is large.
- Decide to whom the centerpiece at the head table will go. It is customary to offer it to the principal guest if there is only one who is clearly the most important VIP. Otherwise, determine to whom it will go.
- Hold door prize awards until the end of a session or party. It is not unusual to ask a guest star to make the drawings and presentations. But be sure that the guest knows about it in advance, or he/she might decide to leave early.

Entertainment Check List

Most parties and receptions have some form of entertainment. It might simply be a pianist or small combo. Or it might be a major band, special star or well-known performing group. Here is a checklist for choosing and arranging for such appearances:

· Analyze the nature of the event, its purpose and the schedule to determine where guest performers might be appropriate or make a significant contribution to the affair.

· The normal range to chose from includes comics, small bands or large orchestras, singing groups, soloists, magicians, fashion shows, marching bands, dance groups (from ballet to modern to country/western), circus acts, local college or community performing groups, satirical revues, and more.

· Prepare a time schedule for each act or event. Stick to it.

· Set up rehearsal times and rooms if needed.

· Allow ample set-up time at the actual location.

· Make sure dressing rooms are properly equipped (mirrors, hangers, make-up, adjacent rest rooms, good lighting, easy access to the performing area, etc.)

· Provide musical groups with suggestions of appropriate types of music, specific songs, and required mood changes (background, dance, fanfares, etc.)

· Establish rates for all talent well in advance, get signed contracts, determine if appearance is guaranteed.

· Check if local license or police in attendance are required.

· Determine if there are religious or patriotic observations on the same day which may provide musical suggestions; also determine if the National Anthem is to be played or sung.

· Determine if prayers are to be offered, and select a member of the clergy from the community to lead them.

· Determine if toasts are to be made, assign someone to handle them, and consider using the band to call attention to them.

· Arrange for platforms, raised stages, ramps, etc.

· If necesary, provide storage area for props and musical instruments. It should be locked or guarded.

· Be sure performers check out sound systems in the actual rooms to be used prior to the event.

· Determine if a Master of Ceremonies is needed. It might be the General Manager, a visiting guest star, a major community figure, or even the Sales Director or Promotion Director—if they are effective in such a role.

Giving a party or holding a major meeting can be one of the most demanding activities—and one of the best opportunities for creative fun—that a Promotion Director will face. Imagination, professionalism, leadership and patience are all necessary in large quantities. A final word on parties comes from veteran Director of Advertising and Promotion Harry Honig, at KSDK in St. Louis, who sums up one of his recent presentations—to have been a multiscreen preview party by the pool at a local country club, featuring a fashion show and on-air personalities. "But the real highlights," says Honig, "came when a sudden wind blew the screens and projectors into the pool minutes before the presentation was to start, and shortly after when toy sailboats with new show's names printed on the sails began to sink.'' Honig's warning: ''Be ready for any and all unforseen events. And don't overlook the possibilities for disasters when you plan. If it happens and you're ready for it, no one may notice. And you may get credits for preparedness and effective planning.''

More about Meetings

Many elements of meetings have been covered in the preceding section. There are a number of additional suggestions listed below:

• Schedule in plenty of free time and travel time. Jamming up a schedule just to cram more into it is folly for a good meeting planner. Have plenty of time for not only the presentation but for a Q & A period. Make sure to arrange the schedule so there is ample time for personal time—changing clothes, visiting rest rooms, and traveling from one meeting room to the next. Even for small groups, 10 minutes between meetings is necessary. For larger groups, 15 minutes might be more appropriate. This also allows for slippage if one guest speaker or workshop runs longer than planned.

• Be sure all events at a meeting are well signed. Direction signs, overall maps of meeting rooms, and signs outside each meeting room are very helpful. Panelists and guest speakers should have name signs. The type should be large enough to read from the back of the room.

• Check acoustics in meeting rooms carefully. Be sure speakers can be heard. Check for echos and dead spots in large rooms, and avoid putting chairs in places with those undesirable effects.

• If there are A/V screens in a room the first row of seats should be no closer to the screen that two screen widths.

• Always have extra projector bulbs. Be sure film and tapes are properly rewound from their last showings. Have an engineer or equipment operator on hand.

• Define policies for removal of display and exhibit material and audiovisual equipment.

• Have appropriate insurance coverage for theft and public liability.

• Set up a lost-and-found area.

• Event organizers should have lists of all phone numbers which might be needed in emergencies: police, fire, doctors, hospitals, ambulance services, drug stores.

• Advise local police fully about the event and any problems expected.

• Limit keys to locked security areas to event organizers and security people.

Security Tips for Meetings and Parties

Security is a special problem when audio-visual equipment must remain in place overnight, while rooms are unoccupied, when exhibitors have displays, and when events occur in areas accessible to the general public, such as hotels, restaurants, and convention centers.

The following is a security check-list:

· Assign guards or attendants to all exits as needed.
· Study applicable fire regulations to know which exits may be closed and secured.
· Determine if your own station personnel can perform adequate guard service, if the site staff is equipped to handle such security, or if an outside firm must be hired.
· Determine to what extent local police can be of assistance.
· Check for anticipated trouble areas (pickets, protestors, demonstrators, hecklers, etc.)
· Make sure all undesirable people are watched closely by security staff.
· Arrange for a system for alerting the police, if they should be needed for any reason. Frequently a hotel will have such procedures. Know them, and be sure appropriate station staff people do to.
· Determine if bodyguards are needed for VIP or "star" guests.
· Arrange for special entrances to be used by such stars.
· Check out a hotel's fire prevention systems in advance. Be sure all public areas, hallways and meeting rooms have sprinkler systems, and guest hallways and private rooms have smoke detectors.
· Walkie-talkie communication between meeting or event organizers and guards may be adviseable.
· Arrange for safety deposit storage of valuables.
· Establish a replacement procedure in case items are lost or stolen.

Publicity Appearances

Guest appearances by "stars," VIPS, and station talent can often attract press and media attention to a station. Visiting recording artists and interview-program guests get many radio stations into the newspapers. Visiting TV personalities do the same for TV stations. The clever Promotion Director knows how to use such visits to maximum advantage.

At the same time, such guests must be treated with appropriate courtesy and respect. Proper treatement reflects well on the station, encourages the visitor to assist the station with its publicity efforts in all possible ways, and ensures that the guest will want to return at some time in the future.

A performer entrusts both time and talent to the Promotion Director when visiting a station and its city of license. It isn't fair to leave any detail unattended. The potential for problems is always present. Only careful pre-planning can ensure a profitable visit.

First, how can the visiting star be effectively used? Here are the most common station-organized activities:

1. Individual press interviews.
2. Personalized on-air promotion spots.
3. Mass press conferences.
4. Personal appearances on local radio and TV shows, including those on the host station, itself.

There are numerous ways stars can serve the local station when they come to town for a station visit. Top left, Lorne Greene attends a station cocktail party for clients and press. Top right, Chad Everett lunches with the local press. Middle left, Ron Howard suits up for a game with a local station's softball team. Middle right, Steve Allen poses beside a billboard promoting his show. Lower left, Bob Clayton rides in a parade in a station car, and lower right, Batman and Robin attend a community function to meet with children and sign autographs.

5. Press-covered visits to locales similar to those where the star's program is filmed.
6. VIP treatment at civic functions and organization meetings.
7. Client cocktail parties.
8. Motorcades to and from places where these events are staged.
9. Charity events.
10. Razzle-dazzle stop-offs at major department stores and shopping centers, frequently in conjunction with program-related books or items for sale. Stars with books (Steve Allen, Julia Child, etc.) can hold autograph sessions.
11. Blood donations, or appearances at them.
12. A flow of photographs and feature stories and news items about the visiting star to the city desks and appropriate editors of local press.

The Schedule. A complete schedule, or itinerary, of the star's visit is a must. It should be completed and sent to the visitor's network or trip sponsor before the guest has departed for the visit to the station. It should be in chronological format, telling everything the stranger in town will want to know about the visit:

- Who to see.
- Where to stay.
- Where to go and at what time and for how long.
- Who to talk to.
- How much time will be spent on each scheduled activity.
- How much time there'll be between activities.
- What groups to appear before, along with any relevant side notes of interest about the groups and their current activities, special interests, etc.

In preparing the schedule, here are several key points to remember:

- Avoid big gaps. The visiting celebrity will feel time is being wasted.
- Avoid schedules that are too tight. The visitor will not have time do an effective job at any stop along the way if there isn't room to get from one event to the next, or to have a little breathing and thinking room along the way.
- Avoid events that are unproductive in terms of publicity, promotion, or sales. Experienced celebrities know when an event is designed just as "filler," to take up slack time in a schedule with little productive purpose, and they resent it.
- All events should be firmed up in advance of the trip. Last minute changes can cause complications and confusion for the visitor.
- Copies of the schedule to go to all appropriate people at the station involved with the visit, and to the station's newsroom.

In supervising the star's visit, here is a set of basic rules:

· Contact the airline in advance for special handling, quick deplaning, expedited luggage removal, easy access by welcomers, unawkward movement through the airport, and a convenient approach to ground transportation. (Some "extras" that might be arranged: a red carpet; a motorcycle escort for a limousine, which meets the celebrity at the plane's ramp and whisks him directly to his hotel; a small jazz or ragtime band to march him through the airport; members of his local fan club on hand with banners and an official welcome; and a city official on hand to present the keys. All are possibilities that can get a visit off to a great start, provide useful photo opportunities for the press, the station's photographer, or the station's news cameras or microphones.)

· If at all possible, provide a chauffered limousine. If that's not possible, a shiny, new car. Often a station auto dealer client will provide one free.

· The star should be met at the plane and accompanied during all official parts of his/her visit by a station person thoroughly knowledgeable about the schedule, the city, and the star's personal interests.

· Book a suite in the best hotel in town, if at all possible. Two adjoining rooms or a two-room suite provide interview space for the visitor for hosting members of the print or broadcast media. Flowers or fruit should be waiting in the room.

STATION SPEAKERS BUREAU

At larger stations, a speaker's bureau is often handled by the Community Services (or Community Relations) Department. If there is no such department, responsibility for a speakers bureau might rest with the Promotion Director. It is included here because it can be an important part of the station's overall public relations.

Over a period of years, station staff members or people speaking on behalf of the station can establish personal contact with tens of thousands of individuals in the community through an organized speech-making effort. This kind of contact enables a station to help viewers and listeners to understand the station, its goals, activities, programming, needs, and problems. It can also introduce audiences to personalities in a first hand way that encourages familiarity, admiration and loyalty.

Broadcasters have important messages for the general public that can be effectively communicated through speeches made to local community groups. Public broadcasters need direct financial support from people, as well as volunteers; and they need to generate a groundswell of favorable public opinion to influence local, state and national legislators, from whom much support comes. Commercial broadcasters, in the words of then ABC President James E. Duffy at a 1980 BPA Convention, "Need to make the public more conscious of the values of the unique system we have today, in the face of growing competition." Cable and new low-power broadcasters have specialized interests as well which can be effectively communicated in a direct and personal way through public appearances.

How does the Promotion Director shape such a public speaking effort when time is so precious and limited? There are two frequent approaches: use of the station staff, and use of outside volunteers. For both kinds of speakers, the Promotion Director must supply materials, training, and an organized structure.

The formation of a "speakers bureau," headquartered in the Promotion Department, is a logical first step. The Promotion Department is usually privy to most information about programming, station policies, and network or group activities. The Promotion Director maintains constant contact with all other senior staff members, with the press and public, with other broadcasting organizations, and network or group officials.

The requirements of a speakers bureau are:

- A list of people who can speak well and represent the station impressively.
- Several basic speeches on important topics.
- A flyer or brochure used for generating speech invitations.
- A schedule of speaking engagements.

Here are five steps to follow to set up and run a station speaker's bureau, provided by Promotion Director Linda Nix of public station WYES, New Orleans.

1. *Know what it is you want to communicate to the public.*

Make a list of key points the station would like to get across to audiences. In WYES's case they were:

- That public station WYES's is a ready resource providing viewers with excellent and diverse programming.
- The sources of WYES's funding, programming and strength.
- Ways people can help ensure the station's growth and strength through viewing and contributing money and time.

For a commercial television station, the possible key points might be:

- The quality and quantity of the station's services to the community, including local news, local programming, and entertainment programming.
- The valuable role that commercials play in the local economy.
- The fact that broadcast TV, as a resource to the community, is free.

Other stations might have different, or more specific lists, or might include additional points. As part of this first step, a detailed briefing paper should be prepared explaining and documenting each of the points listed. It might run three-four pages typed.

2. *Pick the right people to speak.*

The first choices are key station executives and personalities who can speak well and make good impressions. Selections might include the General Manager, Promotion Director, Community Services Director, Program Director,

Sales Director, and on-air talent. But don't overlook the Design (or Art) Director, program directors and producers, the News Director, key assistants in many departments, and anyone else with special interests or activities outside the station which might provide useful contacts. For example, a station might have a technician who could speak to his flying club. Or the film department manager might address his local P.T.A.

Don't be limited to station personnel. Attend a meeting of the local Toastmasters organization. Outline needs for one or more qualified speakers to represent the station before the community on a regular basis, and ask for volunteers. Other similar resources might include the Jr. Chamber of Commerce, the Advertising Club, or an organization of community businesses. People like to be associated with broadcast organizations. Many will volunteer.

3. *Training sessions and a "speaker's kit" are essential.*

With so many volunteers, the station will need to be sure that speakers actually selected can, in fact, speak well; and that their material is accurate.

Training sessions run by the Promotion Director are used to weed out those who can't speak well, those who don't seem able to grasp the nuances of the station's messages, and those who are unreliable or unenthusiastic. First sessions should have a great deal of specific instruction in speaking and speech preparation. Later sessions should provide small audiences to give a flavor of reality.

Actual speech training must concentrate on allowing ample time for speech preparation, knowing the occasion and the audience, keeping material simple and direct, providing specific details, keeping visuals clear and easy to see, allowing time for questions, and more.

The speaker's kit should include a sample speech, an annual report (if the station has one), a station brochure, the purpose of the speakers bureau, a list of esoteric broadcast terms and phrases, clichés to avoid, suggestions on how to counter oft-repeated criticisms (such as "I hate commercials. They waste my time!"), a coverage map, and any other specialized information you might have.

TV stations can, if they are members, turn to the Television Information Office (TIO) for specialized information. Radio stations can get significant useful material from the Radio Advertising Bureau. In addition, all commercial and public networks can provide recent speeches by their executives, and relevant information for speeches on a wide variety of topics.

4. *Provide the speaker with additional materials.*

Slides, or a slide/tape presentation; a videotape; brochures; give-away premiums; photos of station talent. All can be useful. WDCN-TV provides its speakers bureau with a 20-minute film (or tape) "Television Is For Learning," and a seven-minute slide show loosely based on the sample speech in the kit. A Fall preview tape might be useful. Again, ABC, NBC, CBS, PBS, NPR,

TIO, RAB, TVB, station ownership groups and other organizations might have presentations that can be used as is, or adapted to suit station needs.

5. Promote the speakers bureau.

The local Chamber of Commerce undoubtedly maintains lists of civic and professional groups who are frequently looking for speakers. PTA chapters, large companies, and schools can provide speaking dates. Send out an inexpensive direct mail piece to these organizations outlining the speakers service. Public stations can mention the service in the station's monthly program guide. And a station's own air can be a good place to promote the speakers bureau.

Promotion Director Nix points out that the amount of work needed to get a speaker's bureau started can rob a Promotion Director of some evening hours and definitely requires extra effort. "But," she points out, "once things are in place, the process nearly takes care of itself. You need to schedule your speakers when the requests come in—unless you have an assistant or volunteer to handle scheduling—and you need to periodically review and renew the speech material in use. You need to provide specialized material when there are special messages to get to people. But you don't have to write and deliver speeches every week on your station's behalf."

Most important, the active speaking effort opens up two-way lines of communication to the community. The station can get messages out, and can get feedback from the community at the same time.

PUBLIC RELATIONS AGENCIES*

Station Promotion Directors are frequently involved in the planning of major publicity and promotional campaigns. Due to the importance of some campaigns, stations may elect to seek the guidance and support of a full-service public relations agency. Now the major decision: which agency should be selected, why, and how will it work with the promotion staff?

What a PR Agency Does

Professional public relations agencies serve as a valuable asset in expanding and extending the impact and penetration of publicity and promotional campaigns. An agency's expertise in reaching desired target audiences in vast numbers can be critical to a successful campaign and works to complement the station image.

The agency must, however, be carefully selected with the final decision based on a variety of key factors. The overall effectiveness of an agency is critical in making the decision, which may be based on: a list of clients both

*This section of Chapter 18 was written especially for this text by Gary Claussen, Sr. Vice President, Stone, Associates Public Relations, Los Angeles, California.

past and present, areas and diversity of specialization, reputation with the media and in the community, and its past campaigns and how successful they were.

Big is not always best, particularly when selecting a public relations agency. In most cases the promotion budget will dictate the size of agency to be employed and the project will determine the type of organization to be hired. Most important, however, is knowing how to successfully and effectively select and use the agency in order to generate the desired mass public and press awareness.

Advantages of Using a PR Agency

With the escalating costs of operating a broadcast station, maintaining a large public relations department can be difficult. Stations today generally are not equipped to handle major national publicity campaigns. Often it is a case of too few people doing too many jobs within the station. The staff is spread thin performing the necessary tasks to keep broadcast log editors updated about frequent program changes, publicizing the weekly program schedule, maintaining and planning on-air promotion, designing and implementing the station's advertising plans and actively participating in the steps necessary for license renewal which, with strict Federal laws, has become a day-to-day activity simply to preserve the right of broadcasting.

Public relations agencies are not beset with the heavy demands of operating a station and therefore are able to work daily with members of the print and electronic media, cultivating and cementing important relationships with the press. Consequently, the agency remains in a position to complement its client's image by bringing the project into frequent and clearer perspective with journalists and, through them, to the public.

Equally important is the fresh perspective an agency can apply to an issue or situation. In addition to serving as an invaluable extension of the promotional efforts of a station, the agency representatives can see ''other'' sides of an issue or campaign and evaluate both the objective and subjective positions. This neutral ability results in keeping the campaign aimed in a positive direction. The agency remains alert to pending conflicts or questions in order to prevent possible confusion and a negative press.

An experienced agency with extensive background in conceiving and executing major television and radio promotional campaigns has the basic formula down to a science. All of the publicity and promotion elements, however, must include an exchange of ideas and review by you as client and key representative of the broadcasting outlet.

The hiring of an agency and affording its staff *carte blanche* is unwise and is asking for problems. The Promotion Director is the intermediary and serves a vital function between the agency and station management and the production unit. This is not to say that all of your time will be consumed by the project. It should not be, since the professional agency has been hired to handle the project and produce results. But there are times from the beginning of the campaign to its conclusion when station philosophy and politics must be shared with the agency representatives.

Selecting the Best Agency

Public relations agencies generally specialize in one, or at the most two, key specific fields. The categories are numerous and include corporate affairs, non-profit and fund-raising organizations, performing arts, entertainment, celebrities and personalities, politics, marketing, visual arts, music, business, dance, et al. Therefore, the first determination to be made is a full evaluation of the project, what the station expects in terms of returns, which publics must be reached, and how may both the station and project best be served.

Often a highly experienced and well-qualified agency that offers some variety, through its past successes and its client list, can bring greater depth to the campaign by simple cross-pollination. This is where a medium-size agency with a solid background in handling a varied list of missions can be most useful. An agency of this composition may focus on well-known personalities and entertainers, corporations (business and financial), commercial and public television specials and series, theatrical motion pictures, and all areas of the arts including major museum events. By hiring this type of agency the station not only has immediate use of the agency representatives in the broadcasting division, but their counterparts in the other areas as well who can involve their respective clients on behalf of you and your station's campaign.

Assume, for example, that in the planning stage there is a major station event that also includes a broadcast special which calls for reaching the business and financial press, as well as the on-air and print television press. The additional support of the agency's stable of personalities used during the pre- and post-launch phases of the campaign will always generate increased interest with the press and the public.

By having the option of incorporating more than one of the agency's areas of specialization, the campaign takes on a multi-dimensional profile injecting color and interest and opening additional avenues of exposure to imprint a lasting effect on the target publics.

Employing an agency with solid strength in a number of areas is similar to hiring one agency and having two or three working for the station for the price on one. A well-structured, highly organized agency which provides this full-service approach is worth its weight in gold. The best agency is one that is creative, aggressive, effective and thorough. The final result is rewarding to both the Promotion Director and the station.

When the selection process has been narrowed to two or three public relations agencies, a preliminary meeting with each should be planned. This is an excellent opportunity for the Promotion Director to discuss the project, test the creative atmosphere, and generally explore the chemistry between station staff and agency representatives. Positive client-agency relationships and trust are essential and usually are obvious from the initial meeting. Remember, the station will be working with the agency for a specific period of time—normally for several months—and constant responsiveness, harmony, creativity and input are vital in the day-to-day operation of an effective campaign.

The "first meeting" is critical. Invite agency representatives to discuss the project and to return with a thematic promotional plan, a breakdown of projected publicity and promotion elements, recommended fee for a set period of time, an estimate of expenses, and brief description of the campaign's intended outreach. Be alert to the agency's grasp of the project's subject matter and assess its ability to create a campaign beyond the ordinary treatment. If the project is one which lends itself to reaching specialized organizations and groups like educational institutions, libraries, and hospitals, this is an opportunity to test the agency's imagination and creative skills.

Though the budget can maximize or minimize the number of promotions in a campaign, a "thinking" public relations agency will try new ideas within budgetary limitations—ideas for making the campaign appealing, varied and far-reaching. Be on guard to identify agencies that promise the impossible but are only prepared to deliver the very minimum.

Another important consideration when selecting an agency is its location, both in the station's city and in terms of its offices in other states.

The value of retaining an agency with offices in Los Angeles and New York cannot be overstated if national or trade publicity is needed. Many agencies are headquartered in only one major city, with "auxiliary" offices in other states. Often these "branch" offices operate independently of the agency and provide support on a special sub-contract basis. The single-city agency usually cannot provide the response, coordination and extensive penetration nationally that a multi-city agency can.

Evaluate the size of the agency, the cities in which it has offices, successes of past and present campaigns that are similar to the one you are proposing, and its working client list. A credible and growing agency that is interested in serving the station in a dedicated manner will openly share this information.

The Agency PR Campaign

There are scores of vital and interconnecting elements that must be planned for and implemented in advance to meet deadlines.

The agency should provide a calendar timetable that outlines all the steps in the promotion. This includes the activity, the date to be submitted for station approval, and the date of distribution to the intended media or special organizations. The calendar should be carefully reviewed during a meeting between the agency and you to ensure that all parties understand the process and deadlines.

Too often, producers, directors, executive producers et al do not understand long deadlines inherent in a successful promotional plan. Arrange an early, pre-production meeting so the program manager, producer and director can get to know agency representatives. During this valuable time station needs and those of the agency should be made clear so the best possible results may be achieved. This meeting is instrumental. It stresses the importance of scheduling time on the set during dress rehearsals and tapings for shooting black-and-white photographs and color transparencies of the performers in character. These set-ups are critical to the visual needs of most program campaigns (press kits, posters, exclusive plants etc.) and also serve as an important ''record'' of the production on behalf of the station—for annual reports, sales brochures, educational flyers and other institutional pieces.

In addition to the importance of access on the set for photography purposes, it is equally important that time be made available to the agency representative to interview stars and key production staff during rehearsals to obtain background facts for press materials. During this time the agency can also gather production notes and feed them to columnists. These short ''quick takes'' keep mention of the production alive in the press and provide an important, on-going build-up leading toward the campaign's crescendo.

Early education of the production staff to the significance of cooperation and access eliminates missed opportunities and misunderstanding as the production gets underway.

Special programs that are filmed or videotaped three of four weeks prior to telecast create an extremely tight calendar in which to promote it to the press. This type of tight schedule, of course, results in a variety of missed deadlines and calls for even closer rapport among Promotion Director, agency, production staff and station management.

With short-deadline projects, work closely with the agency—on a day-to-day basis—to maximize use of available time and talent. Part of the Promotion Director's game plan should include helping the producer and program manager to understand the type of promotional campaign and expected results of the short-deadline approach. The average station staff often fails to comprehend how its ''outstanding'' special missed editorial coverage in a publication with a six-week deadline, regardless of the fact that the program was produced only three weeks before air. Normally, a producer dreams of having his special air shortly after the production has concluded—and wants, at the same time, the results of months of careful publicity and promotion planning. Unrealistic? Yes. But since there is no way to require being a Promotion Director as a prerequisite to being a producer, it is the Promotion Director's responsibility—and that of the agency—to ''retrain'' the creative minds at the station.

The ideal campaign, however, is one which permits the necessary time for meeting all deadlines, both in print and for on-air. A television station that invests in a ''special'' must consider the significance of that investment in terms of planning for ample time to include an effective promotion to ''get the word out'' and get ''the numbers.'' Without publicity to generate the audience and the numbers, the game is lost and the investment in a PR agency—and in the show—may be wasted.

To claim that advertising alone can save a program by generating viewers is idealistic and often a losing gamble.

While advertising can prove a valuable asset in supporting the campaign, it cannot carry the mission alone. The value of publicity *with* advertising is best summed up in noting that the average newspaper or magazine devotes 40%

of its space to editorial information and approximately 60% to advertisements. Of the 40% of editorial stories, 20% will have been written by staff writers and 80% will come directly or indirectly from publicity representatives. By *directly,* the publicity office for either a firm or an individual has written the entire story and submitted it as a finished work. By *indirectly,* the publicity person has approached the editor, or a reporter, with an idea for a story, which was then written by an actual media person.

These percentages represent an important overview of the impact of the agency. Without question, the quality of the written materials—from announcement stories and special features to biographies, captions and, yes, even pitch letters—is a critical factor. Make sure the agency hired to do the job can also write, *and write very well.*

Regular progress reports from the agency throughout an entire campaign should be automatic. They take time, but when coupled with frequent telephone communications between the Promotion Director and the agency representative, they are invaluable and keep the station effectively briefed. Additionally, throughout the contract the agency will provide regular press clipping reports which should point out key elements that a Promotion Director, in turn, can present to station management. These significant elements can include mention of the station, call letters, management personnel, reprint of press kit materials including artwork, reprint of the specially designed logo (this happens frequently), sponsor or underwriter identification, producer's name, etc. When the important elements are high-lighted and accompany the press clip, your need to read all the materials that appear in print is eliminated, thus saving valuable time.

There is no need to explore and delineate each obvious step in a promotion and publicity campaign. As a working professional in the promotion field, they are tools which, when used to cultivate the barren terrain, result in a full harvest if employed properly. These ingredients include: gallery photo sessions, full production coverage, special graphic design, writing of all press materials, stunts, promotional events, posters, bookmarks, exclusive and non-exclusive art selection, press screenings, celebrity tours, special mailers, flyers, and preparation and distribution of educational materials. Many of these elements are discussed in detail elsewhere in this handbook.

The key, however, to successful use of a PR agency by a broadcast stations is: will its efforts enable the station to generate significant additional exposure and publicity, while saving the station Promotion Director staff time for other on-going projects? The answer is usually "yes," so the hiring of an outside agency is dependent on the need for that extra measure of publicity.

CHAPTER 18

Station Promotions

In addition to on-air promotion of specific programs and station image, and in addition to advertising and publicity, broadcast stations frequently engage in other activities designed to call attention to themselves, their programming and personalities, and so attract audiences. Among the possibilities are contests, direct mail promotions, staged community events, station presence at community events, and creative uses of premiums and give-aways.

CONTESTS*

High on the list of these other station promotions are contests. Contests are especially popular with radio stations. Over the years stations have come up with thousands of different contests involving large and small prizes, catchy gimmicks, and personalities.

Listener-participation contests can be time-consuming for Promotion Directors and others on station's staffs. The following guidelines, the product of years of experience by a number of broadcasters in the U.S. and Canada, can help make contests meaningful to both the station and the audience, and can help keep station efforts reasonable.

These guidelines were compiled by Lee Pocock, Promotion Director of KSL Radio, Salt Lake City, Utah. Strongly recommended for all broadcasters involved in contest promotions is the National Association of Broadcasters'

*This section on "Contests" was edited from material prepared by A. Lee Pocock, Promotion Director, KSL Radio, Salt Lake City, Utah.; and from a Radio Bureau of Canada booklet entitled 150 Sound Ideas For Retailers, written by RBC's Larry Heywood, Vice President of Creative Services.

booklet, "Lotteries and Contests: A Broadcaster's Handbook." Both Pocock and the NAB strongly recommend consulting the station's legal counsel regarding all station contests to ensure that no federal, state, or local regulations or laws are violated.

Determine Promotional Goals

Contests should not be aired haphazardly or simply because someone had a "good idea." Contests should reflect the station's image, or improve it. They should be directed toward the audience the station wants to influence, and designed especially for that particular audience.

With a clearly defined audience objective and station goal decided upon, some contests will seem ideal, others inappropriate. The Promotion Director must decide what the contest is to accomplish. Is it to be an audience builder, a programming element, or an image reinforcer? What should it achieve? In what time period should it accomplish its objectives? The answers to these questions form the basis for examining contest concepts and carrying contest planning forward.

Contest Concepts

Simplicity is usually a key element in effective promotion contests. On-air delivery and explanations must be simple. The workings of the contest must be easily understood by station employees as well as listeners, so try them out on colleagues first. See if they understand everything clearly.

Vicarious enjoyment by non-participants is another useful element of contest design. People who don't enter should be able to have fun listening to the contest along with those who do enter. If it is a hidden sound contest, for example, the non-participating listener can play along even though he has no intention of entering. Contests which can be enjoyed for information or trivia fall into this category. When a contest engages the interest of all listeners, contest "tune-out" is avoided.

Take a minimum of air time. A one-minute maximum per announcement is suggested by many experts. Be able to explain the rules—or where to get them—as well as the prizes, participating sponsors, and other information in that amount of time.

Run it long enough. For a major contest, two weeks might be considered a bare minimum. The exceptions are fun, lightweight contests involving trivia contests with movie ticket prizes, or similar promotions. These are simple "program fun" contests.

Test the contest. Once the rules are set, test the contest with station staff, a business or church group, Scout troop, or other similar test "audience." Take care not to reveal information that could lead to winning the actual contest. Just test the design, not the actual contest.

Explain it to the staff. It is usually best to have one or two station staff members designated as the people who answer audience questions about the contest. These people are the "experts." But all station staff members should understand the contest thoroughly so they can "talk it up" accurately with friends in the community without giving mis-information.

Spell out everything to clients/sponsors. If a merchandising client or co-sponsor is involved, full documentation should be presented to them prior to releasing information on the contest. Define their responsibilities and the station's. Discuss all aspects of the contest with them. Discuss the model number, taxes, delivery, color, repair, warranty, and other relevant prize information with them, then put it all in writing.

Beware of Lotteries

Before going further, the following caution about lotteries is imperative.

U.S. and Canadian Federal law, and many state and province laws prohibit the broadcasting of information about lotteries. The regulations can be complex, may vary from location, and may be subject to unique legal interpretations.

FCC sanctions for violation of U.S. federal lottery laws range from fines to station license revocation. Canadian stations and personnel may be liable for punishment under Canada's criminal codes.

It does not matter whether a contest is station sponsored, or sponsored by a station client. The station is still responsible for any lottery information it broadcasts. So all contest rules and regulations should be cleared by a station's legal counsel.

There are three elements that must be present to constitute a lottery: prize, chance, and consideration.

Prize. This is the easiest to define and understand. A *prize* is anything of value offered to the contestant. It doesn't matter what the prize is, or how much it is worth. If there is no prize, then a planned "contest promotion" does not constitute a lottery. However, discounts or refunds *do* count as prizes.

Chance. This second element of a lottery is a more difficult concept. Basically, the element of chance exists if either the winner, or the value of the prize, is determined *in whole or in part* by chance. (In Canada, skill questions following random drawings can enable a contest to avoid the "lottery" label, but this is not true in the U.S.)

If the selection of the winner is determined by chance rather than by skill or other factors within the contestant's control, then the second element of a lottery exists. Conversely, if skill—or factors under the control of the contestant—determine the winner, the lottery element of chance does not exist.

Examples of chance include: wheel-spinning, random drawings, being the 3rd person to call in, being at a given place when a random event occurs, or guessing sports scores in advance.

If a contest enables everyone who enters to win something, but some peoples' prizes will be worth more than others, that, too, involves the element of chance.

And so also do skill contests which have random tie-breaking procedures for more than one first-place winner.

Consideration. The least understood of the three elements of a lottery is consideration. The term is applied to anything of value that a contestant must spend—or expend—in order to be a part of the contest. The element of consideration is present if a competitor must furnish money or something else of value, must be in possession of any product sold, manufactured, furnished or distributed by a sponsor of a program broadcast by a station, or meet any other requirement which involves a substantial expenditure of time and effort.

Examples of "consideration" include: agreement to make a purchase; the need to purchase a product or service; or a *substantial* expenditure of effort, either by work or travel.

However, the cost of postage to enter the contest or travelling to a convenient location to pick up an entry blank are not considered "consideration." Neither is the requirement to "be present in order to win," unless, of course, the travel requirement is ludicrous.

Many other factors have been explored before the FCC in test cases and decisions. Communications lawyers should be consulted to be sure the elements of prize, chance and consideration are not included. Again, the NAB's regularly updated book, "Lotteries and Contests: A Broadcaster's Handbook" examines the subject and recent decisions which affect it in detail.

It is always advisable for the station's legal counsel to be consulted in formulating contest rules. The following reminders about rules, controls, on-air, prizes and follow-up were prepared by Lee Pocock, Promotion Director, KSL Radio/Salt Lake City, (and BPA officer). They represent many years of broadcast contesting experience.

Contest Rules

One of the most difficult and exacting elements in designing a contest is the correct preparation and distribution of the rules. A contest should never be undertaken without printed rules, even if they only apply for in-house use. Contests should not go on the air without having on file at the station a full description of all aspects of the contest, including:

- How it is to operate, with a complete list of rules.
- Who will be in charge.
- Who is eligible, and who is ineligible.
- How prizes will be obtained, and where they will be stored.
- Where prizes will be awarded.
- How contest will be judged, and by whom.
- Rules should clearly state how (on what basis) the winners will be chosen.
- Rules should be clear on how second, third, and other placing contestants are chosen.
- Policy for breaking ties should be clear.
- If a skill test question is used to break ties or decide between semi-finalists, the test question should be a genuine test of skill. Simply asking "Who is buried in Grant's Tomb?" is not sufficient. However, a question

such as "Who was the fifth President of the U.S.?" probably would qualify as a skill question.

• When dealing with written entries to a "write in 25 words or less . . ." contest, specify if spelling, punctuation, and grammar will be considered.

• Rules should explain very clearly what audience members must do to participate, or enter.

• Publicly announce (or state in the rules) when winners will be announced and how they will be informed. If a winner is notified on the air, follow up with a certified letter.

• Have a policy that the station owns all entries. This is especially important in song-writing, photography, art, and other contests calling for individual original creativity.

• If entries must be fully original, it should be so-stated in the rules. Require winners to sign waivers assuring originality.

• Specify exactly where, when and how entries will be accepted.

• Exclude station personnel, agencies, clients, if involved, and relatives from winning.

• Be sure the closing date and deadline are precisely defined.

• Require entries to be "received at the station" by a certain date, rather than "postmarked," to avoid problems from late mail deliveries.

• Do all that is possible to be sure that all contestants have been given the same contest information.

• Announce and publish how many prizes will be awarded to one person or household. (A household is usually defined as all parties living at the same address.) The prize limit should be clear. Many stations have a policy that limits to once a year the number of times a person or household can win. Others state once a month, or some other time period.

• Clearly state what constitutes an entry: size, shape, etc. Does it need postage? What address must it have? What information needs to be on the entry?

Contest Controls

Contest controls are procedures that ensure the contest can be easily and effectively managed by the Promotion Director and station staff. Pocock lists the following as important, often necessary controls:

Make sure that only qualified people at the station answer contest questions—preferably the Promotion Director or the promotion staff. It is a good policy not to give out contest information on the phone that isn't given out on the air. Many stations have a special recording device that restates all elements of the contest, outlining all rules. The number for this recording can be given on-air.

A staff meeting held before the start of the contest should fully explain all elements of the contest to all station staff members. They should be told how the contest operates and other pertinent information, even though they are not to give it out. Having the proper information in advance ensures that no one will inadvertently give out mis-information.

Clear the contest with any applicable local, state, federal, or provincial officials.

Treasure hunt contests call for special care to prevent contestants or participants from digging up or damaging property or destroying possessions of others . . . in the wrong part of town, far from where the real treasure is hidden.

Be sure any contest does not encourage participants to interfere with, violate, or infringe upon the rights or privacy of others.

The station might want to consider working with the telephone company to obtain a contest line that is numerically protected by at least 100 digits from other existing exchanges to prevent frequent mis-dials. A commercial exchange should be used.

Notify the mail room, the receptionist, and station switchboard operators so that they will be prepared for a heavy volume of incoming mail, visitors or calls.

Do not let a client or an outside party use the entries as an address or telephone list. The entries are from the station's audience members. They keep the station in business. Their privacy must not be violated.

Make sure that adequate security measures are taken to guard confidentiality of entrusted information, especially information crucial to winning the contest. Don't, for example, leave contest answers (or tomorrow's clues) in the control room. The fewer people who have access to such information, the more protected the contest . . . and the station . . . is from criticism.

Not just winners, but all entries should be kept in safe storage for a considerable time after the contest in case there are challenges to the winner and verification is necessary. None should be lost.

More about the telephone company: it should always be briefed in advance about any contest that will generate more than a routine number of calls. Tell them what lines will be used, what numbers will be given out, what dates and times are involved. Legally, a contest can be stopped if there is interference with telephone traffic. A large number of calls coming in on the same trunk line, exchange and prefix at precisely the same instant creates problems. The phone company can advise ways to prevent problems, or help solve them before they occur.

Contest Judging

Printed rules should state that "the decision of the judges is final." After winners have been announced, never, never change the decision. If it is changed for one contestant, others will demand the same. (The exception is if a contestant is disqualified for, as an example, submitting non-original material when the rules called for original work.)

Make sure that judges are selected who are honest, fair, and impartial.

Make sure that the judges are the best qualified available, having specific credentials in any skill areas to be judged.

Make sure that the judges fully understand the criteria on which they are to select the winner.

It is recommended, through much experience in contest design, that station personnel should never be used to judge a contest.

The judging should not be open to the public. Though it appears to be more honest to judge in the open, the procedure causes more problems than it solves. Some people will demand explanations of why one person won over another. This can generate negative reactions.

When drawings are held, it adds authenticity to use a public official or other prominent person to actually do the drawing. The drawing should be conducted in the privacy of an office or control room.

Station mangement should not do the drawing. If it is deemed necessary, however, other station managers should be present for the station's protection.

Above all, judging must be 100% honest and fair, according to all rules and criteria set up and published in advance.

Contest Prizes

Prizes provide incentive to participate in station contests. To avoid embarrassments and misunderstandings regarding prizes and make them effective motivators, here is a check list of points to consider.

In announcements about contest outcomes, never imply that there were losers. When possible, make everyone a winner in some way. Consolation prizes, small gifts or premiums for entering, and on-air mentions of runners' up are all possibilities.

Award a number of prizes, not one gigantic prize. Listeners want to think they have a good chance for a prize, even though it may not be the big one. Few listeners visualize themselves as the winner of a "grand prize." So more participants will enter if they perceive they have a chance to win one of the several—or a large number—of prizes.

Most effective is the awarding of a large number of identical prizes, such as 10 $1,000 bills; or 20 round trips to Disneyland.

Award prizes exactly as publicized and award them exactly per contest schedule and rules.

A gift release statement should be used in awarding prizes. The statement simply notes that a prize has been awarded for participating in a contest. It describes the prize. It asks for a signature upon receipt. Prize winner should be notified by certified mail. The release, presented at the time the award is actually made, should include permission to tape the award and use it on the air. The release serves two purposes: There is a signed document on file certifying that the prize has been received; and the station has permission to publicize the winner.

Do not depend on the vendor or co-op sponsor to fulfill prize requirements. This is the station Promotion Department's responsibility. The best approach is to request and receive the prize(s) in advance of announcing and publicizing the contest, and keep them in secure storage (locked up at the station, in a bank vault in the station's name, or another secure place). This avoids embarrassments that can come from delays in receiving promised prizes on time, or co-sponsors which might dishonor commitments.

When the winners receive or redeem prizes, there should be no attempt by the station or co-sponsor to coerce them to buy additional goods or services, or to accept substitute prizes.

Do not substitute prizes. Even slight differences between what is promised as a contest prize and what is delivered can cause ill-will and hard feelings and may result in negative publicity. If it is appropriate, state in the rules that there will be no substitutions. Many stations have found that if a cash award is allowed instead of a trip for one winner, many others may want the same treatment. This is especially important when prizes have been traded for by the station, rather than purchased by cash outlay.

When a trip or merchandise is awarded, state in contest rules that they must be redeemed by a specific time and date. Time limits may dictate whether or not people should enter, and will save later embarrassment to notify the United States Internal Revenue Service of all winnings over $600. (This limit is subject to change by the IRS on an annual basis. Check with station attorneys.) The contestant must be made aware that the station is obligated by law to notify the federal government of such awards. Many stations, upon awarding a prize, will state this in the notification of winning and state it again when the prize is awarded.

Prizes should be accurately described in all contest promotion.

Prizes should be useful, functional, and not easily broken or damaged. They should be free of negative racial or religious connotations, or any overtones which may be offensive to winners. They should be as attractive as possible to a wide audience, or to specified targeted audiences.

Indications from BPA member stations is that the number one prize prefered by audiences is money. Travel is the second-favorite prize.

Be prepared to deliver the prize, no matter where the contestant lives, unless contest rules indicate otherwise. Much publicity can be gained from weekly and even daily newspapers when prizes are delivered to the winner's home by station personalities. Be sure to have a photographer and tape recorder on hand.

Contest Follow-up

When the contest is over, winners chosen and the prizes awarded, the Promotion Department's work is not finished.

Prepare a recap of contest details for station management, co-op sponsors, and the Sales Department. Stress advertiser involvement and advantages of participation (exposure in print and on-air, for example). It will be much easier to launch another contest for a co-op sponsor who is satisfied with the results of a previous experience with the station.

Review the contest in detail for station personnel. Explain the elements that worked successfully and those that did not. For Promotion Department files, recap in writing the full range of details for future reference, emphasizing contest objectives and how well they were achieved. Honesty is imperative in evaluating the planning and execution of a contest.

Remember, seasoned professionals in Promotion develop new ideas with each contest. Much can be learned from the experiences of others who have launched similar contests. Each month the BPA's *Newsletter* briefly summarizes many station promotions and contests. A phone call to the station's Promotion Director can yield much useful information.

Sample Contest Ideas

Here are a number of examples of contests stations have run, drawn from BPA Seminars and the BPA *Newsletter*. They are included to give a quick idea of the range of ideas that are possible. More ideas—specifically ideas with advertiser tie-ins—are available from the Radio Advertising Bureau, TVB, and the Radio Bureau of Canada.

> *Cash Quiz:* Announce a dollar figure, call out to see if the listener can tell the amount. Or, translate the station's frequency into dollars made up of 1's, 5's, and 10's. Listeners have to guess how many of each.
>
> *Quotable Quotes:* Pick out a quote, give one word per hour from the quote (out of correct sequence), and take calls after each word. Reduce the jackpot after each word.

Two contest ads, one radio and one television, show the importance of simplicity in detailing contest instructions.

Country Music Month: An annual celebration, with the station giving away an album a day, a vacation a week, and other prizes.

High-Low: Listeners guess a dollar amount and are told "high" or "low" as they call in, until someone finally gets the exact figure.

Parade of Prizes: An audiotape of up to 500 prizes is compiled. Listeners who qualify with a certain phone number digit call in and can receive the prize number for the hour—whatever it is. Run prizes for women in daytime, mens' prizes in evening.

The Great Egg Drop: People are invited to come to a public place (i.e, a shopping center mall) and catch eggs the station will drop from a specified height (relate it to dial position). Any device can be used to catch eggs. A crowd-pleaser because most miss. Get releases. Provide helmets, face masks, padded jacket. Invite winners back for larger prizes if they can repeat their successes.

Dart Game: Easy to do for a public place: put up a green felt, attach 45 and LP records to it. Award records to those who can put a dart into the center hole.

The Big Ice Melt: Listeners must correctly guess when a big block of ice will melt; or, put a barrel on a frozen river or lake and have them guess when it will fall through as the ice melts.

DIRECT MAIL*

Direct mail is a promotional or marketing tool intended to elicit a response from the reader. As such, it covers a variety of purposes. Public television and radio stations use it for new member solicitation, upgrading and renewing memberships, and fulfillment, underwriting solicitation and volunteer solicitation. (Commercial stations use it for sales promotion. Both occasionally use it for direct program promotion to community leaders and special interest groups.)

Traditionally, a direct mail piece consists of a "sell" letter, outer envelope and response device which may be incorporated into the business reply envelope.

However, the general guideline is: *design the mailing to fit the special purpose.* Someone may well read the mailing simply because it is on the station's letterhead. On the other hand, the mailing may require more of an inducement via copy, illustration, design, color or a "teaser" line.

Direct mail packages come in an endless array of shapes, sizes, colors and forms. Packages may be as simple as a self-mailer or post card, or as complex as a kit composed of letters, brochures, order forms, press releases, reply envelopes, special inserts, catalogues and so on. In fact, testing often shows gimmicks, such as cutouts, pop-ups, tokens, stamps or simulated checks, contribute to a higher response. No matter how sophisticated readers are, they still might enjoy playing games.

*Chapter 19 (p. 437—Direct Mail)
This section on "Direct Mail" was edited from PBS Television Network Public Information Department papers on the subject prepared by Dan Agan.

The key word is *appropriateness*. The mailing should be tasteful, fit the purpose, be attractive yet not extravagant, and meet legal requirements.

Direct Mail Allows Targeting

Assuming lists are current, direct mail reaches virtually everyone selected to receive the message. The alternative to selected lists is bulk mail delivery. It uses a cheaper "shotgun" approach. It must be understood, however, that not everyone who receives a direct mail package will read it, although some mailings can be successful with a response as small as 1%.

Audience members differ. Some respond well to on-air messages. Some respond best to direct contact. Others like to see, hold, read, and even save messages.

Direct mail can reach people who are not yet members of the station's normal audience but who share the same demographics and interests as the audience. Public broadcasters have discovered that people who respond by mail sometimes become viewers or listeners *after* they become station members or subscribers. They can be reached because they subscribe to the same or similar publications, are members of the same organizations, or support the same charities as the station's audience. Also, there are those people who seldom want or listen to public broadcasting, but are willing donors simply because the "collect" memberships or contribute for a variety of personal reasons. Admittedly, these groups of members are small.

In commercial broadcasting, specific kinds of sales promotion information is often designed for specific target audiences: media buyers, clients, ad agency personnel, and community leaders—governmental, civic, business or religious.

In these categories, direct mail can widen audiences by introducing station programming (series or specials) through mailed promotional pieces. The station either acquires viewers especially interested in the topic of the special programming, or increases its potential for future income from donor/members or advertisers.

Direct Mail and Other Media

Direct mail works best when combined with other advertising and promotion efforts. On-air, personal contact, special events, and trade press or consumer-oriented print ads all reinforce direct mail, and in turn are reinforced by it. This is especially true when campaigns are coordinated—that is, when the look, style, and copy treatment are similar.

When to Use Direct Mail

There are many factors which affect how often and for what purpose direct mail can and should be used. These factors vary from station to station. Such things as available budget, staff size, financial need, market characteristics and station philosophy will all have an affect upon a direct mail program.

SEASONAL INFLUENCE IN MAIL ORDER

100 = average response

Data from large mail-order mailers, compiled by O. E. McIntyre, Inc., indicates peak mail months for merchandise to be January, February and August. Small competitors may prefer to mail "out of season" when the competition is less active.

Timing, of course, is very important. Direct mail, when used in concert with other media and promotions, must appear concurrently with the others to be effective and efficient reinforcement. However the chart above shows that there are "seasons" which provide more response to mail solicitations, regardless of supporting campaigns, and station mailings may want to take these into consideration.

Budgeting

The budget available for direct mail campaigns directly affects the quantity and quality of those mailings. Conversely, as the quantity and quality of the mailings increases, so does the financial demand. Research has shown that a higher per-piece cost contributes to an increase in response to the mailing. But because quality and timing are also considerations, it does not automatically follow that the more a station spends on a direct mailing, the more response it will get.

For an in-house mailing, it is wise to prepare a projected budget, such as the one shown below, so that costs will fall within acceptable limits. If the mailing is to be produced by an outside agency, the per unit or per thousand cost should be a part of the contract.

A commercial station might prepare a similar budget, substituting advertising income generated by a mailing to clients; or other appropriate response yardsticks.

PROJECTED BUDGET, PTV STATION MEMBERSHIP MAILING

Direct Mail

Mail Quantity:	50,000
Return %:	2%
#	1,000
$	$20,000
Average Gift:	$20.00
Total Cost:	$6,650
Net Revenue	$13,350
Ratio: dollar invested/dollar returned	$1/$2

Cost Breakdown:

Design, typography	$ 500
Production:	
Letter @ $10 per thousand	500
Mail Envelope @ $25 per thousand	1250
Reply Envelope @ $15 per thousand	750
Brochure @ $25 per thousand	1250
List Rental/Addressing @ $25	
(25,000 rental)	625
Mailing @ $13.50	675
Postage @ $22	1100
TOTAL	$6650
Per Thousand	$133

PLASTIC CARD PROMOTIONS

Plastic card promotions have become very popular with radio stations in recent years for several reasons.

Giving listeners credit-card sized plastic cards directly involves them with the station. People like to belong. Having a station card is like having a membership, and there is the possibility of tangible rewards.

Plastic card promotions are usually advertiser funded. Advertisers cover the cost of the cards as well as prizes that are given away to card holders, and—in addition—many buy additional time on the station.

Plastic card promotions provide demographic information the radio station can use to increase its sale of time to advertisers.

Plastic card promotions can be tailored to individual station's needs, and they are easily changed for new promotions.

In short, they are the kind of promotions that please stations, listeners, and advertisers.

The cards with the station's logo imprinted, each with a separate "membership number," are usually distributed to listeners via newspaper, direct mail, point of purchase, and/or on-air promotion spots.

To "activate" the card, each listener must fill out a reply card and return it to the station. The information thus gained may be used in a number of ways: demographic information for sales; client mailing lists; station newsletter mailing lists, and more.

Making a plastic card promotion a success involves several important principles.

First, get the card into listeners' hands as quickly and easily as possible. A proven way to do this is by using a local newspaper. Supply the paper with the station's cards affixed to 8½ x 11" "carriers," or stiff paper sheets which explain the plastic card promotion. (See illustration.) Newspapers charge a nominal fee for inserting these carriers into the papers, and this expense can sometimes be traded for air time.

This kind of distribution is quick, comprehensive, and—because it happens so suddenly, creates word-of-mouth promotion.

If a plastic card promotion is held in conjunction with a particular advertiser, such as a department store chain, provide distribution "take one" displays, and offer newspaper advertising support or ad mattes.

Direct mail distribution is more expensive, but may be useful to reach certain smaller target audiences.

Plastic card promotions should be unique and impressive. As many listener benefits as possible should be provided: grand prizes, many smaller giveaways, savings on merchandise, discount on concert tickets, and more. All this should be presented to the listener in a memorable package. "Super Saver Card," "Magicard," "Star Card," and "Someone Special Card" are but a few examples of promotion titles that capture the essence of station plastic card promotions.

The "carrier" or an attachment to the plastic card which must be returned to the station to "activate" the card is critical: it provides an accurate count of people using the card and tuning in to the station, provides data on where these people live and other information that can be useful to the station's sales staff, and provides a mailing list for followup promotions.

Finally, plastic card promotions are not "one-shot" station efforts, but can become a permanent part of the station's contact with its listening public.

Sample Plastic Card Promotion

In May, 1980, radio station WLS in Chicago began one of the industry's largest plastic card promotions by inserting one million cards on "carrier" inserts in the *Chicago Tribune* newspaper. Within two days more than 25,000 activator cards (entry forms provided as part of the "carrier") were returned to the station. In the months that followed, another one million cards were distributed. They continued to come in at a rate of approximately one thousand per week.

In addition to cards distributed in the *Times*, another 500,000 were distributed through retail stores including a major local food chain and a national hardware chain.

Plastic card promotions are growing in popularity with radio stations and will undoubtedly be used by many TV stations in the future as well. An endless variety of card titles and designs offer discounts, prizes, reduced rate or free concert admissions, and more special features. WLEC's "Someone Special" card is shown on a newspaper insert "carrier," complete with a return "activator" card which gives the station valuable listener age and address demographic information for use in sales efforts.

Dear Listener:

Your permanent Q CARD is attached. Keep it with you at all times and listen to either KHQ-AM or Rock 98 Q-FM for exciting ways to use it.

Thank you for listening to Q!

Sincerely,

President and General Manager

The "Fantastic Plastic" card was introduced to Chicagoans with a high impact, multi-media ten-day tease campaign which included five 600 line ads in the *Tribune,* a full-page two-color ad in the paper the Friday before the card insertion, a schedule of ten-second television commercials, and sixty-second promotional spots around the clock on WLS Radio.

For two months following the initial card distribution, WLS ran weekly, 600-line ads in both the *Chicago Tribune* and the *Chicago Sun-Times.* The ads told readers what values the Fantastic Plastic Card would be good for during each respective week; and also contained coupons which, when mailed to the station, requested a card.

The card was designed to have two primary uses:

- The awarding of large prizes, i.e., trips to Acapulco, $1,000. gift certificates to a jewelry store, Walt Disney World vacations, etc. Plastic card numbers are randomly drawn and their numbers read on-the-air. The card holder has thirty minutes to call the station and claim the prize.
- The card also permits discount values on merchandise or services. Since the promotion began, the card has been used at theatres, restaurants, sports shows, and concerts for free or discounted admissions, product discounts on items such as albums, clothes and sports equipment.

Listeners are told what the cards may be used for via on-air announcements, encouraging more listening.

WLS began the card as a summer promotion, but continued it following its tremendous success as a regular, on-going station promotion.

BUMPERSTICKERS

Many radio stations and some television stations, distribute bumperstickers to increase awareness of the station's format or a particular program. This encourages audience identification with the station or its personalities or programs.

Bumperstickers are useful for logos, slogans, call letters, dial position, channel numbers, and sometimes a personality's name and face. Short program titles and air times for continuing programs might be used. But the stickers must not be crammed with so much information that printing is too small to be read. Bold colors with contrasting lettering shows up well, and many stations have used day-glo colors for more reflectivity at night.

They are best used as reinforcement for campaigns which include outdoor ads, newspaper ads, on-air, and other components of a total campaign.

Country and Western station KEBC-FM in Oklahoma City has used this technique heavily. Promotion Manager Jane Graber, working with Dr. Donald Patton, Professor of Mathmetics at the University of Oklahoma, has devised a formula for determining how many bumperstickers should be placed on cars in any given community to effectively reach all its population.

The formula below uses the following components:

- Average number of miles a car is driven per year (12,000).
- Number of square miles in the station's coverage area.
- "Cover Factor," or the desired reach.
- Average number of miles an automobile is driven per year in the particular coverage area.

To obtain the average number of miles an auto is driven in a particular community, state, regional or local motor vehicle or traffic officials can be consulted. Square mileage of the coverage area can be determined from ratings books, coverage maps, local officials, or "The Statistical Abstract of the United States."

Here is the "Graber-Patton Formula:"

$$\frac{12,000 \times A \times F}{M} = N$$

12.000 = represents the average annual mileage of an auto in the U.S. This figure remains constant, no matter where the formula is used.

A = The number of square miles in the populated area to be included. This is usually the station's coverage area.

F = "Cover Factor." To date, the formula has been worked out to provide "cover factors" for reaching 65%, 85%, or 95% reach in a market. For 65% reach, F = 1. For 85% reach, F = 2. And for 95% reach, F = 3.

M = The average number of miles an auto is driven per year in the coverage area.

N = The number of bumperstickers to be actually placed on cars in the coverage area to obtain the desired reach of 65%, 85%, or 95%.

Example

If a station's coverage area is 250 square miles, cars are driven an average of 9,000 miles each year, and the station wants to reach 85% of the market through its bumpersticker campaign, the formula would worklike this:

$$\frac{12,000 \times 250 \times 2}{9,000} = 666.66$$

In other words, approximately 667 bumperstickers actually placed on cars would reach 85% of the people in the market in a year.

Promotion Manager Graber claims that since she began using this formula and maintaining a 95% reach, coupled with a strong, simple, unified "Keep Every Body Country" campaign which includes outdoor print and on-air ads, her station has risen to the number three position in the market. She gives a large amount of the credit for the rise in audience to the bumperstickers.

In other markets, radio stations have numbered bumper stickers for "lucky car" contests, with numbers being drawn and prizes awarded; or stickers being spotted at specific locations and awarded prizes.

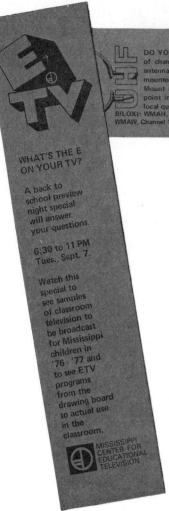

DO YOU KNOW HOW TO GET ETV ON YOUR TV SET? Mississippi ETV stations with the exception of channels 2 and 12, operate on UHF (Ultra High Frequency) channels. If your indoor or built-in antenna proves inadequate for UHF reception, you should install an outdoor UHF antenna. It can be mounted on the same mast you may be using for your VHF antenna, or it can be installed separately. Mount a high-gain antenna as high as possible, use shielded lead-in wire and make sure it's installed to point in the direction of the broadcasting station's transmitter. If you need help getting ETV, call your local qualified TV serviceman!!!   JACKSON: WMAA, Channel 29; GREENWOOD: WMAO, Channel 23; BILOXI: WMAH, Channel 19; OXFORD-UNIVERSITY: WMAV, Channel 18; BUDE: WMAU, Channel 17; MERIDIAN: WMAW, Channel 14; MISSISSIPPI STATE: WMAB, Channel 2; BOONEVILLE: WMAE, Channel 12.

WHAT'S THE E ON YOUR TV?

A back to school preview night special will answer your questions.

6:30 to 11 PM Tues., Sept. 7.

Watch this special to see samples of classroom television to be broadcast for Mississippi children in '76 · '77 and to see ETV programs from the drawing board to actual use in the classroom.

MISSISSIPPI CENTER FOR EDUCATIONAL TELEVISION

These bookmarks were mailed to all schools and libraries in Mississippi. On the backs of the bookmarks are directions for receiving UHF channels.

BOOKMARKS

Bookmarks imprinted with a station message—usually about a program series—can be supplied in quantity to libraries and school systems. Both sides can be used, and there is ample room for detailed program or series descriptions, schedules and specific program air dates and times, as well as the station's logo, call letters, and channel number or dial position.

Bookmarks do not need to be colorful to attract attention, since they are distributed directly to library patrons, teachers, or students and will be placed in a book. However, a bold heading should call attention to the principle copy element, for example, a series title, or a provocative, program-topic related question.

BILL STUFFERS

Many station clients associated with specific programming as a sponsor or underwriter, or with a schedule of advertising which regularly includes one or more specific programs, will allow the station to provide promotion messages to be stuffed into bills the client sends to its customers each month. These can take the form of separate sheets, or flap imprints.

The Promotion Director should confer with the client to learn the exact size most suitable for easy stuffing into the billing envelope. Lightweight paper should be used to prevent the need for extra postage for the client. In many cases, the client or underwriter can be persuaded to cover all design and printing charges associated with bill stuffers relating to programming with which they are associated. Department and other retail stores, utility companies, and charge companies can include stuffers in monthly bills; and banks and savings and loan companies can include them with monthly statements.

BALLOONS

The advantage of a skyline filled with logo-imprinted balloons is obvious: they are a delight to children and the young at heart, are eyecatching and attention-getting, and are relatively inexpensive.

In a 1981 article in the Broadcasters Promotion Association Newsletter, WFIE Radio Station Promotion Director Joseph Logsdon from Evansville, Indiana, listed important things to consider when involving balloons in a station promotion or presence in the community:

Buy balloons big enough to imprint the station's logo in a clear, easily readable location. A 9″ round balloon is an excellent size and shape. The logo should be towards the middle or bottom. If it is toward the upper part of the balloon, it is less likely to be seen when the balloon is in the air. Larger balloons might seem to catch more attention, but more importantly, they take considerably more time to fill and use up the helium supply more quickly.

Buy enough balloons to fill the demand, and then some. Some will be lost in the blowing up process, and people will almost always want more than is anticipated.

Their cost will vary from place to place. For the first printing there is a charge for the die.

Keep the color selection simple. The station's color (if it has one), with contrasting letters is usually effective. Always remember that when the balloons are inflated, the rubber expands and the station's message or logo may become distorted. Keep the design simple and compact.

Always, always blow up balloons with helium, and tie them on a string for distribution. Helium is readily available from welding shops or industrial or medical gas supply houses. Usually they will have a balloon-inflating device which they will provide free or for a modest rental charge. Or a company can be hired to handle the inflation. Balloon string is usually available from the balloon salesman.

Have plenty of help to blow-up, tie and distribute the balloons. It takes a surprising amount of time to go through this process, and fingers can get very tired after about 30 minutes.

Logsdon points out that balloons are fun, have great appeal for all ages, and are relatively effective as a promotional tool. In addition to being used as give-aways, they serve to colorfully identify a station's exhibit booth or live-remote location, and can be released from overhead at indoor parties or special functions at a critical moment to provide a gala atmosphere.

OTHER PROMOTION MATERIALS

Successful station promotions can call on any number of additional promotional materials which have two basic functions: to call attention to the station, its programming or personalities, and to focus attention on a station theme, program, or personality. Some of these materials include:

Table Tents

These printed cardboard sheets are usually about six inches long by five inches wide, folded in half pup-tent style, and placed on restaurant tables, store counters, registration desks, or other convenient places.

Gummed Labels

Paper or foil lables can be imprinted with a station logo and message and used in literally dozens of ways to extend the reach of a station's promotional message. They can adorn station equipment (cameras, carrying cases, etc.), notebooks, plain press kit covers for special uses, envelopes for station mailings, store windows, new TV or radio set cartons in dealers' stores, and more. They can even be made available to listeners or viewers for use in car and home windows.

Overprinted Letterhead

A station can overprint its own letterhead or press release stationary with a special, bold color to call attention to a unique promotion, event, or activity. This is especially useful when promoting an anniversary week, month or year, new season programming, or a special station event.

Imprinted Novelties

Pencils, pens, coffee mugs, scratch pads, T-shirts, and sports schedules are among the more popular of dozens of items which can be purchased in quantity imprinted with the station's logo. These can be distributed to people at community or station-sponsored events, sold at a company "store"—either at the station or at a rented downtown location, or delivered to agency personnel, clients, and influential media representatives. Stations usually look for items which will receive constant use, preferably on a desk, in the office, or around the home. They are intended to be constant reminders of call letters, dial position, logo or theme of a campaign, or a personality. If items are not prohibitively expensive, enough extra should be ordered so that one can be given to each station staff member. This promotes pride in the station, and a feeling of belonging.

Many station Promotion Directors maintain "prize closets," small rooms for storage of station-imprinted items, and gifts or prizes of more value (portable radios, jewelry, etc.). Well-stocked prize closets come in handy when there are unexpected visiting dignitaries, community or business leaders, or other guests of the station.

STATION PRESENCE AND COMMUNITY EVENTS

Television, and especially radio stations have found that audience loyalty is effectively cultivated by maintenance of a strong, positive station presence in the community which includes station participation in existing events, as well as events, activities and sponsorships initiated by the station. Station and network personalities play an important, and sometimes catalytic role.

Several elements, evident at numerous successful radio stations, contribute to promotional success in station community involvements. Chief among them are: Activities which benefit the community, use of personalities, continuity, and strong promotion.

Community Benefits

Stations should make every effort to tie promotions in to the community in some meanngful way. The most usual way is to structure a promotion which raises money, or provides services for a local charity. Blood drives, United Way, Red Cross, Salvation Army, Scouting, Goodwill, Cancer Society, and many other groups in cities across America benefit each year from radio station—and to a lesser degree, television station—promotional events. Promotion, publicity and advertising support are easier to get for such events. And they leave audiences and community residents with a positive feeling about the station.

Personalities

The use of station personalities in community activities where the station has a presence has a cumulative effect over the years. Continuing exposure of the station's people to different groups . . . and to the same group year after year—give many people the chance to feel that they actually "know" the personality. Audience loyalty to the personality becomes loyalty to the station.

Personalities can take on the roles of host, guest speaker, honored guest, visiting celebrity, or active participant.

Continuity

One-shot community involvements can be modestly effective but a station makes the most impact by repeating successful promotions year after year, or season after season. Members of the community learn to associate the station with a particular charity, charitable fund-drive, or community event. The resulting good-will can help in attracting audiences and in attracting advertisers. A station should pick particular charities or events, spaced throughout the year, and work closely with each to help the group or activity achieve its goals. Strong support on-air and a physical presence (with banners, balloons, booths, and on-air talent and live broadcasts at the event give the station visibility, and generate valuable publicity. It is best to limit the number of such annual or regular community involvements. Too many can confuse the audience, or diffuse the station's identification with a particular activity. One technique is to allow each of the station's air personalities identification with one major annual activity. Each can also take on a number of other one-time only activities during the year.

Promotion

The station must not be shy about its community involvements. They are not done from purely altruistic motives, but rather because they help the station build audience and garner advertiser support. As it inevitably turns out, when the station sets out to serve its own needs through community involvement, it benefits the community too. That is no reason to be modest.

Stations use ads, on-air promotion, posters, target mailings, booths, balloons, banners, and any other means at their disposal to tie themselves in with the activities they support. And after the event, make hay by touting the success and the resultant benefit to the community. Ad copy reporting such successes might be humble and deferential to the benefiting organizations but it should be present, bold, unmistakeable.

In Part Five of this Handbook, a section on community involvement details a number of activities by ten radio and television stations which have benefited both the station and the community. These case studies contain a wealth of specific ideas and details on how many were carried out.

THE STATION AS A FRIEND

Station promotions which position the station as a friend of the community, and an aid to individuals in the community, are common. There are many promotions stations can do which have such benefit, from fund-raising campaigns to useful booklets and brochures.

Examples of the latter variety are shown in the illustrations that follow. They are offered on air, and frequently at the location of participating sponsors. Bulk mailings to schools, hospitals, or any community groups and companies can help spread distribution.

WGBS Radio in Miami offered a hurricane tracking chart, in cooperation with Whirlpool Home Appliances. On the back fold is a reminder that "WGBS keeps a watch on weather, traffic and sports . . ."

WJKW-TV, Channel 8 in Cleveland, Ohio, provided a tip sheet letting its news viewers know how to avoid being taken by car repair dealers, and what they could do about it if they were.

WJBC Radio in Bloomington, Illinois, offered a "Constituent's Guide" to local and national officeholders, with a map clearly showing local districts and listing names and addresses of all local and national representatives.

KOIT Radio in San Francisco provided a folder calling attention to fine dining spots in town . . . ones which advertise on the station, of course.

WJKW-TV, Cleveland, provided its viewers the opportunity to receive, free, an 11-page booklet on how to buy a car, including checklists and a price comparison chart. The same station also provided a "Tornado Map and Guide," tagged with the slogan, "Look for Dick Goddard with current weather conditions on Newscenter 8 at 6 & 11 p.m.

WTCN-TV, Minneapolis, Minnesota, in conjunction with a series of health-related programs, provided "Breast Cancer: The Silent Ordeal," listing both facts, controversial issues, and local resources.

CBC Radio in Toronto, Canada, made available a "Cope Kit," a pocket-sized 43-page booklet providing a wealth of local advice: How to get around, how to get help, things to do, places to go, landlord/tenant information, adult and continuing education information, and tips on how to break through the red tape of local bureaucracy.

The nationally syndicated "H.O.T. Car" program is subscribed to by many local stations. With guidance from its syndicators, this program enables a local station to provide special kits to local viewers or listeners containing a variety of anti car-theft tips and devices. In markets where it has been in use, car theft has dropped—sometimes' dramatically.

These are but a very few of the countless promotions undertaken by local stations which provide something valuable to the audience, closely associated with the station and/or its programming.

Sales Promotion

As stated in Chapter 2, sales promotion classifies that type of promotion and publicity which is directed at advertising agencies, clients and others who influence or have a part in buying time on the station. Sales promotion is a simple result of the fact that a station's promotion department is a service-oriented department, drawing on its many skills to work closely with the Sales Department to bring added business to the station.

In its simplest form, sales promotion includes such things as printed flyers and biographies on various station personalities. Most stations have a sales promotion kit which also includes the station's coverage map, program schedule, other program highlights and, usually, the station's rate card for commercial time.

MATERIALS

In addition, many stations must sell not only the station but the market, or city as well, in trying to appeal to national or regional advertising representatives (reps) which purchase time on the local station for major national advertisers. The national sales rep for a medium or small market station very much appreciates the added sales promotion material which tells all the good things about that particular market, such as its purchasing power, population, median income, types of local manufacturing firms, and various other details. The station has hired the rep to seek national companies to buy its commercial time. With proper sales promotion materials, it can help the rep do the job most efficiently by giving it the tools necessary to give the potential advertiser a favorable impression of the market.

THE 10 O'CLOCK NEWS

It's 10 P.M. . . . do you know where the news viewers are? They're tuned to Channel 5 and the brisk, news-packed hour that's a full 60 minutes ahead of the late-night newscasts. And it's not just entertainment . . . it's choice.

Its reporters are uniquely experienced . . . because they know and understand New York City and the whole Metropolitan area . . . because they're skilled at simplifying even the most complex news events of the day – international, national and especially local – for New York's great tri-state audience.

Anchored by John Roland with co-anchors Bill McCreary and Judy Licht, this hard-hitting, factdigging program doesn't cover the news; it uncovers it. Its exposes of corruption in both high and low places makes it the best kind of investigative journalism.

For people who aren't yet home when the early news goes on, and just don't care to wait for the 11 o'clock newscasts, the prime time "10 O'Clock News" has done more than answer a need. It has earned the unshakable loyalty of millions of viewers, the news curious and the news addicts.

For Life Your Choice is

5
WNEW-TV
Metromedia New York
205 East 67th Street, New York, N.Y. 10021-212-535-1000 · Represented by Metro TV Sales

ALL IN THE FAMILY

"All In The Family" – winner of 18 Emmys and a 1978 Peabody Award for "establishing the right to express social comment in a novel comedy" has won the hearts of all America and most especially New York. It captured the number one show spot on WNEW-TV, and is the number one show in the market, 6-8 PM Monday-Friday, with the utterly uproarious way it has managed to spotlight some of the most sensitive issues of our time.

Carroll O'Connor is the brash, opinionated Archie Bunker – a name that has become part of our language. The hilarious foils to Archie are the marvelously drawn characters of Edith, his wife (Jean Stapleton); daughter, Gloria (Sally Struthers) and his son-in-law Mike (Rob Reiner) who complete the most argumentative quartet in the nation. The point at which there is no argument at all: "All In The Family" is a comedy classic!

For Fun Your Choice is

5
WNEW-TV
Metromedia New York
205 East 67th Street, New York, N.Y. 10021-212-535-1000 · Represented by Metro TV Sales

THE BIONIC WOMAN

When Lindsay Wagner guested as a "bionic woman" on "The Six Million Dollar Man," the soaring ratings for the two-parter made a spin-off inevitable.

In addition to her natural equipment, "Jaimie Sommers" has bionic legs for speed, a bionic arm for power, and a supersensitive bionic ear, which makes her ideal for taking on super risk missions.

Normally engaged as a teacher in a California air force-base school, "The Bionic Woman's" double life is chock-full of adventure and intrigue. Some of the most wondrous special effects to be seen on any screen are standard fare on "The Bionic Woman." It has also had a very special effect on huge audiences: it has made them confirmed, completely captivated fans!

For Thrills Your Choice is

5
WNEW-TV
Metromedia New York
205 East 67th Street, New York, N.Y. 10021, 212-535-1000 · Represented by Metro TV Sales

M·A·S·H

[. . .]-based laugh fest led by [. . .]up Alan Alda, has won [. . .] 8 Emmys and a George F. [. . .] you can shake a scalpel [. . .]e high with Channel 5 au-

[. . .]dially - will never win is a [. . .] The wacky carryings-on of [. . .]ile-hospital staffers are [. . .] to hold on to their sanity.

Most irreverent of Alda, as surgeon "[. . .] masking with absol[. . .] protocol. He and [. . .] acters (Hot Lips, R[. . .] Radar, Klinger, M[. . .]er, Father Mulcah[. . .] tive that imagine[. . .]

For Fun Your Choice is

5
WNEW-TV
Metromedia New York
205 East 67th Street, New York, N.Y. 10021-212-535-1000 · Represented by Metro TV Sales

THE MERV GRIFFIN SHOW

Orson Welles calls Merv Griffin "the best of all the talk-show hosts." Phyllis Diller calls Merv "the most talented man I know." Millions of viewers just happen to share these sentiments.

Merv is a genuine innovator. "The Merv Griffin Show" introduced such unknowns as John Davidson, Woody Allen, Richard Pryor, Dick Cavett and Lily Tomlin to the television public. Merv initiated the "theme" show concept. It was Merv who first televised exciting "remotes" from such

places as Monte Carlo and Israel.

Merv's award-winning, enormously popular show is, today, the only talk-variety program in prime time in New York and the only one to originate regularly from the entertainment capitals of the world - Hollywood, Las Vegas and New York. That's where the talent is. And talent simply can't resist "The Merv Griffin Show." Neither can audiences.

For Life Your Choice is

5
WNEW-TV
Metromedia New York
205 East 67th Street, New York, N.Y. 10021-212-535-1000 · Represented by Metro TV Sales

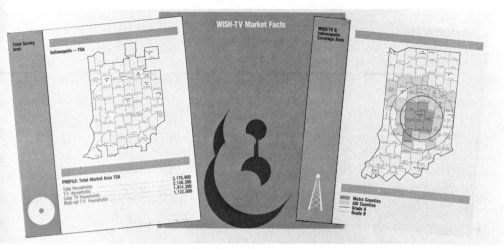

Station WISH-TV designed this kit's contents to help national time buyers realize the specific advantages of the Indianapolis market.

Television has the added responsibility of providing flyers or whole promotion kits on each major program and/or star appearing on the station. Particular attention is given to the local station's biggest money-makers, usually local news programming and prime-time access shows.

The keys to deciding how much sales promotion is required are:

- How strong the station is in the market? Stations with small audiences have little to crow about. Stations with large, or valuable audiences, have more to say.
- What is the demand for air time? If there is a great deal of advertiser demand for air time in the market, and considerable competition from other stations for those advertiser dollars, sales promotion materials are especially valuable.
- What percentage of the station's air time is sold out? If the station has very few available positions to sell to advertisers, the expenses of producing elaborate sales promotion pieces are probably not justifiable. The sales people at some highly successful stations enjoy the position of simply quoting to clients advertising costs and the few available remaining positions for sale.

But most stations, at least some of the time, have to prepare competitive sales promotion tools to carve out their share of available ad dollars. How many times have you read or heard that a station is "Number One"? Well, that is the research part of sales promotion at work. Researchers go through rating books to find where and when a particular station is very strong (hopefully number one.) They then work with the sales department to find ways to drive the facts home to time buyers. This approach is not deceptive. Most clients are looking for specific audience targets for their ad dollars. For example, a savings and loan company may not care if the station is number one in teen-aged audience—or number one overall, for that matter. They may only be interested in how many people watching or listening to the station have incomes of $25,000 or more and are in the 35+ age group. When a station knows its particular areas of strength, much of the sales promotion material that is cranked out supports these specific areas.

A sales presentation might include just computer printouts on a sheet comparing various stations in the market. More often, this type of information is dressed up in a brochure with graphs, pictures, and other attractive ways of saying the same thing. In other words, the *"Life Magazine* approach" is used, rather than the *"Wall Street Journal* approach," to attract attention and make information stand out.

Stations with heavy play-by-play sports have other interesting responsibilities in the sales promotion area. These types of sales promotion materials often include printed team posters and game schedule cards with sponsor tie-ins. Often, a "kick-off" party for broadcast sponsors of the game, trips, and merchandise prizes are part of the overall sales promotion effort. It is important to create a lot of excitement about play-by-play sports on broadcast stations, not only for the audiences, but for advertisers so that they feel a part of the "team" that includes both players and the station as well.

PREVIEW PARTIES

Most television stations are involved in the pageantry of the annual Fall Preview Party, at least once a year. Some stations hold a smaller party at the start of each "new season" of programming. These parties, described in greater detail in chapter 17, involve a theme built around the biggest "happy hour" for clients and agencies that the station can possibly dream up. The trick is to make the presentation of programming elements entertaining and informative, while making the party an event of such fun, surprises, and imagination that it is eagerly looked forward to each year. The Fall Preview Party sales promotion is one of the grandest and most complex forms of presenting programming to agencies and clients. The promotion department is busy with everything from the menu to the guest list to taking care of invited stars and praying that all 25 slide and film projectors in the audio-visual presentation will do their little but very important part in making the overall evening a big success. Clients must be impressed not only with the programming itself but with the station's overall effort in the way it is able to successfully make such a big party work.

SALES PRESENTATIONS

The more theatrical side of sales promotion continues when the promotion department is asked to create a slide or film presentation for station sales people to use in widescreen format, or in one-on-one presentations across a desk.

There are drawbacks and advantages to each approach. A slide presentation can be interesting and colorful, but rarely will it have as great an impact as a slick and exciting film or videotape presentation. However, slides are more changeable and the presentation in an office can be more intimate. Slide presentations can be easily altered by changing slides or their order; and the salesperson can rewrite the words used with the slides to match what the client needs to hear. Slide productions are less costly than tape or film and are easier to revamp when station personalities suddenly change, or programs are dropped from the lineup.

The more intimate slide presentations usually range from five to fifteen minutes. Larger impact film or tape presentations can be limited to that, but often run up to a half-hour. It is generally accepted that no major film or videotape sales presentation should run longer than 40 minutes. It's hard to hold peoples' attention for even that long at a Fall Preview Party, or other major event with distractions such as liquor, stars, games, and a party-like atmosphere. Less than 20 minutes, however, is rarely enough time to do the necessary informing and selling job. Most presentations end up between those two extremes, and many producers shoot for program-length presentations which might be aired on television for audiences as well as clients, just by changing the announcer's copy. Program-length is approximately 28 minutes.

Outside professional help is frequently needed in preparing this kind of sales promotion tool, especially at radio stations. But whatever the medium or the message, keep in mind that as far as Sales Department people are con-

Parties have been held on planes, buses, and boats; in studios, restaurants, hotels, and caves. This KDKA-TV party featured a "Showboat" theme and included a river cruise in Pittsburgh.

'Vegas on the Suncoast' was the theme for WTSP-TV's 1980 Fall Premiere party. The Tampa-St. Petersburg station invited guests to spend $2,500. each in 'play money' in a 'casino-restaurant atmosphere,' following a 45-minute presentation of upcoming local and ABC Network programs.

cerned, the Promotion Department is providing them with tools they can use to sell commercial air time.

At public broadcasting stations, the parties and the sales promotion tools are very similar; but the emphasis is on acquiring program or day-part underwriters rather than selling commercial time. For more information, see chapter 20.

TRADE ADVERTISING

Advertising in the trades is another important part of sales promotion activities. The type of ads run depend on the station's strengths or needs. Management may feel it is important to tell prospective time buyers that the station's news has been voted the best in the community for ten straight years.

Or perhaps the message might be that the station, and not its competition in the market, is number one in a highly important daypart. If a small or medium market station is involved, the ad will frequently position not only the station, but also the market as one that shouldn't be ignored.

Sales promotion ads are placed in trade press publications which media buyers and potential advertisers are likely to see. *Broadcasting Magazine* is a

High scorer for special needs

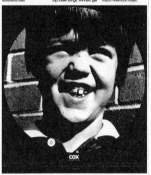 **Good for kids' teeth**

 KFI: A gusher of information

These ads were placed by KFI Radio, Los Angeles, in the trade publications indicated to attract advertiser interest, and let the broadcasting industry know what the station and its ownership are doing for the community.

frequently used publication for both radio and television stations. In addition, *Advertising Age, Adweek, TV/Radio Age, Madison Avenue,* local grocers' journals and advertising club publications, merchandising newsletters, and similar publications might all have value. Each should be studied with the station's Sales Department for potential value in attracting advertisers.

SALES PROMOTION DISPLAYS

Construction of a station exhibit booth can add an additional dimension to a station's sales promotion effort. As an example, KNX Newsradio in Los Angeles has for years used a "History of Radio News" booth, a simple free-standing display featuring 14 historical news events pre-recorded and played back to listeners on special phones at area trade shows.

The Sales Department uses the booth as a bonus when a trade show client buys a schedule on KNX. Promo spots describing the booth are aired on the station and tagged with the show's location, thereby drawing people to the show. The station is happy with the sale and the client benefits from additional public exposure. In one sense, this type of sales promotion crosses the boundaries of audience promotion and merchandising, as do so many other projects in the sales promotion category.

SUMMARY

Successful sales promotion relies primarily on knowing who a station's listeners or viewers are; knowing what kinds of advertisers wish to reach par-

On these pages are a number of sales promotion efforts by various stations' Promotion Departments. Washington D.C.'s WTTG-TV used very simple flyers to impress buyers with their ratings edge and with specific demographics. This is the most important thing time buyers need to see. WABC-TV (New York) sent out an elegant corkscrew with this small 6-fold brochure graphically displaying its ratings leadership in various key time periods.

WJXT-TV, Jacksonville, Florida, produced this sturdy two-fold showing ratings and demographic information on the numerous sports programs it carries. The station also sent miniatures of its billboard campaign to buyers to emphasis a promotional push, while WSPA-TV in North Carolina sent buyers a dart board to keep programs and rates clearly in mind.

KING Radio in Seattle capitalized very cleverly on the Mt. St. Helens eruption by sending out "soft rock"; and WKQX-FM in Chicago prepares each year a directory of Chicago phone numbers agencies, buyers, and media people use—a valuable tool that remains on peoples' desks year-long. Many stations print four-page "newsletters" which can be used with station staff as well as agency people and media buyers. Several examples are shown above.

ticular categories of the audience, and being able to target the potential advertisers to that audience.

This calls on the research and ratings information detailed in Chapter 11, and the information on how to best use motivational techniques effectively as outlined in Chapter 13. In addition, on-air production skills from Chapter 16 are essential in producing presentations; party-giving skills spelled out in chapter 18 are critical; and knowledge of good advertising design is imperative.

Sales Promotion, as it encompasses advertising, publicity and promotion, draws from the promotion director's knowledge of those skills to aid the station's Sales Department.

Part Four

Special Promotion Challenges

CHAPTER 20

Promoting Public Broadcasting

The person at a public radio or television station in charge of advertising, promotion and publicity is most frequently titled Public Information (or PI) Director. The PI Director's job is similar in most respects to that of the commercial station Promotion Director. The knowledge of basic principles of creating effective advertising, on-air promotion and publicity materials is just as important. Establishing and maintaining good press contacts is, if anything, more important. And, as in commercial broadcasting, it is vital for the public broadcaster to know audiences—real and potential—and program audience targets.

However, there are some key differences for public broadcasting PI Directors. Most of them are also magazine editors, turning out monthly program guides. Dealing with underwriters involves nuances and restrictions with which commercial broadcasters need not contend. Tighter, or even non-existent promotion budgets—and non-profit status—provide both challenges and opportunities their commercial counterparts don't face. The necessity of on-air fund raising provides a quite different set of promotion and advertising opportunities. And the structure of the national public broadcasting system, with its emphasis on local station production of national programming, creates a whole area of advertising and promotion alien to commercial broadcasters.

Each of these differences is examined in the pages ahead.

STATION PROGRAM GUIDE MAGAZINES *

Most public broadcasting stations solicit financial support from viewers in the form of "memberships" or "subscriptions." To partially reward viewers

*Much of the material included in this section on Program Guides was edited or excerpted from *Radio Program Guide Critique*, a 1980 publication of the Corporation for Public Broadcasting, prepared by S. L. Harrison, and Nell Jackson.

and listeners who regularly contribute, most stations print and mail to all members or subscribers a monthly guide to station programming.

These guides become a major part of the station's image to home audiences. In a booklet on radio station guide magazines, the federally-funded Corporation for Public Broadcasting states: "The program guide can be the bridge between programming, audience-building and fund-raising, as well as the catalyst for positive community support. It is a tool for building and retaining the station's constituency—public radio members and business and community groups who support the station with financial contributions." The same holds true for public TV station guide magazines.

The Corporation's booklet, prepared under the supervision of Nell Jackson, CPB's Assistant Radio Development Manager, goes on to point out that the greatest asset in publishing a quality guide is to start by determining the purpose of the guide. Start with these basic questions:

- Who is the station trying to reach? (Identify the Guide's audience.)
- What is the station's message?
- Once the "who" and "what" are decided, the next step is to determine "how" the purpose will be accomplished.

CPB emphasizes that whether guide copy is low-key and factual or emotional, attracting and holding reader attention and interest are paramount. Enthusiasm for the guide at the station staff level will translate into enthusiasm among readers. PI Directors and guide editors should ask themselves these questions:

- If I received this guide, would I be tempted to read it?
- If I read it, what impression would I get of the station?
- What, if anything, would I do?
- Does the guide make it easy for me to do it?

Guide Magazine Content

The chief purpose of a guide magazine is to provide program information. Secondary purposes are to provide information about the station, its staff and activities; to forge an active link between the station and the community; and to enhance fund-raising activities. To help bring a guide magazine's content into focus, CBP recommends asking these questions:

- Is the guide a forceful extension of the station's sound (radio) or look (television), or image (both).
- Does the guide show what the station does for its public?
- How does the public's interest and involvement make a difference?
- Does the guide encourage reader response (through letters, special columns, surveys, etc.)?
- What can be done to make special programs stand out? Are new programs previewed?
- What is there about upcoming program and station activities which will entice guide readers?

PTV Station guide magazines. *Pittsburgh,* a 90+ page full color city magazine, represents the most ambitious guide in the public TV system. It is published by WQED-TV/Pittsburgh. In contrast, WMUL-TV/Huntington, W.Va., publishes a simple, single color 8-page typewritten guide. (Lower left.) Between the two extremes is KLRN-TV/Austin, Texas with *The Schedule,* featuring a handsome full-color photo by a local artist on the front cover. Connecticut Public Television's *Guide* represents a popular alternative to the standard 8½x11″ size. It is 5½ x 8½″.

• Are the basics included? These include station call letters, radio dial position, TV channel number, address, telephone number, a membership/response coupon, and information on how to subscribe to the guide and the station.

Public Participation Elements. The following elements are recommended for radio and TV station guides: Letters to the editor. Volunteer news. Board of Directors lists. Audience surveys. Community Advisory Board involvement. Activities of the station's "Friends Group," or volunteers.

Public Awareness Elements. Coverage of special events. Speakers bureau activities. Information about station advertising campaigns. Station identity elements (look and logo). Comment on the station from other organizations. Information about station tours. Special contest information. A community activities or arts calendar.

Fundraising Elements. Membership activities, a coupon, and membership benefits. Companies which provide matching employee grants. Features on special fund-raising campaigns, auctions, etc. Information on premiums and record clubs. Day, or Day-part underwriters. Paid Advertising.

Station Information Elements. Manager's Report. Call letters and dial location or channel number. Telephone number. Guide staff and volunteers. Features and photos on station personnel. Guide editorial policy statement. Station address, licensee, and guide publishing information. Mission, or purpose statement about the station.

Program Information Elements. Features and photos on network programs. Features and photos on local productions. Interviews. Highlights of all major upcoming programs. Program previews. Program listings. A week-at-a-glance chart (especially for radio stations.) Program personality features and photos. Station-produced program ads.

Here are more details on some of these content areas.

Program News and feature stories are usually about important special programs and series premieres. Included are photos of major stars and action sequences from programs. Stories and photos should inform readers about the series and entice them to watch.

Production features highlight programs the station is producing. These stories are based on an intriguing aspect of production, that is: unusual locations, extraordinary makeup or costuming, difficult working conditions, or anything which sets the production apart from others and has human or visual interest. Such stories raise expectations, encourage word-of-mouth promotion, and improve the climate for station fund-raising by showing the local community significant projects in which the station is involved.

Promotion and coverage of special station events includes auctions, pledge or fund-raising drives, and season premieres—all activities which involve the entire station's staff and which need public support. Both news and feature articles can help keep station contributors aware of station needs for money and volunteers.

Staff features with photos highlight members of the station's staff—usually those who have made significant contributions to station efforts or the community. They can help personalize the station to guide magazine readers. They can also be real morale boosters for all the staff. Everyone likes to see the accomplishments of others recognized.

Features about local personalities who have given significant help to the station reinforce the station's ties with the community and underscore the need for public support.

Special messages from the station's General Manager make guide magazines useful tools in explaining station actions, such as cancellations of popular series, an urgent need for volunteers for a specific project, the reason for yet another on-air pledge drive, or the reason why a network program is not being carried. Some stations establish a regular monthly channel of communication between the General Manager and guide readers. Others prefer only to bring the weight of that position to bear when there is a special need. Either way, it is yet another means of making contributors feel a part of the station.

Letters from viewers. Invariably, more letters come to the station each month from viewers and contributors than can possibly be printed. This feature gives the station the opportunity to use such letters to reinforce other messages it wishes to communicate. Critical letters should be mixed with letters of praise to maintain reader interest, assure station contributors that their voices are listened to, and display fairness.

Paid advertising can reduce costs. Producing and mailing a monthly guide can be costly. To minimize the impact on the promotion department's budget, the station can solicit advertising for its magazine. For many advertisers, the up-scale, money-contributing station guide magazine reader is an especially attractive target. Research on rates other station's charge is available from the PBS network and CPB. Pricing of ad space might be keyed to magazine production costs and should anticipate ad volume.

Program promotion. Whether or not the station solicits outside advertising, its magazine should run most ads the station is placing in local newspapers and TV Guide. These reinforce the image of the ads seen elsewhere and help readers remember upcoming programs.

Guide Magazine Format & Production

Format includes size, paper stock, layout, binding, typeface, and general makeup of the program guide. At public stations, guide formats range from a standard 8½ × 11″ self-fold brochure to slick, sophisticated magazines of 56 or more pages. The most popular size is 8½ × 11″. Second most popular is 5½ × 8½″. These two sizes are also the most economical in terms of paper usage. Other sizes require paper waste from trimming.

Paper is one of the most critical factors to consider in evaluating guide magazine costs, representing as much as 50% of the total cost of producing the magazines. And since paper comes in a bewildering array of colors, finishes, sizes and weights, the PI Director must know the kind of printing equipment that will be used, in order to match the right grade and weight of paper to it.

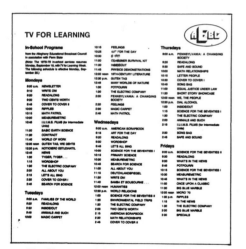

Four guide magazine features. Upper left, a program ad placed in KOCE-TV's *Forum Fifty* by the local underwriter of the program. Upper right, the same magazine displays premiums viewers can earn with their contributions. Lower left, WPSX-TV's program guide features a page showing daytime educational and in-school programs. And WNMU-FM's guide features a schedule-at-a-glance.

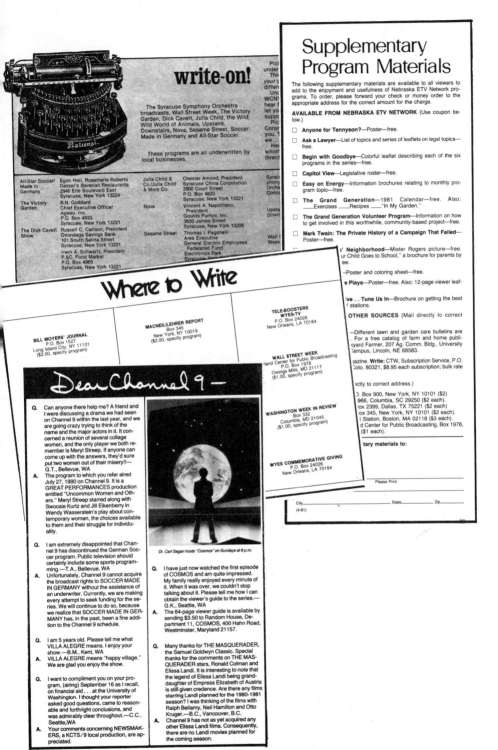

Useful Guide Features. The "Where to write column provides addresses where station members can write for program transcripts. "Write On" urges viewers to write to program underwriters and provides names and addresses. "Supplementary Program Materials" gives viewers a chance to extend their enjoyment of programs to tangible reminders they can acquire free, or at minimal cost. "Dear Channel 9" is typical of many reader columns in program guides.

A suggestion in dealing with printers is to request samples of their work for other customers.

If color is to be used in a guide magazine, here are several "musts":

- When more than one ink color is involved, determine at the outset the best type of art or color separations.
- Use the available ink charts (from the printer) to combine inks when possible.
- Make certain that separate color proofs are required; prepare all separations early.

Ask the following questions regarding the use of color:

- What has been done for other customers with similar budgets? (Look at samples.)
- Are more color options available? (For example, a 16-page guide with a second color on the cover might allow for color on several additional pages at no extra cost.)
- Can money be saved on color costs? Can screens and halftones provide more visibility from a second color?

Type talks. Especially in small publications. No matter how stunning a guide's layout or eye-catching its artwork, the typeface used must transform that copy into lines of type which entice the reader.

Type comes in endless varieties. Phototype has expanded the number of typefaces beyond the capacity of today's type books. A guide editor must select the most legible and economical typeface possible, or ask the advice of a graphic designer.

Many printers supply typesetting services. Most provide estimates that include typesetting. Many offer wide varieties of type. Printers will not be offended, however, if the editor buys typesetting services elsewhere and presents clean paste-up, camera-ready artwork to process and print.

The most economical way to determine the best type buy is to get competitive bids from two or more type houses or printers. Look at options such as saving type from month to month for repeated headlines and program listings.

Attractive printed pieces employ few typefaces. Type must be used sparingly and thoughtfully. Type strengthens the appearance of skillful design, but it should not be the guide's most outstanding topic of conversation. That goes for cover and headline type, too.

Layout and design are critical format elements. Professional advice is essential in developing a guide's basic layout. The layout is a road map—the piece of paper everyone (writer, photographer, artist, typesetter, printer) will follow in producing the guide.

How detailed should the layout be? That is a question all editors face. It must be detailed enough for the station manager to be able to visualize it. Yet, since art preparation time can be expensive, it should not be so detailed that it adds significantly to the guide's cost. Some basic suggestions:

Selecting Type

Type faces fall into five general classifications: Old Style, Modern, Square Serif, Sans Serif, and a miscellaneous group which may be termed "Special." These groups are not rigid, and some type designs have characteristics which may place them in several of these categories.

Old Style: The type faces in this group are classics. Most old style types are used extensively in fine book work because of their readability and because they print well on book papers. We see in many old style faces a hand-made, calligraphic quality, which makes them particularly suitable for formal copy and dignified layouts when used in advertising design.

Garamond Old Style: ABCDEFGHIJKLMNOPQRS abcdefghijklmnopqrstuvwxyz

Caslon 540: ABCDEFGHIJKLMN abcdefghijklmno

Original Old Style: ABCDEFGHiJKLMNOPQRSTUVWXYZ abcdefghijklmnopqrstuvwxyz

---

Modern: Basically two groups combined into one. *Transitional* types are the intermediate step in the evolution of old style faces into that group which we call modern. Widely used for general advertising and printing work, modern faces are up-to-date and precise, having greater contrast between thick and thin strokes, straighter serifs, and rounder, more mechanically perfect curved letters.

Bodoni: ABCDEFGHIJKLMNOPQRSTUVWXYZAB abcdefghijklmnopqrstuvwxyzab

Caledonia: ABCDEFGHIJKLMNOPQRSTUVWXYZabcdefghijklmnopqrstuvwxyz

Century Expanded: ABCDEFGHIJKLMNOPQ abcdefghijklmnopqrstuvwxy

---

Square Serif: Although this design dates back to the mid-nineteenth century, it is a contemporary face and a true reflection of our scientific age. Layouts using this group are usually severe and geometrical, with emphasis on straight lines and angles.

Memphis Medium: ABCDEFGHIJKLMNOPQRSTUVWXYZ abcdefghijklmno

Beton Extra Bold: ABCDEFGHIJKLMN abcdefghijklmno

Cairo Bold: ABCDEFGHIJKLMNOPQRSTUVWXYZ abcdefghijklmnopqrstuv

---

Sans Serif: In this group we have letters reduced to their pure form, without serifs, shading or ornamentation. Copy implications are modernity and functionalism. This group is unexcelled for reproduction by lithography and gravure.

Futura Demi Bold: ABCDEFGHIJKLMNOPQRSTUVWX abcdefghijklmnopqrstuvwxyz

News Gothic: ABCDEFGHIJKLMNOPQRSTUVWXYZ abcdefghijklmnopqrstuvwxyz

Franklin Gothic: ABCDEFGHIJKLMNOPQRSTabcdefghijklmnopqrstu

Special: As the name implies, each type design in this group has its own function—to imitate handwriting or lettering (Brush), for copy written with a religious quality (Goudy Text) or just to tease and catch the eye. The type specifier chooses from this group whenever he desires a special effect.

Brush   *Commercial Script*

Goudy Text   P. T. Barnum

Rondo   Remington Typewriter

Tuesday 3

morning & afternoon

6:45 A.M. WEATHER

7:00 SEE CHILDREN'S GUIDE AND ITV SCHEDULE ON PAGE 22.

evening

6:00 OVER EASY (C. Cap.)
Steve Allen and Jack LaLanne are guests.

6:30 THE MACNEIL/LEHRER REPORT
A thorough, thought-provoking examination of one timely news story each night, with Robert MacNeil in New York, Jim Lehrer in Washington and correspondent Charlayne Hunter-Gault reporting on the stories behind the headlines.

7:00 LEGISLATIVE HEARING ON LB 319, SCHOOL DISTRICT CONSOLIDATION BILL

10:00 NOVA (C. Cap.)
The sophisticated instrumentation used by astronomers enables us to see beyond the once cloudy barrier of the Milky Way. NOVA takes a trip to the perhaps 100 billion other galaxies in the universe, as old as time and several million light years away.

11:00 MYSTERY! (C. Cap.)
Leo McKern as "Rumpole of the Bailey" is called away to serve as junior counsel to an actress accused of the backstage murder of her husband. The leading lady soon fires her leading counsel and asks Rumpole to defend her alone.

KYNE-TV

11:00 PSYCHOLOGY 101 (45 min.)

11:45 UNO SPECTRUM (15 min.)

Dance Specials

Two unique dance programs, "Screenplay" and "A Ceremony of Dreams," produced by the cultural affairs unit of University of Nebraska Television, will be broadcast on WEDNESDAY SHOWCASE, Wednesday, March 4, at 9 p.m.

Members of the Omaha Ballet Company and the Creighton University Dance Company perform two jazz ballets on "Screenplay." Job Sanders choreographed the title ballet, with the other dance piece, "Zampur," choreographed by Tibor Zana.

Five of Nebraska's Interstate 80 sculptures provide the environment for "A Ceremony of Dreams."

The music and dance theatre performance features the musicians and dancers of the Entourage Music and Theatre Ensemble of Maryland, under the direction of Joe Clark.

The dance performance follows the group through their dreams and fantasies utilizing the sunset, nighttime hours and sunrise with various Bicentennial and sculptures serving as the ceremonial grounds.

Wednesday 4

morning & afternoon

6:45 A.M. WEATHER

7:00 SEE CHILDREN'S GUIDE AND ITV SCHEDULE ON PAGE 22.

evening

6:00 OVER EASY (C. Cap.)
Parent-child relationships.

6:30 THE MACNEIL/LEHRER REPORT

7:00 THREE HOSTAGES
An Oxford student, a millionaire's daughter and a ten-year-old boy are all kidnapped and held by a powerful crime syndicate planning a major coup in Europe and America.

8:30 THE PICNIC
The Two Ronnies—Ronnie Corbett and Ronnie Barker—present this comedy special about a summer day with a crusty general and his son.

9:00 WEDNESDAY SHOWCASE
"Screenplay" is a program of two dances by members of the Omaha Ballet and the Creighton University Dance Company in 1975.

"A Ceremony of Dreams" presents dance and music, with five of Nebraska's Interstate 80 Sculptures as the settings, performed by the Entourage Music and Theatre Ensemble of Maryland.

10:00 THE DICK CAVETT SHOW

10:30 CAPITOL VIEW
Coverage of the day's activities in the Nebraska Unicameral.

11:00 HUMANITIES THROUGH THE ARTS
Repeats from Saturday at 1 p.m.

"A Ceremony of Dreams" was taped at the following sculptures: "Roadway Confluence" near Sidney, "Crossing the Plains" near York, "Nebraska Gateway" near Brady, "Erma's Desire" near Grand Island, and "Arrival" near Seward.

Cultural affairs unit senior producer Gene Bunge produced and Ron Nicodemus directed "Screenplay." Special projects unit senior producer Rod Bates produced and directed "A Ceremony of Dreams."

Thursday 5

morning & afternoon

6:45 A.M. WEATHER

7:00 SEE CHILDREN'S GUIDE AND ITV SCHEDULE ON PAGE 22.

evening

6:00 OVER EASY (C. Cap.)
A look at pioneer photographer Edward S. Curtis and his photos of American Indians.

6:30 THE MACNEIL/LEHRER REPORT

7:00 DATELINE NEBRASKA
Panelists Don Walton, *Lincoln Star,* Dick Herman, *Lincoln Journal,* and Frank Partsch, *Omaha World-Herald,* question national and local newsmakers.

7:30 OUTDOOR NEBRASKA
Tonight's program from the Nebraska Game and Parks Commission includes a viewers' phone-in on any topic, plus features on spring turkey hunting and the Blue Hole State Wildlife Management Area.

8:00 SNEAK PREVIEWS
Co-hosts Roger Ebert and Gene Siskel provide viewers with candid critiques of newly released movies.

KYNE-TV

7:00 WOMEN'S BUSINESS (30 min.)
"Stress in Business" deals with the causes and means of coping with pressures in the business world.

7:30 UNO SCENE (15 min.)

7:45 ON CAMPUS (15 min.)

8:00 MAVERICK BASKETBALL (30 min.)

8:30 THE 100th ANNIVERSARY OF THE AMERICAN ASSOCIATION OF UNIVERSITY WOMEN
Dr. M. Anne Campbell, Nebraska State Commissioner of Education and former national president of the AAUW, hosts this panel discussion in commemoration of its founding. The A.A.U.W., a group of women graduates of accredited colleges and universities, provides scholarships and fellowships for women, as well as grants for individual research.

9:00 THE PAPER CHASE
Elizabeth Logan accuses a respected law professor of sexual harassment, but Professor Kingsfield does not believe her.

10:00 THE DICK CAVETT SHOW

10:30 CAPITOL VIEW

11:00 MASTERPIECE THEATRE (C. Cap.)
Repeats from Sunday at 8 p.m.

KYNE-TV

11:00 PSYCHOLOGY 101 (45 min.)

11:45 DATELINE NEBRASKA (30 min.)

CHOICE/March 1981

A typical guide magazine page features program descriptions, photos, and highlights of special programs. This page is from *Choice,* the magazine of the Nebraska Educational Television Network.

- Ask the designer to spend time creating layout ideas rather than final meticulously detailed layouts.
- Make the first layout clear and clean, but just complete enough to gain the approvals needed.

Most effective program guides have consistent, orderly and surprisingly simple layouts. The reader is usually unaware that the designer has created each page and each section on a grid system. A grid keeps future issues of the guide organized and readable. It makes the monthly production schedule easy; it puts a pattern on all the future guides and helps to create an identity for the publication.

Some pointers:

- One large photo or line drawing is usually more effective than a group of smaller pictures.
- Artwork that bleeds off the page edge makes a page visually dynamic. It makes a photo grow miraculously. But it costs more.
- For readability, the length of a line of type should never be more than 75 characters.
- Another small incentive for the reader: use ragged lines of type on the right-hand side of the copy block, but not on the left, except for photo cutlines. This "rag right" approach gets rid of the breaking (hyphenization) of words, for the most part.
- Photos deserve their own cutlines. They work better together.
- Do not overprint (overlap) type and photos unless the words are brief and big.
- Long sections and paragraphs of reverse type (white on black) are difficult to read unless the type is big and bold.

Printing techniques affect the look of the guide magazine. The size of the press run, paper, special effects, and other costs all influence the choice of printing technique.

Offset lithography gives high-quality, high production runs, at economical cost. Because of its ability to produce sharper images, offset is probably the most popular and economical method of flat surface printing. Numerous ink combinations and quality reproduction of typefaces, line work and photos make this the "workhorse" of printing techniques. Based on the lithographic principle that grease (ink) and water (aqueous solution) do not mix, this process "offsets" the image from flat plate to a rubber blanket and then to paper. The operating sequence of plate to blanket to stock (paper) gently places the image on the sheet and produces sharply printed type faces and realistic artwork.

If the job is a small press run, letter press might be considered. In this process, plates are made in relief and the image is transferred directly from the plate to the paper. Printing from this raised surface produces a sharp image in addition to the advantage of a wide selection of typefaces and ink colors.

Guide Production Checklist

Here is a quick checklist for the production of public station program guides. These are basics which help produce a cost-effective, efficient, productive magazine each month:

• Coordinate all aspects of production by setting and meeting all deadlines. This reduces production problems and costs for corrections. Write out job instructions so that all concerned fully understand what is required; correct all proofs so that misunderstandings are avoided. Above all, enforce the schedule. One of the most severe and common problems involved in guide magazine production is getting program information from the Programming Department, the network, or other outside program suppliers in time to meet monthly deadlines. The PI Director and/or Guide Editor must be firm with the Program Director, and, if necessary, the General Manager. One way is to show how much extra late changes can cost the station.

• Evaluate available printers for the equipment—web or sheet-fed presses, for example—for the most economical choice. What papers are best suited for the presses available? Check samples.

• Determine costs by getting a price break-down on all components—makeready, plates, schedule lags and the like. Discuss fully with vendors the range of cost options. Get competitive bids. Have a written contract that explains all cost items.

• Select typeset sources, whether hot type or cold type; decide whether or not computer setting will help save money; make full use of artist aids that can be found in-house; evaluate the best source of art preparation for the station's needs.

• Copy preparation should follow a clear layout before writing begins; character-count all typewritten copy to fit layout; prepare all copy for typeset on white paper, double-spaced, one side only, and marked correctly on a standard-sized piece of paper.

• Lay out the publication before attempting to fit copy into pages; artwork can be fitted into the layout without expensive revisions; photos can be scaled and keyed in as well and page makeup will be quicker and easier. Never proceed to final printing without a full check of a finished proof.

• Multicolor printing is more costly and requires an early determination of the best kind of artwork for color separations. Use the available charts to combine inks when possible; make certain separate color proofs are required and prepare all separations early.

Useful References:

The Pocket Pal. International Paper Co. 220 East 42nd St. New York, N.Y. 10017

Imagination. Champion Paper Marketing Services. 245 Park Avenue. New York, N.Y. 11017

A Comprehensive Sampler and Dictionary of Predictable Results. Hopper Paper Company. P.O. Box 369. Taylorville, Illinois 62568

How To Plan Printing. S.D. Warren. 225 Franklin Street. Boston, Mass. 02101

Controlling Your Composition Costs. National Composition Association. 1730 North Lynn Street. Arlington, Va. 22209

Paper'n Graphics Miniguide. International Paper Co. 220 East 42nd St. New York, N.Y. 10017

LOW BUDGET, OR NO BUDGET PROMOTION

Along with some commercial radio stations and a few small commercial television stations, a larger number of public radio and TV stations have to advertise, promote and publicize with very low budgets, or—in rare cases—no budget at all.

Dawn Stowe DeLong, Assistant Director for Public Affairs for the Communications Center of the University of Texas at Austin, which encompasses KUT-FM, a National Public Radio (NPR) member station, has put together the following advice for stations in such circumstances.

"First," she says, "the PI Director has to believe in the station and what public broadcasting stands for. Second is the ability to relate station needs to the interests and needs of corporations, other media, and the public.

"A 'What can you do for us?' attitude or 'How can you help us?' approach is more effective than 'Can you do anything for us?' The former questions initiate action in thought; the latter creates the opportunity for a 'no' response."

Free Promotion

Because public radio and television are non-profit, there is a certain amount of promotion that can be arranged for free. Banks, libraries, theatres, schools and shopping malls often offer display space. The display may take the form of a bulletin board, table display, or in the case of some malls, a booth available to non-profit organizations. Such display can be used for station public awareness or to promote specific programs. Use of audio or videotape cassettes of programs for on-the-spot playback on recorders or monitors can make such exposure especially effective.

Posters are available from both the NPR and PBS networks and from program producers for many network series and specials free of charge. The station may pay a small cost for overprinting its local air date and time. These can be put up on bulletin boards in schools, libraries, and in book, record, video, and other appropriate stores.

There is the obvious on-air promotion on the station, itself. Thirty- and 60-second spots are used not only for specific and generic promos, but also to inform people of membership and the station's program guide.

Frequently, local commercial radio and television stations will provide public service announcement (PSA) time. They will use audiotapes, copy, and/or slides to create spots without cost. The Public Information Director should find out from each what their services are for non-profit organizations. Public radio and television stations should be sensitive to the fact that commercial stations are competition, and should limit requests for PSA time to important specials and services, such as radio programming for the blind, captioned TV for the deaf, and service-organization related programs.

Presentations before organizational meetings are good promotion. Speeches to local PTAs, volunteer groups, service organizations, social work groups, retirement centers, and unions can pay off in goodwill, recognition, and increased audiences.

If the station tapes local concerts for delayed broadcast, the PI Director should request free ad space in the printed program. Since the station is promoting the concerts or the organization by airing the event, it can certainly feel justified in requesting program space. Such ads may advertise the station, related programming, or the airdates of other station concerts.

Trade-out advertising is another method of obtaining space without paying cash. If the station has a program guide, arrangements can be made with local drama theatres, music festival groups, and others for a trade: the station places its ad in their programs, and they place ads in the station's guides. Both receive added promotion without ad space costs.

Trade arrangements with other broadcast stations are also possible, with on-air funding or presentation announcements being traded by the public station for advertising time on the radio or television station.

Break-Even Promotion

There are many promotion products that must be purchased in the first place, but then "break even" in the end. For instance, T-shirts promoting the station or specific programs can be ordered and sold at cost or small profit. It is better to sell more and charge less, because the product is publicizing the station for free everytime the T-shirt is worn.

In addition to items such as T-shirts and tote bags which sell well in any part of the country, close attention should be paid to the interests of people in the station's particular locale: visors, for example, in a sunbelt community, or umbrellas in a rainy climate.

Carefully choose premiums for on-air fund-raising which will also continue to promote the station. If people in the community use bumper stickers, give them free with membership, along with more valuable items such as program-related books, tote bags, lightweight jackets—all with the station's logo imprinted.

Normally Paid-for Advertising

Advertising that is usually paid for can sometimes be obtained at no cost. And when "free" is not possible, deals can be made. Never assume that any advertising is out of reach financially until all possible arrangements have been pursued. It is possible, in fact, to take a certain amount of money—$2,000, for example—and begin to spend it on a campaign and discover after several weeks that half of it is still left and the station has received more than $2,000 in advertising.

For example, outdoor companies would rather have billboard space filled than vacant. It's often possible to arrange to have station material available if and when a vacancy occurs. The station gets the advertising and the billboard company has its spaces filled *and* earns a tax write-off. One station Public Information Director asked about a small billboard and was told that it was $300 for one month, but could be donated free. She then asked for one month free and one month to be paid for. The billboard was put up two weeks early by the cooperative company, and kept up for four months. The station received four-and-a-half months of outdoor advertising ($1,350 worth of space) for the cost of one month ($300).

It is worth asking commercial stations their rates for advertising. In some cities, for example, it is less costly to have 10 TV ads than one newspaper ad, depending on the airtime. Again, the public station can offer to pay and place its spots at the exact times most beneficial to its needs, rather than having them placed as PSAs. PSAs will be aired, but at times convenient to the commercial station. Specific target audiences are missed. The public station Public Information Director should make a point of letting the commercial station know that he or she is appreciative of the PSA opportunity, but would still like to spend some of its very limited advertising budget with the commercial station. They might well be willing to make a special deal, such as two spots for the price of one, making the buy particularly attractive.

Some commercial stations will even produce promotion spots for a public station at very little cost, or free-of-charge.

Local artists and advertising agencies often give their services as a tax write-off and contribute artwork, logos, and even whole campaign ideas.

Newspaper ads can be costly. One way to avoid the expense is to see if underwriting the cost of newspaper advertising will be done by local businesses or foundations. For their contribution, copy at the bottom of the ad states that it was "paid for by Rooster Andrews Sporting Goods, Inc." The station can also give underwriters on-air mention before and after the program for which the underwriter has provided advertising money: "Promotion of this program was made possible with funds from Rooster Andrews Sporting Goods, Inc." The company receives mention both on-air and in print, and gets a tax write-off, as well as the good-will of listeners who enjoy the program.

Newspaper space can also be had by obtaining a special weekly column in a local newspaper's entertainment section. Editors can be convinced, with the help of samples from other papers which serve other public radio and TV stations. The NPR and PBS networks will help by supplying samples.

Another source of valuable, relatively inexpensive, even productive advertising service is the local university, especially if the public station is a university licensee. The imaginative PI Director can often enlist the aid of various university departments. For instance, a marketing professor may have a class conduct a listener or viewer or market survey. Advertising professors may assign students to sell advertising for the station's program guide. English and journalism professors might assign students to research and write guide magazine articles, feature articles for campus newspapers, and special features for general release to local magazines or newspapers.

Cooperative Ads. During major fund-raising or public awareness campaigns or for special programs, public stations in a given region or state may find it helpful to pool their financial resources into one ad in a regional or statewide publication. In Texas, for example, during a recent national public awareness campaign by the National Public Radio Network, seven Texas public radio stations got together to run an ad in *Texas Monthly* magazine.

PROMOTING FUND-RAISING EVENTS

The two main kinds of fund-raising events public station PI Directors must promote are auctions and pledge weeks. While the events are unlike most activities at commercial stations, most of the tools and skills used to promote them are the same as those used to promote programming and image: the station's own air, advertising, station guide magazines, and publicity.

Auctions

Many public stations have skilled teams of staff members and community volunteers who spend most of the year combing the community—especially businesses—for donations of products and services to be auctioned off on the

THE ANNUAL KQED AUCTION JUNE 5-10

An auction announcement brochure/flyer prepared by KQED-TV/San Francisco, for mailing to members, businesses, and community groups. Note that copy, layout, and printing were all donated, with thanks given in small print on the flyer.

**WHEN YOU GIVE
TO THE KQED AUCTION,
YOU ALWAYS GET MORE THAN
YOUR MONEY'S WORTH!**

One of the highlights of the Northern California television season is coming June 5 - 10th.

The KQED Television Auction: The frantic fun-filled extravaganza viewed by more than 3,000,000 from the Oregon border to San Luis Obispo.

50 telephones are kept constantly busy taking bids from 2 p.m. to midnight every day of the Auction.

Just think of the TV coverage you get when you donate your product or service to the KQED Auction. Over, 3,000,000 viewers and *your gifts are tax deductible!*

air. Proceeds, after expenses, go to support programming and other station activities. As auction time approaches, articles in the station's guide magazine begin to create a climate of mounting excitement and anticipation at least a month in advance. At least two weeks in advance, on-air announcements begin to appear, with increasing frequency as the beginning of auction week nears. A stream of news and feature releases will have started going to the press at least a month in advance, with features highlighting unusual, expensive and desirable auction items, acution personalities, volunteer efforts, and the like. If the station has a speaker's bureau, its members will concentrate their public speechs on the need for volunteers to work at the auction; the need for donation of items to be auctioned off; and the need for people to watch and bid for items. Many broadcast stations will provide PSA time for auctions.

The involvement of a large number of volunteers and viewer/bidders year after year makes many people in the community aware of the auction as fascinating programming and an annual event in the community to anticipate. Promotion efforts stress both the spirit of fun and the value to the station.

Auction donors are a good possibility for extra advertising and promotion dollars. The companies which have donated goods and services to be auctioned off on the air might:

· Take out their own ads to build public station audiences.
· Turn over some of their own contracted ad space to the public station as an additional donation.
· Put money into a pool, along with other donors, which the station can then use to advertise the audition.

Pledge Weeks

At least twice a year most public stations hold "pledge weeks," special periods of time during which the station appeals to audiences to become contributing members or subscribers. The on-air appeals are done between programs. While little is done to promote the pledge breaks themselves, a major portion of the station's annual program advertising budget is used during these periods. Pledge weeks are to public broadcasters what ratings periods are to commercial TV: the time when the stations needs to attract the largest possible audiences, for reasons of economic survival.

Just as commercial stations reserve their best programs, series, and contests for ratings periods, so public stations reserve their best programming for pledge weeks.

And, of course, the biggest advertising and on-air promotion efforts of the year happen concurrently.

Public television's national "Festival Week" traditionally occurs in early or mid-March. Winter is ending. People are beginning to recover financially from Christmas giving. Competition from the commercial networks' ratings wars in February is over and their reruns are starting. And public television takes a "week" (usually about 15 days) to sustain a coordinated national effort

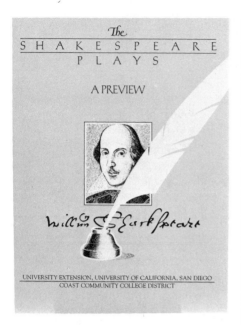

The

S H A K E S P E A R E
P L A Y S

A PREVIEW

William Shakespeare

UNIVERSITY EXTENSION, UNIVERSITY OF CALIFORNIA, SAN DIEGO
COAST COMMUNITY COLLEGE DISTRICT

COURSE CONTENT

The course, which is divided into six units corresponding to the biweekly television programs, presents a balance among the histories, tragedies, and comedies of Shakespeare. The six units are:

1. *As You Like It*, the first play in the series, is a sophisticated Shakespearean comedy about love.
2. *The Tragedy of King Richard the Second*, written in the middle of Shakespeare's career, is set in 1398. The events of the play, a history, are the continuation of quarrels, rivalries, and claims that Shakespeare's audience knew had begun much earlier.
3. *Romeo and Juliet*, one of the world's great love stories, is a Shakespearean tragedy, set against a vivid background of civil strife and domestic controversy in fifteenth-century Italy.
4. *Measure for Measure* is a comedic play that examines many issues found in Shakespeare's tragedies.
5. *Julius Caesar*, a tragedy, deals with the conspiracy against Caesar, his assassination, and the subsequent defeat of the conspirators.
6. *The Famous Life of Henry the Eighth* depicts the pageantry of the court of King Henry VIII and the historical events surrounding his turbulent reign.

COURSE GOALS AND OBJECTIVES

The basic aim of the course is to introduce students to the world of drama, especially that of William Shakespeare, and to enable the students to experience a play with understanding and appreciation. Specifically, by the end of the course, the student should be able to:

1. Cite examples of the ways in which Shakespeare's text is a script that gives clues for performance.
2. Identify major characters, discuss the problems they face, and show how they deal with them.
3. Describe the various groups of characters and discuss their interaction.
4. Identify the main locales of action and explain their significance.
5. Trace the sequence of events and suggest why the scenes are ordered as they are.
6. Identify differences in the ways the various characters speak, and show how language—metaphor, diction, verse and prose forms, jokes, wordplay, etc.— contribute to the interest and meaning of the play.
7. Explore the relationship between the printed text and the televised performances.
8. Discuss the various possible interpretations of scenes, characters, and entire themes which are supported by the evidence of the text.
9. Relate the major themes of the various plays to human experience.

One of Hollywood's oldest film lots is now one of Hollywood's newest video production centers.

Film,Tape & Post-Production

These two pages give just a brief sampling of the many kinds of program-related materials public station PI Directors must create. The Shakespeare Plays Telecourse Guide was prepared by University Extension, University of California, San Diego, and Coast Community College District, to supplement the TV series. The Production brochure (above) helps KCET-TV/Los Angeles, rent its studio facilities. "Why Me" was a special on breast cancer. The brochure shown helped public stations share in discovering ways to reach out into the community with special events and activities related to the program. KUSC-FM's quarterly publications, "Soundings," is sent to leaders of corporations, business, financial institutions, foundations and government to inform them of the activities and progress of the station. And the 1979–80 season program proposals prepared by New York's WNET were colorful six-inch square three-folds, printed front and back.

OUTREACH WITH "WHY ME?"

POV: MPBN

As with last year's eminently successful utilization project "Drink, Drank, Drunk", the emphasis of the Maine Public Broadcasting Network will be on coordination and joint efforts with the appropriate agencies and service organizations throughout the state. This will differ from an approach to a single metropolitan area because of widespread population locations and especially because of the essentially rural character of Maine.

It is the rural character of the State of Maine, in fact, which is often cited as one of the indirect causes of the high number of breast cancer deaths in Maine. Maine has the third highest death/rate per 100,000 population in the nation for cancer. According to the American Cancer Society, there will be an estimated 89,000 new cases of breast cancer in 1975 in the United States. Of this number an estimated 33,000 will result in death. Maine will have around 500 new breast cancer cases in 1975, of which an estimated 175 will be fatal.

The basic thrust of this utilization project is to provide the Maine viewer (women in particular) with access to information and services dealing with breast cancer. MPBN will function as an "information broker," outlining the services available through on-air and print promotions, as well as broadcast activities surrounding the airing of "Why Me?".

The specific objectives of this utilization plan include the following:

* To develop a coordinated approach toward reaching women in Maine, who are the potential victims of breast cancer.

* To help bring to bear on the public awareness as much information about breast cancer as is possible within our timetable of activities.

* To impress upon the viewer the importance of monthly breast self-examinations.

* To impress upon the viewer the importance of having annual medical examinations.

* To obtain the cooperation of as many media agencies as possible in providing referral

information, urging women to contact the American Cancer Society and/or their physicians.

The Main Public Broadcasting Network will attempt to achieve these objectives in the following ways:

BROADCASTS

* The broadcast of "Why Me?" on Monday, November 24 at 8 p.m.

* The broadcast of "One Eight Hundred: Breast Cancer", a statewide phone-in program that same evening at 7:00. (One Eight Hundred is a weekly series that regularly airs each Monday evening on both MPBN TV and radio.) The phone-in will feature a physician and a representative of the American Cancer Society. They will briefly discuss the topic and open the program up for questions from viewers and listeners.

* MPBN will produce a separate follow-up phone-in program at 9 p.m., which will follow the fo 'mat outlined above. For this program, however, we hope to add to the panel of guests a woman who has undergone a mastectomy.

* The production of television and radio spots about "Why Me?" for broadcast at station breaks before the broadcast, encouraging people to view the program, as well as the phone-ins and emphasizing the seriousness of the breast cancer situation in Maine.

* The airing of short films dealing with breast cancer. The following films are available from the American Cancer Society and are being considered:

BREAST CANCER: WHERE WE ARE
30 min. TV program narrated by Jennifer O'Neil demonstrates new detection techniques of mammography and thermography. It answers the questions women need answered to rid themselves of unnecessary fear, and to be prepared to respond rapidly

---

FALL 1979
91.5 KUSC FM

soundings

Corporate Support Vital to Public Radio

The support of private business and industry is essential to the survival of public radio in America. Corporate underwriting ... and specific programs is relatively ... lic radio itself has only recently beg... achieve the impact of its elder relative, public television.

We are proud of the support of those corporations and businesses which have already invested in KUSC. Their contributions, combined with the individual donations of KUSC subscribers and financial assistance from the University of Southern California, have enabled us to emerge as both a major National Public Radio station and as an important service to the citizens of Los Angeles.

Public radio is a community asset. Executives who value the quality of life in the areas where they and their employees live and work increasingly recognize its merits. Commercial radio is vital to America and will always provide the major program service to a community. Public radio enhances the total output of the medium by using its noncommercial advantage to deliver special events not available on commercial broadcasts.

KUSC's comprehensive appeal is demonstrated by its singularly distinctive programming. We bring to Los Angeles features such as the highly acclaimed national news magazine All Things Considered, regular season broadcasts of the Los Angeles Philharmonic, Mobil's Masterpiece Radio Theatre, and our daily classical music programs.

We hope you are familiar with KUSC and we encourage you to listen to us at 91.5 FM. Our goal is to provide an important music, arts and information alternative for Los Angeles that will enhance the cultural advantage of living and working here. The support of public radio by you and your colleagues is an essential component in achieving that objective.

Wallace A. Smith
Wallace A. Smith
General Manager, KUSC

Atlantic Richfield Foundation Leads Philharmonic Series Funding

Atlantic Richfield Foundation has taken a leading role in support of nationwide radio broadcasts of the Los Angeles Philharmonic with a grant of $65,000. This landmark radio series includes the Philharmonic's entire 1978-79 season under the aegis of its new music director, Carlo Maria Giulini. The performances, produced by KUSC and distributed by National Public Radio, were broadcast from April through September in 140 U.S. communities.

KUSC's general manager, Wallace A. Smith, describes the series as a joint effort on the part of the Philharmonic, the foundation, and NPR. "We join the Philharmonic in thanking Atlantic Richfield Foundation whose $65,000 grant has helped to defray performance rights for the 26 broadcasts," he says. "We are also pleased that NPR is helping to fulfill the desire of Southern Californians to share the music of their great orchestra with the rest of the nation."

Atlantic Richfield Foundation's grant not only enabled KUSC to move ahead with recording the series, it provided leadership which was instrumental later in the year in attracting a major contribution from the United California Bank Foundation in support of the broadcasts (see accompanying story). The investments of these two foundations boosted the project from its proposal stage to the series heard across America.

For Atlantic Richfield Foundation, this project is an extension of a long-standing commitment to the cultural life of Southern California. Walter D. Eichner, executive director of the foundation, explained, "The Los Angeles Philharmonic is an absolutely outstanding orchestra. We hope that this radio series will make that fact abundantly clear to serious music enthusiasts everywhere."

KUSC's development director, Susan Stamberger, summarized, "The initial response to this series has been extremely pleasing. Both the orchestra's performance and the quality of the production have been praised by listeners across the country. With the substantial help of Atlantic Richfield Foundation and now the United California Bank Foundation, we have launched the first Los Angeles Philharmonic radio broadcast season, an event we hope will continue for many years to come."

Nonesuch Develops Record Coupon Premium

Over the past few years, Nonesuch Records, distributed by Elektra/Asylum Records, a division of Warner Communications, Inc., has made a major in-kind contribution to KUSC by donating records for use as premiums. Premiums are offered as incentives for new listener subscriptions during KUSC's on-air fundraisers. The Nonesuch records are especially popular with KUSC's classical music audience.

For the spring '79 fundraiser, Nonesuch created an innovative variation on the record premium — a coupon which could be redeemed for a Nonesuch recording. This allows subscribers to select records of their choice. And, since the subscriber chooses the premium at one of six retail outlets (Tower Records coordinates this effort for Nonesuch), costs to KUSC for packaging and mailing are sharply reduced.

KUSC's development director Susan Stamberger credits Keith Holzman, vice president, production, Elektra/Asylum/ Nonesuch, for these premiums. "It was Mr. Holzman who offered to donate the recordings, and he who developed the coupon idea," she says. "An avid fan of KUSC, he has actively and imaginatively supported our efforts to develop a financial base from listener subscriptions."

Opening night of the Los Angeles Philharmonic's 1979-80 concert season will be broadcast live, Thursday, October 18, at 8:30 on KUSC. Carlo Maria Giulini will conduct Verdi's "Requiem" with soloists Renata Scotto, Lucia Valentini-Terrani, Veriano Luchetti, and Martti Talvela, and the Los Angeles Master Chorale. The program will be produced by KUSC.

1979-80
SPC 6

Program Proposals

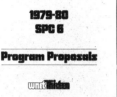

Bill Moyers' Journal

KTCA-TV CHANNEL 2 AUGUST PLEDGE DRIVE
August 17 - August 26

ANOUNCER SCRIPTS

(Daily programming spots - to be read alone or as tag to pre-recorded spots)

FOR FRIDAY, AUGUST 17
TONIGHT, THE BEST SEAT IS IN THE HOUSE...YOUR HOUSE...WHEN CHANNEL 2
BRINGS YOU "THE BANDWAGON"...WITH FRED ASTAIRE, NANETTE FABRAY, AND JACK
BUCHANAN. TUNE IN AT 9 AND PLEDGE YOUR SUPPORT TO KTCA-TV, CHANNEL 2.

FOR SATURDAY, AUGUST 18
TONIGHT, CHANNEL 2 BRINGS YOU THE "SUPER BOWL" OF DRUM CORPS COMPETITION...
"THE 1979 DRUM CORPS INTERNATIONAL COMPETITIONS"...LIVE, FROM BIRMINGHAM,
ALABAMA. TUNE IN AT 7:30 P.M. AND PLEDGE YOUR SUPPORT TO KTCA-TV, CHANNEL 2.

FOR SUNDAY, AUGUST 19
TONIGHT, CHANNEL 2 BRINGS YOU A PORTRAIT OF "MR. POPS"...THE LATE ARTHUR
FIEDLER. TUNE IN AT 9:15 AND PLEDGE YOUR SUPPORT TO KTCA-TV, CHANNEL 2.

FOR SUNDAY, AUGUST 19
TONIGHT, THE MONTY PYTHON GANG IS BACK ON CHANNEL 2...TUNE IN AT 10:20 FOR THE
WILD AND ZANY ANTICS...AND PLEDGE YOUR SUPPORT TO KTCA-TV, CHANNEL 2.

FOR MONDAY, AUGUST 20
TONIGHT, CHANNEL 2 BRINGS YOU "AMERICA AT THE MOVIES"...A SHOWCASE OF
HOLLYWOOD'S BIGGEST BOX OFFICE SPECTACULARS. TUNE IN AT 7...AND PLEDGE
YOUR SUPPORT TO KTCA-TV, CHANNEL 2.

FOR TUESDAY, AUGUST 21
TONIGHT, CHANNEL 2 BRINGS YOU "THAT GREAT AMERICAN GOSPEL SOUND"...WITH
TENNESSEE ERNIE FORD AND HIS SPECIAL GUEST DELLA REESE. TUNE IN AT 8...
AND PLEDGE YOUR SUPPORT TO KTCA-TV, CHANNEL 2

FOR WEDNESDAY, AUGUST 22
TONIGHT, CHANNEL 2 BRINGS YOU A STAR-STUDDED CONCERT..."NEWPORT JAZZ AT
SARATOGA"...WITH DAVE BRUBECK GERRY MULLIGAN, B.B. KING, GEORGE BENSON,
MUDDY WATERS' BLUES BAND, AND MORE. TUNE IN AT 8, AND PLEDGE YOUR SUPPORT
TO KTCA-TV, CHANNEL 2.

Announcer copy such as shown above provides daily reminders to audiences of special pledge-week programming, and of the station's need for viewer support.

to get new members and re-enlist existing ones. Festival planning begins at least five months earlier, as the network and local stations begin the search for or production of special programs. By early January, most of the programs are locked into place and PI Directors are given their first look at network-developed advertising and on-air promotion materials which can be adapted for local uses. Traditionally, PBS supplies its stations with press kits, camera-ready ad mats for all major Festival Week programs, and ad-building materials such as

Public Television Festival '79
TV worth staying home for.

"LIVE FROM THE GRAND OLE OPRY®"

THIS AD MADE POSSIBLE BY THIS STATION AND THE CORPORATION FOR PUBLIC BROADCASTING.

6:00 p.m.   Featuring two full shows
in one grand ole evening.

Yes, I'm happy to support the quality programming on
Channel 12 and join the **Friends of WILL.**
Name
Street
City   State   Zip
$120 Patron $60 Sustaining Member
$30 Family $15 Individual
Clip this coupon and mail with your check to: Friends of WILL
1110 W. Main St.
Urbana, IL. 61801

Channel 12

This *TV Guide Magazine* ad from WILL-TV, Urbana, Illinois, typifies a common public television station approach of coupling its ad-space with fund-raising appeals by including a coupon as part of the ad.

logos and type so stations can design their own ads for locally produced or acquired Festival programs. Animated on-air promotion spot openings/closings (called wrap-arounds, or donuts) and related theme music are also provided, along with themed television promos and radio spots. Often there is a cooperative advertising arrangement, as well. The PBS Network provides or arranges for money to be alloted to each station to match what the local station puts up itself, for print, outdoor and radio advertising. In this way the network encourages local stations to spend the maximum amount possible for ads, and the local station is able to nearly double whatever ad budget it can come up with.

A similar, but smaller pledge drive is held in late November or early December. And local stations hold even briefer pledge nights or weeks on their own as their budget needs dictate. But in each case, as with Festival Week, larger than normal audiences are crucial to fund-raising success, so advertising, promotion and publicity—the jobs of the PI Director—take on their greatest significance.

Again, many broadcast stations will cooperate by providing PSA time for pledge periods, though most are reluctant to use their public service time to actively promote specific public broadcasting programs during fund-raising drives. Requests should be for generic time to merely let the public know that the station has a pledge drive on the air.

WORKING WITH UNDERWRITERS

Corporations and foundations provide a significant portion of public radio and television station income. Large companies underwrite the costs of broadcast days and portions of broadcast days, provide matching grant incentives for viewers to donate funds, match employee contributions, and donate acquisition, production and presentation costs for program and series. They can also be an important source of dollars to advertise and promote programs.

Development Departments are the public station equivalents of commercial station Sales Departments, charged with responsibility for all fund-raising including solicitation of underwriter support.

Public Information Departments and PI Directors must work closely with Development Departments to see that when an underwriter provides money for program production, it protects its investment by also providing adequate money to let the public know about the program. Specific dollar amounts vary widely and are dependent upon the nature of the program or length of the series, or the total amount of the production grant. Some underwriters have provided more money for advertising and promotion support than was made available for the production of the program. However, a very basic rule of thumb which serves well as a minimum is to suggest to the underwriter an amount equivalent to 10% of the total program production grant. Less money is usually not enough to do an adequate job; more money usually enables a better job to be done. A number of large corporations work on 30% to 50% estimates. The PI Director should start by drawing up a list of what materials, space, and administrative costs the 10% figure would cover, and increase the amount as the program or series deserves, and the underwriter can afford.

It also falls to the Public Information Director to see that a corporate underwriter adheres to specific and strict advertising and promotion guidelines. These usually include:

Avoiding the use of the word "sponsored" in advertising and promotion. Because of the connotations of program content control implicit from early days of commercial television, public broadcasters insist on a number of alternate phrases for use by corporate underwriters in program ads as well as before and after programs, themselves. Among the acceptable alternatives:

"This program made possible by a grant from . . . (XYZ Corp.)."
"Funding for this program was made available by . . . (XYZ Corp.)."
"This advertisement made possible by a grant from . . . (XYZ Corp.)."

On-air promos for programs on the public station may not mention the corporate underwriter. Ads for use on commercial TV, however, may. If a company provides only advertising money for a program, that fact may be announced before and after the program on-air. This is especially common on public radio stations.

Corporate ads must not give the impression that program content or scheduling are under the control of the underwriter.

Most large corporations which provide significant amounts of money for public broadcast programs retain their own advertising agencies and public relations firms. These corporations frequently involve their agencies and PR firms in advertising/promotion/publicity efforts for programs. The Public Information director must see that these organizations, in their zeal to help, do not violate rules, principles or traditions which circumscribe such activities in public

"World" press kit, prepared for PBS and PTV stations by WGBH-TV/Boston, contains photos, news and feature releases, listings, promotion slide, and 4x5″ color transparency. "La Giaconda" kit from KCET-TV/Los Angeles and BankAmerica Corporation, provided PTV stations with materials to distribute to local teachers, including a teachers guide, poster, sample shooting script, audio-tape, and color character cut-outs.

broadcasting. For example, if the program is for network use or national distribution to other public stations, the PI Director at the originating station must see that all other public station PI Directors are informed of all advertising and promotion efforts in behalf of the program. This enables the other stations to capitalize on such efforts, or to prevent them if they are not carrying the programming.

NATIONAL PROGRAM PRODUCTION: PUBLIC TELEVISION

Most programs seen on local public TV stations via the PBS Television Network were produced or acquired for the network by local stations. This is unlike commercial television network affiliates, which contribute very little to their networks. There is a concurrent responsibility of the local public TV station, which falls on the shoulders of the PI Department, to provide the network advertising, promotional and publicity materials for the program or series it is producing. These materials are then made available by the network to other public stations which will carry the program, and become the basis for any network campaigns. Such arrangements are also necessary when the local station supplies programs to any other national or regional distribution service.

Such materials traditionally include:

- A press kit with releases and photos.
- An on-air promotion slide with corresponding copy.
- Videotape on-air promotion spots.
- Audiotape radio ads.
- A 4" x 5" color transparency for guide magazine or Sunday newspaper supplement cover use.
- A brief one-paragraph listing suitable for TV Guide or Sunday supplement and station guide magazine use.

The PBS Network Public Information staff serves as a clearinghouse for local station PI Directors, providing guidance about specific needs for particular programs and series. As soon as a PI Director knows his or her station is to provide the network with a program or series, contact is made with the appropriate people in PBS advertising, publicity and on-air promotion areas.

Other elements in such campaigns can include educational materials, posters, ad materials, and special feature articles.

The Station Program Cooperative

Universally referred to in public television as the SPC, the Station Program Cooperative is a complicated bidding system by which all public television stations decide how an available pool of local station money will be spent on national programming produced by local stations.

Reduced to its basics, the SPC works like this: public stations wishing to produce programs for the national system submit proposals to the PBS Net-

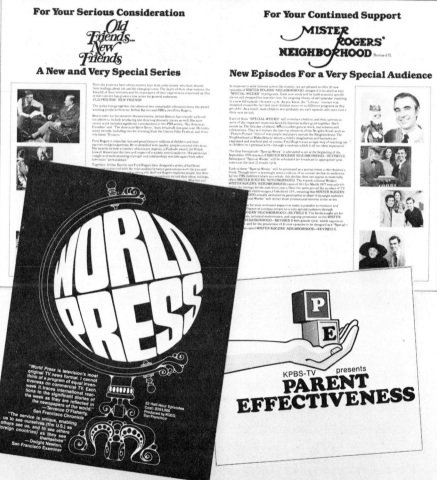

Public station PI Directors must produce "sales promotion" pieces to interest other public stations in their Station Program Cooperative (SPC) program offerings. Above are samples from Family Communications, Inc., WNET-TV/New York, WETA-TV/Washington, D.C., KPBS-TV/San Diego, and KQED-TV/San Francisco.

work. The network narrows the list of proposals down by pre-established criteria based on system needs to about twice what the system can afford with its collectively pooled money. PBS then submits that list to a series of station votes, eliminating the low vote-pullers and guaranteeing the high vote-getters until the pre-determined amount of money is spent.

The significance of this to the PI Director at a would-be producing station is that "sales promotion" materials must be developed to attract other stations' interest in the program offerings. These are usually developed by the PI Department. And the PI Director must develop the promotion budget that becomes a part of the program-offer package. A fine line exists between providing enough money to give a series good advertising and promotion support; and putting too much ad/promo money in the budget, effectively raising the price of the program or series beyond the system's ability to afford it in the SPC. Again, close consultation with the PBS Network PI staff is very helpful in reaching the right balance.

The "sales promotion" materials developed to interest other stations in the SPC offering can range from simple single-sheet flyers to elaborate full-color brochures or press kits. They are distributed to Program Directors and/or General Managers of all other public stations to call attention to production quality, stars, and how the program will meet PTV station needs.

PUBLIC BROADCASTING PI VEHICLES

Summarizing the vehicles public broadcasters have at their disposal with which to reach audiences and potential audiences, the following list was used at a recent public broadcasting conference:

Print Advertisements—On-air promotion—Press Releases (photos, and press kits)—Press Contacts—Press & Community Leader Previews—Company Newsletters in the Community—Flyers & Posters—Brochures—Color (for cover placement)—Audience Mail—Audience calls—Direct or Target Mailings—Station Guide Magazines—Program Schedules—Guest Stars of Dignataries (Talk shows, phone interviews, etc.)—Community Events (Station sponsored, auctions, pledge periods, etc.)—Speakers Bureaus—Station Tours—Station Brochures, Flyers, etc.—Display Booths or Exhibits.

RECEIVERS OF PI INFORMATION

Accompanying the above list of PI Vehicles is a list of target audiences who should be receiving the various pieces of information:

Major Newspapers—TV Guide Magazine—Individual viewers or listeners—Other public stations—The PBS or NPR Networks—Other local radio stations—Other local TV stations—Wire Services—Magazines (Local and regional)—Suburban Newspapers—Umbrella Organizations—Corporations & Foundations—Community Leaders (Civic, business, religious, and governmental leaders).

Checking each program promotion activity against both these lists provides the public broadcasting station PI Director with the widest possible range of options for promoting a program, series, fund-raising activity, or the station's image in general.

And it can be seen from the lists that nearly the same contacts and information vehicles are equally important to commercial broadcasters.

USEFUL REFERENCES

Public Information Department
  (or Development Department)
PBS Television Network
475 L'Enfant Plaza, S.W.
Washington, D.C. 20024

Radio Development Department
Corporation For Public Broadcasting
1111 16th St. N.W.
Washington, D.C. 20036

Public Information Department
  (or Development Department)
NPR Network
2025 M Street, N.W.
Washington, D.C. 20036

CHAPTER 21

Marketing Cable Television*

The broadcast Promotion Director and the cable television Marketing Director would find most of their skills and selling problems very compatible. Both have the need to move potential audiences to action. Both must plan, organize and control marketing plans to achieve specific objectives. Both depend very much on their station or system delivering constant satisfaction to the viewer/subscriber.

An award-winning cable marketing campaign can be smashed by delayed and sloppy installation of equipment, just as an exciting promotion campaign for a new TV anchorman is a waste when he quits in a contract dispute, or worse yet, jumps to the competition.

Both are dealing in a very perishable commodity. The subscriber can disconnect without penalty about as easily as he can switch channels with a remote control unit at his easy chair. There are, however, certain distinctions that the cable marketer must face.

MAJOR DIFFERENCES

The first major difference lies in the multi-points of subscriber contact with the system which provide potential problem areas. While the station viewer gets his or her full impression of the station and the program through the single dial position on the set and related media advertising, the cable subscriber has more opportunity to judge good or bad. In short, there are more chances for things to go wrong. For example:

*This chapter was written especially for this text by Rod Warner, Cable Marketing Consultant based in Sarasota, Florida.

The billing process each month inevitably generates errors which are frustrating and annoying to subscribers. A call to the system to correct the error is a test of the politeness and salesmanship of the billing clerk.

Any outage on the cable is usually blamed on the cable company—whether it's the fault of the power company, their own TV set failure, or a direct lightning strike on the tower of their favorite network affiliate, and service response is expected whenever they call—even if it's 11:50PM Friday night.

The serviceman who entered the house to reconnect the cable that was pulled from the TV when run over by the vacuum cleaner may have just come over through the rain from replacing the squirrel-chewed cable in the crawl space under the house next door and left some of the mud and water on the carpet where the errant vacuum cleaner can't get it out.

The next area of difference is in pricing sensitivity. The cable marketer must always weigh the price in every promotion/marketing action. While the broadcast Promotion Manager may have critical input into the station programming decisions, he is usually out of the advertising rate debate. The cable marketer will play a role in system judgment as to programming *and* pricing. This can be very complicated as the modern cable system adds more "tiers" (sets of one or more channels available for additional cost). How much an average cable home is willing to spend each month in home entertainment via the local cable system is currently under test in the industry and likely will always be a test subject in individual cable markets. These pricing strategies need to be sensitive to theories of "elasticity and inelasticity" (the reader is advised to turn to economic texts to more fully understand the difference). Now and then, a cable operator will choose a low price or, more likely, increase the programming (and costs) at the same price, only to find that the increased number of subscribers was not enough to increase profits.

A third area of difference is in the importance of local politics. The federal government's regulatory control over broadcasters also includes rules for cable operators. But cable franchises also have obligations to meet promises made to local community governments, which retain the power of reviewing and approving rates charged to subscribers. The cable marketer must continually be sensitive to this local regulatory environment and also be certain that selling practices meet the letter of the ordinances that give the company the right to do business. And these particulars vary considerably from community to community.

Let's examine the various aspects of selling cable to the public: these include approaches taken to make the initial sale, and ways of keeping subscribers in the system and persuading them to increase, or upgrade, their levels of service.

There's a world of difference in selling cable television in an environment where cable has never been seen before versus persuading a previous subscriber to reconnect or an existing subscriber to add new programming tiers and premium channel options. Each situation deserves its own "unique selling proposition" and a commentary on effective approaches to each problem.

THE NEW BUILD

Somewhere between six and nine months after a cable franchise has been awarded, all the red tape and pole clearances have been accomplished, and enough strand and cable will be in place to serve a home with cable signals.

The first realization is that an advertising campaign cannot be used yet because, although the community or city may be waiting in anticipatory delight for cable service, media use can generate a demand that will overwhelm the system's switchboard. The marketing must be controlled so that any calls coming in should be from those who can immediately be served with cable signals. Even without media, there will be inquiry calls of the "when will I get cable?" type absorbing valuable phone time. When the inquirer is on the line, it stops a legitimate potential sale from coming in or the telephone sales person from calling out.

This problem can be so great that some systems have published a timetable map in the newspapers to show the progress of cable through the city, hoping to forestall this kind of phone call. The map, when used, is the limit of mass media use in a new-build.

The new-build marketer looks at the problem as a series of neighborhoods turning on one after the other, cable spreading throughout the city in an orderly pattern like a giant amoeba. The marketing problem is zeroed in to block-by-block areas. This is most efficient for both selling and installing, for it is most critical that the installation of cable service follows as quickly as possible after the sale. The longer the delay between sale and installation the higher the cancellation rate.

Every purchaser of any moderate-to-high priced item experiences a psychological second thought called "buyer remorse." There are remedies for this (that will be addressed later) to retain customers, but the first and most effective remedy is the quick installation.

Some cable operators choose to use a combination of direct mail, followed promptly by telephone calls to each home. This procedure is less expensive but will not generate the higher penetration that comes from the one-on-one sale, door-to-door: the complete antithesis of the television promotion manager's orientation to mass media.

The direct mail-phone technique tends to average around 30% penetration of basic cable to homes passed, with the marketer intending to return later to remarket for higher penetration. The door-to-door sales teams have been getting penetrations around 60% or so, but are more expensive. But the user of door-to-door is willing to take the higher sales expense to get penetration up immediately, with less of a remarket problem later.

The door-to-door sales approach here has several advantages:

The cable company is given a "personality" when the sale is made in-person. That person may be the first and last time the customer ever has personal contact with the company.

The in-person sale is more lasting. That's important when what you're selling can be disconnected at any time without penalty.

More contacts can be closed. The salesman can take more time with his in-person pitch than can be done by phone, and he can be more sensitive to opportunities for closing the sale.

There is not the normal resistance to door-to-door salesmen. Cable has been big news in town for some time and, with an introductory postcard mailing, salesmen will be expected and welcomed. Door-to-door sales people for cable have little difficulty no matter what the size of the community is.

New builds present a unique sales opportunity to the marketer. For here, the potential customer has no real perception of the value of what he or she is getting. One can't imagine what it's like to have 35 channels of television to choose from and doesn't know what it's worth, having nothing to relate the price to. The marketer is in a unique position, a position he or she may never again enjoy, and it must be handled well, for the opportunity is fleeting.

The marketer can sell 35 channels from a menu of several increasingly higher priced tiers, plus a special price on each of the premium "pay" channels. These stairsteps may run from $5.45 for 12 channels all the way up to over $40.00 per month for everything offered.

The most successful presentation of these options is to start by offering no options. The cable television being introduced has 35 channels for the price of $40.00 per month. Service is to be paid in advance each month and can be disconnected at any time without penalty. The entire content of all the channel services is briefly described and if agreeable for the price, the sale is closed. Resistance to the price would prompt the salesman to retreat back one step, and, if necessary continue backward until reaching a point of no price resistance. This process is called selling "from the top down," presenting "the full boat" or going "for the whole enchilada." It requires the customer to say "yes" only once. Conversely, working up the steps means a "yes" at every level and an infinitely more difficult sales chore, guaranteeing a lower revenue per cable home.

THE MATURE SYSTEM

Once the customer has lived with cable service he or she will have absorbed mentally the concept of price versus service that was introduced with the new subscription. In one town, four channels are worth $7.50, in another people might think of cable as 35 channels for $7.50. Whatever the case, the marketer must face this as an obstacle in selling additional services.

This hurdle was there when pay channels first came on the scene in the late 1970s. "If I pay $7.50 for 12 channels, why should I pay $9.00 for one channel?" When multi-pay channels came later, the marketer had to go back to the $9.00 Home Box Office subscriber and request an extra $9.00 for another premium opportunity. Even before pay, basic cable had the same dilemma when going for rate increases. Cable operators know today that underpricing their product can lead to years of marketing difficulty and lost revenue. In the 1980s, marketers realize that pay services were underpriced initially.

Introducing Pay Television

The most effective and efficient technique used today for introducing pay channels is the "sell-a-thon." Usually, this is two days of feeding the premium channel unscrambled to basic cable subscribers with "call now" sales pitches between the features. Although billed as a "free preview," it's actually the use of blockbuster titles to draw attention of viewers to the channel so on-air pitchmen can ask for their order.

With the advent of three or more pay channels on the system, the sell-a-thon produced by the program supplier is fading as a useful technique for a single service, since the cable operator does not want to promote switching from one premium channel service to another. To continue, cable operators must devise, with the aid of the premium services, sell-a-thons that push all the premium options in one marathon session of big titles common to all.

Increasing Penetration

Increasing basic penetration can be achieved by occasional sales and special offers. These promotions have been carried on by cable operators from the days of classic systems when good reception was the primary benefit of cable. Their sales were much like small retailers, keyed to holidays and the changing of the seasons. Indeed, some systems were always running some kind of special; if someone came in insisting on paying full price, the counter clerk would not know how to handle it.

Today, with programming choices moving cable into the home and rapid growth in the large markets attracting trained marketing specialists to the field, this approach has evolved into sales techniques that can best be characterized by these fundamentals:

It is important that the integrity of the system's price for services be protected. Price communicates value. Consistent giveaways degrade the customer's value perception of the service. During significantly extended time periods for most of the year, the full rate card for the system's services should be observed without exception. That sets the stage for an effective sale.

The sale should be keyed to product benefit. It may, for example, be a month-long promotion of cable service as the remedy for the long summer of television reruns. An August promotion of cable programming choices as an alternative to political convention coverage is another example of a sale opportunity.

The offer needs only to be "special." The exact amount of a price discount is not really significant. The fact of "special" cost savings will be effective. The trend is to make the price discount off the first month's service, rather than the traditional half-off installation. Paying the full install price reminds the customer that he has an investment in cable that he will lose should he consider a later disconnect.

Awareness

The grease that makes the period of price integrity a successful product-related sale is the use of media to gain a high awareness of continuing benefits of cable. This might be regular insertion of tune-in ads or radio spots for programming not available off-the-air (such as Madison Square Garden events, or the unique programming of the superstations).

The Sales Opportunity

Year-round, the best and easiest sales opportunity for the mature cable system is also the most frustrating one for every marketing manager and the most difficult to use: the normal contacts the public and subscriber have with the employees. Every viewer contact with the system is a sales opportunity. A technician goes into the home to service cable and uses the opportunity to promote additional TV outlets for sets in the bedroom. A basic cable customer calls to inquire about his billing and the clerk uses the opportunity to point out the current sale on premium services. The manager who keeps employees alert on these points is bound to achieve a new subscriber gain each month. A test on whether this is working is to have someone call the system as if they were just moving into the area and inquire about cable. Many system managers are shocked by the no-sale response heard from the system's employees.

The Marketing Audit

Approximately every three years, an audit of the system should be conducted to verify legitimate subscribers, uncover bootleggers and discover illegal subscribers occuring through system fault. An example would be a move-in using cable service that the cable company neglected to disconnect when the previous resident moved away. (See how complicated running a cable system can be?). The marketing challenge is not to send the bootlegger to jail but to turn him into a paying subscriber to the "whole enchilada." Sales-trained audit personnel can make the auditing chore lucrative, rather than an unpleasant necessity.

RETENTION

Since most cable marketing managers earn a bonus based on system net subscriber gain, retention efforts should be applied to retain the customer once sold. The cable industry has fallen into the syndrome of billing customers monthly, creating for themselves a monthly disconnect opportunity as the subscriber looks at the bill and judges whether or not to disconnect this non-utility luxury and go back to an antenna, which is most likely still fixed to the roof. Or, as video-disks, STV and other competitive entertainment opportunities proliferate, the system will need to work harder to retain revenue allegiance.

Awareness advertising, previously discussed, serves this end. In addition, the system can install "verification" contacts after the sale and "save-a-customer" steps after the subscriber announces an intention to disconnect.

Verification

Verification addresses buyer remorse. Whenever anyone makes a commitment that parts a significant amount of dollars from his pocket at one time or on a continuing basis, he goes through a remorseful period seeking reassurance that he made a wise decision. Surely, you have gone to your friends to show off the new car you have purchased or the new suit you put on the charge account. You were experiencing buyer remorse and looking for reassurance that you made a wise decision and sent your money off to a worthwhile purpose. Treating the symptoms of buyer remorse and solidifying the sale are accomplished by these usual steps:

> The installer reviews the benefits of cable service with the subscriber, ensuring that he understands how to use the converter, if one is required, and points out the phone number to call if one is required, and points out the phone number to call if service is needed. He reviews the dial positions of all the channels and ensures that the new purchaser is comfortable with his buy. In the process, the trained installer reassures the subscriber that he has made a wise choice.
>
> A few days after the installation, not more than ten, someone from the cable system calls to verify that the installation was satisfactory. Was our installer polite in his work? Are the pictures clear? Any problems? Questions may come up such as network-duplication protection, or the caller may discover that a lug has come loose on the connecting compacitor, causing a poor picture. Some systems routinely make this verifying call

throughout their system on a regular basis. This step is particularly ingratiating and appreciated by the customer. (When did your department store call you last to see if you were pleased with the refrigerator you purchased from them?) This verification call, besides preventing a disconnect can be a revenue producer as an opportunity to sell an upgrade in service to pay channels or add outlets.

The next productive step is the letter from the system manager about five days prior to the customer's receipt of his first bill. In this letter, the manager welcomes the subscriber to the system, again reassures that the customer made a wise decision, and briefly describes the billing practices and what to expect on that first invoice.

Save-a-Disconnect

The term "churn" is used by the cable industry to describe the effect of customers leaving the systems while new customers come on. It cannot be totally prevented. There are bound to be deadbeats who don't pay their bills and some 20% of households move every year. But there is always a group that disconnects for product-related reasons and/or system-related reasons. System-related provocations come in several forms, such as repeated billing errors, rude personnel, poor installation work, or badly maintained system subject to outages and poor pictures. Cutting down "churn" through a "save-a-disconnect" program always assumes that a subscriber who doesn't pay is not necessarily a deadbeat but may be a symptom of system or product dissatisfaction expressed in not paying one's bill. There are steps of remedy:

The phone call. When the disconnect notice is received by mail or phone, a system employee advises the disconnect possibility that someone will call to make a disconnect appointment, and in the process will endeavor to learn the real nature of the complaint.

The phone call out. A trained employee reviews the nature of the complaint and calls to make the disconnect appointment, prepared to counter the problem or objection. Hopefully, the disconnect will be saved at this point and a disconnect date will not need to be set.

The letter. Should step number 2 fail, a letter quickly goes out to arrive before the disconnect date. This letter from the manager addresses the problem, based on information gained from the previous steps and expresses the manager's dismay that the system is about to lose a customer, asking the customer to call and "stop everything."

The disconnect. Should step 3 produce no response the system technician dispatched to the residence can make one last attempt to save the customer.

Systems that have employed these steps report 40–50% "saves." The steps take some doing to get under way and much of the effort is realized only in the long term: two reasons why many managers postpone them forever. Not doing them can, however, be disastrous in the long run.

MULTI-UNIT SALES

This area deserves separate comment because of its growing importance as cable moves into more urban areas where it's a simple fact that there are more hotels, motels, hospitals, nursing homes, condominiums and apartments than the industry has had to deal with heretofore. Sales people especially trained to pitch both basic and premium cable packages on bulk rates are coming on board to meet the need and the demand to extend cable beyond single residences. The industry, as a matter of dire necessity, needs to mobilize for this market to prevent others (including master antenna companies and direct broadcast by satellite outfits) from pre-empting the opportunity. The premium programming services are developing sales programs and presentations for these markets of considerable aid to the local operator.

Condominiums and Apartments

Soliciting here has always been an access problem. Bulk rate discounts can be justified by a single bill to the condominium association or apartment owner with a convincing position that the service cost can be acceptably added to the monthly rentals or condo maintenance fees. The condominium association usually needs only a majority of votes to impose the bulk rate on the total building. Apartment owners or managers can often be persuaded by the availability of cable attracting renters, and/or the offering of a free cable service to the apartment manager.

Hotels and Motels

Two major problems in this area are stopping the decision-making buck from being passed to the home office; and making the case that the service fee is not an additional "cost" without generating revenue for the house. The premium program suppliers have developed attractive occupancy-based rates that keep the cost in line, and several major hotel and motel chains are using the availability of cable services in their national and local advertising. One successful sales method is to invite all the town's hotel managers to a cocktail affair in which an elaborate audio visual presentation is made, previous hotel buyers testify as to the value of the service, and a mass sign-up is attempted.

Hospitals and Nursing Homes

Here the competition is usually a master antenna system operator and/or a TV rental company. Some cost objection, as with the hotels, arises. There is also a privacy problem of R-rated movies in the wards. However, cable service does tend to increase TV rental revenues to the hospital, and a bulk rate proposal may provide a better deal than a master antenna operator can offer.

BUDGETING

This can be a frustrating dilemma for the new marketer in today's fast-changing cable environment, with seemingly every "Broadcasting" or "Cablevision" magazine announcing new premium services and basic cable channels.

A traditional and conservative approach to budgeting involves a review of marketing expenditures for the previous year and relating that amount to the net gain in basic and premium subscribers during the same period. Net gains, of course, are the difference between subscribers installed and subscribers disconnected. In that particular market, an historic marketing cost per net gain can be used as a rule for projecting subscriber growth in the coming year. Whatever the manager settles upon as a subscriber net gain goal, this cost per net gain will compute to be the marketing budget for the coming year.

Another approach is to decide what the system is willing to endure in per sale marketing costs. Some idea of the subscriber life is required for this decision.

SUMMARY OF CHURN AS EXPRESSED IN SUBSCRIBER LIFE

If: Churn is		subscriber life is
1.0% month	it is 12% year	6.5 years
1.3% month	16% year	5.1 years
1.5% month	18% year	4.8 years
1.8% month	22% year	3.8 years
2.0% month	24% year	3.5 years
2.3% month	28% year	2.9 years
2.5% month	30% year	2.7 years
2.8% month	34% year	2.4 years
3.0% month	36% year	2.2 years
3.3% month	40% year	1.9 years
3.5% month	42% year	1.8 years
3.8% month	46% year	1.6 years
4.0% month	48% year	1.5 years
4.3% month	52% year	1.3 years
4.5% month	54% year	1.3 years
4.8% month	58% year	1.2 years
5.0% month	60% year	1.1 years
5.3% month	64% year	1.0 year
5.5% month	66% year	.9 year
5.8% month	70% year	.8 year
60% month	72% year	.8 year

Major Assumption: Churn remains constant for the life of the subscribers

Subscriber Life* is the length of time a subscriber is actively on the service. Gauging this for the system' subscriber mass, one has to have a reading

*Don Mathison
Vice President, Marketing
Times-Mirror

on "churn," i.e., the rate (expressed as a percent) that subscribers are disconnecting the service. This churn rate is determined by:

$$\frac{Current\ month's\ disconnects}{Subscriber\ count\ end\ of\ previous\ month}$$

To save the further computation, the table above can be used as a guide to the effect of churn on subscriber life.

Once knowing the system subscriber life, the cable Marketing Director can determine the revenue subscribers will generate and decide how much per subscriber the system is willing to invest in acquisition. Marketing budgets for this approach will undoubtedly be higher than the historical cost per net gain, but they offer the potential of faster and farther growth.

This latter approach to budgeting makes it reasonable to consider promotional opportunities that may come along in the coming year that are unbudgeted, and there are always bound to be some for thinking marketers. When these special promotion opportunities appear, the marketing budget can be set for them based on the projection of subscriber growth to be gained by the special promotion. Those subscribers gained thus pay for the marketing costs incurred. And little damage is done to the budget—assuming of course that the marketer has skillfully projected his anticipated subscribers gained from the promotion.

At this point, it might be well to use an old illustration for establishing the marketing budget. Like a bonfire that one knows will be put out by dousing it with water, one is confident marketing techniques will make the sale. The question is how many buckets of water are required to put the fire out? One short of enough and the fire will continue to burn, making a total waste of all the water sloshed to that point. So, one must consider whether it's better to spend a little too much yet get the subscriber, or spend not quite enough and miss the sale.

SUMMARY

This chapter has briefly reviewed a few of the fundamentals of cable marketing, noting similarities and differences to the techniques of broadcast promotion. Cable television marketing is a vastly complicated matter with far more variables involved than might first be imagined. Although, initially, it would seem that promotion managers and cable marketers might easily make a transition between fields, the reality is that each field has unique selling problems and requires its own special skills. However, both need a thorough knowledge of broadcast advertising and good public relations techniques to perform their jobs effectively.

CHAPTER 22

Identity Changes & Anniversaries

Promotion Directors are continually facing certain kinds of station identity changes. TV stations hire new anchorpersons for the local news program; radio stations bring in major new personalities; logos are changed; call letters are changed; channel numbers or dial positions are swapped with another station (a rarity, but a potentially confusing nightmare); or the station moves to a new building.

And at regular intervals, stations reach anniversary dates from the day, week, month or year they signed on the air. These are opportunities to call attention to a station's service to the community, and to the station's personalities, programming, and physical presence.

Both identity changes and anniversaries call upon most of the tools of the trade elaborated upon in earlier chapters. But since both are inevitable challenges for the Promotion Director, this chapter will provide some basic guidelines in dealing with such situations.

IDENTITY CHANGES

Changes of call letters, channel number, dial position, format, or logo can be disrupting to members of the station's audience and the community. Rarer but potentially even more confusing, is a television station channel swap.

There are several things a broadcast statio must do when changing its identity:

Keep as many members of its old audience as possible.
Use the event to attract as much positive publicity as possible.
Attract as many new audience members as possible.

A key element in achieving all three of these goals is the clarity with which a station makes a change. It must be perfectly clear to members of the community what the station is doing, and why.

A second key to success with an identity change is making sure that members of the community (and the potential audience) understand the benefits of change.

New call letters should be memorable. Several years ago long-established WTOP-TV in Washington, D.C., underwent an ownership change which required new call letters. The station chose—and widely publicized—WDVM-TV. The D, V, And M stand for the District (of Columbia), Virginia, and Maryland—the three major political entities in the station's coverage area. In the same market at about the same time, long-established WMAL-TV had to make a similar change for similar reasons. The station chose—and also widely publicized—the new call letters, WJLA-TV, as being the initials of the station's new owner, Joel L. Albritton. Because Albritton had received considerable publicity relating to the station purchase, his name was well known.

In both cases, the letters chosen were not arbitrary, but were memorable because of association with places or people with whom the community was familiar.

Radio stations frequently attempt to relate their call letters to their format. Thus a format change can frequently be tied to a call letter change. An easy-listening station, therefore, might try to get EZ into its call letters; a rock-music station tries for ROQ or ROC or ROK. Oklahoma City's KEBC has staked its identity to the slogan "Keep Every Body Country," promoting its country-western music format.

A new dial position or channel number might provide improved reception, a clear promotable audience benefit. A new format might provide better service to the community. In fact, new formats are usually chosen after careful research of the community to discover an area of need currently unfilled in a given listening area. Once a station discovers what kind of radio or television service would better serve the community and commits to a format change that will presumably draw larger audiences, format-change promotion should emphasize the benefits.

Station logos are symbols which visually represent the station in a variety of ways: letterheads, ads, station vehicles, station equipment, building signage, and TV on-air identification all bear this station mark, and can help audiences remember the station, its format, its news, its location (channel number or dial position), its personalities, its image.

Since logos are the visual identification of the station, they should encompass the most important thing about a station: where it can be found (channel number or dial position) as well as call letters. In fact, in recent years many radio stations have decided that their complete call letters are not even essential. In advertising, publicity and promotion they drop the K or the W, and use the letters which have meaning coupled with the station's dial position; or they keep the K or W and substitute dial position for the other letters, as did San Francisco's K-101.

Consequently, logo changes are frequently coupled with other identity changes—format, channel number, or network affiliation. Advertising and TV on-air promotion can, of course, show off a new logo. But, in addition, press coverage can be useful in letting the audience know what the station is doing. Some kind of event should be scheduled which attracts media attention and results in press coverage of the station's change in its visual symbol. At its simplest, a detailed press release explaining the new logo, how it was conceived and designed, by whom, and how it symbolizes the station's relationship to the community, accompanied by a clear, reproducible photo of the logo, should be delivered in person to major press contacts and mailed to other station mailing lists. Additional photos showing how the logo is used on station vehicles, equipment, and on the building itself, might also be supplied.

The station which is tying a logo change in with an image or format change, or significant programming changes, will want to go much further. A party for press, clients, agencies, and community leaders might be appropriate, with logo-imprinted mementos (paperweights, pens, memo pads, coffee mugs, etc.) for guests. For radio stations, such an event might best be held about a week before the public introduction of such a major change, allowing ample time for appropriate press coverage. For a television station, three weeks in advance is more appropriate to allow time for Sunday Supplement TV magazine coverage of the change, as well as of new programs and personalities.

Specific publics which need to be informed about any station identity change include:

· Station boards of directors, ownership groups, or owners. Usually, these people have been involved in the decision to make a change. If they have not, they are the first who should learn about it, and understand all related financial and legal ramifications. Print pieces, mailings, and updates from the General Manager are sufficient.

· Advertisers, agencies, station reps, and underwriters must be told what is happening, and how changes will benefit them, or make the station an even better "buy" than it was before. Will there be positive effects of station audience size, size of viewing area, or signal quality? Personal contact, with "leave-behind" printed information or followup mailings, conducted by the sales staff are the proper approach.

· Current viewers must be prepared for certain kinds of changes. Format changes, channel swaps, new call letters—all can be reasonably explained beforehand both on-air and through ads and publicity.

· Potential audiences must learn what the new identity means in terms of different, perhaps more appealing programming. Ads and publicity are the most effective means of communication to reach these people.

· The station's network operations, promotion, sales, and station relations departments should be advised, because of possible impacts in all of those areas.

· Local cable companies which carry the TV station making changes should be notified in advance, in case there is an impact on their operations or advertising.

CHANGING NEWSPERSONS

All television and many radio stations inevitably undergo what might be a traumatic experience: the change of newspersons, especially popular news anchormen or women. It is a time when many in the audience will be upset because they regard the departing person highly, perhaps have even come to view the station personality as an unofficial member of the family.

Naturally, there are also many in the audience who don't care, and some who will be glad to see a replacement. In any event, during the change the station has three principal goals:

· To avoid losing some of its audience.
· To establish the credentials, and for television, the face of the new personality.
· To use the opportunity to attract new audience.

Emphasis should always be on the new person and his or her unique strengths. Things to promote, when they apply, include the newcomer's experience, popularity in a previous market, new depth in reporting or analysis available to the station, or any unusual perspective the person brings to reporting. Billboards, on-air promos, and print ads can combine to make the community aware that there is a change, a fresh face, a potential benefit in terms of more effective news coverage by the station. Audiences should be invited to sample the news with the new reporter or anchor.

Loss of audience can occur if a particularly popular newsperson leaves or goes to another station in the market; or if the departure is an unpleasant one and newspapers pick up and report acrimony between the station and the person who is leaving, has been fired, or not rehired.

In such cases, all the Promotion Director's skills in dealing with the press come into play. Members of the press will be curious, and will probe. The honest and skillful promotion director will emphasize positive aspects of the change, and trade on a long-established positive rapport to minimize any negative aspects of the situation. If, for example, a newsperson is departing because of salary or contract disputes, it might seem easy to blame that person for the problem. The station, after all, has power and prestige on its side. However, the proper course would be to share responsibility for such a dispute, where it is appropriate, and not assume the appearance of a big guy (the station) going after a little guy (the individual). Honesty, candor, and asking the press to see both sides of a complex situation are usually the best approaches to minimizing the negative aspects of a story and receiving fair treatment.

Having its own new reporter or anchor on the air as quickly as possible, with an accompanying announcement campaign is one good way of minimizing the impact of a popular personality defecting to the competition. Show the public the station has replaced someone good with someone better.

General Image Changes

A move to a new building might be the perfect time to make one of several other changes: new logo, special address, or phone number.

If a new logo is going to be part of the move, planning must begin far in advance for new stationary, business cards, building and vehicle logos a multitude of station forms, and advertising and on-air materials.

It might be possible to make an arrangement with the post office for the new facility to have a very special address: "Broadcast Lane," "Signal Hill," "Radio Road," or one of hundreds of other possibilities.

And the phone company might have a number available which relates to the station's channel number or dial position; or they might be able to reserve one.

Any new number or address that will help the community remember who and where the station is and where it can be found on the air are useful promotion tools in the long run.

Historic and On-Air Materials

Assign one news photographer to film the new building's construction. Select a permanent vantage point for filming construction progress, to be later edited into a "construct-before-your-eyes" film or tape for use on-air or at the dedication . . . and at future anniversaries. Still photos should be taken to match the film's vantage-point.

Let the audience share the move, but be careful not to over-do it. Sneak previews of a new TV facility a week or so in advance of a move, and station ID's of the new building during the week before and after the move can provide the right emphasis. ID's can be still slides or brief :03–:10 second clips with announcer voice-over highlighting those things of special interest to the viewer—especially new equipment that enables the station to do a better job on-air. Always focus on audience benefits.

Dedication Program

In Janet Lane-Tornell's two station moves, she used two different approaches to the on-air dedication program.

The first was a half-hour pre-taped show hosted by the station's chief anchorman, covering station history and a tour of the new building by the General Manager. For the second move, she planned a one-hour show with live coverage of the actual dedication ceremony hosted by the chief anchorman, followed by a pre-taped tour of the new building hosted by the weathercaster and local public-affairs program host.

The easiest way to make such a program work is to assign it to a competent writer-producer, perhaps the station's on-air promotion person, and the station's best director.

The station might even want to consider offering commercial time in the program to contractors, plumbers, electricians, furniture stores, etc., giving first option to the companies which helped build and furnish the new facility.

Dedication Ceremony

A number of decisions need to be made about this event.

First, will it be an "invitation-only" affair for VIP's? Or will it be an "open house" for the general public? Or both? Be careful not to let publicity of the event confuse the two, or thousands could turn up at the station's doors when only hundreds are expected.

Will a meal—luncheon or dinner—be served? From the following list, who will be included? Board of Directors, community VIPs, major agency and client personnel, station department heads, station employees, employees' families, others?

Who will the principal speakers be? How long will they speak? Will there be any celebrities present? Who will write the speeches? Again, the Promotion Director should be prepared to suggest answers to all these questions to the General Manager.

Commemorative Gifts

A commemorative gift with the station's logo and or a representation of the new facility is appropriate. A limited number of costly items might be prepared for Board Members, the General Manager, and special guest speakers or political officials. Framed photos, special plaques, or dozens of other possibilities exist.

If an open-house for the public is planned, a souvenir commemorative booklet and, perhaps, a key chain or similar item for each person who attends might be appropriate. Balloons for the kids, and some clowns, and refreshments for all add to the festivities.

For the station staff, coffee mugs, T-shirts or jackets, or other mementos can help instill pride.

Advertising and Publications

There are a number of decisions to be made, whether radio or print ads, or both, are used.

- Should "teaser" ads on the new building be planned?
- Should the station advertise the dedication ceremony? The dedication program?
- Which publications and stations should be used? What audiences does the station want to reach?

Don't forget the station's own internal public. In a recent move to a new building in downtown San Francisco, KPIX-TV prepared a booklet for employees telling the history of various buildings and landmarks in the new neighborhood, with a map locating high, medium and low-priced nearby restaurants, and nearby shopping facilities.

Other publications might include a map of the new facilities, invitations to various ceremonies, and a special map of the city showing how to get to the new building.

Budget

Six months in advance of the dedication, the Promotion Director should have a completely prepared budget for all necessary events and elements of the ceremonies surrounding the move. The budget should include:

On-Air Promos & Programs
Newspaper Ad Buys
New Building Booklet, Map,
   Other Printed Materials
Bar
Invitation List & Guest Expenses
Security & Traffic Control Costs

TV Guide Ads
Radio Buys
Caterer
Tour Costs
Gifts & Commemorative Items

Lots of Extras

What else is there to do? Lots! Don't forget to order "Our New Address Is . . ." cards for sales and promotion uses; new business cards for the entire staff; flowers for the dedications and/or open house; other personalized items such as station napkins, matches, pencils, pens, etc.; begin training station tour guides if tours are on the program. Mail invitations at least a month in advance; write the necessary speeches; and after the affair, don't forget letters and notes of thanks to all who helped make the affair go well, from the parking lot attendant to the General Manager's wife.

ANNIVERSARIES

Most radio and television stations find that certain anniversary dates provide a way for the station to reinforce its record of service and commitment to, and presence in, the community. Tenth, Twentieth, Twenty-Fifth, and Fiftieth Anniversaries call for major celebrations. Intervening years may call for smaller notice, usually with on-air station-break slides on the anniversary date or during anniversary week.

For the large-scale celebrations, many elements are the same as for a building move. Again, the Promotion Director is usually asked to head up a station task-force to focus attention on the anniversary.

In addition to open houses with station tours, some stations sponsor parades in the community; others hold giant birthday parties; and still others arrange major contests with extravagant prizes.

There are several "musts." For publicity purposes, to call attention to the nature of the event, a birthday or anniversary cake must be ordered. Cakes have been in the shape of the station building, the tower, the channel number, call letters, dial position numbers, and the number of years in the anniversary. Be sure photographers are present when the candles are blown out and the cake cut.

The station's publicity effort around an anniversary can make a critical difference in public recognition of what the station means to the community. Releases, brochures, and sometimes even commemorative books should recount the station's

- History.
- Public services to the community over the years.
- Personalities who made—and make—the organization great.
- Outstanding community events sponsored by the station.
- Awards and honors the station has won.
- Local advertisers with whom the station has had a long and successful association.
- Outstanding or unusual or memorable local programs over the years.

Again, all the tools a Promotion Director normally has to use can be brought into play. Billboards, bumperstickers, newspaper ads, on-air promotion spots, press kits, press lunches, parties, and more all contribute to a campaign climate for the anniversary.

For 25th and 50th anniversaries, stations may want to make the celebration year-long by incorporating a "50 Years of Service" kind of slogan into the logo. It can be used occasionally on air, more frequently in other station advertising, and all-year long on stationary, postage meters, balloons, lobby signage, vehicle signage, T-shirts, pens, and more. Such a slogan is a constant reminder to the community, and begins the momentum-building for actual Anniversary month, week and day.

Station anniversary parties range from outdoor picnics or barbeques for the community to elegant formal dinners for community leaders. Party decorations range from folksy banners to crystal-like ice carvings. But the emphasis should always focus on service and commitment to the community.

Part Five

Case Studies in
Broadcast Promotion

On the pages which follow are a number of specific case studies of radio and television station Promotion Director efforts. These examples have been submitted by stations, or have been drawn from the Broadcasters Promotion Association Library at San Diego State University. The library material in turn comes largely from BPA's annual awards competition. Most materials entered in the competition go on file in the Library in a variety of categories, listed in the appendix of this text. They are available for use by BPA members, including student and academic institutional members.

These case studies represent a cross-section of the kinds of activities broadcast stations and station promotion departments routinely become involved in, from promotion of single programs to entire series; and from community involvement activities to fund-raising support by public stations, and sales promotion by commercial facilities.

Editor:

Enclosed please find WLS-TV'S 1979-80 PREMIERE PRESS KIT announcing all our current Channel 7 personalities, top management and locally-produced programs and special features.

We have designed the PRESS KIT so that it can be easily utilized for print purposes. On the left side of each page you will find a black and white photograph of the subject; to the right, a short description of the person or program. The perforation should make it easy to separate the description for informational use and the photo for re-print in your publication.

We hope you find this PRESS KIT easy to use and informative. If you have any questions, don't hesitate to call me at Ext. 311.

Sincerely,

Charlotte J. Koppe
Manager,
Public Relations

Diane Allen
EYEWITNESS NEWS Anchor/Reporter

Diane Allen joined WLS-TV in January, 1979, as anchor/reporter for WLS-TV's Saturday EYEWITNESS NEWS broadcast. In May, 1979, she assumed the additional responsibility of anchoring the 5 pm news, Monday through Friday. Other responsibilities include co-hosting "EYEWITNESS CHICAGO," Channel 7's weekly magazine-format show which airs Saturday at 6 pm.

Prior to joining WLS-TV, from 1976 to 1979, Allen co-anchored the Eyewitness Noon News and was general assignment reporter for KYW-TV in Philadelphia.

Along with appearances on the Eyewitness Noon News, she hosted "Morning Live," a half-hour daily public service program.

From 1975 to 1976 Allen co-anchored nightly news at New Jersey Public Television Network. In addition, she was a feature reporter and a State House reporter.

Her first job in the media was with a small radio station in Mt. Holly, New Jersey, at WJJZ-AM from 1970 to 1972 as news anchor. After one year she was appointed news director.

In 1978 Allen received the Women in Communications SARAH Award for a special report entitled "Teasing a Dream: Impact." In 1975 Allen was awarded an Emmy for a series called "Assignment New Jersey" at WOR-TV in New York.

Diane Allen is a native of Newark, New Jersey. She presides in Hinsdale with her husband and two children.

Jay Berry
EYEWITNESS Sports Anchor

Jay Berry joined WLS-TV as EYEWITNESS NEWS sports anchor in May, 1979. Currently he anchors the 5 pm EYEWITNESS sports and covers all areas of s...

Prior to joining Channel... reporter for KHou...

Jay Berry
Contact: Public Relations, WLS-TV, 190 N State St., 263-0800

History of WLS-TV

Experimental television station W9XBK began operation in the fall of 1939, as the first TV station in Chicago and the third in America. At the time, W9XBK telecast 15 minutes per day with a program consisting solely of a newscast and a film short. Often, the place of a test pattern, the camera aimed at the Wrigley Building and the Chicago River; and the response at seeing "downtown life" was nothing short of phenomenal! The late John Balaban, president of the Balaban and Katz Corporation, owned W9XBK.

In August, 1943, W9XBK obtained an FCC license and a construction permit for a commercial television station, and two months later, on October 13, 1943, newly titled station WBKB made its debut.

Ten years later in 1953, United Paramount Theaters, Inc., owners of Balaban Katz Corporation, merged with the American Broadcasting Company to form American Broadcasting Paramount Theaters, Inc. Balaban and Katz owned WBKB then became one of the five Owned and Operated Stations of the ABC Television Network.

In Chicago, WBKB-TV merged physically with the then ABC owned Station, WENR-TV, and the combined station facilities assumed the WBKB call letters.

In October, 1968, another milestone occurred in Channel 7's story when the FCC authorized the change of call letters from WBKB-TV to WLS-TV.

WLS-TV is now in the third ranking television market in the United States, covering a 75 mile radius and reaching parts of three states — Illinois, Indiana and Wisconsin.

Currently, WLS-TV is the only VHF station in the country to transmit using an antenna system known as circular polarization. The station's circularly polarized antenna, located on top of the Sears Tower, reduces "ghosting" for reception of multiple images on home television received in large cities where there are tall buildings. The system, received a special engineering achievement Emmy Award in 1977.

What started as 15 minutes of broadcasting time a day has expanded into a state-of-the-art and local programing schedule every night covering 20 to 23 hours each drop as achievement... the total hours of receiving are in the Chicago area having added 1.5... daily. Currently, WLS-TV reaches almost three million total homes in the Chicago area alone.

Contact: Public Relations, WLS-TV, 190 N. State St., 60601, 263-0800

Station Press Kits—WLS, Chicago

1. AUDIENCE PROMOTION

Station Press Kit, WLS-TV, Chicago, Illinois: Fall, 1979

In November, 1979, the Public Relations Department of Chicago TV Station WLS distributed the press kit shown here to more than 300 local and national press contacts and community groups. The purpose of the press kit was to introduce all talent, top level management, programs and specials that were currently appearing on the station's air.

The entire project was conceived, designed, written and executed by the station's PR Department in cooperation with the Art Department, a printer, a photographer, a photo reproduction company and a bindery which perforated the final copies to facilitate their use.

Until November, 1979, local and national press contacts and important community leaders, their groups, and station clients were supplied with photos and biographical information on WLS-TV personalities and programs on a random basis, as shows and talent began appearing on-air. This press kit changed the haphazard approach into an organized one, and brought the station a better response.

It took one year to pull all the kit material together and complete the project. More than 50 personalities and program producers had to be interviewed, and past bios and show information consulted. Photo appointments were scheduled for all the people included to provide up-to-date likenesses that were uniform in style and presentation.

The folder shown represented the station's answer to the problem of creating a holder for the photos that was easy to file, easily accessible, attractive enough to stand alone, and which clearly identified the station.

The pictures and bios were reprinted on photo paper and perforated for easy use for reprint purposes. On the left side of each page was a current photo of the subject; to the right, a short description of the program or biographical sketch of the person. The unique perforation format made it easy to separate the description for informational use and the photo for reprint in any publication or community newsletter.

The file folder design made it easy to update the information. In a quickly changing business such as television or radio, this was a prime design consideration. The station provided updated material in a similar perforated photo format at least twice during the year, adding new talent, management personnel and programs when necessary. Alphabetical arrangement of photos in the kit made both finding needed material and inserting updates quick and easy.

WLS reports considerable favorable reaction to this press kit format, both from its own personnel, and in the form of increased attention in the press. The station also noted use of more accurate, updated information about its programs and people in press stories about station programming and activities.

Shown are the press kit folder, several sample photo/bios, and a letter which accompanied the mailing from WLS-TV PR Manager Charlotte J. Koppe.

2. TOTAL IMAGE & AUDIENCE BUILDING CAMPAIGNS, RADIO

KNX Newsradio, Los Angeles: 1977 and 1978 "Look Who's Listening" and 1980 "Who" Campaign

During the latter part of 1976, the management of KNX Newsradio in Los Angeles began plans to try and change the image of the station. The feeling was that the Newsradio format, while extremely successful, had some negative aspects associated with it, primarily due to the fact that a news station reports the news as it is and as it happens. Much of the news is "bad" by description. "Good" news, most of the time, just doesn't make headlines. Unfortunately floods, homicides, inflation, tax increases, and the like make most of the headlines and are reported.It does not imply manufacturing or sensationalizing events. This is reporting the news "as it is." One can easily imagine the impact on the listener of hearing a series of not-so-good news. It is disastrous for the station if the listener tunes out. But it is equally bad for a newsradio station if the listener begins to get an overall bad feeling about the station. Many news formated stations try to counter this type of programming by inserting all types of features, i.e. sports, weather, travel reports, fashion news, consumer tips, etc. In the latter part of 1976, KNX decided to go one step further in trying to create a new, good feeling about the station.

The promotion department devised what became a 2-year "Look Who's Listening" campaign. The strategy was to show people from various walks of life (in a lighthearted manner) listening to KNX Newsradio. The light approach, carried out in all mediums, was replaced in the second year of the campaign with a more straightforward manner. The key to both campaigns was to involve the listener. This campaign case study is broken down by year, then by medium, as follows:

1977
On-Air Promotion

KNX decided to poke a little fun at itself and the listeners as well, hoping to generate a new interest in the format. The key to the strategy was to use puns. Research showed that people liked puns and KNX hoped for a high degree of audience involvement. The first phase called for writing and airing 500 different puns relating to KNX. They were aired twice each hour, 24 hours a day, along with appropriate musical bridges. Some examples included:

"Archaeologists *dig* our coverage . . ."
"Artists *brush up* on our news . . ."
"Policemen find our news *arresting* . . ."
"Sailors like our *anchormen* . . ."
"Housewives are at *home* with us . . ."

The effect was immediate and overwhelming. Not only did these 10-second spots create a little humor in the news format but the audience responded with over 5300 on-air suggestions for KNX to use on the air. The best were indeed used along with the station's internally-developed puns. Special form letters were used to thank listeners for their suggestions and to screen the puns scheduled for use.

TV Advertising

Four separate 10-second film spots, using the music beds already airing with the radio announcements, were used in a two week campaign on local television stations, coinciding with the rest of the promotion effort. Due to budget limitations only limited animation, using artwork generated for the print phase of the campaign, was used on the air. The results were still very clever short TV spots.

Newspapers and Magazines

Twenty different 3-column by 8-inch ads were used in newspapers and full page ads were used in the regional editions of national magazines such as Time and Newsweek, as well as the locally-produced Los Angeles Magazine. The print vehicles were chosen primarily because of the ability to deliver an affluent readership, the type which studies showed also listened to a news format on radio. In a mammoth saturation effort, KNX ran nearly 50 separate ads in the print blitz. The readership response was again immediate and overwhelming. Hundreds of unsolicited ad suggestions poured into the station.

The print campaign was capped by a full page newspaper ad showing all the ads in the campaign and this time asking for reader response. In all KNX received well over 7,000 puns from listeners and readers. Morever, KNX received hundreds of letters and calls commending the station for such an uplifting promotion. Even young children got into the act as local school teachers assigned pun studies to their students. Many excellent puns were received by KNX via this route and the best were chosen for airing.

The overall good will generated by the "Look Who's Listening" campaign cannot be measured in a ratings book but it certainly was there nonethe-

less. And, as KNX suspected, local listeners and readers loved being a real part of the promotion through their participation.

KNX showed a significant ratings gain as a result of the campaign. Further, the CBS Radio Network, in an unprecedented move, adopted the KNX campaign for all its affiliated stations. Finally, the campaign won several top regional and national advertising awards such as: the Art Directors Club of Los Angeles Exhibition Award; two Broadcasters Promotion Association Gold Medallion Awards; the Advertising Club of Los Angeles Belding Award; the Society of Illustrators of Los Angeles Exhibition Award; and the Art Directors Club of New York Exhibition Award.

1978

Due to the initial success of the "Look Who's Listening" campaign, KNX decided to expand on the original concept and run a new phase in 1978. The decision was to select a cross section of listeners and actually use their pictures and quotes about the station in the ads. The promotion department developed 25 separate ads in this style.

On-Air Promotion

Several promotion spots were prepared in 30- and 60-second versions, using a montage of actual quotes from listeners telling why they listened to the station. To obtain meaningful quotes the promotion staff spent several days in the field interviewing listeners in order to obtain the best for broadcast.

TV Advertising

Four separate 10-second TV spots depicting listeners (portrayed by actors) in humorous situations, were used. The 10-second spots were combined to form different 30-second announcements. KNX used the segments to promote its different features such as sports, traffic, weather, etc.

Newspapers and Magazines

KNX ran a total of 76 448-line ads in this campaign during a two-week period in Los Angeles area newspapers. Twenty two separate ads were prepared, each showing a listener from a particular walk of life, listening to the station. The ads further contained an actual quote from that listener, telling why he or she listened to KNX.

In addition, 19 full-page ads appeared in the regional editions of national magazines. They were exactly the same as the smaller ads, except in size. Running a total of 96 print ads in the Los Angeles market was no small expense but the resulting effect was what the station wanted. The penetration was extensive and readers quickly "got the picture" of the mammoth proportions of the promotion campaign.

The results of the second year "Look Who's Listening" campaign were not as dramatic as the first. Perhaps one reason is that the idea was no longer new. Also the humorous puns were not used. Although many listeners called

or wrote in asking to be used in the next ads, the response was less than the year before. One very important thing was accomplished, however. KNX wanted the public to see a cross section of the station's upscale audience and perhaps encourage ad readers to be a part of what was depicted as an elite listening group. Note that KNX included a dentist, lawyer, pilot, stock broker, etc., in the campaign; all upscale and affluent positions. Again, KNX was creating an image, somewhat different than the year before, but nonetheless powerful. The two-year results of the "Look Who's Listening" campaign were very positive. Ratings and sales definitely improved.

1980

KNX's award-winning "WHO" campaign was begun in 1979. It was so successful, the station continued it through 1980, with a few changes. The campaign was appropriately named, because it focused on the "who," "what," "when," "where," and "why" of the news. Promotion included heavy use of outdoor, very heavy use of television, and moderate use of other media. As in the first year of the campaign, the target was the Los Angeles metropolitan area.

Television

The "Who" 30-second spot was a highly sophisticated production involving a parody on the lyrics to the Jerome Kern hit, "Who." This was coupled with state-of-the-art animation to produce a captivating, exciting, memorable commercial. In its first year, the campaign involved a large schedule placed over a four week period. In the second year, 1980, KNX purchased time on every commercial station in Los Angeles, stretching over an eight week period. *The buy delivered nearly 1,100 gross rating points.* The schedule concentrated spots around news-oriented programs such as "Good Morning America," "The Today Show," "60 Minutes," and all local TV station's news programs, as well as focusing on many early fringe and prime time programs with the appropriate audience demographics.

Outdoor

The outdoor aspect of the campaign took advantage of the tremendous traffic on Los Angeles streets and freeways. "WHAT" designs were placed on 30-sheet outdoor posters; "WHO" designs were placed on 8-sheet posters; and "WHERE," "WHEN," and "WHY" designs were used on king-sized bus panels. All the outdoor designs were taken from the TV spot to give the campaign a coordinated look.

The 30-sheet showings from January through April were estimated to reach 7.6 million adults approximately 29.8 times each, for 2,709 gross rating points.

The 8-sheet posters, also showing from January through April, were estimated to reach 3.8 million adults an average of 15 times each.

The King bus panels during the same time period reached an estimated 10.2 million adults with an average frequency of 15 times for an estimated 2,520 gross rating points.

The station also used "Triosk" posters in 20 area shopping centers. These were estimated to deliver 32.9 million exposure opportunities in the four month showing.

For illustrations, see pages 151 and 379.

Magazines

As with the outdoor ads, magazine ads repeated the artwork from the TV commercial. However, only "WHO" and "WHAT" designs were employed, to reduce production costs. Regional editions of *Newsweek, Los Angeles Magazine,* and *TV Guide* were used, though the TV Guide ads were for a KNX contest rather than the "WHO" campaign.

The station purchased four full-page ads in *Newsweek* and 4 full-page ads in *Los Angeles Magazine* during the campaign, for an estimated 1,300,000 impressions.

Newspapers

Newspaper advertising during the "WHO" campaign was reserved for promotion of special programming and station contests.

On-Air Promotion

For the 1980 version of the "WHO" campaign, KNX used three versions of the 30-second "WHO" spot and one 60-second version with a donut so live announcements about upcoming program features or special reports could be inserted. The spots were scheduled to air in all day-parts to provide strong support to the overall campaign.

KNX also added a radio station ad buy to the mix, using a much listened-to station between Los Angeles and Las Vegas, catching the many motorists traveling the desert between these two cities.

KNX NEWSRADIO 10.70

(sung :30) "Who . . ."

". . . has gone where today?"

"What did they have to say?"

"Where, how, why . . ."

". . . what happened to who?"

"You should listen and . . ."

"you would know too."

"When is what's happening . . ."

". . . who did that crazy thing?"

"Things you always wanted to know . . ."

"are all right here at 10.70 . . .

". . . KNX NEWSRADIO!"

KNX NEWSRADIO 10.70
6121 Sunset Blvd.
Los Angeles, CA 90028

Fred Bergendorff
Director of Advertising & Promotion

Designed and Produced by:
Future Media Corporation, Los Angeles

Agency: Bell Advertising

Other 1980 KNX Promotions

While the "WHO" campaign set the image for KNX, the station also ran a number of additional promotions: two 20-week contests, one of them a traditional "1070" contest (the station's dial position) and the other a travel contest; distribution of a unique directory of all major ad agencies and media outlets in the Los Angeles area, and a "History of Radio" Newsbooth set up in numerous trade shows and manned by hostesses.

Finally, KNX makes frequent use of a large private bulk mail firm to deliver millions of promotional flyers.

KNX ratings remain strong in a highly competitive market by continuing strong creative approaches that are well thought out, well targeted, and well executed.

3. LOW BUDGET PROMOTION, SPECIAL PROGRAM

WTTV, Indianapolis, Indiana: "Solid Gold" Promotion

Promotion Director Joe Logsdon was faced with a very typical problem: a potentially audience-attracting special program coming up on his TV station, and little extra money with which to advertise or promote it. The program was a March, 1980, special called "Solid Gold '79," a pop musical showcase of the top 50 records of 1979, featuring a galaxy of stars.

Logsdon knew that the program would have special appeal to people who listened to radio stations which played pop music. So he devised an inexpensive promotion that would elicit considerable on-air comment on the upcoming TV show by radio station DJs.

He produced fake gold bullion bars (ingots) and printed information sheets in the form of stock certificates. Imprinted on the bars were the words "Solid Gold '79" and Channel 4's logo. A pretty girl was hired as Ms. Solid Gold and, with Logsdon, she arrived at each major radio station in a police-escorted, chauffer-driven limousine to make a presentation of the gold bar and certificate to the "solid gold" DJ on the air.

Logsdon took along a videotape crew to tape the "presentations," for later use in making an on-air promo. All the DJs were flattered, allowed the presentation—and mention of the TV Special—to take place on their air, and most continued to talk the show up for the rest of the day.

A visit to the Indianapolis mayor's office produced similar results: photos for the press, and videotape for the promo.

The result: independent station WTTV beat all three commercial network stations in the ratings during the show's time period, with a 38% percent share of the audience.

SOLID GOLD '79

This certifies that

_____

is a Solid Gold Personality with WTTV, Channel 4.
(S)He is entitled to one (1) Solid Gold bar courtesy of Channel 4,
and unlimited shares of pleasure while viewing SOLID GOLD '79
Saturday, March 29th at 10:00pm on Channel 4
(Right after the Boys IHSAA Basketball Championships
that begins at 8:00pm.)

MUSIC **4**

Indianapolis Mayor William Hudnut (top, center) receives "Gold Bar" from WTTV Promotion Director Logsdon, and Solid Gold Personality certificate from Ms. Solid Gold.
Above, left, WIKS DJ Dave Dugan is surprised on-air by Ms. Solid Gold. Above right,
the promotional certificate awarded to local DJs, dignitaries and the press.

24 October 1980

FOR IMMEDIATE RELEASE
For further information please contact
Judy Johnston, Promotion Director

WALLY AND SHARON HATE WNYR

IT WAS A LONG SEARCH, BUT WE FINALLY FOUND TWO ROCHESTERIANS WHO HATE WNYR.
AS A RESULT, WE ARE OFFERING WALLY AND SHARON BOCK A CHALLENGE. BEGINNING
TUESDAY, 28 OCTOBER AT 10 A.M. THEY WILL BE LIVING IN A TENT ON A BILLBOARD
AT THE RIDGE DEWEY SQUARE (NORTHWEST CORNER). THE ONLY ENTERTAINMENT THEY
WILL HAVE IS MUSIC PIPED IN 24 HOURS A DAY: WNYR. WE ARE BETTING THAT
GIVEN ENOUGH TIME - AND WE CAN HOLD OUT FOR AS LONG AS THEY CAN - THEY WILL
LEARN TO LOVE US.

WALLY AND SHARON WILL LIVE IN A FULLY EQUIPPED TENT, IN FULL VIEW OF THE
PUBLIC, FOR AN INDEFINITE PERIOD OF TIME. THEIR ONLY COMMUNICATION WITH
THE WORLD IS BY A DIRECT TELEPHONE LINE WITH THE STATION, AND AN HOURLY
LIVE BROADCAST ON WNYR DURING WHICH THEY WILL BE ALLOWED TO "AIR" ANY GRIPES
ABOUT THE STATION.

ROCHESTER MEDIA ARE INVITED TO MEET THE BOCKS TUESDAY MORNING WHEN THEY
BEGIN THEIR SOJOURN OF TRUTH. THEY WILL BE UP THERE THROUGH SNOW, RAIN,
HAIL, BUS FUMES, UNTIL................

4. LOW BUDGET AUDIENCE PROMOTION, RADIO

WNYR, Rochester, New York: "Wally and Sharon Hate WNYR"

The best way to explain this highly unusual, tremendously popular and
attention-getting promotion is to reprint station WNYR's press releases on the
on-going event, designed to generate larger audiences and call attention to the
station's format.

90/WNYR Fresh Country Air

29 October 198

FOR IMMEDIATE
For further in
Judy Johnston,

WALLY AND SHARON HOST HOLLOWEEN PARTY

Wally and Sharon Bock are still up on the billboard camping-out for WNYR
And they still hate us, so they won't be coming down for
Since 10:22 a.m. Tuesday, they have been
they are hearty folks.
love us or

990/WNYR Fresh Country Air

31 October 1980

WALLY AND SHARON VOTE FROM ATOP BILLBOARD

Since Wally and Sharon are stubborn, claiming they still hate WNYR, they'll
on the billboard at least through election day, November 4. So that
considered anti-American as well as anti-WNYR, they'll be

tance had to be overcome by
had the right to use
genuinely

990/WNYR Fresh Country Air

5 November 1980

FOR IMMEDIATE RELEASE
For further information please
contact Judy Johnson,
Promotion Director

WALLY AND SHARON LOVE US!

Wally and Sharon have spent a long 13 days up on their platform. But
they're only coming down because they lost their challenge; they listened
to WNYR for 312 hours and couldn't help but like us, nay, love us. They
found the station they thought they couldn't live with is actually the
station they can't live without.

This is the challenge (though not through such extreme measures) that we
offer to everyone in the greater Rochester area. Just give WNYR a listen;
it begins to grow on you.

Wally and Sharon have made this special promotion a great success. They
genuinely disliked country music and WNYR when they first climbed up onto
the billboard. Now they know better and truly enjoy Winner radio. They

5. COMMUNITY INVOLVEMENT

WJBC Radio, Bloomington, Illinois: Variety of Community Involvements

WJBC Radio (1230 AM), Bloomington, Illinois, is an Adult Contemporary (MOR, or Middle of the Road) station in the heart of one of the nation's biggest agriculturally producing counties. Its prize-winning news staff combines with the ABC Network for more than 20 newscasts each day. On-air personalities are each individual in their approaches to the listening audience but all encourage call-in conversations in addition to the music they play. A six-day-a-week talk show, "Problems and Solutions," has open lines to allow listeners the freedom to call and voice their opinions and question guests. However, since 1975, Arbitron surveys have consistently rated WJBC very high nationally for average share of the listening audience available. Few privately-owned stations can compete with WJBC because it is known and loved as part of most McLean County Families. Why? Because of its strong commitment to effective community involvement.

The station's slogan is "The Spirit of McLean County." Everything WJBC does strives to exemplify that feeling. Some of WJBC's annual projects include the "Spirit of McLean County Award," presented at the local Association of Commerce and Industry Dinner to a McLean County resident "for significant contributions to the improvement in the quality of life in McLean County . . . for actions and deeds which best exemplify the initiative, industry, imagination and compassion that we at WJBC call 'the Spirit of McLean County.' " Listeners are asked to write letters of recommendation and a panel selects the award recipient, who is feted at an awards dinner and receives a framed parchment award and silver engraved tray.

Another popular project is the WJBC "Brotherhood Tree." Starting with the Christmas shopping season, huge trees are located in the two area shopping malls, as well as one each at the radio station and at a home for the elderly. These trees are used as drop-off points for gifts to be distributed to the needy. Names are received from social service agencies and from individuals who know of people in dire economic straits. Gifts are collected, sorted, bagged and delivered by volunteers a day or so before Christmas. This project grew to the point where by the early 1980s nearly 600 families were receiving gifts, and more than 2500 separate donations were being received, more than 100 volunteers were involved. All of these people—donors, recipients and volunteers—develop a particularly close attachment to the station.

Don Munson, Operations Manager and early morning personality, planned, researched, wrote and produced a three-month series of Sesquicentennial Stories for McLean County. These were published with the assistance of the county's Historical Society, with profits going to the Historical Society. The book was published to coincide with the county's anniversary date.

For the past several years, WJBC has sponsored, in cooperation with a local shopping mall, an "Amateur Moment." Listeners call the station's automatic recorder to audition. Station DJs listen to the auditions and select a pair of contestants to compete by phone on the air during their time slots. The audience picks winners by call-in ballot. The winners go on to the semi-finals which are live performances at the shopping mall. Ten are selected to return for final competitions. Prizes are awarded at various levels consisting of cash and merchandise provided by the Mall Merchants Association. The 1st place winner goes on to perform live at local Fall Festivals and County Fairs, on behalf of the station.

Other WJBC community projects include Free-Throw contests with the proceeds going to Muscular Dystrophy; a March of Dimes Auction; a Haunted House at Halloween, and various additional fund-raisers or attention-getters for local groups. A spirit of McLean County Band Day gives local bands and cheerleaders a chance to perform with the Illinois State University Big Red Marching Machine (the world's largest marching band). And Tournament Trial Sheets for the High School Basketball tournament are printed each year so the community can follow the progress of local teams through playoffs to the championship.

Another practice that WJBC has tied in with the Sales Department and various advertisers is sponsorship of Great Escape Trips. WJBC coordinates and sells group vacation trips to all parts of the world (London, Paris, the Alps, Carribbean Cruises, San Francisco, etc.) several times each year. A WJBC personality travels with the group and acts as host or hostess. The Sales Department sells advertising packages to help promote one trip each year. People enter by going into participating stores to sign-up for a drawing which produces four Great Escape winners. "The WJBC Great Escape" has become a well-known phrase in the station's listening area: It means 'a good trip and lots of fun.'

WMAL-AM Radio, Washington, D.C.: Variety of Community Involvements by Station Personalities

Like WJBC, WMAL Radio is a dominant MOR station in the Washington D.C. area. The station's Executive Vice President, Andrew M. Ockershausen, has spent his entire broadcasting career—31 years—at WMAL. He firmly believes that the station's success rests on twin cornerstones of service to the community, and announcers who are strong, well-liked personalities.

Over the years, WMAL has become *the* radio station in the Washington, D.C. area that genuinely cares about the community it serves. That image has been developed by the station's personalities serving as "goodwill ambassadors."

The pioneers in this effort, according to Ockershausen, were Frank Harden and Jackson Weaver. Arbitron reports have consistently shown theirs to be the most listened-to radio program in the market since 1965, when Arbitron started measuring Washington, D.C. Harden and Weaver's community involvement stems from a deep-rooted love for the area. (They have even turned down work in New York to stay there.)

Above, WMAL Radio's premiere and beloved morning men, Jackson Weaver (l.) and Frank Harden (c.) present a check to a representative of D.C.'s Children's Hospital . . . the funds raised at the annual Harden & Weaver Golf and Tennis Tournament. Below, WMAL Radio personality Bill Trumbell participates in a celebrity softball game he helped organize to benefit Latin American Youth Center. These typical contributions of time and energy by station staff members have paid off in audience loyalty for the station and the affection and respect of the entire community.

Says Harden, "We realized early on that if one is going to broadcast one-on-one, in other words—make a listener a *friend* of yours, someone with whom he can identify, someone with whom he relates—you must meet him, you must do more than just being an unattached voice on the air."

Weaver continues, "And so we've attempted, wherever two or more people are gathered together in the name of anything, to be there, Harden & Weaver, to shake hands, to say 'hello.' And this has really paid off."

Harden adds, "The people do indeed identify with us, can relate to us. They count us among their very good friends. It's been our experience over the years that people getting in touch with us—through the rapport of Harden & Weaver and the audience—have told us many very, very personal things that people tell only their own family and close friends."

Concludes Jackson: "Since we started making personal appearances 20 years ago, the other personalities on WMAL have picked up the same campaign. And they have also garnered very fine results."

Every year, Harden & Weaver receive thousands of dollars in unsolicited contributions for Children's Hospital/National Medical Center in D.C.

Tom Gauger, WMAL's midday man since the late 60's, does remote broadcasts from shopping malls every December to promote the efforts of the Salvation Army. In 1980, the organization honored Tom with its "Blood and Fire" award. Tom has also broadcast his program from local scouting Camporees and other community events. He is a past president of the nearby Fairfax County Symphony, and has broadcast concerts by the excellent Fairfax High School Orchestra and Chorus. Tom has real credibility in the performing arts area and is involved in music in the schools. He has accompanied high school organizations on trips, as well as featuring them on his program. He was even asked by famed composer Marvin Hamlisch to appear with him at a benefit performance at the Kennedy Center.

His involvements encompass other local entertainment groups: he is regularly requested by the various military bands in Washington D.C. to narrate works at their performances.

Bill Trumbell and Chris Core are WMAL's afternoon drive team. What began for them as a fascination with trivia and "boring facts" grew into regular "Baffle Bowl" competitions, with school or organization teams competing in an "It's Academic" or "College Bowl" type of format. The events always prove successful for the groups involved, and are a good way to get the station's talent out in situations where they can enjoy themselves and meet their listeners.

WMAL Vice-President Ockershausen stresses the importance of continuity. "The same person at the same annual event builds identification and contributes to the station's community-oriented image. Some radio people like to hide behind the anonymity of the medium," says Ockershausen. "The trick for a station is to work with its talent to find something the talent can associate with, and break them in gently. Once they get a taste of the outpouring of affection, they'll enjoy going out. People love their favorite radio personalities—people who are part of their daily lives. Our Harden & Weaver have likened them-

For nearly 15 years, Tom Gauger has taken an active role in community activities, and his audiences on WMAL RAdio have grown increasingly large and loyal. Above, he leads a "safari" on inner-city youngsters to Lion Country Safari Entertainment complex, a coop venture with an advertiser. Above right, he does a live concert with the National Children's Choir. Right, he hosts a musical program at Wolf Trap Farm Park for the Performing Arts. Lower right, Gauger narrates a program by the U.S.A.F Band. And below, he hosts a local public television on-air fund-raising drive.

selves to a public utility—people expect the light to come on, the bus to show up, and Harden & Weaver to be on the radio in the morning.''

In fact, WMAL Radio translated its warm personality-listener identification into a major promotional campaign. In 1980, the station took a close look at itself, its image in the community, and the way it interacted with members of its audience and community in a search for a slogan that would encapsulate and promote that interaction. One word kept coming to the mind of station staffers . . . "family."

WMAL concluded that it served as a family member, a constant companion, a reliable friend. Once that conclusion was reached, the slogan was simple: the station became, to the people of the Washington, D.C., area: "The Grand Family Station."

Subsequent promotions and even programming picked up this image theme. "The Great Family Airloom" encouraged listeners to phone in personal bits of family folklore, cherished family memories or traditions passed down from generation to generation. A recognized folklore expert helped select memories for airing, and chose 50 to be reprinted in his forthcoming book. Every voice used received a gift certificate good for a family 8x10" color family photo. The comments were aired at the rate of eight per day, for three weeks. The response was immense. More than 1,500 memories poured in. Many people contacted the station with thanks just for providing an opportunity or excuse for them to remember things long past.

Continuing the "family" kind of promotion, the station staged a "Grand Ol' Swapry"—a giant garage-sale-style fundraiser to benefit the Lions Eye Bank and Research Foundation. Instead of asking people to buy, the station offered an opportunity for them to swap items, making up value differences in cash. Two cash-only auctions were held, and hot dogs and soft drinks (donated by local merchants) sold, with proceeds going to the charity. The event was held outdoors with a live remote broadcast, square dancers, bands, and all of WMAL Radio personalities present. More than $4,300. was raised in one afternoon.

Coupling public exposure of personalities with events and activities that have meaning and value to the community are the proven secret of success for WMAL, as well as for WBJC and a number of other successful radio stations. Listeners send in anniversary or birthday wishes for their relatives or the station airs public service announcements for bazaars and bake sales, and usually there's a check in the envelope for Children's Hospital. It has developed into a regular part of the Harden & Weaver program.

In the early 70s, a group of community leaders, working with the station, created the Harden & Weaver Golf (now Golf and Tennis) Tournament to benefit Children's Hospital. Local celebrities, major sports figures, religious, political and community leaders participate alongside Washingtonians who come to represent their office or golf club, or who just want to be part of the fun. Harden & Weaver broadcast their program live from the Tournament both mornings, and people get up early just to come and watch the show. The station always has a live band and enough "drop-in" guests to keep things running smoothly. And a lot of money is raised—$111,313 in 1980 alone, and over ten years, more than half a million dollars. The hospital dedicated a wing to Harden & Weaver in 1973, a permanent monument to a couple of guys whose concern for people is only exceeded by the loyalty and affection that is returned to them by faithful listeners and the community at large. This kind of acceptance doesn't happen overnight, and it doesn't happen at all unless the personalities are sincere. "An audience should never be patronized," says Ockershausen. "There's nothing it dislikes more."

6. RADIO FORMAT CHANGE & TOTAL CAMPAIGN

KBIG FM, Los Angeles: 1974-5 Campaign

Los Angeles is a market with over 70 radio stations competing for audience and a share of the advertising revenue that is placed in the market both locally and nationally.

In late 1974 one of those stations was KXTZ-FM . . . a superior technical facility with a good music format. There was one major problem . . . not enough people knew about it. Research showed that the call letters were hard to say and even harder to remember.

The ratings were less than average and the station had to fight for its share of local and national advertising revenue.

The decision was made to change the call letters and then promote the station. The call letters were changed to KBIG-FM 104 in the second half of 1974. A multi-media promotional campaign was designed to introduce listeners in the Southland to the new name. The format was not changed.

The immediate goal of the station was to become the #1 FM good music station in Los Angeles. The long term goal was to become the #1 radio station in the market.

It was decided that the creative approach should follow the same theme in all media using a minimum amount of copy for outdoor and transit and to use television and newspaper as well as radio to sell the format.

A logo was established showing the call letter, dial position and format and this logo was used in all media.

A new copy line was introduced every several months, such as "The Leader," "Follow The Leader," "First Choice," and Everyone's Favorite."

Color changes were made in the transit and outdoor every three months for a fresh look, but the logo remained the same to give constant awareness of the call letters and dial position.

Transit was used throughout the year as a constant reminder. King size and taillight spectaculars were utilized.

A heavy television schedule of 30- and 10-second spots, with on-camera spokesman Henry Mancini, ran on five Los Angeles television stations during the first part of 1975. During the fourth quarter a 30- and 20-second computer animation spot was used, giving the campaign a fresh approach.

Billboards were employed as part of the outdoor campaign in June and September. Painted spectaculars were also used.

Henry Mancini was used as a station spokesman in newspaper ads as well as on television. Periodic newspaper ads were used throughout the year including a double truck ad listing a full day's programming. The ad used stars featured on KBIG-FM.

Research showed that good music stations share audience with the Spanish stations, so KBIG advertised to these potential listeners in their own language using Spanish newspapers and Spanish radio.

Other radio was also utilized. Spot schedules ran on one of the AM news stations in Los Angeles and also on KBIG-FM's sister station, KBRT-AM.

It's Beautiful

YOU'LL NEVER HAVE TO SWITCH YOUR RADIO DIAL AGAIN

K-BIG FM 104

just beautiful music ...*always*

HENRY MANCINI
has another beautiful idea

LISTEN TO KBIG
my station for
just beautiful music

Henry Mancini

The result of this campaign was a dramatic increase in ratings. (See chart.)

In the Oct/Nov '74 ARB, KBIG-FM was the 6th ranked station in the market with an Average Quarter Hour listening estimate of 50,300 adults 18 +, Mon-Sun, 6AM-MID. In Oct/Nov '75 ARB, KBIG-FM was the #2 station in the market with an Average Quarter Hour listening estimate of 73,700 adults 18+, Mon-Sun, 6AM-MID . . . an increase of 46.7%. The immediate goal was reached, KBIG-FM was the #1 good music station in the market. Sales improved very rapidly as the station's numbers increased.

In the Jan/Feb '76 ratings KBIG-FM was the #1 radio station in the market with an Average Quarter Hour listening estimate of 83,600 total persons 12+, Mon-Sun, 6AM-Mid. This included both the total survey area and the metro area.

The long term goal had been reached.

One of the most important factors in the rise of KBIG-FM's good fortunes was the full scale promotion campaign that apparently got the message across. Shown here are posters, newspaper ads, outdoor and transit ads, a TV spot and envelope advertising that did the job.

ANIMATED TELEVISION
COMMERCIAL - 30 Second
& 10 seconds
with recorded sound
track using the
KBIG FM Station
Jingle

7. COMMUNITY SERVICE, RADIO: BZ LIVING CAMPAIGN

WBZ Radio, Boston, Massachusetts

A radio station promotion is something that calls attention to the station in a positive way. It is possible to create promotions which also serve to benefit the community. In fact, many radio stations around the nation do just that. This case study is but one example.

Boston station WBZ Radio learned that health care costs in the U.S. were rising dramatically; that Americans spent more than 25 billion dollars annually on junk food, tobacco and alcohol; that 90% of Americans were not physically fit, and fewer than 45% engaged in activities promoting a healthy lifestyle. Further, no-one in the media was providing any serious comprehensive health education that promoted a healthy lifestyle.

So station Promotion Manager Doranne Jung created a four-month "BZ Living" campaign in the first half of 1977 that stands as a landmark in major radio station community service promotions.

Using every facet of WBZ's programming as well as off-air promotion, the campaign covered these topics: fitness, exercise, activity, diet, nutrition, stress, relaxation, sleep, dreams, snacks, breakfast, smoking, drugs, aging, and more.

WBZ distributed all campaign materials free, and paid for all ads relating to the campaign.

CAMPAIGN ELEMENTS

Kick Off

Newspaper ads. On February 23, 1977, a 1,500 line ad was run in the *Boston Globe* and *Herald American* which asked readers to answer seven questions and send in for a free "BZ Living Calendar." More than 2,000 responded.

Magazine & Tabliod Ads. The February and March issues of *Boston Magazine* and the February 22 weekly issue of the *Phoenix* carried a full page ad similar to the one in the newspapers.

Television Spots. The week prior to the beginning of the campaign, two 30-second spots were aired on WBZ-TV. The station aired the spots throughout the campaign.

Fitness Testing. To involve the WBZ Radio staff, a day of fitness testing was conducted in the station by Barbara Zenker, fitness consultant. Staff members participated in the written and physical exams.

Calendars

The "BZ Living Calendar (or BZ Living Guide) was keyed to on-air programming. More than 25,000 were distributed to individuals, companies, organizations and schools free.

WBZ RADIO 1030

1170 SOLDIERS FIELD ROAD BOSTON MASSACHUSETTS 02134 787-7000

30 SEC. TV,   CARL de SUZE,   "BZ LIVING"

HI, I'M CARL de SUZE. THROUGHOUT THE DAY

ON WBZ RADIO, WE'LL BE GIVING TIPS ON HOW

TO STAY HEALTHY, AND HAVE SOME FUN WHILE

YOU'RE AT IT. WE CALL IT BZ LIVING. FOR

INSTANCE, HERE ARE TWO WAKE-UP TIPS.

FIRST, WHEN YOU GET OUT OF BED, SWING YOUR

ARMS VIGOROUSLY. IT'S GOOD FOR YOUR BACK

AND SHOULDERS. THEN, TURN YOUR RADIO DIAL

TO BZ-1030. THAT'S GOOD FOR HEARING ME AND

THE MORNING TEAM GIVE YOU MORE HEALTH

HINTS.

IT ALSO STRENGTHENS YOUR GRIP.

(MUSIC TAG)

On-Air Programming

February. The fitness consultant spent a full day on the air giving shape-up advice to all on-air personalities.

For one week, the morning personality was served a different breakfast each day.

Personalities talked about ways to become active, and gave exercise information.

Two editorials were run 11 times each, setting the stage for the campaign by talking about the physical fitness problem.

March. Nutrition: for one week dietitians gave nutrition tips each hour and took listener calls.

Diet: Personalities taked about counting calories, fad diets, substitutions, etc.

Weight Loss Contest: One station personality went on a diet, listeners invited to guess how much weight he would lose by May 2. The winner won a 10-speed bike.

Snacking: Each day a personality was served with two snacks, and asked to select one (one was good, one was unhealthy.)

New Series: The station aired a five-part series on heart attacks.

Editorials: Six more were aired on such topics as exercise, diet, and healthy living.

April. Stress/Relaxation: Air personalities talked about ''type A'' people and how they could learn to relax.

Sleep and Dreams: Personalities talked about getting enough sleep, how to remember dreams, and numerous sleep-related topics.

Food Day: On April 22 (National Food Day) personalities gave a countdownwn of the 10 most-bought vending machine foods.

Boston Marathon: WBZ covered the Boston Marathon with newscasters, helicopter, and a special kind of commitment because of the ''BZ Living Campaign.''

Jogging and Sports: A medical expert on jogging provided on-air advice on getting into shape for summer sports.

And still more editorials—four of them—touted exercise-related topics.

May. Drugs: Personalities talked about abuses of over-the-counter drugs.

Aging: Personalities talked about ways to grow old gracefully, and talked about people throughout the world who are over 100 years old.

Smoking: For two weeks the entire station devoted energies to a unique smoking-cessation program based on a behavioral modification model, concentrating on listeners who were ready to stop. The first week included tips on how to prepare to stop on ''Quit Day.'' After that, air-personalities provided helpful advice on how to avoid starting again.

Results

WBZ concluded that it was ''impossible to assess the effects of this campaign.'' However, the station reached more than 1.5 million different listeners each week in 38 states. Feedback from the public, companies, organizations, schools and the press was overwhelmingly positive. It included dozens of offers of assistance, thousands of requests for information and letters of thanks, and editoral praise.

All these sources indicated that WBZ had achieved its objectives:

> To decrease personal expenditures on health care.
>
> To convince individuals to engage in healthy lifestyles and to accept responsibility for their own health.
>
> To promote "lifestyle"—a total personal preventative medicine program which would result in one becoming "fit."
>
> To motivate people to act, or at least become aware of the basic keys to healthy living.

Implicit in all these goals was WBZ's desire to be known as a station that is working in a positive way to benefit the community. In the long run, such an image creates an aura that advertisers, community leaders and potential listeners are drawn to, respect and admire.

8. RADIO STATION AWARENESS/AUDIENCE PROMOTION

Hot Air Balloon, "Orville" CJOR/60, Vancouver, Canada

As lower age demographics became increasingly important to advertisers during the '70s, "talk" radio station CJOR in Vancouver, Canada, became aware it had to broaden its audience base from a "talk" station's traditional older listeners, and go after people in the 35–55 age range.

With the help of a new ad agency, CJOR began planning for the future by:

> Creating a new multi-media marketing plan to sell the station's new image.
> Making programming changes to moderate the "all-talk" image. More contemporary music was played, there was less talk, and the station devised a new approach to handling traffic reports during peak drive periods.
> Commissioning a customized *hot air balloon* to represent the station at many high traffic, public gathering happenings in and around Vancouver.

It is the balloon, named "Orville," which is the focus of this case study, because it became the focal point of CJOR's new, aggressive approach to programming, audiences and advertisers.

The balloon was planned to make a lasting impact on the general public, serve as a reminder of the new programming, represent the station in a positive way, and remind the Vancouver public that the station was innovative. It reflected the vitality, imagination and appeal of the station, and created an aura of fun and excitement. "Orville" was launched in July of 1979, and exposed to about 3,212,500 Vancouver area people during that summer, plus another 18,000,000 on U.S. national television.

Fully inflated, "Orville" stood seven stories high; its gondola held three people; its ascent was controlled by propane gas. It could be used in free-flight across the city and surrounding countryside, or serve as a tethered reminder of the station at specific locations, rising and descending as much as 250 feet, allowing the station to give rides to the public.

USAGE

A breakdown of the exposure looked like this:

Event	Audience Size Estimate
N.A.S.L. Vancouver Whitecap Home Games	90,000
Remote Broadcasts	1,500
Disco Receptions	10,000
Fraser Valley Raft Race	5,000
Canada Sings	1,003,000
Vancouver Sea Festival	800,000
Fifth Annual World Belly Flop & Cannonball Championships	3,000
Pacific National Exhibition	1,300,000

Additional U.S. Viewers of Belly Flop
   Contest on NBC   18,000,000

At Vancouver Whitecap home games, "Orville" was inflated an hour before game time behind the scoreboard. As the national anthem was closing, it rose above the stadium, displaying a "Beat the Cosmos" (or other competition) banner.

In the summer, CJOR made remote broadcasts available to clients which included three live 60-second cut-in commercials per hour, hostesses to serve coffee, talk to the public about the client, and distribute giveaways and major prizes. As an added feature, "Orville" was made available to the broadcast location site, tethered at the client's location. Rides were offered to the public. It became a real crowd-attractor and client-pleaser.

At the finish line of the 24-kilometer Fraser River Raft Race, "Orville" soared aloft in salute to each finishing entry.

"Canada Sings" was a celebration of Canada's 112th birthday, held in Empire Stadium, featuring guest celebrities and more than 100 musicians, carried in part on the entire CBC-TV network. When the national telecast began, the first thing Canadians saw was "Orville," with its red and white Canadian colors, above the center of the stadium.

The "Sea Festival" was a nine-day celebration of living by the sea in Vancouver. Rides on "Orville" were offered daily, at a prime festival location.

At the Belly Flop contest, the first contestant made his dive from "Orville," tethered over the pool.

Costs

The following costs were involved in constructing and operating "Orville" for the year:

Manufacturing costs	$ 7,675.
Pilot Fees (12 months)	12,000.
Propane (per flight)	50.
Insurance covering public liability, public damage, and third party claims (for 12 months)	1,633.
Flight permits and licensing fees (12 months)	500.

Third Party Promotions

"Orville" enabled CJOR to structure third-party promotions by using hang-down cloth banners custom-painted for each client.

Such promotions enabled the station to recoup many of the expenses and operating costs, while still getting station recognition.

With its height, "Orville" could be seen for up to 12 miles—generating considerable interest for the client, who paid $800 to cover "Orville's" presence and a remote broadcast, in addition to commercial costs.

An alternative for clients was an in-depth, long-term association. In conjunction with a time-buy on the station, the client could choose to sponsor the balloon for an extended exposure, such as the 8-day Sea Festibal, or 16-day Pacific National Exhibition. The surcharge also covered the cost of a banner for the client to hang from the balloon.

Neil Soper, General Manager of CJOR, noted that the station's hot air balloon had one additional feature: exclusivity. Since the station was the first in the area to use such a promotion, any other would have been regarded as a copy of the original. And he feels the spirit, look and excitement created by "Orville" went a long way toward helping the station underscore its new, contemporary image.

9. FALL SEASON CAMPAIGN—PUBLIC TELEVISION

"Brighten Your Night" WWVU-TV, Morgantown, West Virginia

Many small and medium-sized TV stations face major program or season promotion campaigns with extremely limited budgets. This 1976 effort cost WWVU-TV just under $8,000., but was highly effective.

"Brighten Your Night" was a short, positive, flexible theme, selected to underscore the strength of the evening broadcast schedule which included an assortment of national PBS programs and local station productions. Because dollars were limited, the campaign concentrated on the station's own air, adding print and radio advertising. To keep costs down, the campaign was structured to maximize use of existing materials including network-supplied on-air promos, pre-printed posters, and news releases. These items were edited or customized to WWVU-TV's needs by Community Relations Manager Gary Watts.

Objective

The station's objective was to increase viewing by the current audience while attracting new viewers throughout the coverage area.

In the November, 1976, Nielsen Station Index Weekly Cume, WWVU-TV reached 51% of the metro households between sign-on and sign-off. This was a considerable increase over previous ratings which were so low they were unreportable, and proved the campaign's success.

On-Air Promotion

On-air promotion was used as the campaign's cornerstone. The images and impressions created were then transferred and reinforced through print, radio, and other media. The "Brighten Your Night" theme was adaptable and flexible when coupled with existing videotape promos and slide/audio-tape spots.

Video animation was used to introduce all station breaks and promos. Night-of-the-Week promos were used to highlight entire evenings' line-ups. Subject-area promos were used to spotlight categories of programs—i.e. performance programs, documentaries, etc.

Campaign station IDs were used to end each station break. A typical station break contained a 10-second "Brighten Your Night" animation, one or more promotion spots for upcoming programming, and the themed ID. Campaign music was used under all ID's, animations, specialized promos, and radio spots.

Print Ads & Publicity

A series of print ads and promotional pieces were developed and placed in area newspapers, *TV Guide* magazine, TV sections of Sunday papers, company newsletters, and the station's magazine.

A generic ad was scheduled in 26 area newspapers to kick-off the campaign.

A total of seven newspaper ads were scheduled to promote various programs during the subsequent four months.

Four *TV Guide* ads were run in conjunction with the generic newspaper ads.

The station's quarterly program guide was distributed to 10,000 area residents.

Four pre-print posters were customized with the campaign message and distributed to area schools, libraries, etc.

Numerous press kits, news releases and photos were prepared and distributed to area newspapers, radio stations, cable companies, colleges, and company newsletters.

Radio

Five 30-second spots were developed and placed on 20 commercial radio stations (see market map). Each spot was scheduled to complement the station's print and on-air efforts. In addition, stations provided some PSA time for WWVU-TV's radio spots. The total frequency of play for the five spots: 1,466 times.

This is the kind of campaign many small stations must mount each year, and for not much more money—though media costs are escalating each year. However, as station market size and promotion budgets grow, the basic elements of a campaign—publicity, advertising, and on-air promotion—remain the same.

10. AUDIENCE PROMOTION, TOTAL CAMPAIGN—RADIO

"Everything's Beautiful" WLOO-FM, Chicago, Illinois

The 1979–80 promotional strategy developed by WLOO-FM, Chicago, and its advertising agency, Bentley, Barnes & Lynn (also Chicago) had one prime objective:

To create a simple, yet memorable campaign which would be fun to look at while subliminally creating in the mind of a *prospective* listener a feeling of "there's the place I have been looking for on my radio," while at the same time causing *present* listeners to think, "that's why I listen."

To keep the theme fresh, it was decided to create two interlocking campaigns within the year: one for Fall and Winter—"Beautiful Music Above the Noise"—and one for Spring and Summer—"A Beautiful Place To Be." In both cases the station is positioned as "beautiful"—an escape from unpleasantness, whenever or wherever it appears.

Creative Approach

The television and outdoor advertising creative copy were carefully married to each other. Three 30-second TV spots were created during 1979 and 1980 for this campaign. Each contains a little animated person who always ends up listening to FM 100 by turning a small radio knob on an outdoor sign. The billboard contains the copy line which is subsequently on display throughout the Chicago area on 24- or 30-sheet outdoor posters, on transit ads, and in print.

The creative approach was deliberately simplistic, according to Promotion Manager Lynn Christian. For television, animation was selected over live-action to avoid making the spots appear as editorial comments about Chicago's noise or high density traffic.

The outdoor and transit copy reinforce the TV campaign. The copy on all outdoor and transit boards is easy-to-read type, in eye-appealing colors. Print ads in consumer and trade publications either support the TV and Outdoor copy or reinforce the slogan.

The TV spots, print ads and merchandising were produced for WLOO-FM by its agency, Bentley, Barnes & Lynn, while the outdoor layouts were developed by Foster & Kleiser Outdoor Advertising, in association with the station and the agency.

In all cases, both WLOO-FM and parent company Century Broadcasting promotion people were involved on a day-to-day basis in creating the "Everything's Beautiful" campaign, as it came to be called.

Media Used, and Budget

The following media were used in the campaigns:

Television. Three spots were created and placed on network channels 2, 5 and 7, and independent stations 9, 32 and 44. Each spot focuses around a billboard, calling attention to the station's outdoor campaign, and each spot uses the flower at the center to reinforce the station's centered dial position on the radio. Budget: $150,000.

Outdoor. The outdoor campaign for the "Beautiful Music Above the Noise" 30-sheet campaign was designed by the agency, based on a concept prepared by the Art Department of Foster & Kleiser Outdoor Advertising. Copy and design were coordinated with the TV spot and print ads to be mutually supportive. Outdoor posting dates were timed to coincide with the TV campaign, and 300 boards were used in the Chicago Metro area. Budget: $74,000.

Transit. Exterior signs on the sides and backs of Chicago Transit Authority buses were used throughout the city for both campaigns. The black background was especially effective during bad winter months as city streets tend to make bus signs difficult to read. More than 400 bus sides and 200 backs were used while the TV and outdoor campaigns displayed the same graphics. In addition, vertical posters were used near exits inside both Northwestern and Illinois Central commuter trains for 60 days. The same posters were used during station media parties, such as the one shown aboard a Chicago River Boat. Budget: $30,000.

Print. North Shore and the regional edition of *Time* magazines are consumer publications which read a large, affluent segment of WLOO-FM's potential audience. Again, the station decided to reinforce the TV and outdoor with a "storyboard" print ad. The reference to "We Light Up Your Life" was directed to the little FM 100 Character lighting up the outdoor sign on the TV spot, just as the music of FM 100 lights up the lives of its listeners every day.

Crain's Chicago Business is a specialty publication which reaches an upper income listenership. Its use daily by WLOO-FM also reinforced the station's sales efforts. Use of the back cover of Standard Rates & Date Service's Spot Radio Book invoked a different connotation for "A Beautiful Place To Be" for media buyers planning a Chicago radio buy.

Also included in the print buy were *Playbill, Chicago Symphony, Lyric Opera,* and *Ravinia Outdoor Festival* programs. This aspect of the campaign was created to assure the current listener of FM 100's intent to maintain its quality image. In this situation, the station hoped that listeners would assume the "noise" referred to in the ad was Rock & Roll or excessive talk on other Chicago radio stations, not the "noise" of the city. Print budget: $20,000. (See illustration, page 405.)

Merchandising & Promotion

Beautiful music stations traditionally do not become heavily involved in merchandising or contests. But WLOO-FM feels that its high ratings and ranking compared to other major-market beautiful music stations is due in part to the station's willingness to promote, contest and merchandise like a Rock, Talk, or Middle-of-the-Road station. Such "foreground" elements have helped the station develop a reputation as an FM station that can produce advertising results, create store traffic and deliver mail or phone responses.

T-Shirts, custom-made stereo albums recorded for WLOO by Vic Damone, and tote bags are a few of the merchandising items the station has created.

The station also ran a "Mystery Song" contest twice, drawing an average of 60,000 pieces of mail each. For each contest, 1,000,000 flyers were stuffed in Dominick's In-Store grocery sacks during the first two weeks of each three-week contest. Different prizes and in-store coupons were featured in each of these on-air promotions.

Total budget for merchandising and promotions: $25,000.

Total campaign budget: $300,000.

Results

When this campaign began, WLOO FM was already the leading Beautiful Music station in Chicago. But in subsequent Arbitron rating books, the station's audience continued to grow.

	Jan/Feb '79	Apr/May '79	July/Aug '79	Oct/Nov '79
Metro Share,	6.3	6.9	7.4	8.2

Total Persons 12+:

In the process, FM 100 moved from the #3 to the #2 radio station in metropolitan Chicago, just 2.3 shares behind the perennial #1, WGN. Promotion Director Christian attributed the increases in ratings and ranking to the "careful use of a limited promotional budget," "continuing promotion," and the station's "excellent on-air product."

Part Six

Your Future in Broadcast Advertising, Promotion and Publicity

A SPECIAL MESSAGE TO STUDENTS

by Tom Dawson, Vice President,
CBS Radio,
Past President, BPA (1980)

Well, where do you go from here?

A career in broadcast advertising and promotion awaits your answer. What is your response to this all important question?

First, let us consider the probable demand for broadcast advertising and promotion executives in the years ahead. This will give you an opportunity to put your career objectives in perspective.

You will find the need for radio and television promotion professionals is going to increase substantially. The reason is competition.

There will be many additional voices on an already crowded radio dial. Television viewers will be wooed by cablecast, pay TV and satellite to home transmission.

These emerging competitors will seek trained broadcast advertising communicators. In addition, independent program packagers and syndication companies will have to sell their product to broadcasters, cablecasters and the public.

Advertising and promotion will need to be employed with great sophistication to attract the eyes and ears of listeners and viewers. It will have to be engaging, inventive, imaginative, distinctive, persuasive. It will have to be well written, well designed and well produced whether the message appears in print, on-air, or in multi-media.

407

These skills demand the training of a promotion specialist by whatever title: creative services director, promotion director, information services director, advertising director.

The challenge to increase audiences and sales will be fierce. You will need all of the talents detailed and explained in this textbook.

There will be a greater reliance on research and copy testing. This will sharpen the communications resultfulness of radio and television promotion. There will be less advertising that is approved by management just because it looks and sounds right. Much of this kind of noncommunication is just that, and it is worthless.

The effective promotion person will know how to use research to develop an advertising campaign. Research will be commissioned to make sure a campaign is actually communicating the desired message to its target audience.

Advertising communicates when the listener, viewer or reader is given a self-interest reason for doing what you want done.

That is why special studies will be used to search out the emotional reactions which listeners and viewers have to individual television programs and personalities as well as radio formats. Advertising based on emotional appeals, promotion that promises a benefit, will result in campaigns that are far more persuasive than traditional announcement copy.

In addition, an understanding of research will enable the advertising and promotion executive to be of much greater value to the program and sales departments. Telephone, mail or personal interview surveys can develop audience reaction to new programs and personalities. Such studies can also be used to determine advertiser awareness and acceptance in the marketplace as well as product usage.

Sales promotion will be required as never before. Apart from on-going competitive pressures, this will come about as television stations join radio stations in targeting their programming to specific audiences. This is called narrowcasting as contrasted with broadcasting.

New sales promotion materials will be required. These will enable an account executive to articulate why a particular audience is of prime importance to an advertiser.

Much of this promotion information will be organized according to listener and viewer demographic and lifestyle characteristics.

The sales department will increase its demands on the promotion department to help it prepare a comprehensive new business campaign. This requires an intelligent evaluation of the audience a station can deliver an advertiser.

For example, almost every successful radio station targets its format to serve the interests of a specific type of listener by age and lifestyle. Advertisers, in turn, determine who are their best prospects by age and lifestyle. Directing a station's sales promotion effort to those specific advertisers it can best serve in terms of audience delivered by the station will result in many new customers and sales dollars.

An aggressive sales department will additionally call on the promotion department for support materials which help increase the use of television and radio by large retailers. These are the traditional big newspaper users.

Information prepared by the promotion department will be used by sales people to show existing retail customers how they can employ the broadcast media much more effectively by doubling or tripling their radio or television budgets. Most of these retailers have just tapped broadcasting's true communications capability to generate store traffic. A steady sales promotion effort should also be directed at radio and television retail store holdouts.

Successful stations will become more committed to helping solve community problems. Involvement in major special events requires huge amounts of time if the community and station are going to derive maximum benefit. The creation and implementation of such projects will most often be the responsibility of a promotion executive.

This person must work with station management to establish a meaningful relationship with elected and appointed public officials, community opinion leaders and local institutions. Station executives should be encouraged to appear before local civic, charitable and fraternal groups. Organizing a station speakers bureau can be most rewarding in this regard. The promotion department should prepare presentation material for use by station executives in their speeches.

None of this will happen by luck or chance. It requires a great deal of planning to be effective. The promotion department at most stations will be the logical area to assign such responsibility.

The full scope of what is expected of a broadcast advertising and promotion specialist should now be in focus.

Well, where do you go from here?

If you continue to be intrigued by the challenge of a career as a promotion professional, here are some additional considerations.

Your learning experience is an on-going process. Your skills must remain current, contemporary.

You must seek out opportunities to enrich your understanding and knowledge of promotion disciplines. Study ads in newspapers and magazines. Carefully review editorial layouts for articles, check headline and picture placement, the choice of type. Give special attention to book covers as well as record album jackets. Monitor broadcast advertising on-air and in print. Collectively, these are the state of the communications art.

In particular, examine advertising for motion pictures. Look at the typeface that is used. See how it is incorporated into the design together with a picture or illustration. Go to as many movies as you can. Watch the design elements utilized for titles and credits.

Take a night class if you need to sharpen your production, typography, design or language skills. Seek out advice from your printer.

Encourage sales calls by representatives of suppliers. These include producers of station identification and image campaigns, jingle packagers, manufacturers of merchandising materials, sales presentation and promotion specialists, trade publication sales people. Ask them questions, explore their proposals. You will learn a great deal in the process.

Ask others questions! How can I help? Ask this question of your station manager. Ask it of your associates in news, programming, sales. Make yourself an invaluable member of your company's management team.

Become an expert on the advertising as well as broadcast industry. Read *Advertising Age, Broadcasting, Marketing and Media Decisions, Television/Radio Age, Variety.*

Be sure to keep this handbook within easy reach. It is actually a broadcast advertising and promotion workbook for ready reference. Use it often. It can be an important idea resource when you are under pressure to complete a project.

Join the Broadcasters Promotion Association. The BPA is responsible for this handbook.

You will find membership in this organization will help you to creatively meet the challenge of change. The BPA's monthly publications are planned to enable you to sharpen your audience, public relations, research and sales promotion skills.

Your attendance at the BPA annual Seminar is important to your career development. You will gain resultful, new ideas, insight and information.

Participation at the BPA Seminar will help you fine-tune your ability to compete aggressively for your company in the demanding days ahead. You will meet with the most talented people in the broadcast industry. You'll find you share many problems and challenges. You'll discover solutions during the workshops, at mealtimes, between sessions, by visits with exhibitors and in suppliers' suites.

Is a career in broadcast advertising and promotion right for you? There is no more dynamic business than the broadcast industry. Competition for viewers or listeners and sales is intense.

The future promises much more of the same. It will require your commitment to excellence, your desire to be a dedicated advertising and promotion professional.

Well where do you go from here?

Useful Forms

PROGRAM PROMOTION PLANNING GUIDE

PROGRAM/PROJECT: _____

AIR DATE: _____ TIME FRAME: _____

PROMOTION COMPLETION DATE: _____

BUDGET AVAILABLE: _____ ACCOUNT: _____

	PRIMARY	SECONDARY	OTHER
1. TARGET AUDIENCE: Who will be interested? Who cares? Who do we hope will watch?			
2. BENEFIT OR NEED PROGRAM SOLVES: Why would audience be interested? What is motivation to watch?			
3. DEMAND: Among which groups would the demand, or interest be highest? Moderate? Lowest?			
4. HOW/WHERE DO WE REACH THIS AUDIENCE? Which media do they use? What vehicle might reach them more effectively? Any unique ideas?			
5. PRODUCT UNIQUENESS: Is ther a loyal audience? Is the production unique or spectacular? Is the content unusual or controversial? Is there a star?			
6. WHAT IS THE BEHAVIORAL OBJECTIVE OF THE PROGRAM WITH REGARD TO THE AUDIENCE?			

PROGRAM/PROJECT, CONTINUED:_____

	PRIMARY	SECONDARY	OTHER
7. CREATIVE STRATEGY: What ad theme, press angle, or special promotion is appropriate?			
8. MEDIA SELECTION: (Based on available budget.) On-air/radio/TV Guide/ releases/target mailing/other.			
9. RESOURCES: Information and/or materials about this program is available from where? Network/local produ- cer/distributor/ PR Firms/other.			
10.MEASUREMENT: Both short-term and long-term. How can we track success? Ratings/Primary research(question- naire)/letters/calls/ other.			
11.COMMENTS/EVALUATION: After program notes on what might have been done better.			

Program Promotion Planning Guide. This form, developed by Linda Nix, Public Information Director at public station WYES-TV, New Orleans, is useful for organization the thinking that goes into the planning process for a program or series. It can also be a valuable tool in training promotion department members in thinking in logical, organized patterns, without stifling creativity. Finally, it is a way of keeping track of Promotion Department efforts on various programs and projects during the year.

DATE _____ REVISION _____

ADVERTISING ACTIVITY PLANNING CHART

1981

Program Area: _____

MEDIUM	JAN				FEB			MAR				APRIL				MAY				JUNE				JULY				AUG				SEPT				OCT				NOV				DEC		
	28	4	11	18	25	1	8	15	22	1	8	15	22	29	5	12	19	26	3	10	17	24	31	7	14	21	28	5	12	19	26	2	9	16	23	30	6	13	20	27	4	11	18	25	1	8	15	22	29	6	13	20
ARB Rating Period																																																					
NSI Rating Period																																																					
PRINT																																																					
Newspaper - regular																																																					
Production																																																					
Supplements																																																					
MAGAZINES																																																					
TV Guide																																																					
Production																																																					
RADIO																																																					
Media																																																					
Production																																																					
OTHER MEDIA																																																					
Billboard																																																					
Transportation																																																					
All Else																																																					
Production																																																					
TV PRODUCTION																																																					

KRON-TV PRODUCTION REQUEST

Title:		SUBJ		Start
Slate	Rec Date		Time:	Stop
Dir.		Talent		TRT

No.	Description	Length	Distribution:

Distribution:
White=Bul/Bd | Yel=Dir.
Blue = Art | Pink=E.N.G.
Green=Engr | Gold=Vtr Sup

FACILITIES

Cam _____ TLEPRM _____
Vtr _____ E.N.G. _____
Film Chn_
Lav _____
Hand _____
Stand _____
Other _____
CG _____
Easel _____
Teleprm Opr _____

NEWS SET ☐
INTRVW SET ☐
WX SET ☐

notes:

Production Facilities Request. All television stations have production facilities request forms. This one from KRON-TV, San Francisco, enables the Director of Creative Services, or the On-Air Promotion Writer/Producer to order specific equipment, facilities, and studio space. Various colored copies are for distribution to the department bulletin board, the Art Department, Engineering Department, the director who will be working on the project, the videotape production crew, and the videotape editing supervisor.

Specific facilities which can be requested include camera, teleprompter, videotape recorder(s), electronic newsgathering equipment (mini-cams and recorders), film chains, mikes (lavaliers, hand mikes or stand mikes), easels, a teleprompter operator, news set, weather set, or other studio settings.

←————————————————————————————

Advertising Activity Planning Chart. This form, in use by KRON-TV in San Francisco, is an aid to the station's Director of Creative Services in planning advertising expenditures for the year. The form can be used for specific programs, program areas or dayparts, or for an entire year's schedule. Multiple copies in various colors can be directed to others at the station who need to share this information, including the General Manager, the Business Affairs office, and others in the Creative Services (Promotion) Department.

ART ORDER

REQUESTED BY: _____DEPT:_____DATE_____NEED BY_____

TO BE FILLED OUT BY ORIGINATOR	ART PERSONNEL ASSIGNED_____
PROGRAM OR USE:	TO BE FILLED OUT BY ART DEPT.

CLIENT: _____

AGENCY: _____

BILLING ADDRESS: _____

_____

_____

CAMERA CARD: COL ☐   SUPER ☐

CENTER ☐   LOW 3rd ☐   OTHER ☐

SLIDES: COL ☐ SUPER ☐ LOW 3rd ☐

DUPES ☐   FREEZE FRAMES ☐

CUE SHEETS ☐   TELEPROMPTER ☐

CRAWL ☐   CAMERA PREP ☐

CAMERA CARDS:

FSC ☐   W/OVERLAY ☐   LOW 3RD ☐

SLIDES: COLOR ☐ SUPER ☐ DUPES ☐

KODALITH NEGS ☐   COLOR KEY ☐

CAMERA PREP ☐   FILM FTGE ☐

TELEPROMPTER ☐   TED IMPUT ☐

CUE SHEETS ☐   MAKEUP ☐

STORYBOARDS ☐   OTHER ☐

SHOP OR SCENIC JOB: ☐

* NOTE:

FURTHER DESCRIPTION OR DETAIL REMARKS

	COMPLETED BY:	TIME:
ART DIRECTOR	PRODUCTION MANAGER COSTS	

Graphics (art) Order Form. Station Design Departments provide Promotion Department with order forms for ordering a variety of items for use in productions. (These forms are also used by all others at the station whose production depends on graphics.) This form from KRON-TV, San Francisco, is typical.

CONSENT AND RELEASE

By signing this form, I give consent to Chronicle Broadcasting Company (KRON-TV) to use and reproduce my name, voice and picture in a program to be broadcast over KRON-TV or the facilities of any other television station. I also agree to the use of my name, voice and picture

- in program publicity materials

- for non-broadcast showings to private groups.

By signing this form, I also release

- KRON-TV from any claim I might have against it because of the use of my name, voice and picture, including, for example, any claim based on defamation, slander, libel or invasion of privacy

- KRON-TV's affiliated companies and businesses, its advertisers and agencies, and any stations or networks making use of my name, voice and picture

- the directors, officers, employees or agents of any of the above organizations.

I acknowledge that I

- will receive no money from KRON-TV for giving this consent and release

- am an adult (18 years or older)

- have read and understand this form.

_____	_____
Date Signed	Signature
	_____
	Name (please print)
_____	_____
Signature of Witness	Address

Consent and Release Form. When members of the public are included in still photos, video tape or film in station promotion material, a consent and release form similar to this one used by KRON-TV, San Francisco, is a must. It prevents the signer from later stopping the station from using the material, or suing the station for its use. Without such forms, all the money, time and effort put into a promotional project might be wasted if someone included in the project later decides he or she just doesn't want to be included.

INSERTION ORDER

CREATIVE SERVICES INK
KRON-TV
1001 VAN NESS AVE.
SAN FRANCISCO, CA 94109
561-8653 OR 441-4444

TO:

DATE: _____

CONTRACT NO. _____

LINE RATE: _____

INSERTION DATE	SIZE	CAPTION	AMOUNT

MATERIALS DUE DATE: _____

☐ YOU HAVE MATERIAL

☐ MATERIAL BEING SHIPPED SEPARATELY

☐ MATERIAL ENCLOSED

TOTAL GROSS

MINUS COMMISSION

TOTAL NET

POSITION REQUEST _____

PLEASE SEND 2 TEAR SHEETS WITH BILLING,
TO THE ABOVE ADDRESS, ATTENTION _____

IF YOU HAVE ANY QUESTIONS REGARDING THIS
INSERTION ORDER, OR THE AD MATERIALS, PLEASE CALL _____

NOTE:

AD Insertion Order Form. Also from KRON-TV, San Francisco, is this general-use form for advertising orders. It can be used for newspaper or magazine insertions, outdoor ad orders, and any other ad insertions.

KRON-TV San Francisco

TV GUIDE INSERTION ORDER

CREATIVE SERVICES:
441-4444
561-8653

ORDER DATE: _____

PAGE _____ OF _____

ISSUE DATE: _____

TRADE OR PAID	INSERTION DAY & DATE	PLACEMENT	AD SIZE	CAPTION/ART	FOR STATION USE ONLY	
					ART DUE	NET ✓

TV GUIDE **Magazine—Ad Insertion Order Form.** This form, designed and used by KRON-TV, San Francisco, enables appropriate record-keeping and planning in placement of *TV Guide* Magazine Ads.

419

TELEVISION COMMERCIAL PRODUCTION

STUDIO COST SUMMARY

Date:

Production Co:		Agency:	Agency job #
Address:		Client:	Product:
Telephone No.:	Job #		
Production Contact:		Agency prod:	Tel:
Director:		Agency art dir:	Tel:
Cameraman:		Agency writer:	Tel:
Set Designer:		Agency Bus. Mgr:	Tel:
Editor:		Commercial title:	No. Length:
No. pre-prod. days	pre-light/rehearse	1.	
No. build/strike days	Hours:	2.	
No. Studio shoot days	Hours:	3.	
No. Location days	Hours:	4.	
Location sites:		Agency supplies:	

SUMMARY OF ESTIMATED PRODUCTION COSTS					
1. Pre-production and wrap costs	Totals A and C				
2. Shooting crew labor	Total B				
3. Studio costs: Build / shoot / strike	Totals D, E, and F				
4. Location travel and expenses	Total G				
5. Equipment costs	Total H				
6. Film stock develop and print: No. feet	Total I				
7. Props, wardrobe, animals	Total J				
8. Director/Creative fees	Total K				
9. Payroll taxes, P & W and misc.	Total L				
10. Insurance					
11.	Sub-Total - Direct costs				
12. Mark-up (% of direct costs)					
13. Talent costs and expenses	Total M and N				
14. Editorial / Videotape	Total O and P				
15.	Grand Total				
16. Contingency Day					
17.					
18.					

Comments:

Television Commercial Production—Studio Cost Summary. This set of forms, originally designed in numerous variations for use in producing TV commercials, can be invaluable in planning the production costs of elaborate promo spots. Many stations use this kind of form, with variations to suit local needs.

PAGE 1

A: PRE-PROD'N / WRAP   B: SHOOTING

CREW	ESTIMATED				(Actual)			ESTIMATED				(Actual)		
	Days	Rate	O/T Hrs	Total	Days	Rate	Total	Days	Rate	O/T Hrs	Total	Days	Rate	Total
roducer:														
sst. Director:														
r. Photography:														
amera Operator:														
sst. Cameraman:														
utside Props:														
side Props:														
lectricians:														
ips:														
xer (or Playback:)														
ecordist:														
oom Man:														
ake-Up:														
air:														
ylist:														
ardrobe Attendant:														
ript Clerk:														
me Economist:														
enics:														
TR Man:														
FX Man:														
urse:														
elepr. & Operator:														
nerator Man:														
ll Man:														
oc. Contact/Scout:														
A.														
d A. D.														
eamsters														
	SUB TOTAL A								SUB TOTAL B					

scription / Schedule Breakdown

PAGE 2

PRE-PRODUCTION & WRAP/MATERIALS & EXPENSES	Estimated	Actual	
31. Auto Rentals (Cars @ $ x days)			
32. Air Fares: No. of people ( ) x Amount per fare ( )			
33. Per Diems: No. of people ( ) x Amount per day ( )			
34. Still Camera Rental & Film			
35. Messengers			
36. Trucking			
37. Deliveries & Taxis			
38. Home Economist Supplies			
39. Telephone & Cable			
40. Art Work			
41. Casting (Days @ $)			
42. Casting Facilities / Equipment			
SUB TOTAL C			

SET CONSTRUCTION (CREW FOR BUILD, STRIKE)	# MAN DAYS	Estimated	Actual	
43. Set Designer Name:				
44. Carpenters				
45. Grips				
46. Outside Props				
47. Inside Props				
48. Scenics				
49. Electricians				
50. Teamsters				
51. Men for Strike (___grips,___props,___elect.,___misc.)				
52.				
53.				
54.				
SUB TOTAL D				
# man days........................				

SET CONSTRUCTION MATERIALS	Estimated	Actual	
55. Props and Set Dressings			
56. Lumber			
57. Paint / Wallpaper			
58. Hardware			
59. Special Effects			
60. Special Outside Construction			
61. Trucking			
62. Messengers / Deliveries			
63.			
SUB TOTAL E			

STUDIO RENTAL & EXPENSES - STAGE:	Estimated	Actual	
64. Rental for Build / Strike. (days @ $)			
65. Rental for Pre-Lite Days (days @ $)			
66. Rental for Shoot Days (days @ $)			
67. Rental for Shoot O. T. (Hrs.)			
68. Rental for Build / Strike Days O.T. (Hrs.)			
69. Total Power Charge & Bulbs			
70. Misc. Studio Charges & Service			
71. Meals (Lunches & Dinner for Crew and Talent)			
72.			
73.			
74.			
75.			
SUB TOTAL F			

PAGE 3

ION EXPENSES		Estimated	Actual	
Location Fees				
Guards				
Car Rentals				
Bus Rentals				
Camper / Dressing Room Vehicles				
Parking, Tolls, & Gas				
Trucking				
Other Vehicles A /				
Other Vehicles B /				
Special Crew Equipt. / Clothing				
Air Freight / Customs / Excess Baggage				
Air Fares: No. of people ( ) x cost per fare ( )				
Per Diems: Total No. man days ( ) x amt. per day ( )				
Breakfast: No. of man days ( ) x amt. per person ( )				
Lunch: No. of man days ( ) x amt. per person ( )				
Dinner: No. of man days ( ) x amt. per person ( )				
Gratuities, Tips and Misc. Outside Labor				
Cabs and other passenger transportation				
Limousines (Celebrity Service)				
	SUB TOTAL G			

PMENT RENTAL				
Camera Rental Type:				
Sound Rental				
Lighting Rental				
Grip / Dolly Rental				
Generator Rental				
Crane / Cherry Picker Rental				
VTR Rental				
Production Supplies				
	SUB TOTAL H			

RAW STOCK DEVELOP AND PRINT				
Purchase of Raw Stock: footage amount ( ) x per foot				
Developing and Printing: footage amount ( ) x per foot				
Studio for Transfer: No. of hours ( )				
16mm or 35mm Mag Stock: No. of hours ( )				
Sync/Screen Dailies				
	SUB TOTAL I			

PS AND WARDROBE				
Location Props				
Costume/Wardrobe Rental & Purchase				
Animals & Handlers				
Wigs, Mustaches / Special Make-Up				
Color Correction				
	SUB TOTAL J			

PAGE 4

DIRECTOR / CREATIVE FEES:	Estimated	Actual
121. Prep Days		
122. Travel Days		
123. Shoot Days		
124. Post-production Days		
125.		
SUB TOTAL K		

MISCELLANEOUS COSTS	Estimated	Actual
126. Total Payroll & P & W Taxes % of total of A, B, D, & K		
127. Air Shipping / Special Carriers		
128. Phones and Cables		
129. Misc. (Petty Cash)		
130. Misc. Trucking & Messengers		
131.		
132.		
133.		
SUB TOTAL L		

TALENT	No.	Rate	Days–Fees	Travel	O.T.	Estimated	No.	Days–Fees
134. O/C Principals								
135. O/C Principals								
136. O/C Principals								
137. O/C Principals								
138. O/C Principals								
139.								
140.								
141.								
142. General Extras								
143. General Extras								
144. General Extras								
145.								
146.								
147.								
148. Hand Model								
149. Voice Over								
150. Fitting Fees								
151. Audition Fees: No. of talent ( ) x Amount ( )								
152. **SUB-TOTAL**								
153. Payroll & P & W Taxes								
154. Wardrobe Allowance: No. of talent ( ) x No. of garments ( ) x fee per garment ( ).								
155. Agents' Commissions								
156. **SUB-TOTAL**								
157. Other								
158. Handling Fee (____ %)								
SUB TOTAL M								

TALENT EXPENSES	Estimated		Actu
159. Per diem: No. of man days ( ) x amount per day ( )			
160. Air fare: No. of people ( ) x amount per fare ( )			
161. Cabs and other transportation			
162.			
163.			
164.			
SUB TOTAL N			

PAGE 5

IAL COMPLETION	Estimated	Actual	
iting			
st. Editor			
ding			
ojection			
twork for supers			
ooting of artwork			
ock footage			
ll photographs			
ticals (incl. pre-optical)			
imation			
ock music			
iginal music			
und effects			
ibbing studio			
idio for narration - including transfer to mag. No. of hours ( )			
idio for mixing - including transfer to mag. No. of hours ( )			
egative tracks			
iswer & corrected prints			
ontract items			
lm to tape transfer (incl. reprints & masters)			
lm to tape transfer - editorial fee			
Editorial Handling Fee:			
SUB TOTAL O			

TAPE PRODUCTION AND COMPLETION	Estimated	Actual	
asic crew (No. of men:)			
dditional crew (No. of men:)			
abor overtime			
TR/Camera rental			
dditional VTR's/Cameras			
quipment overtime			
pecial equipment (specify)			
pecial processes (specify)			
rucking			
obile unit			
tock (rental ☐ purchase ☐ No. of hrs:)			
creening			
n-line editing No. VTR hrs:)			
ff-line editing (No. of hrs:)			
ideotape A/B roll preparation and stock			
udio mix with VT projection			
ideo air masters			
ideo printing dupe			
/4'' videocassette			
ape to fim transfer			
larkup			
SUB TOTAL P			

No. of hours in basic day: _____

No. of travel hours: _____

No. of setup/wrap hours: _____

No. of net shoot hours: _____

Crew O.T. rate per hour: _____

Eqpt./stage O.T. rate per hour: _____

Comments:

KABC–TV
4151 Prospect Avenue
Hollywood, CA 90027

ADVERTISING ORDER FORM

	Order Number
	KCS–

ISSUED
TO

Date: _____

Attn:

DESCRIPTION:	AMOUNT:

Vendor No.

Oper Unit	Cost Center	Account Corp	Sub	Prog.	SL # or W/O	Amount	Oper Unit	Cost Center	Account Corp	Sub	Prog.	Amo

Disc.	Disc.

Approval: _____

Approval: _____

A form such as this is used by the station when placing an ad with media, ie, newspaper, TV Guide, or an outdoor company.

TELEVISION/RADIO COPY

Date_____
Production_____
Title_____
Length_____

Video   Audio

1

2

3

4

5

6

7

8

9

10

11

12

13

14

15

16

17

18

19

20

21

22

This slightly whimsical form is used by KNXT-TV, Los Angeles, for preparation of copy for on-air promotion spots. The form is used in-house only.

KNXT, CHANNEL 2

Program Changes

FROM: Jay Strong
TO: ALL DEPARTMENTS
DATE: Nov. 17, 1981

WEDNESDAY, NOVEMBER 18, 1981

    7:00-9:30AM   -Delete- PRESENT SCHEDULE
    7:00-7:30AM   -Insert- PRESIDENT REAGAN ADDRESS
    7:30-9:00AM   -Insert- MORNING
    9:00-9:30AM   -Insert- WAKE UP WITH THE CAPTAIN

SATURDAY, DECEMBER 12, 1981

    10:00-11:00PM   -Delete- NETWORK TBA
                                -Insert- CBS REPORTS

SATURDAY, DECEMBER 19, 1981

    3:00-5:00PM   -Delete- PRESENT SCHEDULE
    3:00-3:30PM   -Insert- 2 WITH YOU
    3:30-4:30PM   -Insert- DANCE FEVER CHRISTMAS SPECIAL
    4:30-5:00PM   -Insert- 1981 KODAK ALL-AMERICAN FOOTBALL
                                         TEAM

A bold, easily recognized form is important for making all departments at the station aware of late program changes. KNXT-TV uses a very bold and distinctive heading, and prints the form on pink paper for quick recognition and action by all affected departments. Such forms are initiated in the Program or Operations Department of a station, but usually have immediate impact on Promotion, Sales, and Technical Operations activities.

SHOW   PROD. NO.   DATE RECORDED   AIR DATE   CUSTOMER P.O./AUTHORIZATION   COST CENTER   DATE

187 - 162

TO BE COMPLETED BY OFFICE

| EMPLOYEE NAME / EMPLOYEE NUMBER | MACHINE NUMBERS 1ST 2ND | REQUISITIONED TIME FROM / TO | SET UP TIME | ACTUAL TIME FROM / TO | OPERATING UNIT | COST CNTR | PROGRAM NUMBER | PRODUCTION WORK ORDER NUMBER | FUNCTION CODE |

HOUR MIN. A OR P   HOUR MIN. A OR P

2 3 4 5 6 7   31 32   54 55 56 57   18 19 20 21 22 23 24 25 26 27   33 34 35   37 38 39   40 41 42 43 44   45 46 47 48 49   58

WORK INSTRUCTIONS

CIRCLE DAY WORKED
SUN MON TUE WED THU FRI SAT
1 2 3 4 5 6 7

MO.   DAY   WK#

1
2
3
4
5

ENGINEER WORK PERFORMED

LIBRARY INSTRUCTIONS   LB   HB

15
30
60
90
120

1 - RECORD AND PLAYBACK FOR PRODUCTION   2 - EDIT   3 - SWEETEN   4 - COMMERCIAL
INTEGRATION   5 - PLAYBACK FOR NETWORK ORIGINATION   6 - DELAYED BROADCAST DUB
7 - SCREENING   8 - SPECIAL PROJECTS

RELEASED

PRODUCTION AD: _____ DATE: _____

INTEGRATION AD: _____ DATE: _____

HPR-59 (5-73)

Work orders can be complex or simple, depending on station operations and accounting procedures. This example, used by KABC-TV''s On-Air Promotion staff, serves all producing entities of the station as well. It enables accurate record-keeping necessary for union requirements, as well as later budget planning for production and staff time.

Broadcast Promotion Curriculum

Based on
BROADCAST ADVERTISING & PROMOTION!
A Handbook for Students and Professionals

NOTE: Clearly, this course outline will need to be expanded or contracted to fit the actual number of classes in the semester, quarter, summer program, or other time period. Also, specific instructors or part-time teaching professionals from the industry will have areas of strength in which they want to concentrate, and will expand those areas.

This outline is meant only as a guide to the first-time teacher of a course in Broadcast Advertising and Promotion, and an indication of the kinds of guests who might be invited to participate in the classroom.

CLASS #1: Part One. Chapters 1–4.
The opening lecture should familiarize students with the terms introduced in Chapter 2; and provide background and historical information on promotion, and BPA. Local station resources and historical examples should be worked into the lecture, after consultation with local stations.

CLASS #2: Part Two. Chapters 5–7.
Focus here is on the broadcast station Promotion Director, the job and the staff. The chapters give students a further familiarization with the categories of work involved, and how they might best be divided among available staff. A guest lecturer from a TV or radio station might focus student attention on a real-life situation.

CLASS #3: Part Two. Chapters 8–10.
This lecture broadens the scope of the Promotion Department by locating it within the station and exploring the relationships between promotion and other stations

departments, and between the Promotion Department and the network or group promotion function. A station General Manager might be a guest lecturer.

CLASS #4: Part Two. Chapter 11.
Emphasis is on management skills as they apply to promotion people. A management expert might be the ideal guest in the classroom.
This is a good point to summarize and solidify what has been learned to date by giving a test or extensive quiz.

CLASS #5: Part Three. Chapter 12.
Ratings and research go hand in hand, and are crucial foundations on which Promotion Directors build their efforts. Carefully go through the processes involved; bring in a market research, or station ratings expert as a guest.

CLASS #6: Part Three. Chapter 13.
Because of the importance of ratings and research, a quiz on those subjects at this point will help fix the principles in students' minds. The budget planning process is an essential to management team members; and junior-level management people should also be familiar with this material. A station financial officer might guest.

CLASS #7: Part Three. Chapter 14
This material is the key to successful advertising, promotion and publicity. At least one, and probably two class periods should be spent on these principles.

CLASS #8: Part Three. Chapter 14
Continuation of previous class. An ad agency creative expert might make a superb guest.

CLASS #9: Part Three. Chapter 15
Advertising is a major concern for Promotion Directors. At least one class period should be devoted to the characteristics of various media.

CLASS #10: Part Three. Chapter 16
Promotion people usually function as their own media buyers. A knowledge of how to select media for campaigns is vital. A local media buyer might supplement the text and instructor's lecture.

CLASS #11: Part Three. Chapter 17
On-air promotion is the station Promotion Department's most cost-effective resource. Knowing what it is and how to use it effectively is critical. A local station may be able to supply examples, or the instructor might request samples from the BPA library.

CLASS #12: Part Three. Chapter 18
All stations depend upon publicity. How to get it deserves at least one entire class. A local TV columnist might make a good guest lecturer.

CLASS #13: Part Three. Chapters 19 & 20
Station promotions and sales promotion activities are becoming increasingly important. A radio station Promotion Director might make a good guest for the class.

CLASS #14: MID-TERM EXAM

CLASS #15: Part Four. Chapter 21.

Public broadcasting has its own unique set of challenges for the promotion expert, or Public Information Director. This chapter explores them, and the local PBS or NPR station PI Director would be an ideal guest.

CLASS #16: Part Four. Chapter 22.

Cable, too, has unique marketing and promotion challenges. A local cable system marketer could bring the class up-to-date on the rapid growth and changes which are taking place in this still-young field.

CLASS #17: Part Four. Chapter 23.

A discussion of identity changes and anniversaries can be used to bring into play many of the techniques of motivation, advertising, promotion and publicity learned in earlier chapters as the class approaches these typical Promotion Department challenges.

CLASS #19: Part Five

The instructor will have made use of some of the case studies included in this section as the course has progressed. However, this time is for reviewing the rest of the specific station activities. It might also be used to give a quiz on material presented since the mid-term exam.

CLASSES #20–22: STUDENT PROJECTS

It is recommended that early in the semester, students be given promotional project assignments . . . either as individuals, or as Promotion Department groups. In the latter concept, each group might have a Promotion Director, Advertising Manager, On-Air Writer/Producer, Publicity Manager, and Sales Promotion Manager; and be required to produce a campaign, Fall Preview Party, Anniversary Celebration, or solve another specific promotional problem.

Presentation of these projects can take up to several class periods, and might include critiques by guest Promotion Directors or other members of the class.

FINAL CLASS: Final Exam

The BPA Resource Center, housed at San Diego State University, is part of BPA's member services, and is available to all members. The resource center houses video, audio, and print material in all areas of promotion for the media. The material is catalogued under these reference headings: **Videotapes** Awards, Reference Material, Seminars, Instructional; **Audiotapes** Awards, Reference Material, Seminars; **Print** - Index, Slide Index; **Premiums; PBS Program Press Kits and Folios; Distribution Company Press Kits and Folios; Vendor File; BPA Publications; Related Publications.**

Videotapes

1976-79 BPA Awards compiled entry tapes currently being re-catalogued.

1979 BPA Awards Convention Banquet, Nashville: Tape 1 - 60:00; Tape 2 - 60:00; Tape 3 - 60:00.

1980 BPA Awards Competition Compiled Entry Tapes:
C-1 Tape 1 Large Market TV—News and Public Affairs - 30:00; C-1 Tape 2 Large Market TV—News and Public Affairs - 30:00; C-1 Tape 3 Large Market TV—News and Public Affairs - 30:00; C-2 Tape 1 Medium Market TV—News and Public Affairs - 30:00; C-2 Tape 2 Medium Market TV—News and Public Affairs - 30:00; C-3 Tape 1 Small Market TV—News and Public Affairs - 30:00; C-4, 5, D-4, 5, 6, Tape 1 Radio on TV - 30:00; D-1 Tape 1 Large Market TV—Other than News and Public Affairs - 30:00; D-1 Tape 2 Large Market TV—Other than News and Public Affairs - 30:00; D-1 Tape 3 Large Market TV—Other than News and Public Affairs - 30:00; D-2 Tape 1 Medium Market TV—Other than News and Public Affairs - 30:00; D-2 Tape 2 Medium Market TV—Other than News and Public Affairs - 30:00; D-3 Tape 1 Small Market TV—Other than News and Public Affairs - 30:00.

1981 BPA Awards Competition Compiled Entry Tapes:
Cat. 1 Tape 1 Multi-Media Campaign Large Market TV - 60:00; Cat. 1 Tape 2 Multi-Media Campaign Medium Market TV - 30:00; Cat. 1 Tape 3 Multi-Media Campaign Small Market TV - 30:00; Cat. 1 Tape 4 Multi-Media Campaign Large/Medium Market Radio - 30:00; Cat. 2 Tape 1 Multi-Media (In-House) Large Market TV - 60:00; Cat. 2 Tape 2 Multi-Media (In-House) Medium Market TV - 30:00; Cat. 2 Tape 3 Multi-Media (In-House) Small Market TV, Radio - 30:00; Cat. 3 Tape 1 Limited Campaign, One Medium Large Market TV - 60:00; Cat. 3 Tape 2 Limited Campaign, One Large Market TV - 30:00; Cat. 3 Tape 3 Limited Campaign, One Medium Market TV - 60:00; Cat. 3 Tape 4 Limited Campaign, One Medium Market TV - 30:00; Cat. 3 Tape 5 Limited Campaign, One Small Market TV - 30:00; Cat. 3 Tape 6 Limited Campaign, One Small Market TV, Radio - 30:00; Cat. 4 Tape 1 TV Announcement for News/Public Affairs Large Market TV - 60:00; Cat. 4 Tape 2 TV Announcement for News Medium Market TV - 30:00; Cat. 4 Tape 3 TV Announcement for News Small Market TV, Radio - 20:00; Cat. 5 Tape 1 TV Announcement Other Large Market TV - 30:00; Cat. 5 Tape 2 TV Announcement Other Medium Small Market TV, Radio - 30:00; Cat. 8 Tape 1 In-House Produced Announce. Large Market TV - 40:00; Cat. 8 Tape 2 In-House Produced Announce. Medium Market TV - 30:00; Cat. 8 Tape 3 In-House Produced Announce. Small Market TV, Radio - 10:00; Cat. 9 Tape 1 Local Use-Syndicated Materials Large/Medium Market TV - 20:00; Cat. 9 Tape 2 Local Use-Syndicated Materials Small Market TV - 20:00; Cat. 11 Tape 1 Sales Promotio Large Market TV - 60:00; Cat. 11 Tape 2 Sales Promotio Large/Medium Market TV - 60:00; Cat. 11 Tape 3 Sales Promotion Medium/Small Market TV, Radio - 60:00; Cat. 14 Tape 1 Promotion, Other Large/Medium Market TV - 30:00; Cat. 14 Tape 2 Promotion, Other Medium/Small Market TV, Radio - 30:00; Cat. 15 Tape 1 Program Distributers - 30:00; Cat. 17 Tape 1 Community Involvement Large/Medium Market TV - 30:00; Cat. 17 Tape 2 Community Involvement Medium/Small Market TV - 30:00.

1981 BPA Awards Competition Winners:
Tape 1 Cat. 1, 2, 3, 4, 5, 8, 9, 11 - 60:00; Tape 2 Cat. 11 60:00; Tape 3 Cat. 11, 14, 15 - 60:00.

Awards, Other
1979 IBA International Broadcasting Awards 21st Annual, World's Best Commercials - 20:00;
1980 IBA International Broadcasting Awards 22nd Annual, World's Best Commercials - 18:00;
1976 NAEB Design and Graphics Awards - 60:00.

1979 ABC Closed Circuit News Advisory Service Affiliate News Promotions: Tape 1 - 30:00; Tape 2 - 60:00; Tape 3 - 30:00; Tape 4 - 30:00; Tape 5 - 30:00; Tape 6 - 30:00.

1979 CBS "Looking Good" Campaign - 30:00.

1980-81 BPA TV Reference Promotion Tapes:
General News - 60:00; News Anchors - 30:00; Weathercasters - 15:00; Sportscasters - 15:00; Program Promotions - 30:00; Movies - 40:00; Sports Programs - 10:00; General Station Image - 60:00;
Community Involvement;
Tape 1 - 30:00; Tape 2 - 20:00;
Sales Promotions (Awards 1981 BPA Compiled Cat. 11):
Tape 1 - 60:00; Tape 2 - 60:00; Tape 3 - 60:00;
Special Reports:
Tape 1 - 60:00; Tape 2 - 9:00;
Political Coverage - 6:00;
Holidays - 12:00;
Contests, Give aways - 12:00;
Station Produced PSA's - 30:00;
Helicopters, Equipment and Awards currently being catalogued.

1980-81 BPA Radio Reference Promotion Tapes:
General Format Promotions - 25:00; News/All News - 10:00; Personalities/Programs - 10:00; Contests - 10:00; Sales Promotions (Awards-1981 BPA Compiled Cat. 11 Tape 3) - 60:00.

1975 BPA Denver Convention:
"A Survey of Canadian TV Promotion" - 37:00;
"Stategy of On-Air Promotion" - 20:00.

1977 BPA Los Angeles Convention:
"General Session: Radio" Part 1 Tape 1 - 60:00;
"General Session: Radio" Part 1 Tape 2 - 30:00;
"General Session: Radio" Part 2 Tape 1 - 60:00;
"Effective On-Air Promotion-Radio" - 60:00;
"Animation and Other Interesting Phenomena" - 60:00;
"If you don't Promote, Something Terrible Happens..." - 60:00; "The General Manager and You" - 60:00;
"Banging Your Head Against the Wall" - 60:00;

"Effective Advertising in the Trade Press" - 60:00; "How to Turn 1,000 Ping Pong Balls into Research" - 60:00; "Back to Basics-Promotion" - 60:00; "Promotion People and Their Stations-Promoting You" - 60:00; "The Great Hollywood Ripoff: Let Hollywood Help" - 60:00; "Let a Style Be Your Umbrella" - 60:00.

1980 BPA Montreal Convention:
"101 Great Ideas to Show and Steal" - 60:00.

1981 BPA New York Convention:
"In-House Production: A Craftsman's Approach" - 15:00; "The Impact of Animation on Promotion" - 15:00.

1977 National Public Television Promotion Conference:
"Sample Promotions from PBS Stations" - 60:00.

1981 National Association of Broadcasters Convention:
"Television Promotion: Samples From . . . " (Not Narrated) - 40:00.

Instructional
1980 "BPA Special Promo Briefing"
Steve Sohmer, CBS, Los Angeles: Tape 1 of 2 - 30:00; Tape 2 of 2 - 60:00.
1981 "T and A: Trageting and Audience"
Dave Course, KARK TV, Little Rock - 34:00.
1977 "What Is A Promotion Manager"
Rod Warner, WJW TV, Cleveland - 30:00.
1976 "Small Market Television Production"
KARK TV, Little Rock - 15:00.
1976 "TV Station ENG Equipment"
Tom Batista, KMOX TV, St. Louis - 10:00.
1981 "Behind the Local News"
Robert Phillips, SDSU, KFMB TV, San Diego - 30:00.
1981 "PBS Program Title Slides: How to Work with what You've Got" - 30:00.

Audiotapes

1978 BPA Awards Finalists, Radio on Radio, TV on Radio - 20:00.

1978 BPA Awards Competition Compiled Entry Tapes:
Large Market TV using Radio - 60:00.

1980 BPA Awards Competition Compiled Entry Tapes:
A-1 News and Special Reports: TV on Radio - 60:00; A-2 News and Special Reports: TV on Radio - 30:00; A-4 News and Special Reports TV/on Radio/Radio on Radio - 60:00; B-1 Other than News and Special Reports: TV on Radio - 60:00; B-2 Other than News and Special Reports: TV on Radio - 30:00; B-3 Other than News and Special Reports: TV on Radio - 30:00; B-4 Other than News and Special Reports: Radio on Radio - 60:00; B-5 Other than News and Special Reports: Radio on Radio - 60:00.

1980 BPA Awards Winners Radio and TV on Radio - 30:00.

1981 BPA Awards Winners Radio and TV on Radio:
Tape 1 Cat. 1, 3, 6, 7, 8, 10, 14 - 60:00; Tape 2 Cat. 14, 15, Misc. - 60:00.

Awards, Other
1978 IBA International Broadcasting Society 19th Annual, Radio Commercial Trophy Winners - 60:00.
1979 IBA International Broadcasting Society 20th Annual, Radio Commercial Trophy Winners - 60:00.
1980 IBA International Broadcasting Society 21st Annual, Radio Commercial Trophy Winners - 60:00.

Reference

1980-81 Radio Reference Promotion Tapes:
Programs/Personalities - 5:00; Speciality Programming/Special Reports - 14:00; Contests - 45:00; Community Involvement/Fundraisers - 11:00; News/All News; General Format Ads; Sales Promotion - 8:25; Give Aways/Sales Items - 4:00; PSA's - 7:00; Station/Program Awards - 3:05; Anniversaries.

1980-81 TV Reference Promotion Tapes:
News, General News; Testimonials - 4:00; News Anchors - 6:00; Weathercasters - 4:30; Sportscasters - 8:00; News Teams; Special Reports - 45:00; News Expansion - 1:40. Programs Promotion - 46:00; Movies; Sports Shows - 3:30; General Station Promotions - 11:00; Sales Promotion - 1:30; Contests - 4:00; Community Envolvement/Fundraisers; Give Aways/Sales Items; Equipment; Public TV/General Station; Public TV/Auction, Pledge, Etc.; Change of Station Number; Number Change (station) - 3:00.

Seminars

1977 BPA Los Angeles Convention Seminar (Each 90 minutes long): "Key Note Address—John H. Schneider"; "Panel Discussion—Radio"; "General Session—Jack Yianitsas"; "Luncheon—Connie Chung"; "The General Manager and You"; "If You Don't Promote, Something Terrible Happens . . . "; "Off the Wall, Off Air Promotion"; "Effective On-Air Promotion"; "Ping Pong Balls into Research"; "Batting Your Head Against the Wall"; "Animation and Other Phenomena"; "The Syndicator and You"; "The Hollywood Ripoff: Let Hollywood Help"; "Let a Style be your Umbrella"; "Advertising in the Trade Press"; "Back to Basics—Promotion"; "Major Market Research"; "Luncheon—Willie Davis"; "Promoting the Independent"; "Graphic and Logos"; "Promoting Yourself at the Station".

1978 BPA St. Paul Seminar Convention (each 90 minutes long): "'Get the Message . . . '"; "General Session—Stephan B. Labinski"; "TV is for Learning"; "Time Management: Art and Science"; "Sales Presentation: Right and Quick"; "PTV Station Guide Magazines"; "How to Compete against the Big Three"; "Board Casting Broadcasting"; "How to Deliver a More Effective Presentation"; "Development and PI-Working Together"; "Drawing a Line of Communication"; "Why an Agency? Why Not?".

1979 BPA Nashville Convention Seminar (each 90 minutes long): "TV—Management Style"; "TV—What to Promote Besides News"; "Radio—Print Money and How to Get It"; "Public—Legal Eagle Review"; "Design—Animation and Alternatives"; "TV—International"; "TV Communicating Communications"; "Radio —How Does Your Audience Hear You"; "TV—Special Production Workshop"; "Design—Say it With Type"; "TV—The Indies Have Their Way"; "Design—Design Symposium"; "What Makes the Best"; "TV—Outdoor . . . Media's Medium"; "TV—Managing Management Time"; "Radio—How to Make TV Work For You"; "Radio—Finding A Sugar Daddy"; "Design—Arts on Trial"; "TV—The New Promotion Manager"; "TV—Newspaper Ads . . . How to Get Them to Work For You"; "TV—Music and Jingles"; "Broadcast Law and You"; "Radio—Promoting News and Sports".

1980 BPA Montreal Convention Seminar:
"Breakfast with James Duffy" - 90:00; "New Broadcasting Technology" - 90:00; "International Design" - 90:00; "Publicity" - 90:00; "On-Air Promotion" - 90:00; "Radio Contests" - 90:00; "Luncheon—Pete Barbotti" - 90:00; "Limited Resources—Radio" - 60:00;

"Limited Resources—TV" - 60:00; "Computer Graphics Today" - 60:00; "Outdoor Advertising Part 1" - 60:00; "Outdoor Advertising—TV Part 2" - 60:00; "Outdoor Advertising—Radio Part 3" - 60:00; "Designers Talk, Computers Listen" - 60:00; "Budgeting" - 60:00; "Sales Promotion" - 90:00; "Stress" - 90:00; "US Ratings" - 90:00; "Canadian Ratings" - 90:00; "TV News Promotion" - 90:00; "News Set Design" - 90:00; "Radio-On-Air" - 60:00; "Luncheon with AW Johnson" - 60:00; "Radio News and Sports Promotion" -90:00; "TV Guide Ads" - 90:00; "Station Presentations" - 90:00; "Animation and Music—Steve Sohmer" — 90:00; "Design Symposium" - 90:00; "Working With Your Art Director" — 90:00; "101 Great Ideas—Radio Promotion" - 90:00; "Promotion Planning" - 90:00; "More of 101 Ideas for Radio" - 60:00; "Print Ads TV" - 90:00; "Creative Photography" - 90:00; "Luncheon with Lindsay" - 60:00; "Beggers and Mohammad" (General Session) - 60:00; "TV Ideas to Show and Steal" - 60:00; "The Modern TV Art Department" - 60:00; "Radio's Future" - 60:00.

1981 BPA New York Seminar Convention (Each 90 minutes long): "Luncheon With Mayor Koch and J. Caseman"; "Getting Your Act Together . . . New in the Job"; "See Spot Run . . . Right"; "Audience Promotion, The Essential Alternatives"; "Working with An Outside Production Resource—Successfully"; "Using Music on TV, for TV Promotion"; "New Ways to Out Promote Your Competition"; "In-House Production, A Craftsman's Approach"; "Promotion of the Industry, and the Station"; "Research, Programming, and Promotion W#1 S#1"; "How Healthy is Your Radio Station?" W#2; "Luncheon with Richard H. Long"; "How Promotion Managers Can Work w/Music Prod. Co."; "Communications: the Secret to Effective Sales Promotion"; "Media Interview: Paralyzing or Profitable"; "How Would Programmers Promote"; "Advertising That Works"; "Louis Dorfsman: Three Decades of Achievement"; "Cable: The New Industry"; "Publicity and Production Image"; "Breakfast with CC Standen"; "Broadcast Promotion, The State Of the Art"; "Ratings Research . . . New Data Means Strength"; "Television News Promotions . . . A tough Situation"; "Creating Radio Advertising for TV"; "Sales Promotion, Marketing, and the 'Rep' Firm"; "Contest Ideas to Build Audience and Sales"; "Women in the Industry"; "Design Symposium with Tom Carnasse"; "Management and Financial Skills for Broadcast Designers"; "Luncheon with B. Tarkikoff"; "Using Print Advertising for Maximum Impact"; "The Official Rules of Copywriting"; "Putting Out Social Fires With Your Transmitter"; "Research for the Segmented Audience of Tomorrow"; "Advertising to Advertisers—Sales Promo Tools"; "Problems and Solutions of the Small Art Department; "Living Budgets—Small Markets"; "Living Budgets—Medium Markets"; "Living Budgets—Large Markets"; "What to Do When Its Time To Change Jobs, Or You're Fired"; "Radio Sports Promotions, Special Events"; "Scenic New York"; "And In This Corner . . . "; "The Impact of Animation in Promotion"; "Awards Luncheon".

1982 BPA San Francisco Seminar Convention (Each 90 minutes long): "TV: How To's and How Not To's In Print"; "Animation and The Future"; "Radio: Focus Groups"; "TV: The Best Ad Agency for your Station"; "Copyright for Art Directors"; "Incentive Luncheon: Jack Yianitsis"; "New Horizons in TV: On-Air Creative Techniques"; "Design: Case Study of a City"; "Media Relations: Basic Cable and Pay TV"; "Radio Press and Publicity"; "Design: New Trends in Print"; "Understanding Radio Research"; "TV: The Press, From the Other Side"; "Careers in Cable TV"; "Radio: Adver-

tising Alternatives to TV"; "Radio for TV Promotion"; "Keynote Luncheon: Fred Silverman"; "Retailing Radio: Promotion For Profit"; "Cable Research: The Great Debate"; "The TV Design Twins: PBS And Commercial"; "Electronic Still Storage and the News"; "In-House Animation"; "The Promotion Manager Today"; "TV: The New Electronic Media"; "Public TV: Problem Solving: One Person Departments"; "Public TV: Problem Solving: 2-3 Person Departments"; "Public TV: Problem Solving: 6+ Person Departments"; "Animation: Bob Abel"; "TV Station Building for the 80's"; "Radio: Usable Sales Promotions"; "Quick and Inexpensive Sets"; "TV: New Directions in TV News Promotions"; "The Dollars and Sense of TV Promotion"; "Design: The New Image Workshop"; "Luncheon: Jay Finkleman, Tom Elrod"; "Illustrations for TV"; "DBA: Corporate Design"; "TV: Media Buying Madness"; "Design: Commercial Ventures on PTV"; "BDA: From Here to 1990"; "Broadcast Advertising: State of the Art"; "TV: Pressure Group Safety Valve".

Print

PRINT INDEX, TELEVISION

Community:
Commendations; Contests; Involvement; Fundraisers (see Involvement); Give-aways; Saleable Items.

General Station:
Anniversaries; Award Ads; Broadcast Center Folios (see also Anniversaries); Bumper Stickers; Call Letter Changes; Co-ads; Equipment: Buildings, Helicopters, Mini-cams, Motor Vehicles, Radar, Towers; General Station Ads (see also SALES Media Buyer Ads); Historys and Profiles; Holiday Ads; Holiday Cards; House Organs; Image Changes; Invitations; Letterhead (see also Folio Folders, Anniversaries); Logos (see also Letterhead, Bumper Stickers); Newspaper Supplements; Number changes; Production Facilities Ads; Research Studies; Set Design; Transit Ads; Outdoor Ads.

Programming:
News Ads: Feature Reporters, General News, News Expansion, News Newscasters, News Sportcasters, News Weathercasters, Newscasters, News Teams, Political Coverage, Special Reports, Sportscasters, Weathercasters, Outdoor Ads, Transit Ads.

Program Ads:
Children, Comedy, Community Information, Documentary, Dramatic, Game Show, Magazine Format, Movies, Music, Program Line-ups, Public TV Ads, Soap Operas, Specials, Sports, Talk Shows, Variety Shows, Outdoor Ads, Transit Ads.

Sales
Audience Demographics:
Station/Area; Programming; (see also Rate Cards, Program Information sheets); Coverage Maps (see also Rate Cards, Audience Demographics, Station Profile Folios, Programming Info); Folio Folders (see Also Letterhead); Media Buyer Ads; Media Buyer Give-aways; Programming Information Sheets: News; Programming; (see also Audience Demographics, Rate Cards);
Rate Cards: General Programming; Production Facilities; Sports; Schedules; Station Profile Folios (complete sales kits).

RADIO

Community:
Commendations; Contests; Involvement; Fundraisers

(see Involvement); Give-aways; Saleable Items.

General Station:
Anniversaries; Broadcast Center Folios (see also Anniversaries); Bumper Stickers; Co-ads; Equipment-Buildings, Helicopters, Towers; Historys and Profiles; Holiday Ads; Holiday Cards; House Organs; Image Format Changes; Invitations; Letterhead (see also Anniversaries); Logos (see also Letterhead, Bumper Stickers); Newsletters; New Station Ads; Station Award Ads, Survey Analysis, blank samples.

Programming:
Personalities—Print, Outdoor, Transit; Programs—General, Program Line-up, Political Coverage, Outdoor Ads, Special Reports, Transit Ads.

Sales:
Billing Notices; Demographics; Coverage Maps; Media Buyer Ads; Media Buyer Give-aways; Folio Folders; Programming Format Information; Rate Cards; Station Profiles *complete sales kits.

Station Format Ads:
General; Classical; All News; Country; MOR; Rock/AOR; Easy Listening; Public Radio.

SLIDE INDEX

The Slide Index contains slides of many of the print pieces listed in the Print Index. Currently this collection is viewable only at the BPA Library in San Diego.

Premiums

The Library maintains a large collection of premiums, from tee-shirts to paperweights (even a branding iron!). Currently these materials can only be viewed at the BPA Library in San Diego.

PBS Program Press Kits

Most of these materials can be xeroxed for members.

Distribution Co. Press Kits

Most of these materials can be xeroxed for members.

Vendor File

The BPA Library houses information and sample material from companies providing related services in various areas of promotion. Most of these companies are BPA Associate Members.

BPA Publications

BPA Newsletter:
The Library contains copies of almost every newsletter from 1970 to current.

Seminar Reports:
1975 Denver Seminar; 1976 Washington Seminar; 1977 Los Angeles Seminar; 1978 St. Paul/Minneapolis Seminar, 1979 Nashville Seminar; 1980 Montreal Seminar; 1981 New York Seminar.

Seminar Notebooks:
1978 St. Paul/Minneapolis Seminar; 1979 Nashville Seminar; 1980 Montreal Seminar; 1981 New York Seminar; 1982 San Francisco Seminar.

Big Ideas Publications:
"So You Want To Have An Affair?"; "Anniversaries"; "Printed Advertising—Audience"; "Creatively Servicing the Budget"; "Graphics"; "Merchandising"; "Program Promotion Material Supplied by Distributors 1977"; "A Survey of Radio and TV News Advertising"; "Promoting News"; "On-Air Promotion Handbook"; "Outdoor Advertising #1"; "Outdoor Advertising #2"; "Program Schedules"; "Promotion Production"; "Publicity"; "Sales Promotion #1"; "Sales Promotion #2"; "Special Events #1"; "Special Events #2"; "Tune In Ads".

Related Publications

Related publications are also kept on file at the BPA Library, and copies can be obtained by members. They include: 1982 Publications Catalog NAB; Guidelines for Radio: PROMOTION (NAB); Lotteries and Contests: A Broadcasters Handbook (NAB); The Handbook of Radio Publicity and Promotion by Jack McDonald (TAB Books); A Glossary of TV Promotion Terminology (CBS); Broadcast Designers Association 1979 Awards Book—Print, 1981 Awards Book—Print, Designing for TV: News Graphics.

AWARDS COMPETITION

The BPA Library is also compiling a listing of promotion-related competitions that members can enter, and receive recognition for outstanding work.

ORDERING FROM THE
BPA RESOURCE CENTER:

To order, a member can write to the BPA Resource Center with a list of requests along with a check made out to the Broadcasters Promotion Association.

The cost of this service is as follows:
VIDEO: $20.00/half hour OR $30.00/hour. You provide the ¾" cassette.
AUDIO: $7.50 for up to 90 minutes. We will provide the cassette.
PRINT: .06¢ each page, black and white xerox.

Please call if you have any questions, or for a list of current materials in the library. Please send your order to:
BPA Librarian
Department of Telecommunications and Film
San Diego State University
San Diego, CA 92182-0117
(714) 265-6374

NOTE: This catalogue is revised annually. Call or write for a current one.

Index

T